Piccolo

Bassoon

Flute

Contrabassoon

Oboe Clarinet English horn

Bass clarinet

WOODWINDS

Understanding
MUSIC

"Angelic Concert" from Isenheim Altarpiece. *Grunewald, Mathias. Colmar Museum, Germany.*

WILLIAM FLEMING *and* ABRAHAM VEINUS

Syracuse University

Understanding
MUSIC

Style, Structure, and History

NEW YORK · 1958

HENRY HOLT AND COMPANY

Acknowledgments

The authors wish to thank the following publishers for permission to quote copyrighted materials:

Associated Music Publishers, Inc., New York, for the excerpts on pages 411 and 412 from Webern's Concerto for Nine Instruments, copyright 1948 by Universal Edition, Vienna; and from Berg's Violin Concerto on page 415, copyright 1936 by Universal Edition, Vienna;

J. and W. Chester, Ltd., of London, for the excerpt on page 422 from Stravinsky's *Les Noces;* Elkan-Vogel Co. for the excerpts from Debussy on pages 387 and 389, permission for reprint granted by Durand et Cie., Paris, France, copyright owners; Elkan-Vogel Co., Inc., Philadelphia, Pa., agents;

Harcourt, Brace and Co., New York, for the quotation from Louis Untermeyer's translation of Heine's poetry on page 162;

Harvard University Press, Cambridge, Mass., for the material from *Historical Anthology of Music* by Archibald T. Davison and Willi Apel on pages 253–255;

Mediaeval Academy of America for the passage on page 259 from *Notation of Polyphonic Music, 900–1600* by Willi Apel;

New Directions, The New Classics, for the translation of Baudelaire's poem by Geoffrey Wagner on pages 391–392;

W. W. Norton and Co., New York, for the quotations from *Source Readings in Music History* by Oliver Strunk on pages 283, 319, and 320;

G. Schirmer, Inc., New York, for the excerpt from Schoenberg's String Quartet No. 4 on page 414.

Preface

THIS book is designed an an introduction to music. As such, it presupposes no prior technical knowledge on the part of the reader. However, in the course of exploring any art as complex as that of music, it is inevitable that some technical obstacles will be encountered from time to time. When such technicalities do occur, they are presented more as expressions of broad basic principles than as ends in themselves. The principles of polyphony, for instance, lie entirely within the grasp of an inquiring adult who may not have had the benefit of an academic course in contrapuntal writing. When confronted with such difficult subjects, we have avoided deceptive simplicity, since complex concepts cannot be oversimplified without the danger of essential falsification.

This volume is not to be considered as a replacement for the music itself, nor is reading it equivalent to an appreciation of music. It is intended, rather, to provide certain essential information of an analytical, stylistic, and historical nature, with confidence that such approaches will lead ultimately to a critical understanding of the composer and his product. The very word "appreciation" has been

v

rather studiously avoided in the title, and wherever possible in the text, since the appreciation of a piece of music is a highly personal synthesis that each listener must ultimately make for himself. It is hoped, however, that these pages may possibly clarify for the listener some of the various components of a musical situation, without presuming to intrude either upon the privacy of the listener's preserves, or upon his right to react to any specific musical contingency in accordance with his own personal philosophy.

Music, as a creative process, involves the activities of the composer, performer, and listener, who are brought together into a mutual relationship by a social occasion. The process of musical creativity is thus threefold, with the composer as the prime mover communicating his ideas, through the performer as his interpreter, to the listener as his audience. Each, however, participates in the creative process to a definite extent, the difference being one of the degree and intensity of the stimulus and response, the breadth of the background of experience, and the concentrated creative thought each is able to bring to bear on the musical situation.

Music in this sense is a form of communication from the composer through the performer to the listener. The composer's role is, of course, primary. It is he who conceives the musical idea, works it out, and commits it to paper. His score, however, would remain mute and his intentions unfulfilled, were it not for the performer or recreative artist—whether singer, pianist, or conductor. It is the performer, then, who transforms the timeless, silent symbols on the printed page into living sound and flowing movement progressing in time. The activities of both composer and performer, in turn, would be quite in vain without the listener to whom their mutual efforts are addressed. And just as there are good as well as bad composers and performers, there are also good as well as bad listeners. Great music, of course, demands a great deal of its listeners. Granting, however, that the composer is a competent craftsman, his need is for a responsible performer who will reproduce his ideas so as to correspond as closely as possible to his own intentions. And the whole process, in order to be successful, presupposes that both composer and performer will be able to communicate with listeners who are receptive, informed, aware, alert, and intelligent. We earnestly hope, then, that this book will suggest a range of valid viewpoints as well as provide the listener with various types of background material, so that he will be able to receive and evaluate the composer's communications with broader understanding, and hence be able to play his role in the musical process with greater responsibility.

We acknowledge our deep debt to the efforts of the many individuals who have done so much to ease this book on its often difficult way: especially to Frank Macomber for his intelligent and invaluable help in the preparation of the manuscript, the musical examples, and the index; to Dorothy V. Hagan for making available some of her own unpublished material; to Barry Brook for his good counsel along the way; to Arpena Mesrobian for her many helpful suggestions in the galley-proof stage; to Grant Beglarian for his expert craftsmanship in the setting of the musical examples; to Alfred Frankenstein for generously permitting us to use several of his photographs of the Victor Hartmann drawings; and, finally, to our colleagues and students, who have often contributed, perhaps unknowingly, to the clarification and elucidation of many points in the pages that follow.

W. F. and A. V.

Syracuse University
April 1958

Table of Contents

ix

PART I

The Composer
and His Materials

The Raw Materials
of Music

Chapter 1

THE basic raw materials of music are sound and silence. Just as an architect thinks in terms of material masses and voids, so a composer deals with sonorous masses and voids. An architect uses bricks and mortar to enclose space, and a composer arranges tones to articulate the flow of time. An architect defines spatial units, and a composer imposes temporal divisions. An architect tries to make space both useful and meaningful, while a composer endeavors to endow time with significance. An architect makes his intentions known by the lines and spaces on his blueprints, and a composer indicates his ideas by the notes and rests on his scores. And just as an architect must be conversant with the principles of engineering, so also must a composer take certain acoustical factors into account. Music, in fact, is a kind of fluid architecture unfolding in time; and the composer thus becomes the personal force behind these moving patterns of sound, determining their specific musical content and endowing them with human meaning.

The audible raw materials of sound are constantly heard coming from all sides. There are mechanical sounds such as the screech of automobile brakes, the chattering rhythm of a pneumatic drill digging in the pavement, the crescendo of an approaching railroad train, and the chromatic wail of a fire truck's siren. Then, of course, there are the occasional lulls or quiet periods between sounds. Certain recognizable features come out of this world of sound, and the shrill, high pitch of a police whistle is distinguishable from the low, muffled roar of thunder, the quick gallop of a race horse from the slow gait of a draft horse, the softness of distant sounds from the loudness of those close by, and the difference between one church bell and another. The pitch of a human voice can indicate immediately whether the speaker is male or female; the rhythmic fall of footsteps can tell whether the walker is in a hurry or at leisure; the increase or decrease in intensity can reveal whether he is coming or going; and the quality of the voice can disclose whether he is adolescent or adult, calm or angry. Sound, then, is associated with action, silence with respite or repose.

Through the processes of selecting, discarding, refining, organizing, and improving, a language of music has gradually emerged. The elements of sound are present everywhere, and their possibilities have been grasped and forged into art forms that can convey meaning to the minds and hearts of man. A composer can find his rhythms in the beating of a heart, the drawing of breath, the changing of the seasons, or the periodic revolutions of the planets in their orbits. His mediums are derived from the multiplicity of available sounds, which may include human voices, with all their variable qualities, or instruments, with their individual ranges and particular timbres. Whether he uses them alone or blended with others, each can contribute its characteristic color to his work.

Life provides basic experiences that a composer can shape for his expressive needs. The encountering of conflicts and difficulties has its counterpart in such points of tension as harmonic dissonances, while the working out of solutions and settlements is reflected in points of relaxation such as resolutions and cadences. His forms may be based on the universal experiences of recurrence involving both memory and premonition which together may combine to endow a given musical moment with meaning. As his composition unfolds in time, it is always in transition, and any given tone or group of tones can be at once both reminiscent and prophetic. Silences are by no means merely the cessation of sound. Such pauses in the musical progress can arrest the movement temporarily or suggest continuity of motion depending on the memory of what came before and the anticipation of what may come after.

Ultimately tonal relations in music can create their own meaning, and the most abstract aspects of the art can rest on acquired associations and conventions within a given musical context. A composer can thus construct his own world of sound relationships, but he would be powerless to do so unless the experience of pitch, rhythm, intensity, tone color, harmony, counterpoint, dissonance, and consonance were not among the universal aspects of human experience. The musical tone, then, with its definable qualities and characteristics as well as its possibility of infinite variation, is under the control of the composer. The composer himself is seen as an artist endowed with tonal imagination and the power of invention who lives and works in a world of auditory imagery. Communication through sound is as necessary to him as communication through words is to a writer.

When a key on a piano is struck or a string on a guitar plucked, a tone is produced. This single tone is at once both a psychological as well as a physical fact. The vibration sets the surrounding air in motion, and the waves pulsate against the ear drums and thence are conveyed by the nervous system to the brain where, psychologically, they awaken an auditory response. Physically, the quivering string can be described quantitatively, since the vibrations can be counted, the duration of the sound timed, its intensity measured, and its quality analyzed into the complex system of overtones known as harmonics or upper partials. The tone is thus a vibrating, enduring, dynamic, qualitative fact known as a sound wave. Its regularly recurring impulses distinguish it from the unorganized, irregular, confused vibrations of noise, which are also sound waves, though noise as such is by no means excluded from the musical process. The wave frequency, or the number of vibrations per second of the tone, leads to the sensation of *pitch,* its time length to *duration,* its energy to *intensity,* and its overtone structure to *timbre.*

The theoretical basis of music lies in the various divisions of this vibrating string or, in the case of wind instruments, a column of enclosed air. If a low C, for instance, is taken as a ground tone and the string is divided exactly in half, the two equal segments of the string will sound the tone C one octave higher—a relationship expressed by the mathematical ratio of 1:2. If the string is divided into three equal portions, each of the three segments will sound the tone G, an octave plus a fifth higher, or a ratio of 2:3. If divided into four parts, the tone will again be a C, this time two octaves higher than the fundamental, or 3:4, and so on. The distance between these various divisions of the vibrating string define certain intervals. When the mathematical ratios are very close as in the case of the octave (1:2), the fifth (2:3), and the fourth (3:4), the intervals are called perfect. When the ratios are more remote as with the large third (4:5), the small third (5:6), the whole tone (8:9), and the half tone (15:16), they are said to be imperfect.

Many of these divisions are heard when the fundamental tone is sounded, and the richness of the timbre, or tone quality, depends on how many of them are present. For the sake of convenience they have been illustrated here in a horizontal series (Ex. 1:1); actually they should be considered vertically since they are component parts of a single tone and thus are heard simultaneously. This vibrating string, known as the fundamental tone, with its recognizable characteristics of pitch, duration, intensity, and timbre, is really the seed that contains all the other tones, and it thus holds locked within itself the potentialities of the musical art. These

Ex. 1:1

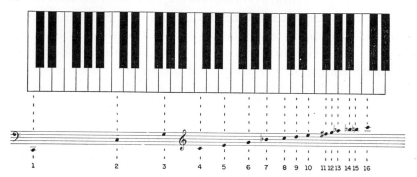

tones then become the source of musical movement when released from their germinal state into a horizontal series of related tones unfolding in time.

The poetic possibilities of this play between a fundamental tone and its overtones have been explored by composers. In the opening of his Ninth Symphony (Ex. 1:2), Beethoven chooses the fundamental tone A

Ex. 1:2 Symphony No. 9. First Movement (Bars 1–5). Beethoven.

in the bass which sounds together with E, the fifth above it. Over them at the end of the second bar the upper fifth plunges downward to the octave, the octave in turn moves to the fifth below, and then to the ground tone. Here the three perfect intervals, the span covered by the first three overtones of the series, are spun out horizontally in time to produce a musical statement. Symbolically the upper and lower limits of the harmonic space are defined, thus creating a certain mysterious emptiness which demands fulfillment in the future course of the composition.

The Prelude to Wagner's *Das Rheingold,* the first opera of his cycle, *The Ring of the Nibelung,* opens with a motive (Ex. 1:3) derived from a fundamental tone of E flat, followed in rhythmic succession by its closest overtones. The Prelude precedes a scene in which the Rhine Maidens are discovered swimming around as they guard their gold in the depths of the river. This so-called "Nature" motive suggests the indefinite, shapeless, fluid mass of water as it flows, swells, and ebbs. Coming as it does at the opening of a vast work that has to do with the mythological beginnings of the world, it symbolizes the evolutionary origin of life emerging from the primeval waters. As Wagner himself has commented, "From the funda-

Ex. 1:3   Prelude to *Das Rheingold* (Bars 1–8) . Wagner.

mental note of harmony, music has spread itself into a huge expanse of waters, in which the absolute-musician swam aimlessly and restlessly to and fro. . . ."

The single fundamental tone is thus dominated principally by quantitative characteristics—that is, the number of vibrations, the length of duration, the degree of intensity, and the constitution of its harmonics. When two or more tones are heard succeeding each other in time, comparison becomes possible. A change in the number of vibrations either higher or lower marks a movement in *pitch;* a shift in the time values by making them either longer or shorter becomes a movement in *duration;* an increase or decrease in the degree of energy means a movement in *intensity;* and a shift from one sounding body to another is a movement in *timbre.* To proceed now into the perception of qualities: pitch, perceived as the relative highness or lowness of two tones, is heard as a *line* moving upward or downward; duration, perceived as the relative longness or shortness of two tones, is felt as *meter;* intensity, perceived as the relative loudness or softness of two tones, is sensed as *dynamics;* while the distinction between timbres becomes the experience of *tone quality.* To go one step farther: the extension of linear movement becomes *melody;* the continuation of metrical movement becomes *rhythm;* the increase or decrease of intensities becomes *dynamics;* and the organization of timbres becomes *tone color.* Together the totality of this four-dimensional melodic, rhythmic, dynamic, and qualitative movement is the raw material of music, hence its fluidity and versatility as a medium of expression.

As extended in time, melodic movement has its directional tendency; melodies have their characteristic shape as well as design, and they can be classified into types. Melodies move by steps or skips. The various distances between the tones are referred to as intervals, and the related tones can be organized consecutively into a system of modes or scales. Such intervals, when combined and heard simultaneously, become the basis of harmony; while the combination of one or more melodies becomes counterpoint. Rhythmic movement grows out of the sequence of simple and compound meters, regular and irregular beats. Tempo evolves from the pace or relative speed of the units of movement, and the experience is based on the perception of the passage of events within a given time period. Dynamic levels have their accents and gradations as well as tidal waves of tonal ebb and flow; while the organization of tone qualities stems from the exploration of the color capacities of individual voices and instruments all the way to the complexities of instrumentation and orchestration. Each element and complex adds, in turn, its particular vocabulary to the overall language of music.

The obverse side of this coin is, of course, silence, which, by inference, has its line, meter, dynamics, and tone color depending on the circumstances that precede and follow it. According to an old proverb, speech is silver but silence is golden. Lucky is the composer who understands the use of silence, for it is one of his most eloquent means of expression. As in speech, a composer must allow for breathing pauses at the ends of phrases —a literal necessity in the case of singers and wind players and a figurative one for clear articulation in that of other instrumentalists. Music also has its innuendoes and implied meanings, and sometimes what is left unsaid in either a conversation or composition assumes greater importance than what is actually stated. Composers also employ rhetorical pauses for purposes of emphasis that can have real dramatic implications when they occur at climactic moments in the build-up of a composition.

To cite some specific uses of silence: Beethoven's Piano Sonata in E-flat Major, Op. 7, contains an expansive slow movement, Largo con gran espressione (slow—literally large—and with great expressivity). Fully half of the allotted time in the opening section is given over to a silence that contributes to the conception of spaciousness and grandeur implied in the tempo indication. Silence as a divider in a formal design is also employed to good effect by composers to separate the sections of their compositions. When judiciously used, silence can likewise create a sense of suspense and expectation as does Wagner in the Prelude to *Tristan and Isolde* (Ex. 6:16), where a feeling of longing and unfulfilled desire is implicit in the rests. There are also the pauses that allow the listener's imagination to fill in the empty musical spaces, and Beethoven even goes so far as to place a fermata (hold) sign over the rest at the end of a movement (Ex. 6:11), an implication that the music continues beyond the cessation of physical sound. And lastly, the ideal of full employment at all times may be a happy state for a social order, but when the same principle is applied to an orchestral community, the result is din and complete confusion. Thinning out the ranks by leaving individual parts tacit for at least part of the time is one of the necessities of good ensemble writing.

Movement as the outward manifestation of all life is externalized in space and time. Spatialized movement as in the dance is visible to the eye, while temporal motion as in song is audible to the ear. Far from being mere idle motion and dull duration, however, life is made significant by its aims and objectives. Musical motion likewise derives meaning from its direction. From a melodic phrase to a complete form, the musical entity, in the classical sense at least, has a beginning, a middle, and an end. With the flow of lines, rhythms, and harmonies and with the apprehension of their force and direction, the incipient tendency of a musical idea is discerned and its shape becomes clear. The form may then be discovered as the musical idea unfolds, and its potentialities are realized in various stages from the motive, phrase, and section to ever-widening horizons. A basis for the understanding of the spirit of a work can thus be established.

As Stravinsky has aptly said: "The elements of sound given us by nature evoke music in our minds, but sound is not yet music. It is for man to grasp and develop the inherent possibilities of this promise—man who is not only sensitive to all the values of nature, but also capable of organizing them. There is no such thing as music without the working of a mind that creates, orders, vivifies." In listening to a piece of music it is in order to ask such questions as: Does the regular rhythmic repetition of strong and weak beats bring to mind patterns of motion such as the stamping of feet and the gestures of the hands as in the dance? Or does the motion conjure up a stream of emotion and thought activity that is internally rather than externally oriented? Does the melodic and rhythmic motion tend toward the finite and complete, toward rest and repose? Or does it move in the direction of the infinite and incomplete, toward action and further motion? Does a pregnant pause here arrest the action momentarily? Or does the silence promote further unheard motion as it moves beyond the limits of physical sound? Types of musical motion can thus express anything from the image of a simple work song, such as "I've Been Workin' on the Railroad," all the way to such exalted visions of the emergence of a great and free humanity as in Beethoven's mighty symphonies. Furthermore, since each individual composer, each generation, each age expresses itself in its own concepts and formulates its own aspirations and ideals, each musical work becomes the key to the understanding of the meaning of an individual attitude toward life, the spirit of a creative artist, the essence of a generation, a period, an age.

Tone Color

Chapter 2

———————————————————————————

Tone color is the musical element that permits the listener to distinguish between sounds of different quality. Tones of the same pitch, duration, and intensity vary from one another depending on the source from which they come. Each human voice, as well as each musical instrument, has its own unique and recognizable timbre. Human voices—whether those of children or adults, males or females—differ widely in quality. So also do musical instruments and, more narrowly, individual players on instruments. Each great violinist, for instance, has a characteristic tone quality that is his trade-mark. So also does each singer have his own special vocal quality. Just as melody is based on variations of pitch, rhythm on durational change, and dynamics on fluctuations of intensity, so the experience of tone color is rooted in shifts of the sonorous capacities of voices and instruments, as well as on the more striking changes from one instrument or group to another. Individual instruments in their different registers also have their characteristic sounds. The high tones of some may be described as pure, clear, shrill, or piercing; low tones of others are said to be deep, mellow, resonant, or reedy; loud tones on certain instruments may be considered emphatic, booming, strident or harsh, and so on. The ear is thus capable of comparing the various attributes of sound; and the passage of tone color from one register to another, or the shift from one instrument to another, is a qualitative movement. This characteristic of sound has many potentialities and possibilities that are exploited by composers to convey their particular musical ideas.

A score, once it has been committed to paper by the composer, has at that point a potential but not yet an actual musical existence. To bring it to life, the symbols on the printed page must be translated by a performer through a musical instrument into living sound. Furthermore, no matter how abstractly a composition may have been conceived in its planning stage, it can never become music as sound in general, but only in terms of a specific kind of sound—that is, by means of an instrumental medium. When a melody is played, it must therefore be performed by an instrument, and the particular personality of that instrument then becomes inevitably involved as an intrinsic ingredient of that melody. The two can never be divorced, and the instrument therefore becomes in essence a part of the musical subject matter.

Music in the mind of the composer may well be conceived first in more or less general terms and later refashioned in terms of a specific instrument. Beethoven's Sonata Op. 14, No. 1 in E Major was originally written and published as a work for piano, and the composer just a few years later rewrote it as a string quartet in the key of G major. Bach frequently used the selfsame piece in several different musical situations. His setting of the chorale "Sleepers Awake", for instance, is found once in the cantata of that name where it is scored for tenors and orchestra, and it is used again as a chorale-prelude for organ. In another case he opens a cantata (No. 146) with a large-scale chorus accompanied by orchestra, while in another version the same material becomes the first movement of his keyboard Concerto in D Minor.

Some composers emphasize linear and formal considerations and use color in a secondary sense, while others construct a score primarily in terms of specific instrumental coloration. Some Bach works, for instance, may be transcribed from one instrumental medium to another without losing their basic musical substance, just as a Michelangelo painting may be reproduced in black and white without fundamentally violating the painter's expressive design. On the other hand, some music is often conceived directly in terms of the instrument itself, and the musical ideas are then part and parcel of the manner in which the instrument is manipulated. A composition of this kind differs so noticeably when played on another instrument that it sounds almost like a separate piece. If a piano nocturne of Chopin, for instance, is transcribed for orchestra, or if a Debussy piano prelude is rendered on a harpsichord, most of the musical meaning instantly vanishes. A violin or flute may be interchangeable in a phrase of Bach, and the meaning will not suffer materially. But if an oboe replaces the flute in the opening bars of Debussy's *Afternoon of a Faun,* the subtle and sensuous idea conveyed by the flute will have been irretrievably lost.

Tone color can thus be used both organically and decoratively. In painting, for instance, it is possible to distinguish between the work of Cézanne, who builds a picture with color, and Matisse or Gauguin, who use color not only in an organic sense but decoratively as well. Rimsky-Korsakoff, similarly, has distinguished between the *orchestration* of a work and its *orchestral conception*. In a commentary on his own *Capriccio Espagnol*, for instance, he notes: "The opinion formed by both critics and the public, that the 'Capriccio' is a *magnificently orchestrated* piece is wrong. The 'Capriccio' is a brilliant *composition for the orchestra*. The change of timbres, the felicitous choice of melodic designs and figuration patterns, exactly suiting each kind of instrument, brief virtuoso cadenzas for solo instruments, the rhythm of the percussion, etc., here constitute the very essence of the composition and not its garb or orchestration." So strong, in fact, is the nature of the instrument in the overall stylistic conception of the piece of music, that passages are often described as vocalistic, pianistic, or violinistic, and whole works are referred to in terms of the composer's "vocal style," "choral style," or "orchestral style."

THE HUMAN VOICE

The human voice, because of its intimate association with speech and verbal communication, as well as the fact that a minimum of mechanism interposes itself between the performer and listener, is at once the simplest, most direct in communicative power, and the most personal and expressive of all musical instruments. Though styles of singing vary widely from period to period historically, and from place to place geographically, no instrument has been so universally employed by composers over such a long stretch of time. In the process, the human voice has undergone less basic changes than any other instrument. No new exciting devices are possible; and when a composer writes for the voice, he is apt to be concerned more with universal human experience than with novel modes of presentation. With the advent of opera and oratorio in the early seventeenth century, most composers have accepted the so-called *bel canto* ideal of singing—that is, with the open mouth and throat and the resulting clear and vibrant sound. The range of the voice is, of course, restricted. Most commonly, voices fall within the middle registers of mezzo-soprano and baritone for women and men, respectively. With training, voices can be cultivated in their natural placement, or be pushed upward into the soprano and tenor ranges, or downward into the alto or bass registers. Except in unusual instances, the entire normal scope covered by the four principal voices—soprano, contralto, tenor, and bass—is somewhat less than four octaves, extending from a little under two octaves above middle C to about two octaves below.

Voices, over the years, have become typed and standardized because of the ways composers have written for singers in the song and operatic literature. A *coloratura soprano,* for instance, must develop great agility in the high register in order to perform the rapid, dazzling, cadenzalike passages expected of her. (Examples: the Queen of the Night in Mozart's *Magic Flute* and Gilda in Verdi's *Rigoletto*). Closely related is the *lyric soprano,* whose voice possesses a light texture, considerable brilliance, and a capacity for sustained melodic singing. (Examples: Micaela in Bizet's *Carmen,* and Mimi in Puccini's *La Bohème*). More powerful and declamatory, and with a register extending downward into the mezzo region is the *dramatic soprano,* who is needed for roles in the romantic repertory from Beethoven through Wagner (Examples: Leonore in Beethoven's *Fidelio,* Brünnhilde in Wagner's *Ring of the Nibelung,* and Isolde in *Tristan and Isolde*). The *mezzo-soprano* register encompasses the warm, rich lower regions of the feminine voice, and composers often employ it for such sensuous seductive roles as Carmen in Bizet's opera of that name and Delilah in Saint-Saëns' *Samson and Delilah.* The *contralto* or *alto* voice is still deeper and mellower, suggesting such mature matronly roles as Azucena in Verdi's *Il Trovatore* and Genevieve in Debussy's *Pelleas and Melisande.*

The light *lyric tenor* is the smooth, male counterpart of the lyric soprano, and he needs a comparable fluency and flexibility to meet the demands for fleet passage work (Don Octavio in Mozart's *Don Giovanni,* the Duke of Mantua in Verdi's *Rigoletto,* and Rodolfo in Puccini's *La Bohème*). The *robust tenor,* or *tenore robusto,* possesses a full, powerful voice paralleling that of the dramatic soprano. It must be capable of expressing strong forceful feeling (Florestan in Beethoven's *Fidelio,* Max in Weber's *Der Freischütz,* and Otello in Verdi's opera of that name). The *heroic tenor,* or *heldentenor* is a still more massive vocal type developed especially for such Wagnerian roles as Lohengrin, Tristan, and Siegfried. The baritone found many champions among nineteenth-century opera composers, though seldom in stellar positions (Figaro in Rossini's *Barber of Seville;* Escamillo, the bull fighter, in Bizet's *Carmen;* and the elder Germont in Verdi's *La Traviata*). The *lyric bass,* or *basso cantante,* expresses solemnity and profundity coupled with a cantabile style (Don Giovanni in Mozart's opera of that name, Tsar Boris in Moussorgsky's *Boris Godounov,* and King Arkel in Debussy's *Pelleas and Melisande*). The designation *basso buffo* refers to a type of comic role rather than a vocal range as such (Leporello in Mozart's *Don Giovanni,* and Baron Ochs in Strauss' *Der Rosenkavalier*). The lowest of all voices is that of the rarely

heard *basso profondo*. Composers therefore cannot anticipate the availability of such an unusual voice, though Mozart wrote such roles as that of
Osmin in his *Abduction from the Seraglio* for a singer named Fischer with
deeper tones than are usually found in opera houses today.

When writing for chorus, a composer has to be careful to stay within
the comfortable limits of average voices. Though men's and women's
voices are often grouped in separate choirs, the most usual and universal
choral ensemble is the so-called "mixed" choir with its four sections usually divided into sopranos, altos, tenors, and basses. Choirs are the oldest
and most widespread of the world's musical organizations. In Western
music highly skilled professional choruses are known to have existed since
the great days of the Greek drama some 2500 years ago. Up to the middle
of the eighteenth century, in fact, the dominant ensemble in musical life
—sacred or secular—was the chorus. Only since that time has the star of
instrumental musical organizations gained ascendancy. Pure *a cappella*,
or unaccompanied choral music, represented an ideal of sound associated
with the high point of polyphony attained during the days of the Renaissance. This perfect blending of a small group of voices into a single choral
aggregate, with the resulting quality of disembodied sound, is still capable,
when properly performed, of opening up vistas of ethereal beauty that
rise above anything attainable with mere man-made instrumental ensembles. It is interesting to observe in this connection that the great
Renaissance choruses seldom used more than about sixteen singers, and
even Bach neither had nor needed more than around thirty in his choir.
Quality rather than quantity was the rule in producing this unity of
sound with its resulting clarity of line and shapeliness of proportion. The
large chorus is a product of a more gregarious social viewpoint where
grand collective efforts seem to be more effective in moving large gatherings of people. Choral singing is thus the most democratic of all musical
activities, and it still remains the most accessible medium for amateur
participation in the music-making process.

THE ORCHESTRA

Musical instruments other than the human voice are customarily divided into classes according to their construction and manner
of sound production. Those in which a stretched string is bowed or
plucked are called the *strings;* those in which an enclosed column of air
is set in vibration by blowing are the *woodwinds* and *brasses;* and those in
which tightened membranes, or metal disks, rods, bars, and the like are
struck constitute the *battery,* or *percussion* instruments. In addition to
these traditional members of the musical community, an entirely new

class of instruments is currently being developed through the science of electronics. The Theremin and electronic organ, which produce sound by the oscillation of current via the vacuum tube, are commanding increasing attention. In fact an altogether new method of composing, in which all kinds of sounds are recorded on tape, then mixed, altered, and distorted according to the composer's choice, is now well along in the experimental stage. Rather than dwell on the technicalities of the various instruments and how they are played—something that can be understood in any case only by actual demonstration—the accent in this discussion will be primarily on their expressive capacities and poetic possibilities. Since the symphony orchestra is the most all-inclusive of musical mediums, its structure and organization will prove a convenient way of approaching the various classes of instruments. It will also be seen that the symphony orchestra is divided into *choirs* or *sections* according to the above classifications, while each of these, in turn, is arranged into registers that correspond roughly to the vocal ranges found in a mixed chorus.

STRING CHOIR

The first and second *violins,* though they are the same instrument, serve as the sopranos of the string choir, while the *violas* and *cellos* (short for violoncello) are called upon to assume the roles of altos, tenors, and baritones. In the lowest register is found the *bass viol,* also known as the string bass, double bass, or contra bass. Together they constitute the dominant group of the orchestra and comprise more than half of its collective ranks. Historically the strings are the senior members of the symphonic society, the other instruments being comparative newcomers. String color, coming as it does from a single family of instruments, is more homogeneous in sound than that of the other choirs. The tones of the violin and cello, for instance, are much closer in timbre than, say, those of the flute and bassoon in the woodwinds, or the trumpet and tuba in the brasses. The ear, furthermore, accepts the sustained string tone as a norm and tires of it less quickly than it does of the instruments in other sections.

Normally played by drawing the bow across the strings in a smooth, continuous *legato* or a short, detached *staccato,* the composer also has certain special effects at his command. The whole family of instruments can be played *pizzicato* by plucking the strings like a guitar. Bowing two or three strings at once is known as *double* or *triple stopping.* To give the tone a vibrant quality similar to that of the human voice, the player moves his hand quickly back and forth on the string causing the pitch to waver slightly in the throbbing effect known as *vibrato.* The high-pitched, ethereal tones called *harmonics* are produced by stopping the string lightly with the finger so that it does not vibrate as a whole but in segments. The rapid repetition of the same note with up and down strokes of the bow is known as *tremolo;* while the insertion at the bridge of a *mute,* a three-pronged clamp, thins out some of the overtones to produce a muffled, veiled sonority. Some quite startling effects are occasionally called for such as *col legno,* playing with the wooden side of the bow; *glissando,* running the finger rapidly up or down the string to produce a sirenlike sound; and *spiccato,* rapid staccato notes with a bouncing stroke of the bow.

The *viola* is a little larger than the violin; but with its strings tuned a fifth lower, it has a deeper, richer, and less brilliant tone. It maintains itself discreetly in the middle of the harmony and seldom steps forward into the soloist's position. When it does, as in Berlioz' *Harold in Italy,* it has a quality all its own that no other instrument can duplicate. The *cello,* with strings twice as thick as those of the violin, is capable of broad, sustained melodic utterance and a full-throated throbbing tone. Ernest Bloch's *Schelomo,* subtitled "Hebrew Rhapsody for Cello and Orchestra," exploits the glowing warmth of its rich tenor and baritone registers. The *double bass* earned its name from the usual assignment in the baroque and classical periods of duplicating the cello parts an octave lower. Its deep, heavy tone provides not only the string section but the entire orchestra with the necessary bass support. The violin and cello, and to a lesser extent the viola, are all endowed with a significant solo literature; and, of course, they are indispensable in such chamber combinations as duets, trios, quartets, quintets, and the like.

WOODWIND CHOIR

The *flutes* are the sopranos of this section, while the *oboes, clarinets,* and *bassoons* correspond approximately to the alto, tenor, and bass. The range of each of these four principals, furthermore, is extended by at least one other member of its own family. The *piccolo,* short for "flauto piccolo," plays an octave higher than its close relative; the *English horn,* in reality an alto oboe, exploits the register immediately below that of its counterpart; while the *bass clarinet* and the *contrabassoon* sound an octave below their respective namesakes. The woodwinds are strong individualists in the orchestral community; yet, like good citizens, they can also mix well with their neighbors when necessary. Their family tree can trace its roots all the way back to the mythological soil of ancient Greece, where such instruments as the syrinx, or pipes of Pan, were first fashioned out of the hollow stalks of reeds of varying lengths to become the common ancestor of both the organ and woodwinds. Over the centuries their contours and mechanisms have varied considerably, and at present metal and plastic materials are rapidly replacing the wood that gave them their generic name. In spite of modern manufacturing methods, however, these country cousins of the orchestra still retain something of their rustic origin and pastoral character.

The dextrous *flute,* the coloratura soprano of the woodwinds, is highly effective in rapid brilliant passages. The modern transverse flute, in contrast to the older end-blown recorders, is held sideways; and the tone is produced by blowing across a small hole in its side known as the "embouchure." The more petite *piccolo* is used for shrill, whistling effects, as in fife-and-drum corps situations and the like. The *oboe* is played by blowing a stream of air through two closely fitted flat reeds. Deriving its name from "haut bois," French for "high wood," the instrument distinguishes itself in such poignant passages as the lyrical line in the "Funeral March" of Beethoven's *Eroica* Symphony, and the pastoral duet, with its alto counterpart the *English horn,* in the "Scene in the Country" from Berlioz' *Symphonie Fantastique.* According to the composer's own commentary, "The English horn repeats the phrases of the oboe in the lower octave, like the voice of a youth replying to a girl in a pastoral dialogue." The English horn thus intensifies the oboe's two principal personality traits by assuming such roles as that of the tragedian at the beginning of the last act of Wagner's *Tristan and Isolde,* and that of the rustic pipe in Rossini's Overture to *William Tell,* and more recently it is similarly employed in combination with a guitar by Virgil Thomson in a section called "Cattle Songs" from *The Plow that Broke the Plains.*

The *clarinets* include a whole family of instruments, most of which are still heard in large military bands. Only comparatively few of them, however, survive in the symphony orchestra. Those in B flat and A, with their mellow, limpid tone are the ones most often heard, and they have a wider command of dynamic levels from soft to loud than any other wind instrument. The shrill E-flat clarinet occasionally puts in an appearance in such works as Richard Strauss' *Till Eulenspiegel's Merry Pranks.* The deep-voiced *bass clarinet,* with a sonority resembling the low pipes on the organ, is used by composers for solemn, sometimes ominous, situations. Wagner, for instance, employs its deep tones at the close of the second act of *Tristan and Isolde* where King Mark, with dignified pathos, grieves over the infidelity of his knight Tristan and his consort Isolde. Tchaikovsky also brings it into the somber strains of the first movement of his *Symphonie Pathétique.* Mozart was the first major composer to champion the cause of the normal clarinet, and he incorporated it into many of his orchestral and chamber works, including the well-known Clarinet Quintet (K.581) and a fine solo concerto (K.622).

The *bassoon,* a much underestimated musical personality, is the double-reeded bass member of the oboe family and, in spite of its name, it can also play effectively in the baritone and tenor registers. Besides its workaday chores of blending with and supporting the woodwinds in the bass register, it can step forward on its own in a number of expressive situations. It can be quite comical, as, for instance, in Dukas' *Sorcerer's Apprentice,* or as "Grandpa" in Prokofieff's *Peter and the Wolf;* it can dance nimbly as in the Finale of Beethoven's Ninth Symphony, where the strings take the chorale melody while the bassoon cavorts around it and turns handsprings; it can assume a tragic mien in its somber lower register, as in the opening bars of Tchaikovsky's *Symphonie Pathétique;* it can mourn with gentle melancholy, as in the central episode of the Finale of Beethoven's Violin Concerto, where it takes the melody while the violins spin figurations around it; or, in its high register, it can become the strange, wild enchanted singer of a pagan spring, as in the opening moments of Stravinsky's *Rite of Spring.* The *contrabassoon,* or double bassoon, is the woodwind equivalent of the string bass. Its deep rumbling tone is used, for example, by Haydn in the *Creation* to accent a fortissimo at the point where he is setting the words, "By heavy beasts the ground is *trod."* Though the woodwinds are primarily ensemble instruments, there is a large literature for solo purposes. In the writing of contemporary composers such as Stravinsky, Hindemith, and Milhaud, the woodwinds have definitely gained in stature in both chamber and orchestral combinations.

THE BRASS CHOIR

The *trumpets* are the sopranos of this section; the *French horns* are the altos; the *trombones* cover the tenor and baritone registers; and the *tuba* brings up the bass. Except for the slide trombones, the modern versions of these instruments are all controlled by valve mechanisms. When played together, the vigor and virility of the brasses can provide the thunderous sonorities needed for tremendous orchestral climaxes; or, when required, they can sing out with long sustained organlike harmonies, as, for instance, in the pilgrim's-chorus passages of the Overture to Wagner's *Tannhäuser.*

The silvery soprano register of the *trumpet* shines through any orchestral fabric with assurance and ease. Its bright timbre and good carrying quality have been well-known since antiquity, when it proved its usefulness in signaling battle commands to the forces in the field. Jazz trumpeters have also contributed much to the newer color capabilities of the instrument, and in contemporary orchestrations its tone is often modified by flutter-tonguing technique as well as by the insertion into its bell of various mutes made of metal and cardboard as, for example, at the beginning of the procession in Debussy's *Fêtes.*

The rich, round resonance of the *French horn* is the essence of sonorous nobility. Its many dramatic usages run the gamut from such horn calls as the opening of the "Great" C-major Symphony by Schubert and that in "Siegfried's Rhine Journey" by Wagner, to the full-throated singing of entire melodies as in the Overture to Thomas' opera, *Mignon,* and the Finale of Brahms' First Symphony. Socially speaking, the instrument is one of the best mixers in the orchestra. In this capacity the French horn often deserts its brother brasses to join with the woodwinds, where it softens the rough edges of their reedy texture and generally integrates their separate sonorities into a homogeneous group, often without the listener's being aware of its presence.

The *trombone,* with its slide action and stentorian tone, is somewhat similar in sound to the French horn, but with a deeper and more penetrating quality. Ever alert to the unique possibilities of sound, Berlioz calls it an epical instrument. "Directed by the will of a master," he observes, "the trombones can chant like a choir of priests, threaten, utter gloomy sighs, a mournful lament, or a bright hymn of glory." Wagner employs the trombone to great advantage in the Prelude to Act III of *Lohengrin* as well as in the Overture to *Tannhäuser. Tubas* of varying sizes provide the brass section with the heavy tone and broad volume needed to complete the choir. Seldom used in other contexts, they can be solemn and majestic, as in the Prelude to Wagner's *Meistersinger,* or humorous, as the dancing bear in Stravinsky's ballet *Petrouchka.*

PERCUSSION SECTION

This body of instruments can be classified into those of definite pitch such as the *timpani* (or kettledrums), tubular *chimes, bells, glockenspiel, celesta,* and *xylophone;* and those of indefinite pitch such as the *snare* or *side drums, bass drum, cymbals, triangles, gongs, castanets, tambourines,* and a host of others.

The nucleus of the percussion group is found in the *timpani,* the tops of whose shiny copper kettles or bowls are covered by taut skin. The tension of this head can be controlled to produce definite pitches by adjusting screws or pressing on a pedal mechanism. Different sonorities are possible by striking the membrane with sticks, the heads of which may be equipped with a variety of soft or hard materials. The timpani can punctuate orchestral statements, give sharp definition to rhythms, make colossal crescendos by the drumroll technique, and point up climaxes. The tubular *chimes,* a set of metal cylinders hung on a wooden frame, are used for the clangor of church bells as in the final part of Tchaikovsky's *Overture 1812.* Actual bells of specified pitch are also sometimes employed. More delicacy is possible with the *glockenspiel,* a set of metal bars arranged in a graduated series. Mozart uses their bright metallic sound in his *Magic Flute* when-

ever Papageno needs to summon supernatural aid. The *celesta* is similar
to the glockenspiel but played by means of a keyboard. When Tchaikovsky came upon the newly invented celesta in a Paris shop, its sticky, sac-
charine sound proved just what he needed to portray the sugar-plum fairy
in his ballet, the *Nutcracker.* The *xylophone,* a series of tuned wooden
bars arranged like a keyboard and struck with wooden mallets, gives the
crisp, dry sound that Saint-Saëns uses to suggest rattling bones in his
Danse Macabre as well as for the "Fossils" in his *Carnival of the Animals.*

Percussion instruments of indefinite pitch include the *snare,* or *side
drum,* whose crisp, assertive sound suggests its military origin; the *tambourine,* a small drum equipped with jingling metal disks, is often used
in dance music and for Spanish or gipsy local color; and the booming *bass
drum* provides the heavy artillery of the battery. The *cymbals* are the
slightly concave disks of brass that make a shattering sound when clashed
together at climactic moments. The tinkling *triangles,* single metal bars
bent into triangular shapes of varying sizes, add sparkle and luster at appropriate moments. The *gong,* or *tam-tam,* is a large disk of hammered
brass of Chinese origin. Struck loudly it gives out an ominous, diffused
sound in contrast to the more mysterious quality produced when struck
softly. For extraordinary effects many odd percussive items are available;
and rattles, sirens, temple blocks, whistles, wind machines, and even chains
are occasionally called for in contemporary music. Modern scores such as
Stravinsky's *Petrouchka* and *Rite of Spring* put a heavy emphasis on the
percussion, and in the same composer's *History of the Soldier,* one player
must sometimes perform on as many as four different instruments in the
same bar. In conclusion it should be pointed out that some instruments
which lie outside the usual choirs or sections—the harp, mandolin, organ,
saxophone, and piano, for instance—are occasionally included in modern
orchestral music.

Over this vast mechanism presides the *conductor,* who plays no instrument, yet plays them all. While the individual musician in the ranks is
concerned with but a single part, the conductor is the one musician who
is responsible for all the complex details of the whole score. Technically
he must provide a clear beat, set and maintain the tempo, signal any tempo
changes, cue the entrances of the various instruments and sections, see to
the precision of the ensemble playing, mold the phrases into shapely
melodic entities, adjust the delicate tonal balances, vary the dynamic
shadings, and build up dramatic climaxes. In this sense his business is to
weld the heterogeneous mass of orchestra players into a single, organic,
and responsive instrument, so that the ideas the composer notes in the
score can be realized in sound. Beyond this, he must provide the authority

of knowledge, the personal magnetism of leadership, and the spark of inspiration that ignites the inert pages of the score into musical flames.

Thus by the humanization of instrumental personalities, by historical and psychological association, by suggesting symbolic meanings, or by stark imitative realism, a composer builds a color vocabulary to communicate his particular ideas and to serve his dramatic designs. The orchestral composer must know not only the limitations and capabilities of each instrument, but also how each sounds in the company of its fellows. Some inevitably attract attention to themselves whenever present. The trumpet, E-flat clarinet, and cymbals, for instance, can never appear in disguise, and their company is not always welcome. Others, such as the violas and cellos are essentially good mixers, and their presence would be sorely missed if the composer inadvertently left them off his guest list. Still other instruments, such as the violins, bassoons, and French horns, blend well and tend to merge with the other colors, but they are also able to stand out with pronounced personalities of their own whenever necessary. Furthermore, if a composer is to justify his use of the colossal arsenal of the symphony orchestra with its huge aggregate of strings, reeds, pipes, tubes, and membranes, he must match his mighty medium with some correspondingly great ideas. These phalanxes of fiddles and row upon row of performers should not be bowing, blowing, and beating in vain.

INSTRUMENTATION

The art of *instrumentation* is simply the practice by composers of organizing all these instrumental possibilities for their particular expressive purposes—in other words, choosing the right tools and combinations to do the job. The process of scoring a work might well be likened to the problems that confront the pictorial artist. After he has decided on the scope and size of his design, determined the direction of his lines and the balance of light and shade, he must then proceed to determine the most suitable medium and color scheme. A particular idea, for instance, might best be realized as a black-and-white etching or lithograph, a water color, oil painting, or large fresco mural. In much the same manner a composer takes into account the various avenues open to him and the nature of the ideas he is trying to realize in sound. The variety of color available with a single solo instrument, for instance, is quite restricted, while with an orchestral palette at his disposal, an almost infinite range of hues and instrumental mixtures is at his command. And just as a connoisseur of art can recognize instantly the work of Titian or El Greco by their color harmonies, so also is a discerning listener immediately aware of the characteristic sounds of Beethoven's or Wagner's orchestra. In this way a composer's musical personality is often seen through his idiomatic handling of instruments. Using the piano as an example, Beethoven's explosive accentuation, Chopin's coloratura lyricism, Debussy's mysterious mixtures of tone and overtone, and Stravinsky's brittle, percussive sonorities reveal each composer's personal conception of what constitutes "piano style." In a somewhat broader sense, the profile of a style period is likewise mirrored in the characteristic ways its composers approach the instruments at their disposal. These color images, moreover, are often just as important in the total vocabulary of a composer as are melody, rhythm, dynamics, textures, and formal principles.

Clothes, it is often said, make the man; and in similar fashion the choice of instruments makes the music. A composer dresses his melodies in a variety of sonorities just as a dramatist clothes his characters according to the situations in which they are to appear. Whether a melody is conceived in the mind of a composer with or without its unique color, his choice is always dictated by the context, the sequence of colors in a large-scale work, the need for dramatic entries at particular points, and the color that comes closest to realizing his idea in sound. Schubert, for instance, opens the slow movement of his "Great" C-major Symphony with a quiet, fairly unobtrusive melody. In order to command the necessary attention it needs to be spotlighted, but no very arresting accent is required. It just has to be there from the start, clearly in focus, but without making an obviously dramatic entry. A trumpet would be too much, a flute too little. What choice, then, could be better than that of an oboe with its poignant tone and the cutting edge of its sound quality? No matter how softly it is played, its presence is always felt. The seven introductory bars for low strings provide the background support; contribute to the contrast of string and woodwind color; and further serve to focus the oboe melody by playing low to its higher register, dark to its brighter color, and an even pulsation to the melody's irregular contours.

The vocabulary of instrumental usages locates a musical work in space as well as in time. The passage for four horns in Weber's Overture to *Der Freischütz*, for instance, could refer only to Germany and, more specifically, to its forest locale; the *Homage to Debussy*, written by Falla for the guitar, is obviously a Spaniard's homage to the great French musician; and the "hillbilly fiddler" style of the last movement of Gruenberg's Violin Concerto sets the piece in the Ozark mountain country. Social level can also be suggested by instrumentation. The flutter-tongue trumpeting in the opening measures of Copland's *Music for the Theater*, as well as the jazz style of the "Burlesque" movement, clearly indicates the type of theater he has in mind, which is Broadway rather than the Metropolitan Opera House. Cycles of taste, furthermore, are factors in the fluctuations of musical styles. After the rich, sensuous orchestration of his early ballet, *The Firebird,* Stravinsky moved into a neoclassical phase and favored more austere and minimal instrumental combinations such as the violin and piano, where the emphasis was on line and construction rather than on lush orchestral coloration.

Certain characteristic vocal and instrumental timbres are indelibly imprinted on the styles of various historical periods. Pure polyphonic choral writing sung *a cappella,* for instance, is invariably associated with the Renaissance in the fifteenth and sixteenth centuries, while the antiphonal responses of "broken" choirs recall the setting of St. Mark's Church and the Venetian polychoral style. Instruments and their combinations likewise have their periodic points of popularity. The incisive sound of the trumpet and oboe delighted the baroque ear, while the aristocratic eighteenth-century rococo enjoyed the pure tonal elegance of the agile flute, and the romanticists explored the mellower colors of the clarinet and French horn. The busy, thick, bustling tuttis of a Bach *Brandenburg* concerto contrast fundamentally with the poised elegance and balanced symmetry of those in Viennese classical concertos; the fragile thin sonorities of the harpsichord obviously were not adapted to the thunderous, heaven-storming music the romanticists wrote for the piano.

Historically, the identification of specific instrumental timbres with particular musical ideas is a fairly recent development. Renaissance music, for instance, is often directed by the composer to be played by voices or viols interchangeably. Also in older operatic scores the orchestration was quite haphazard, and composers merely suggested certain instruments and combinations according to what might be available at the time of performance. Even when the choice of specific instruments in this older music can be identified with accuracy, the precise meaning often escapes our modern ears, based as it is on a lost performance tradition. The surviving names of these older instruments, however, indicate that past periods attached definite significance to particular timbres. The *viola d'amore* (love viol), for instance, with its warm vibrant quality was apparently so called because its affecting tone suggested amorous situations. Likewise the flutes that bore such qualifying adjectives as *flûte d'amour* (love flute), *flûte douce* (sweet flute), *flauto d'eco* (echo flute), *Waldflöte* (woodland flute), and *oboe da caccia* (hunting oboe) were apparently all identified at some time or other with particular qualities and musical situations. When these ancient instruments are revived today, either for the performance of old music or when used by contemporary composers, they always have a quaint quality of bygone days and an antique flavor associated with the past. At best, however, a modern performance of eighteenth-century keyboard music on a harpsichord can endow the music with the authentic ring of a true period piece. With its fragile, wiry tone, its two manuals and coupling devices, the harpsichord is ideally adapted for the terraced dynamics, antiphonal effects, echo nuances, and linear clarity of the baroque style.

Many older instruments in their modern forms still retain meanings associated with their origin and early usage. Trumpets, for instance, can be used simply for their bright incisive sound, or symbolically to suggest warlike imagery or the festive fanfares announcing the grand entries of important personages (the "Grand March" from Verdi's *Aida,* and Mendelssohn's "Wedding March" are examples) . French horns were originally hunting horns, hence their association with sylvan settings and the chase (for example, the Trio from the Scherzo of Beethoven's *Eroica* Symphony, Weber's Overture to *Oberon,* and Mendelssohn's Nocturne from the incidental music to Shakespeare's *Midsummer Night's Dream.* The fife-and-drum corps instrumentation of Beethoven's "Turkish March" from the *Ruins of Athens* is also immediately intelligible to the modern listener, as is the country-amateur style of string playing in Mozart's *Musical Joke* (K.522) and in the Scherzo movement of Beethoven's *Spring* Sonata, Op. 24, for piano and violin. The woodwinds likewise retain something of their original outdoor character when heard in the serenades and divertimentos of Haydn and Mozart, where they readily recall the garden parties and street music of their time. Brahms in the Allegretto grazioso movement of his Symphony No. 2 skillfully employs the woodwinds in their pastoral sense as do many modern composers.

Many of the subtler meanings of eighteenth-century instrumentation, however, either escape the modern listener altogether or else must be learned through careful study and constant attention. The use of the trombones in the mourning chorus around Eurydice's tomb in Gluck's *Orfeo,* for example, is associated with the use of that instrument during the Masses for the Dead in the Viennese churches of the time, hence their elegiac character in this context. Likewise in *Don Giovanni,* Mozart uses trombones in the climactic final scene where fate catches up with the gay Don; their sepulchral quality is associated with the appearance of the statue of the dead Commendatore, and they thus bespeak the voice of doom. Beethoven occasionally wrote passages in the purported "Turkish" style, so popular in his time. In the Alla marcia section of the Finale of his Symphony No. 9, for instance, he uses such consciously bizarre effects as the combination of the piccolo and contrabassoon, plus the triangle, cymbals, and big bass drum.

Beginning with Gluck, continuing through the classical and into the romantic period, the expressive capacities of instruments were thoroughly explored and typed. Berlioz became the first composer to make a special study of instrumentation as such and to devote a specific treatise to it. His writings attest to his intense sensitivity to the dramatic character of the various instruments. By careful study of the practices of his predecessors— Gluck and Beethoven, in particular—Berlioz said he began to perceive "the subtle connection which subsists between musical expression and the special art of instrumentation." Gluck, for instance, points out in one of the prefaces to his operas that, "instruments should be used according to dramatic vicissitudes." He thus departed from the stylized continuo accompaniments of baroque recitatives and arias and allowed the emotional meaning to be mirrored directly in the instrumental coloration. Berlioz cites as an example the hatred scene from Gluck's *Armide* where "on the first line the two oboes make a cruel discord on the major seventh, like a woman's cry of terror and keenest anguish." He also points to an oboe passage in Agamemnon's song from Gluck's *Iphigenia in Aulis.* "When played on the piano," he says, "it sounds like a meaningless bell, instead of a plaintive wail. In this way the *idea,* the *thought,* the *inspiration* are either marred or destroyed." He also calls attention to the famous flute solo from Gluck's *Orfeo,* which occurs at the point where Eurydice is discovered amid the blessed spirits in the Elysian fields. "The melody," Berlioz writes, "is conceived in such a way that the flute lends itself to all the uneasy writhings of this eternal grief, still imbued with the passion of earthly life. It is at first a scarcely audible voice, which seems to fear being overheard: soon it laments softly, rising into the accent of reproach, then into that of profound woe, the cry of a heart torn of incurable wounds, then falling little by little into complaint, regret, and the sorrowing murmur of a resigned soul." Thus in the hands of the Viennese composers instrumentation began consciously to assume dramatic importance; and through this individualization of instruments, composers began using them, both in their solo and ensemble capacities, as *dramatis personae* of musical dramas, much in the manner that playwrights handle their human characters on the stage.

Berlioz and the romanticists ceaselessly sought out new sonorities, descriptive effects, and picturesque tonal images for their scores as a means of communicating their poetic ideas more vividly. While color as an element is present to a degree in all style periods, it remained for the romanticists to go a step beyond linear, rhythmic, and dynamic movement and attempt to build a musical style on the qualitative movement of tone color. In this esthetic venture they were aided and abetted by the inventive spirit of the Industrial Revolution. By the use of metal the woodwind instruments could be manufactured with greater precision, and the new valve mechanisms assured more predictable results for such instruments as the French horn. With performers exercising greater control over their instruments, the imaginations of composers were further stimulated, and they were able to call for more and more unusual effects with greater confidence as to the outcome at performance time.

Going hand in hand with this development was the rise of virtuosity. Paganini and Liszt as individual performers extended the resources of the violin and piano, respectively, beyond anything composers had hitherto thought possible. This virtuoso approach was also carried over into the realm of the orchestra by Berlioz and Wagner, who, as composer-conductors, developed the inherent possibilities of their gigantic collective forces into the most complex and colorful of all musical instruments—the full symphony orchestra. Wagner's grasp of the dramatic capacities of individual instruments is unparalleled in the history of music. To portray the proud pageantry of the guild in his *Die Meistersinger von Nürnberg* (The Mastersingers of Nuremberg), he uses the pompous posturing of the wind instruments. For the sword in the *Ring* cycle, his choice is a bugle-like melody sounded by the piercing timbre of the trumpet. For Fafner, the lazy dragon in *Siegfried,* he hits upon the deep snoring sounds emitted by the bass register of the tuba. For the crackling flames of the magic fire scene at the end of *Die Walküre,* he adds the sparkling staccato notes of the piccolo and those of glistening glockenspiel. And to set a scene of melancholy and utter desolation at the beginning of Act III of *Tristan and Isolde,* no instrument could be more effective than the plaintive English horn, alone and isolated from the orchestra. The barrenness of the lonely Norman coast where Tristan has repaired after his disastrous duel, the foreshadowing of his tragic death, the hope for the return of Isolde over the sea, and the misery of his separation from her are all realized by this masterly touch.

From Wagner's time to the present the search has continued for instruments with new resources of personality. To serve their poetic purposes composers employ both symbolism and realism, with the meaning and the mood they wish to convey as the deciding factor. The low, reedy register of the flute solo at the beginning of Debussy's *Afternoon of a Faun,* for instance, places the piece in a pastoral setting; and the association of the flute with the ancient pipes of Pan of Greek mythology—fauns being the wayward progeny of the goat-footed god Pan—connects the imagery symbolically with Mallarmé's poem which serves as the programmatic text. As the lazy, flowing melody continues, Debussy surrounds it with a voluptuous tonal envelope by adding the sylvan touch of the French horn and the watery splash of harp arpeggios. The dominant mood of the composition is thus immediately established.

Greater realism in sound has attracted the attention of many composers. Verdi and Wagner used anvils in the forging scenes of *Il Trovatore* and *Das Rheingold,* respectively. No longer content with nostalgic spinning songs, Charpentier brought a corps of sewing machines onto the operatic stage in his *Louise*. Richard Strauss employed a theatrical wind machine in Variation VII and a special horn technique for the bleating of sheep in Variation II of his *Don Quixote*. Dissatisfied with the conventional rendering of a nightingale's song by the stylized flute trill, Respighi calls for an actual recording of a real nightingale in his *Pines of Rome*. For stark realism it would be hard to equal the crescendo on the bass drum to represent the wild beating of Marie's heart in the murder scene of Berg's *Wozzeck*. And the modern mechanical age with its factories and jet engines is surely reflected directly in the insistent rhythms and percussive sounds so frequently encountered in contemporary musical scores.

Finally, it must constantly be borne in mind that from the simple human voice to the complex symphony orchestra, instruments are, after all, only instruments—that is, means to an end and never ends in themselves. That ultimate end, of course, can only be making music.

Rhythm

Chapter 3

RHYTHM is at once the life's breath that animates the
spirit of every musical organism, the life's blood that courses through the
arteries and veins of its circulatory system, the heartbeat that pulses
throughout the body of a musical composition, and the life cycle that
covers the span between the birth of its initial upbeat and the death of its
closing cadence. Rhythm, in this broadest possible meaning, articulates
the flow of musical time, implies the perception of purposeful movement,
and indicates a sense of progress in certain directions. Just as motion
through space is visible to the eye, so motion through time becomes audible to the ear through the medium of music. Such motion is subject to the
greatest diversification as well as the widest variety; and, of course, rhythm
is inextricably intertwined with all the other musical elements and complexes—tone color, dynamics, melody, harmony, counterpoint, and form.
The esthetic experience of rhythm can be as basic as the insistent "oom-
pah" beat of the common march, or as exalted as the transcendental trills
of a late Beethoven string quartet.

Rhythm, in this most general sense, can best be understood as the perception of duration in the flow of musical time. In no case is time to be
considered an absolute. Clock time, for instance, is based on a number of
generally accepted units of measure, just as in the case of weight and distance. By common consent 60 seconds become a minute, 60 minutes an
hour, and so on. Musical time likewise is a system of mutually accepted
conventions, but of a much more complex kind. The rhythmic moment is

the temporal movement between two terminal tones, however near or far apart they may be. Time, as measured by the clock, for instance, is perceived by the interval between the tick and tock in the case of seconds, and by the lapse between chimes in the case of quarter hours, half hours, and hours. Similarly, rhythm refers to a manner of dividing musical time into intervals of relatively short and long duration, into movement toward or away from stressed and unstressed beats, into the regular and irregular patterns by which the direction and flow of the movement is determined.

Various types of motion are discernible within the tonal continuum. Some are concerned with physical action as in the dance, others with psychological action as in the arousal of feeling. When participating in actual dances and work songs, in the first instance, the rhythmic motion is based on the patterned physical activity that directs the steps and shapes the gestures of hands and body. In the other case, rhythmic motion has to do with the striving of the mind and will. The movement here shapes the stream of thought and emotion of the individual or group. When listening to a dance, the steps, gestures, and body movements are recalled through the process of what psychologists call kinesthetic imagery or muscular memory; while in songlike and more abstract moments, various moods and emotional states are conjured up. In one case the experience moves the muscular memory, in the other it moves the emotions. It is indeed no accident that certain single musical forms are called "movements." In this sense the term refers to a whole or part of a composition in which a certain unity can be found in a type of recognizable, coherent rhythmic motion. The term is also used in cyclical forms in which a movement is a single unit of a larger whole, as, for example, a suite of dances or an overall sonata structure. The esthetic and psychological considerations of these more extended forms demand contrasts of individual movements, thus giving rise to the appellations of "allegro movement," "slow movement," "minuet movement," and the like.

No two writers define rhythm in precisely the same way. In the present instance it is considered to have a dual meaning indicating both the broad time-flow of the art of music as well as the regular or irregular groupings of metrical units as they form themselves into recognizable patterns as in a march or dance. The subdivisions under the general category of rhythm are threefold—meter, rhythm, and tempo. A single beat, just as a single tone, has no musical significance. Two or more beats, however, allow for comparative differences of duration and the distinction between strong or weak, accented or unaccented beats. A *meter*, therefore, is based on some pattern of two or more beats joined together to make a recognizable unit. *Rhythm* refers to the recurrence of these metrical entities as they group themselves into regular or irregular patterns and move along in orderly succession. As an ancient Roman grammarian perceptively put it, "Rhythm is flowing meter, and meter is arrested rhythm." The term *tempo,* then, indicates the pace or relative rate of speed by which these metrical and rhythmic groups proceed. A glance at a musical score should make this triple distinction quite clear.

On the first page of Beethoven's Sonata *Pathétique* (Ex. 3:1) the word *Grave* appears over the top staff of lines to indicate that the tempo is to be slow and solemn. Such tempo markings determine only the rate at which the metrical units within the bar are to proceed. Even when the tempo is altered by an acceleration or a retardation, it points merely to a general change of pace and does not alter the internal metrical or rhythmic relationships. After the clefs and key signature comes the time signature *C* which stands for 4/4; in other words, each measure is to be divided into four quarter notes, hence four beats per bar. Time signatures such as this have nothing to do with tempo or rate of speed, since 4/4 could just as well be found in an *andante* or *presto* movement. All it means here is that each measure is to contain just four quarters, which in turn can be subdivided into 16 sixteenths as found in the fifth measure, or the irregular combination of sixty-fourth notes and one-hundred-twenty-eighth notes in the last bar.

Returning now to measure one, it can be seen that the chord that coincides with the first quarter beat is prolonged by tying it over to the succeeding dotted sixteenth in order that the following beat will be weak. This second chord is thus a short thirty-second note going to a longer dotted sixteenth. When this occurs again with the next thirty-second note moving to a quarter, and so on in succeeding measures, it establishes a metrical pattern of short-long units, known in poetry as iambs, that are to dominate the section. The bar line between measures one and two has no fundamental rhythmic significance, which can readily be seen from the fact that the first iamb of the second measure begins with the last thirty-second note of Bar 1. In earlier times when music was printed in parts only, bar lines were not used. Later when all the parts of an ensemble were grouped together in a score, vertical bar lines were introduced as an aid to the eye. From this procedure are derived the English word *score,* the French word *partition,* and the German *partitur.* This new scored notation took account of certain metrical groupings, and both time signatures and bar lines were then needed to indicate the number of beats within the bar. Still later an effort was made to see that the strong beats, if possible, could be made to coincide with the first beat of each bar; though as it works out, this is by no means always the case. In the *Pathétique,* measures two, three, and four proceed similarly to the first measure, grouping themselves rhythmically into a four-bar phrase. The

Ex. 3:1   Piano Sonata, Op. 13 (*Pathétique*). First Movement (Bars 1–10).
Beethoven.

precipitous run in Bar 4 forms a flourishing upbeat to Bar 5 and the
beginning of the next phrase, which is characterized by the regular pulsation of sixteenths in the bass part while the treble continues the iambic
meters of the opening.

Thus are the tempo, meter, and rhythm distinguished. The slow pace
at which the piece proceeds is indicated by the tempo marking, *Grave*.

The meter in this case is based on the short-long beats of the iamb. The smallest rhythmic grouping occurs with the joining of the metrical units first into that of Bar 1, then into that of Bar 2 which is divided from the first by rests. The rhythm then expands into the half-phrase unit of Bars 3 and 4 which in turn group themselves cumulatively with Bars 1 and 2 to form the first full four-bar phrase. Bars 5 and 6 separately parallel Bars 1 and 2, while Bars 7 and 8 together are the counterparts of Bars 3 and 4. Beethoven, however, extends this second phrase by two extra measures, and the section as a whole thus falls rhythmically into two subdivisions of four and six bars, respectively. Musical forms, in this manner, take on an overall rhythmic character of their own, based as they are on the regular repetition and recurrence of musical materials. This feeling of rhythmical flow from phrase to phrase, onward into sections, and thence to whole movements promotes a sense of progress not unlike the growth of living forms. Instead of static blocks, the basic units of a work then become the underlying rhythmic currents that flow past formal landmarks toward moments of emphasis and eventually to the high points of interest that define the musical destination and impart to the whole the sense of the long line.

TEMPO

Among the several ways by which the passage of music's time-flow is measured, *tempo* represents the more general experience of time, defines the rate at which rhythmic groups progress, and is closely identified with the expressive spirit of a piece. While the internal rhythmic relationships provide variety, tempo promotes the continuity of a musical movement and preserves its basic identity and integrity. A proper tempo should be felt as a natural movement welling up from within a musical work rather than an arbitrary pace imposed on it from without. In this way a tempo becomes an effective means of activating static tonal masses, of bringing elasticity to the metrical and rhythmic organization, of breathing life into the formal structure, and of animating the manner of motion and emotion of the musical organism.

This perception of the passage of musical time is not based so much on such quantitative measurements as those of the clock as it is on the qualitative flow of events within a given temporal interval. In addition to mechanical devices everyone is equipped with various physiological clocks that articulate the flow of time—the beating of the heart, inhaling and exhaling the breath, sleeping and wakeful states, recurrence of meal-times, and the like. Psychological factors also enter the picture, and when a person is participating in pleasurable activities, time seems to pass more quickly than when taking part in less pleasant occupations. When events occur in rapid succession, time seems to fly, but when little happens, it lags. Similarly in a state of agitation a person will talk more quickly and walk more hurriedly, while in calmer moments his speech is slower and he saunters rather than runs. Reflections of all these variable physiological and psychological states are to be found in musical tempos. Heightened emotional tension is usually accompanied by a faster heartbeat and faster breathing. An emotional climax in music is often achieved in this same way—that is, by an *accelerando* or quickening of the pace, or with a *stretto,* a narrowing or shortening of the temporal intervals between beats. Similarly with a slowing up of the pace through a *ritardando,* or a broadening of the interval between tones in an *allargando,* a tendency toward relaxation and repose is brought about. Tempos are thus based on these general experiences of ebb and flow in the temporal dimension and hence can give important clues to the individuality and special character of a musical work.

The wide range of tempos from slow to fast can best be understood when a norm is assumed. Such a normal tempo would correspond to the average pulse or breathing rate, though allowance has to be made for individual variations. Handel, for instance, called this norm, *tempo giusto* (a just or comfortable progress) , and this term is also chosen by Moussorgsky to indicate the casual gait of the "Promenade" in his *Pictures at an Exhibition* (Ex. 3:7) . *Andante,* literally "going" or "walking," is found much more frequently and implies a comfortable pace without holding back or forging ahead. The range of moods in this case would be no stronger than those of ease, moderation, and relaxation. Any slackening of this normal rate implies a certain restraint which becomes associated with dignified or solemn occasions. The moods consequently extend from peaceful contemplation and serenity to gentle melancholy, dejection, and despair. A quickening of the pulse, on the other hand, would indicate agitation, excitement, or joy.

Dances written for group participation must take certain physical limitations into account. Marches, for instance, have many possible tempos, each of them connected with a particular function, pace, and mood. If a military march is taken as a normal tempo, a graduation march, a wedding march, a coronation or triumphal march would then be in varying degrees slower until the heavy measured tread of a funeral march is reached. On the brisker side are quick-step marches and the still livelier cavalry marches. For practical purposes, however, none can be so slow that it is impossible to maintain physical balance, and none can be so fast that it is impossible to keep pace. Other barriers likewise set limitations on the range of tempos in concert music. If the time interval between successive tones becomes so great that the sense of coherence and continuity is lost, the tempo is obviously too slow. On the other hand, when tones succeed each other so rapidly that all articulation between them is lost and the rhythmic relationships become an indistinct jumble, then the tempo is clearly too fast. Within these two extremes fall the various possible concert tempos.

The range of tempos is not so great as might be first imagined. If a *largo sostenuto* or a *molto adagio* is taken as the slowest possible tempo, a *prestissimo* at the other extreme will be only about eight times faster. Several factors must, however, be borne in mind since these tempos are relative rather than absolute, and sometimes they are better understood simply as negative indications. An *allegro* can be paced more or less briskly, but never slowly, while an *adagio* can be slow in varying degrees, but never fast. The following table gives the tempos most commonly employed by composers. In addition to these terms many qualifying adjectives can be used, depending upon various modifications and unusual moods. Since sonatas and suites often include dance movements, the title alone—gavotte, sarabande, gigue, and the like—is often sufficient to indicate the proper pace and character of a piece. Similarly, concert numbers patterned after dance forms often bear such indications as *tempo di marcia* (in march time) and *tempo di menuetto* (in the tempo of a minuet) and so on.

Ever since the early nineteenth century, composers have tried to in-

TEMPOS

Tempo	Italian Term	Literal Meaning	Examples from Beethoven's Piano Sonatas
Very Slow:	Largo	large, broad, spacious	Op. 7, 2d movement; Op. 10 No. 3, 2d movement
	Grave	grave, heavy, solemn	Op. 13, 1st movement, Part 1 (Ex. 3:1)
Slow:	Adagio	at ease, leisurely	Op. 13, 2d movement; Op. 27 No. 2, 1st movement; Op. 81a, 1st movement
	Andante	at a walking or going gait	Op. 28, 2d movement; Op. 79, 2d movement
Moderate:	Moderato	moderate, unhurried	Op. 110, 1st movement
Fast:	Allegretto	slightly on brisk side	Op. 31 No. 3, 2d movement; Op. 53, 3d movement
	Allegro	cheerful, gay, the normal brisk tempo	Op. 28, 1st movement; Op. 81a, 1st movement, Part 2; Op. 106, 1st movement
	Allegro Molto	very brisk	Op. 7, 1st movement; Op. 10 No. 1, 1st movement
	Vivace	vivacious, lively	Op. 79, 3d movement; Op. 109, 1st movement
Very Fast:	Presto	quick	Op. 27 No. 2, 3d movement; Op. 79, 1st movement; Op. 10, No. 3, 1st movement
	Prestissimo	as quickly as possible	Op. 109, 2d movement

troduce some objectivity into the process of setting tempos by means of Maelzel's *metronome,* a mechanical device the clicks off so many beats per minute. When set at 60, for instance, it ticks off the number of seconds in a minute as does the second hand of a clock. Brisk marching time can be indicated in a score as $\quad = 120$, thus marking two steps per second— a tempo that also corresponds roughly to a normal concert *allegro.* In the same manner, $\quad = 90$ would be *moderato;* $\quad = 56$, slow; and from $\quad = 140$ upward, fast. Such straight metronomic time, however, tends to be mechanical and lifeless, and a good tempo always needs a little hurrying here and some lingering there so as to give it sufficient elasticity and room to breathe. Fortunately the choice does not lie with the extremes of mechanical regimentation on one side and rhythmical chaos on the other. Some regularity, however, is needed from time to time if only as a point of departure. Tempos thus have a tendency to vary from the comparatively strict to those of a freer type. The difference is mainly one of style and the tempo should always be an outgrowth of the inner character and the individual expressive quality of the musical work.

It is here that *tempo rubato* enters the picture, a term defined by Tovey as a "rhythmical robbing of Peter to pay Paul." The pianist Paderewski described such rubato tempos as being "energetic or languishing, crisp or elastic, steady or capricious." A balance between strictness and freedom has to be struck, bearing in mind that adhering too closely to the metronome can lead to mechanical rigidity and too much freedom can lead to license. Minor fluctuations as accelerations or retardations may occur when called for, but such changes in momentum, if the underlying unity of a movement is to be preserved, can never be so drastic as to drift from one tempo to a radically different one. The choice between a mathematically more exact tempo and a capricious one depends on such factors as whether a rational or an irrational approach is appropriate, an objective or subjective attitude is called for, as well as on many other historical and stylistic considerations. The rhythmical ratios of a Bach fugue, for instance, would be quite different from those of a Chopin mazurka. A fugue tends toward uniformity and precision, while a mazurka is so capricious and personal that it defies exact explanation. This does not mean, however, that all Bach is strict and all Chopin free. Many Bach preludes and slow movements allow a maximum of personal freedom of expression, while the etudes of Chopin can be quite strict by comparison.

Tempos, finally, vary somewhat with physiological and psychological conditions, with differences of interior and exterior temperature, with youth and age, and even with the time of day. Tempos, moreover, are subject to acoustical conditions and the capacities of various musical instruments, as well as the temperamental differences of performers. Even with the same performer, however, tempos may vary from performance to performance, depending upon his mood, state of relative tension or relaxation, as well as on a host of other esthetic and psychological factors.

METER

The single bricks out of which the rhythmic structure of music is built are the combinations of long and short tones, strong and weak beats, accented and unaccented notes known as *meters*. Single beats, as in the case of single tones, have no musical significance. It is a basic necessity of the human mind, however, to group separate impulses together in certain ways. The tick-tock of a clock mechanism, the clickety-clack of a passing railroad train, the dripping of a water faucet are each ordered into repetitive patterns of one sort or another. A simple experiment with a metronome will show that the clicks quickly resolve themselves into metrical units. Some will think or count ONE-two, ONE-two, others ONE-two-three, ONE-two-three, thus showing the necessity of inferring accented and unaccented beats, even where the impulses are mechanically completely regular. The perception of meter, then, depends upon the recognition of some sequence of strong and weak beats, whether actual or implied.

Basically there are only two possible meters—those with two and those with three beats. These two *simple* meters are variously called duple and triple, or binary and ternary. Any meter of more than three beats is *compound* since it can be broken down into one or another of these simple meters. A simple binary meter consists of a strong and weak beat, ONE-two, or a weak and strong, one-TWO. Compound binary would then be some multiple of two, such as four or eight beats as, for instance, ONE-two-THREE-four. Similarly, a simple ternary meter would be ONE-two-three, and one of its compounds ONE-two-three-FOUR-five-six-SEVEN-eight-nine. Binary metrical signatures commonly found at the beginning of a musical score are 2/4 or 4/4, or less often 2/8 or 4/8. Ternary signatures are usually 3/4, or 3/8, and less often 9/8.

The simplest duple-metered composition would be a march with its alternating LEFT-right, LEFT-right, ONE-two, ONE-two, or, as it appears in rhythmic notation, 2/4 ♩ ♩ | ♩ ♩ . Likewise the simplest ternary dance is the waltz with its ONE-two-three, ONE-two-three sequence, or in notation 3/4 ♩ ♩ ♩ | ♩ ♩ ♩ . In more complex phases of the art, metrical arrangements may proceed with the extreme symmetry of the Allegretto from Beethoven's Seventh Symphony (Ex. 3:2), or with the planned asymmetry of the fugue subject the same composer's String Quartet in C-sharp Minor (Ex. 3:3) in which no two measures are identical.

Ex. 3:2 Symphony No. 7. Second Movement (Bars 1–8). Beethoven.

Ex. 3:3 String Quartet in C-sharp Minor, Op. 131. First Movement (Bars 1–11). Beethoven.

A close analogy exists between poetic and musical meters. Ancient Greek and Roman poetry was constructed on an intricate metrical system consisting of various types of poetic feet whose regular and continuous recurrence determined the rhythm. These meters were made up of units of short and long duration—unstressed and stressed syllables—that closely resemble many of the familiar meters found in music. A bar or measure in music usually corresponds to one or two metrical feet in scanning a poem. The grouping of measures in music into half phrases of two or three bars, and phrases of from four to six bars, parallels the grouping of meters into poetic lines. Poetic lines consisting of two meters, for instance, are called dimeters; three, trimeters; four, tetrameters; five, pentameters; six, hexameters; and so on. The ancient Greeks also distinguished a down-beat by the term *thesis*, taken from the stamping of the dance leader's foot, and an upbeat by *arsis,* meaning the lifting of the foot. Among the most common of these classical meters are the *iamb,* a short-long unit symbolized by ˇ – in poetry, and ♩ ♩ in music; the long-short of the *trochee* shown by – ˇ or ♩ ♪; the short-short-long of the *anapest,* by ˇ ˇ – or ♫ ♩ ; and the long-short-short of the *dactyl,* by – ˇ ˇ or ♩ ♫. Some splendid lines of iambic pentameter (meaning five iambs per line) can be found among Shakespeare's sonnets:

> Ŏ lear̄n / tŏ rēad / whăt sī- / lent love / hăth wr̄it:
> To hear / with eyes / be- longs / to love's / fine wit.
> (Sonnet XXIII)

Many musical equivalents of iambic meter come to mind. Beethoven's famous Minuet in G proceeds in iambs, as does the bass part of the Second

Movement of Brahms' *German Requiem* (Ex. 3:13). In the introduction
to Beethoven's Sonata *Pathétique* (Ex. 3:1), the thirty-second notes followed by the dotted sixteenth and quarter notes are likewise iambic.

The trochee is the meter associated with the strong-weak alternation
of the common march step. Shakespeare, however, used the meter for one
of his most graceful lyrics, which is set by Schubert in one of his most
memorable songs.

Who is / Syl- via? / what is / she,
That/ all our / swains com-/ mend her?

(Shakespeare: *Two Gentlemen of Verona.*
Act IV, Scene 2)

Ex. 3:4   *Who Is Sylvia?* (Bars 5–8). Schubert.

Byron's lines, quoted below, are anapests grouped into tetrameters,
while the two excerpts from Berlioz' *Rakocsky March* (Ex. 3:5) are a musical parallel. Anapestic meters are also found in Bach's C-minor Fugue
from Book I of the *Well-Tempered Clavier* (Ex. 7:11), and they likewise
dominate the opening melody of Mozart's Symphony No. 40 (Ex. 10:1).

Ex. 3:5   *Rakocsky March* (Bars 7–8 and 20–23). Berlioz.

The As- syr- / ian came down /like a wolf / on the fold.
And his co-/ horts were gleam-/ ing in pur-/ ple and gold.

Longfellow's famous lines from *Evangeline,* as quoted below, are based
on dactyls.

This is the/for- est prim-/e- val, the/mur- mur- ing/pines and the/hem- locks

The familiar waltz, with its accented first beat and unaccented second
and third beats, illustrates the same dactylic idea in 3/4 time, while its
use in 2/4 or duple time is well exemplified in both the second movement

of Beethoven's Seventh Symphony (Ex. 3:2) and the melody of Schubert's well-known *Marche Militaire* (Ex. 3:6).

Ex. 3:6   *Marche Militaire* (Bars 7–10). Schubert.

Mode, in the Greek and Roman sense, applied to a system of scales and also to a system of meters, each of which had a distinctive character and particular mood associated with it. Just as poetry has the strict rhythms of scanned lines and the wild rhapsodic outburst of free verse, so music too has its regular and irregular rhythms. The words "mood," "mode," and "meter," as well as "motion" and "emotion," are all derived from the same root word. The terms "movement" and "motion" still indicate action and progress, while "emotion" now applies to a psychological disturbance, an excited or agitated mental state. The choice of poetic meter and mode still depends on the mood or manner of the poem, certain metrical patterns being appropriate to elegies, others to lyric, rhapsodic, and epical poems. This is also true of music, with majestic iambs being employed for dignified marches and the dancing dactyls for lilting waltzes and the like.

Departures from metrical regularity are among the stocks in trade of all good composers. A deliberately ambiguous meter, for instance, is used by Moussorgsky in the "Promenade" sections from his *Pictures at an Exhibition* to create the effect of sauntering casually to and fro in a gallery.

Ex. 3:7   "Promenade" from *Pictures at an Exhibition* (Bars 1–2). Moussorgsky.

He divides the first measure into five quarters and the second into six. No accent, however, falls on the first beat of Bar 2. Curt Sachs in his valuable book, *Rhythm and Tempo*, finds that the only possible solution is "a phrase of eleven quarter beats with a suggested but not realized stress pattern." Some subdivision is, of course, a necessity, but exactly where this should occur is left to the performer who may play the measures differently at different times. Tchaikovsky caused considerable consternation with the dance meter he uses for the Scherzo movement of his Sixth Symphony.

Ex. 3:8   Symphony No. 6 (*Pathetique*). Second Movement (Bars 1–4). Tschaikovsky.

One baffled critic described it as a waltz for a three-legged man. The metrical signature is 5/4, which admits of a breakdown into units of 2 + 3 and 3 + 2. The first measure can be counted 1-2-3 1-2 and the second 1-2 1-2-3 and so on. A 7/4 metrical signature can likewise be reduced to 3 + 4 or 4+3. Many modern composers have gone much farther and employed the highly irregular successions of metrical units known as *polymeters*. Stravinsky in the final "Danse Sacrale" of his *Rite of Spring* has successive measures in which the metrical signature changes with each bar: 3/8, 2/8, 3/8, 2/4, 3/8, 2/8, 3/8, 2/4, etc. Note, however, that the entire sequence consists of eighth notes. If he had varied his metrical values too widely and employed a sequence such as 3/8, 5/16, 2/2, 9/32, 2/4, metrical chaos would obviously have developed.

RHYTHM

Rhythm, used here in its specific sense, refers to the time-flow of music which is grasped by the mind and ordered into meaningful patterns of measured motion. While meters consist of the grouping of single beats into short metrical entities, rhythm has to do with the grouping of meters into an orderly succession so arranged as to produce an overall rhythmic structure. This rhythmic grouping of metrical units constitutes the moving impulse that underlies all tonal motion, and which in turn promotes, carries along, and defines its manner of movement. Rhythms tend to flow in a series of accented beats that form the focal points on which both the metrical motion, melodic line, and dynamics converge as they move together toward high points within the phrase and toward the climaxes in the formal outline. Rhythm thus supports the melodic line, continues its momentum while underway, and eventually terminates it. Both motional and emotional changes in music can be effected by shifts of rhythmic relations within the general rhythmic structure. Since the rhythmic structure reveals so much of the ultimate significance of a musical work, it is pertinent to inquire: In what direction is the rhythmic motion striving? Does the rhythmic motion tend toward balance or imbalance? Does the motion tend toward rest or create the demand for further motion? Toward what high point is the rhythmic progress leading? What is the end and goal of the musical phrase and the overall form?

In music there are the speech rhythms of prose and poetry that are united with tone in such forms as the chant, song, choral motet, oratorio, and opera; and the body rhythms that are reflected in the steps and gestures of the dance. Work songs and folk dances, just as in the case of folk songs, tend toward simpler, regularly repeated patterns, while the choreography of a professional ballet corps may be exceedingly complex. All dances meant for the nonprofessional in the ballroom must, of necessity, be kept within the bounds of possible performance by the group for which they are intended; concert dances, however, can be highly sophisticated as well as free in form, and can merely suggest fragmentary memories or images of dances to those who sit and listen.

Of all basic dance rhythms that of the march is probably the one most often encountered in Western music. Historically, marches were at first purely functional, as most military marches are to this day. Beginning with the Elizabethan era in England, however, and continuing with the baroque period on the Continent, they began to appear in anthologies for performance at the keyboard, in suites of dances, and in operatic scenes. In these various art forms, march rhythms have taken on many different expressive connotations, associated as they are with the character of the occasions for which they were written. The sturdy measures of the Lutheran chorale, *A Mighty Fortress*, assert a firm, unshakable religious conviction; the solemn progress of the funeral marches from Beethoven's Sonata for Piano in A-flat Major, Op. 26, and Chopin's Sonata in B-flat Minor, Op. 58, reveal heroic qualities of monumental proportions; the bizarre broken rhythms that Berlioz writes for the "March to the Scaffold" in his *Symphonie Fantastique* give it a thoroughly grotesque atmosphere; the pompous progress of a "Coronation March" can be heard in Meyerbeer's opera, *The Prophet;* while the light tripping step of Mozart's march in the last act of his opera, the *Marriage of Figaro,* and the fanciful fairy march of Mendelssohn's Scherzo for Piano in E Minor, Op. 16, No. 2, have a sprightly gaiety all their own. Certain marches are based on the progressive trochaic step of left-foot, right-foot; others, such as cavalry marches, on the dashing dactyls that recall the gait of prancing steeds. Schubert's marches, such as the *Marche Militaire,* as well as many others that he wrote originally for piano duet, are usually of this type (Ex. 3:6) . Other cavalry marches are to be found in the final part of Rossini's Overture to *William Tell,* as well as in Rachmaninoff's Prelude in G Minor, Op. 23, No. 5; and, of course, it should be pointed out that the cavalry march is a close cousin to the polonaise.

When a composer needs to set a scene in a past period, dance rhythms become useful devices. That of the pavane, for instance, bespeaks a courtly character, while the elegant minuet recalls the polished floors and powdered wigs of the eighteenth-century rococo style. A time-honored rhythm for pastoral idylls is the old Sicilian rhythm $\frac{3}{8}$ ♫♪|♫♪|♩, which Handel uses for the "Pastoral Symphony" of his *Messiah;* Bach, for the gathering of shepherds in the "Sinfonia" at the beginning of Part 2 of his *Christmas Oratorio;* and Haydn, when the grazing of cattle is mentioned in his oratorio, *The Creation.* Rhythms can also create specific images of motion as the following examples will show:

Ex. 3:9 "Bydlo" from *Pictures at an Exhibition* (Bars 1–4). Moussorgsky.

Ex. 3:10 *Erlking* (Bars 1–3). Schubert.

Ex. 3:11 *To Be Sung on the Water* (Bars 1–3). Schubert.

In the first instance Moussorgsky imitates the lumbering gait of an ox-drawn cart for one of his *Pictures at an Exhibition* (Ex. 3:9); in the second, Schubert in his song, *The Erlking,* reinforces the words, "Who rides so late through night and wind," by a figure suggesting the feverish galloping of horse's hooves (Ex. 3:10); and in the song entitled *To Be Sung on the Water,* the same composer uses a wavelike image to suggest the rippling of water (Ex. 3:11). Rhythmic motion can thus communicate likenesses of natural as well as human movement.

Many techniques are employed by composers to insure rhythmic variety. Frequency of stressed beats can make a rhythm strong and stirring, while the infrequency of accent in slow and songlike movements can promote the feeling of inactivity and tranquillity. When too regular, however, the effect often becomes monotonous. In order to create an element of surprise, composers frequently shift the accent from the expected to an unexpected beat with the rhythmic device known as *syncopation.* Another way of achieving variety is that of combining two or more rhythms so that they are heard simultaneously, as in *polyrhythms*. This technique is highly developed in the music of the Orient, where Sachs calls attention to the "unique complication" of the songs accompanying the "clicking, clattering pestle play of rice-pounding women" in the Malay Archipelago as they grind their flour. Such complexities are also heard in the gamelan orchestras of Indonesia where each percussion instrument plays its own rhythm in concert with the others. In Africa also, tribal drummers, each with independent rhythms, often coordinate their efforts with a leader in extremely intricate polyrhythmic patterns. Compared with such complications as these, the rhythms of recent European music, until the twentieth century at least, seem comparatively simple. Every embryonic pianist has probably struggled with the problem of getting his left hand to play three beats while his right plays two, or four against three, as the case may be. Another type can be heard in Chopin's Waltz, Op. 42 (Ex. 3:12), which has a

Ex. 3:12 Waltz, Op. 42 (Bars 9–12). Chopin.

melody in duple time riding along over a conventional waltz bass in triple time. Upon analysis it breaks down into the two principal ways of dividing a rhythm of six beats in a bar. In the middle voice the 6 eighth notes flow along quite smoothly, while above them the melody proceeds in pairs of quarters equaling 3 eighth notes each and below them the bass moves in groups of three regular quarters equaling 2 eighth notes each. The resulting effect of this interplay of the two rhythms is one of conflict and even some turbulence.

   A sensitive adaptation of polyrhythmic procedures is found in the second movement of Brahms' *German Requiem* (Ex. 3:13). The slow laend-

Ex. 3:13 *German Requiem*. Second Movement (Bars 1–6). Brahms.

ler, ♩|♩♩|♩♩|♩, solemnly pronounced by the bassoons, cellos, and string basses, leads directly into the opening words of the text, which the chorus intones on the same rhythm.

Denn alles Fleisch ist wie Gras und alle Herrlichkeit des Menschen wie des Grases Blumen.
Behold all flesh is as the grass, and all the goodliness of man is as the flower of grass.

Since the laendler is a rustic or rural dance, it serves to signify the rank and file of mankind whose numbers are as the blades of grass on the landscape. Next there follows a reference to the goodliness (*Herrlichkeit*) of man, which in the German version connotes his lordliness or excellence, thereby implying a sense of nobility or moral grandeur which is likened to the flowers of grass. This seems to be symbolized by the courtly sarabande rhythm, ♩|♩ ♫♩|♩, specifically called such by Brahms in the first edition of the score. It appears, appropriately enough, in the highest part, where it is played by the flutes, oboes, clarinets, violins, and violas. In the middle the kettledrums constantly reiterate ♫|♩ ♩, a meter originally derived from the military drumroll. As such it is often heard in eighteenth-century marches as well as in the symphonies of Haydn and Mozart. The latter, interestingly enough, also employs it in connection with the Commendatore, a military figure whom Don Giovanni murders in the first act of Mozart's opera of that name; and it recurs again at the end of the opera to symbolize the stroke of fate which drags the gay Don down to his predestined doom. Beethoven uses it in the bass part of the "Funeral March" in his *Eroica* Symphony; and it also becomes the basic motive of his Fifth Symphony, where the composer likened its effect to that of "fate knocking at the door." Brahms' use of it here in his *Requiem* is therefore entirely in character. It thus completes the picture of mortal man—peasant and aristocrat, common and uncommon, simple and great —bound alike by the limitations of fate, and who must, as the text continues, be patient unto the coming of the Lord.

CONCLUSION

It must always be borne in mind that rhythm is not bound by the points or notational symbols on the printed page. The dial of a clock, for instance, has marks for minutes and hours, but time itself is measured by the movement of the hands through and past these points. Rhythmic movement likewise is felt as the continuous passage of energy between tones and is heard as it progresses toward some goal. Thus instead of becoming a series of stops, as the notes in a score might seem to indicate, rhythm begins to flow, to take on directional tendency and significant life. Rhythms, then, are based on patterns of repetition, variation, and combination, while the experience and perception of rhythm are based on memory and anticipation. When, for instance, the expected comes to pass, it can be quite comforting and reassuring; though if it occurs too regularly, it can be monotonous and even boring. When the unexpected transpires, it can be interesting and surprising; when this happens too frequently, however, it can become disconcerting and confusing.

Rhythmic concepts vary from country to country geographically, and from period to period historically. Rhythm according to the seventeenth-century mathematician Leibnitz was "unconscious counting"; while to the twentieth-century pianist Paderewski, it was "subject to moods and emotions, to rapture and depression." In some periods symmetry and regularity of metrical pattern are more prominent, in others asymmetry and irregularity are dominant. Strong body rhythms and explosive accentuations, as well as flow of rhythm toward points of stress, are characteristic of certain styles, while weak body rhythms and a minimum of accentuation, as well as the directional flow away from stressed points, are a feature of others. In some centuries tempos tend to be strict, rational, and objective; in others, free, irrational, and subjective. The stately measures of a sarabande or the graceful steps of the minuet, for instance, bespeak the etiquette and formal predictability of courtly life, while the nervous syncopations of fox trots, with their terse, fragmentary tunes, reveal the tensions and constantly changing pace of contemporary times. Rhythms thus can reflect and reactivate patterns of motion both present and past, as well as recapture some of the living substance and ideals of the individuals, generations, and ages from which they spring.

Dynamics

Chapter 4

THE element of dynamics is concerned principally with the psychological experience of relative softness and loudness. Under this general category fall the various intensity levels from soft to loud; the fluctuation of the flow of sound in one direction or the other; types of accentuation more powerful or exceptional than those normally associated with rhythmic factors; and the volume or amplitude of sonorities which impart to them a sense of size and space. As such this is the musical material most concerned with energy, force, and power. By increasing or decreasing the level of intensity, the composer is able to achieve such effects as proximity and distance, light and darkness, emotional tension and relaxation. By the use of dynamic accents a melodic line can become sharp and jagged, a rhythm rendered restless and vehement, a dissonance intensified, or a chord progression transformed into a series of explosive outbursts. By his choice of scoring a work for string quartet or full symphony orchestra, a composer can suggest intimate surroundings and inner personal revelations in the first instance, or epical grandeur and oratorical pronouncements in the other. While melody and rhythm remain the more important musical materials, the range of dynamic devices from sudden breathless pianissimos to sweeping orchestral crescendos, the occurrence of surprise accents, and the contrast of tonal volumes can produce certain sure-fire reactions.

The experience of dynamics depends to a greater or lesser extent upon the pitch and duration of sounds, as well as on the tone qualities of various instruments and combinations. A range embracing gradations all the way from the threshold of audibility to the ear-splitting point at which sounds become painful falls within the scope of music. The expressive possibilities of dynamics take on added significance when combined with other aspects of the tonal art. By the placement of accents at certain places in the melodic line, for instance, a composer can clarify the directional tendency and point up a melodic climax, as Beethoven does in Example 4:1.

Ex. 4:1 (*a*) Piano Sonata, Op. 26. First Movement (Bars 1–3 of Variation I). Beethoven. (*b*) *Piano Sonata,* Op. 27 No. 1. Fourth Movement (Bars 13–16). Beethoven.

By varying the degree of stress on particular rhythmic beats, or by vigorous accentuation of downbeats where they normally occur on the first beat of a bar, rhythms can acquire a surging character that imparts to them an impelling sense of forward movement. By shifting the dynamic accent to a normally weak beat, the resulting *syncopation* causes the rhythm to take on an assertive forceful character (as in Ex. 4:1 above). When an accelerating tempo is accompanied by a *crescendo,* the simultaneous effect of getting both faster and louder heightens the climactic impact. Similarly, when a retard is coupled with a *decrescendo,* the dual device of growing slower and softer at the same time produces the effect of coming to a stop and dying away. Many other expressive effects are possible when dynamic devices are coupled with instrumental combinations and contrasting tone qualities.

A sense of size is also associated with sounds. A low organ tone, for instance, comes from a larger pipe than a high one and hence seems broader and greater in volume. Such big tones are quite accurately associated with large sounding bodies such as the long thick bass strings of the piano, the huge bass viol, or the great tuba in the brass section of an orchestra. Pipe organs and orchestras as instruments of massive size are also associated with large architectural spaces, where their ponderous sonorities are capable of filling the vast interiors of a cathedral or a hall. A guitar, on the other hand, because of its delicate tone, is barely able to fill an ordinary-sized room. In the vocal sphere a more powerful voice normally emanates from a larger source than a lighter one, hence an opera composer will cast his mothers and mature women as contraltos, while his lithe young heroines are more apt to be coloratura sopranos. Similarly the parts of important personages, such as kings and high priests, are usually given to the ponderous bassos, while the romantic leads are reserved for the more agile tenors.

While musical scores can convey fairly definite—though by no means completely exact—information about pitch and rhythm, dynamic indications remain relatively imprecise; yet these dynamic and accentuation marks in the score are as important to proper musical performance as any other. In contrast to the indications for pitch and rhythm, those for dynamics are subject to many modifications depending on the size and acoustics of the room, the capacities of the instruments, the musical context in which they occur, the style of the period out of which the composition comes, the personal idiom of the composer, and, above all, the interpretive capabilities and insights of the performer. Historically, dynamic markings in scores are of fairly recent origin, dating as they do from the latter half of the eighteenth century, more particularly from the work of C.P.E. Bach, Haydn, and Mozart. Previous to this time, baroque dynamics were conceived as terraced broadly on different levels without individual tones singled out for emphasis. Bach and Handel, for instance, took care of such considerations by their use of registration and instrumentation. In a concerto grosso, for example, they alternated their full orchestra with a smaller group of from two to four instruments. Dynamic changes were thus effected by the addition or subtraction of instrumental forces. An interesting example of the baroque echo nuance can be heard in the "Echo Chorus" and "Echo Dance of the Furies" from Purcell's opera *Dido and Aeneas,* in which spatial effects are achieved by onstage and offstage choruses and string orchestras, respectively. When more gradual increasing and decreasing of sound levels came into general use in the latter part of the eighteenth century, composers were less inclined to leave dynamics entirely to the caprice of the performer. Henceforward, they concerned themselves more with specific dynamic symbols, such as the terms *crescendo* and *decrescendo* or their wedge-shaped counterparts ◁ ▷.

The two principal accent symbols by which individual tones are singled out from their neighbors for emphasis are the sign > above or below the note and *sf.* The latter, also sometimes abbreviated as *sfz,* derives from the Italian word *sforzando* or *sforzato,* literally "forcing" or "forced." Some composers—Haydn, for instance—seem to have used these symbols interchangeably, while others—notably Beethoven—use > to indicate a normal accent and reserve *sf* for more emphatic and explosive occasions.

The force of any accent is qualified by the musical context, particularly by the level of intensity in which it is found. A *sf* in a pianissimo passage, for instance, would be relatively light, while the same sign in fortissimo would be correspondingly heavy. Accents are further altered by durational and color factors as well as by style considerations. Some accents are accompanied by a shortening, others by a lengthening or sustaining of the accented tone. Some accents are of the sharp percussive type, others have a spread-out, diffused sound. Some accents demand special variations of tone quality to set the note apart from its unaccented neighbors. Such accents are produced by enriching the tone color in keeping with the characteristic capacities of particular instruments, which usually means an increased warmth, vibration, or expressive impact.

Beethoven, in his Sonata *Pathétique* (Ex. 3:1, p. 31), indicates by the sign *fp* (*forte piano*) that the initial chords of the first three bars are to receive an acute accent. After this momentary point of emphasis, the remainder of each measure is soft. The middle chord of the third measure is marked *sf* (*sforzato*), indicating a sharp accent. The first chord of the fourth bar is similarly marked and followed by a wedge-shaped symbol calling for a decrease in tone down to the level of *p* (*piano*). The abbreviation *cresc.* (*crescendo*) calls for an increase of sound culminating in the accented A flat above and B flat below, thus preparing the way for the precipitous scalewise descent and implied decrescendo to the *p* (*piano*) of the fifth bar. In this and the next measure, soft and very loud intensity levels alternate with each other as noted by the symbols *p* and *ff* (*fortissimo*). A mounting crescendo is called for in Bar 8 moving toward the climax in the ninth measure. The melody remains momentarily suspended in Bar 10 until the chromatic descent begins. On the final beat, Beethoven suddenly arrests the downward rush by reversing his direction on the accented A flat, thus terminating the introduction and providing a moment of suspense until the Allegro movement begins, which, as he says, is to be "attacked suddenly."

Since intensity and volume are so closely associated with space, they readily lend themselves to various types of imagery, both literal and symbolic. Beethoven's well-known "Turkish March" from *The Ruins of Athens* shows how the swelling and fading of sound can produce the illusion of simple spatial movement uncomplicated by emotional factors. The composer's dynamic scheme for this march is as follows:

Bars			
1 – 8	8 Bars	*pp*	(*pianissimo*, very soft)
9 –16	8 Bars	*crescendo poco a poco*	(growing louder little by little)
17–28	12 Bars	*f*	(*forte*, loud)
29–31	3 Bars	*p*	(*piano*, soft)
32–34	3 Bars	*ff*	(*fortissimo*, very loud)
35–37	3 Bars	*p*	(*piano*, soft)
38	1 Bar	*f*	(*forte*, loud)
39	1 Bar	*più forte*	(louder)
40–56	17 Bars	*ff*	(*fortissimo*, very loud)
57–64	8 Bars	*diminuendo poco a poco*	(diminishing little by little)
65–70	6 Bars	*sempre più piano*	(always getting softer)
71–72	2 Bars	*pp*	(*pianissimo*, very soft)

By using the entire normal dynamic spectrum from very soft to very loud and back again, Beethoven depicts a military march approaching from the distance to the foreground where it passes by in review, then recedes once more into the distance. It will be noticed, however, that the building of the climax is not so simple as merely to start soft and continuously grow louder without interruption. As in climbing a mountain there are at first the foothills with valleys intervening before the next height is attained, then still another valley before the peak is ultimately reached. Hence Beethoven reaches a 12-bar plateau of forte, descends to piano, rises briefly to the first fortissimo, drops down once more, reaches the 17-bar summit, then rapidly descends to pianissimo once again.

This processional-recessional movement has also been employed by other composers with striking effect. Debussy, in the second of his Nocturnes for Orchestra entitled *Fêtes,* evokes at first a festive, carnival-like atmosphere full of gay anticipation and dancing rhythms. The sound suddenly ceases in mid-air at the fortissimo level (Bar 115). Low drums, harps, plucked strings, and muted trumpets enter *ppp* in the next measure (116). As the procession advances, various instrumental groups are added until the saturation point is reached (Bar 200) with the addition of the full weight of the brass and percussion sections. After passing by in review, a long diminuendo of 78 bars begins tapering off to *pp* 14 bars from the end, where the composer writes "retreating ever more into the distance" (*s'éloignant davantage*). The parade ends as it began *ppp*, fragmentarily and far away.

In a symbolic sense, softness can suggest darkness; and loudness, light. In his oratorio *The Creation,* for instance, Haydn has a narrator declaim in a low voice, "And God said, let there be light." In the same C-minor mode, the chorus softly and mysteriously responds, "And there was LIGHT." On the last word, both chorus and orchestra burst out fortissimo in a blazing C-major chord as if the sun had suddenly appeared in midheaven. Wagner, in the Prelude to his opera *Lohengrin,* also employs dynamic imagery to invoke the illusion of a luminous vision. In his own extensive commentary, the composer reveals his poetic plan. The soft shimmering strings at the beginning suggest the idea of the Holy Grail, which, as he says, is the "sensuous conception of this supersensuous idea, invested with a wonderful form . . . yet unapproachably far off . . ." The sound grows through the addition of the woodwinds (Bar 20), and the cup seems to descend from the heights of heaven as if carried by a band of angels. As the gleaming Grail becomes bathed in bright light, Wagner completes his orchestral picture by the addition of a brass choir (four horns are added in Bar 36, three trombones and a tuba in Bar 45, and three trumpets in Bar 50). The metallic sound of the crashing cymbals finally comes in the climactic Bar 54, and the vision then gradually fades as the Prelude ends and the opera begins.

In dramatic music, overtures frequently terminate with impressive crescendos designed to prepare the listener for the rising of the curtain on a brilliant opening scene; both Rossini's Overture to the *Barber of Seville* and Wagner's Prelude to the *Meistersinger* are cases in point. Needless to say, this effect is somewhat diminished when such overtures are played in the concert hall unless the listener supplies the deficiency by an act of the imagination.

The effect of emotional tensions can also be produced by increasing tonal intensities. The mounting of emotional excitement followed by its lessening and relaxation becomes the psychological counterpart of the forward and backward movement in space. The faint sounds of distant events leave the listener relatively unaffected, while he inevitably becomes involved in a vibrant swirl of sound at a high level of intensity. Beethoven in the Overture No. 3 to his opera *Leonore,* for instance, builds up an emotional climax of enormous force by using wave after wave of orchestral crescendos. Since the Overture is so closely correlated with the action of the opera itself, Beethoven's intentions are quite clear. In this case he is recounting in orchestral terms the climactic dungeon scene in which the unjustly imprisoned Florestan is about to be stabbed by the wicked warden. Just as the dagger is raised, the faithful Leonore herself steps between the two. At this melodramatic moment in the Overture (Bars 272–277), as well as later in the opera, an offstage trumpet fanfare signals the arrival of the governor and Florestan's rescue. The lights go up in the operatic Finale signifying the dawn of freedom after the darkness of imprisonment and tyranny, while the crescendos toward the climax in the Overture reflect the building up of emotional excitement by increasing the tonal intensity over a long span. With the action taking place in an underground cell, the offstage trumpets become a literal device to produce the aural illusion of help coming from outside. The final crescendos—from *pp* (Bar 514) to the *ff* (Bar 534, or 105 bars before the end), then dropping back to *p* (Bar 570 or 69 bars before the end) and reaching the *fff* level (Bar 610 or 29 bars before the end)—reinforced as they are by a shift to a *presto* tempo (125 bars before the end) and a series of rising melodic lines, are a fine illustration of the symbolic use of dynamics to express freedom, hope, and the joy of deliverance. Cumulatively, in this case, these devices constitute a climax of truly triumphant proportions.

It can thus be seen that dynamics are among the most important elements in effective performance and a means of eliciting positive emotional responses from listeners. However, it should be pointed out that, of all the basic materials of music, the element of dynamics loses the most in recording processes as well as in radio and television transmission. When a sound engineer feels the pianissimos are getting too weak, he amplifies them. Similarly, when the fortissimos become too loud for his mechanism, he tones them down to prevent distortion. Only under actual live-perform-ance conditions can the dynamic range and its expressive possibilities be enjoyed to the fullest.

DYNAMIC TERMS

Abbreviation	Full Term	Definition
pp *	*pianissimo*	Very soft
p	*piano*	Soft
mp	*mezzo piano*	Medium soft ⎫ neither soft nor loud
mf	*mezzo forte*	Medium loud ⎭
f	*forte*	Loud
ff	*fortissimo*	Very loud
sf	*sforzato*, or *sforzando*	Heavy accent
cresc.	*crescendo*	Growing louder
decresc.	*decrescendo*	Growing softer
dim.	*diminuendo*	Diminishing, or getting softer
smorz.	*smorzando*	Dying away

| Sign for *cresc.* | Sign for *decresc.* | Accented note | Heavily accented note |

* *ppp* and *fff*, sometimes even four or five letters, are occasionally used to indicate exaggerated or very special effects.

Melody

Chapter 5

O<small>F</small> all the elements of music, melody is perhaps the most mysterious, depending as it docs upon the inspiration of the composer and the intuition of the listener. While rhythms usually represent generally accepted patterns that all composers freely adopt and use, melodies always remain much more unique and personal experiences. Dance rhythms, for instance, are social in origin and quickly become the common property of both the group and composer, but the melodic aspect of the dances is reserved as an individualized expression. Some composers have a happy faculty of melodic inventiveness, others develop different materials and resources. Melodies apparently sprang fully formed from the mind and heart of Schubert, while most of Beethoven's lyrical efforts were subjected to years of painstaking revision and reworking before they took the desired shape. The skill of Johann Strauss Jr. lay in his inexhaustible mine of melody, while his harmonies, waltz rhythms, and dance forms were mere social conventions. The powers of Johannes Brahms, on the other hand, rested more in his broad command of many musical resources and structural devices than on his melodies alone. Among contemporary composers, Rachmaninoff is a persuasive lyricist, while Stravinsky freely borrows his best melodic material from folk sources and excels in the rhythmic organization of his ballets, his harmonic daring, and his tightly knit forms.

The effects of melody on the listener are apt to be equally elusive. Some melodies sing their way straight into the hearts of people, others either die aborning or else, after a period of initial promise, quickly play themselves out. While it will always be impossible to explain a composer's inspiration and some of the intangible effects of his melodic products, it is nevertheless quite possible, and even enlightening, to observe how he organizes their component parts and develops their designs; how he clothes them in vocal and instrumental raiment and provides them with harmonic coloration; and how he presents them initially and transforms them later on.

When two tones succeed each other so as to establish a pitch relation-ship, the result is an upward, downward, or horizontally moving line, de-pending on whether the second tone lies above, below, or on the same level as the first. A composer manipulates this linear movement much as a painter draws his lines or a sculptor molds his clay so as to give it the characteristic profile that is recognizable as a melody. From its beginning to its end, a melody is a continuous movement, and like a moving body is never at any one moment in one place but always on its way. It cannot therefore be considered as the sum total of its component tones, but is rather the progress of the moving line passing through the successive sounds. As with the notes on the printed page, the separate tones are nec-essary as guideposts for the ear so that the course of the intervallic move-ment can be charted as it passes through and between points. Further-more, this linear movement has duration, and as it begins to flow more freely in time, it must acquire a temporal organization as well. Rhythm thus enters the picture and begins to play an important role in the shap-ing of the tonal line as well as leading it toward points of interest and emphasis.

A line of any kind, whether visual or tonal, has direction as one of its basic characteristics. This direction may be upward, downward, or con-verging toward a center. The perception of this linear movement upward or downward is rooted in the experience of singing, since the lower regis-ter of the human voice lies in the deeper chest tones and the higher reg-ister in the head tones. In addition to these spatial connotations there is also the feeling of mounting muscular tension as the voice rises and a cor-responding relaxation as it falls. *"Tension,"* wrote the philosopher and theorist Aristoxenus as long ago as the fourth century B.C., "is the continu-ous transition of the voice from a lower position to a higher, *relaxation* that from a higher to a lower. *Height of pitch* is the result of tension, *depth* of relaxation." Moving from one tone to another thus involves a change of position, and as such it is an action associated with an output of energy. Just as singing upward toward higher notes requires additional effort, the playing of higher tones on wind or string instruments also

means increasing the tension, while moving in a downward direction demands correspondingly less energy as the tension decreases.

This motional tendency of melodic lines, accompanied as it is by actual or inferred muscular tension and relaxation, also has an important
psychological counterpart. Inflections of the voice in ordinary speech
follow emotional states of various sorts. In moments of grief and despair,
the voice tends to be lowered in pitch, while a fear reaction can produce
a sudden high scream. Happy occasions are associated with a heightened
sense of well-being and with rising spirits. A pleasant occurrence, for instance, is said to give one a "lift," to cause one to "hold his head a little
higher," or to give one a feeling of "walking on air." Unpleasant incidents,
on the other hand, are said to give one "a sinking feeling," or to "get one
down"; while, in sickness, a person is sometimes said to be in "grave" condition or to be "very low."

Many striking uses of these ascending and descending lines have been
made by composers for a variety of expressive purposes. In the opening
moments of the Finale of his *Eroica* Symphony, for instance, Beethoven
employs a precipitously plunging line to introduce his Promethean theme.
Since the same passage also appears in his ballet, *The Creatures of Prometheus,* where it accompanies the god's descent with the divine fire from
Mt. Olympus, its meaning is quite clear. The effect has been adopted by
other composers, notably Tchaikovsky at the beginning of the last movement of his Fourth Symphony. In a vocal situation a descending major
scale becomes Handel's choice for his well-known anthem *Joy to the
World, the Lord Is Come,* an aria rejoicing in the Lord's coming down
from on high to dwell below among men. A melody from the *Messiah,*
"Come unto Him," is similarly managed so as to invite the tired and
troubled to sink into the arms of the Lord (Ex.5:1).

Ex. 5:1   "He Shall Feed His Flock" from the *Messiah* (Bars 32–36). Handel.

A sigh, accompanied as it is by a falling inflection of the voice, becomes a melodic means for the expression of certain moods. The aria,
"Cara Nome," that Verdi writes for the heroine of his opera, *Rigoletto,*
moves scalewise downward like the sigh of a woman in love as she ponders
on the name of her beloved. A particularly expansive sighing theme is
found in the first movement of Tchaikovsky's Sixth Symphony (Ex. 5:2),
where it is well adapted to the pathos of the situation.

Ex. 5:2 Symphony No. 6 (*Pathétique*). First Movement (Bars 92–97). Tschaikovsky.

Various degrees of sorrow and grief are also associated with downward movement as seen in the long elegiac descending lines of Chopin's C-minor Nocturne, Op. 48 (Ex. 5:3);

Ex. 5:3 Nocturne in C Minor, Op. 48 No. 1 (Bars 1–4). Chopin.

and Bach expresses the Good Friday grief of Christians at the thought of the Crucifixion and burial of Christ by a chromatically descending bass figure which is repeated thirteen times in the course of this movement from his B-minor Mass (Ex. 5:4).

Ex. 5:4 "Crucifixus" from B-minor Mass (Bars 1–5). Bach.

Rising melodic lines are likewise capable of indicating certain directional as well as emotional tendencies. The upward leaping intervals of Wagner's "Ride of the Valkyries" from *Die Walküre* (Ex. 5:5) are well adapted to convey the flight of winged steeds as the warrior maidens bear the spirits of fallen heroes to Valhalla.

Ex. 5:5 "Ride of the Valkyries" from *Die Walküre*. Wagner.

The vocal line of the opening of Schumann's song cycle, *Dichterliebe* (Poet's Love) on the other hand, shows a more gentle lift, in keeping with the rising thoughts of love that come in the springtime (Ex. 13:2). The soaring, effervescent waltz melodies Johann Strauss Jr. writes in his *Beautiful Blue Danube* and *Voices of Spring* bubble upward like champagne. When a composer depicts a gathering storm, as Beethoven does in his

Pastoral Symphony, the line rises in successive waves as the fury of the elements increases, then falls later as the storm abates. A similar procedure is found in the mounting of emotional excitement as represented by Beethoven in the first movements of both his *Pathétique* and *Appassionata* Sonatas (Ex. 5:6).

Ex. 5:6a   Piano Sonata, Op. 13 (*Pathétique*). First Movement (Bars 11–15). Beethoven.

Ex. 5:6b   Piano Sonata, Op. 57 (*Appassionata*). First Movement (Bars 1–4). Beethoven.

A particularly powerful example of emotional climax is found in the "Love Death" at the end of Wagner's *Tristan and Isolde,* where the scalewise chromatic sequences rise higher and higher and thus create an almost unbearable tension in the process.

Many melodic lines converge toward a central tone without pronounced movement in either direction. Some extreme examples are found in those associated with death, such as the "Funeral March" from Beethoven's Piano Sonata in A-flat Major (Op. 26) where the initial E flat is repeated some thirty-four times before moving onward. In the slow movement of Beethoven's Seventh Symphony (Ex. 3:2), the first note occurs twelve times in succession without changing, as does that of the "Andante Funèbre" from Tchaikovsky's String Quartet, Op. 30. The inexorable line Schubert gives to the voice of Death in his song *Death and the Maiden* (Ex. 13:1), and that Mozart writes for the statue of the dead Commendatore in the Finale of his opera, *Don Giovanni,* are in both cases almost as rigid and stiff as rigor mortis itself. Occasionally, for desired effects of monotony, a composer will cause a single tone to be repeated throughout a piece as does Chopin in the middle voice of his so-called *Raindrop* Prelude, Op. 28, No. 15. In all the above cases, however, composers call upon rhythmic and harmonic variety to relieve the melodic monotony.

Melodies that hover closely around a tonal center are often used for the expression of religious devotion or of quiet meditation. In his *Ave Maria* (Ex. 5:7), the tone B flat serves as the center from which Schubert departs and returns. At first his line dips only a single step, while next it moves a third upward, then a third downward, returning to B flat each time. At its most expansive point it reaches a fifth above and a fourth below, each time converging once more on its center.

Ex. 5:7 *Ave Maria* (Bars 3–4) . Schubert.

Most melodies are not as definite in their downward, upward, and central tendencies as the above, while many are quite indeterminate in their direction. Those of Schubert's "Trout" and Saint-Saëns' "Swan," for example, swim rather aimlessly, but not inappropriately, first this way then that. An interesting instance in this connection occurs with the opening theme of Brahms' Fourth Symphony (Ex. 5:8) . At the time of its premiere the composer was criticized for not being able to make up his melodic mind. Some Viennese went so far as to coin words for the chronic indecision of this theme, "Goes to, goes fro; goes here, then there."

Ex. 5:8 Symphony No. 4. First Movement (Bars 1–8) . Brahms.

Melodic lines perforce must proceed either by steps or skips. Stepwise or conjunct motion, as seen in Example 5:9, follows the closely spaced intervals of a scale; while the disjunct motion of Example 5:10 is spread out harmonically along the tones of a chord.

Ex. 5:9 Symphony No. 9. Fourth Movement (Bars 92–99) . Beethoven.

Ex. 5:10 Piano Sonata in A Flat. First Movement (Bars 1–4) . Weber.

The dominance of one or the other of these types of motion will reveal the inherent character of a melody; and, depending on whether the intervals are wide or narrow, continuous or discontinuous, the melody will be rendered active or passive, tense or relaxed, awkward or graceful. The scalewise intervals of Example 5:9, for instance, hold the movement to a quiet, peaceful course in the manner of a hymn. The expansive, undulating line of Example 5:10, on the other hand, covers much more territory; but since the intervals follow regularly the outline of a single chord, it is still predictable and smooth. By way of contrast, the active line of Example 5:11 gets off to a running start with its rising figure, then proceeds to jump unexpectedly in a series of wide, angular leaps that give it a highly impulsive quality. Such dance melodies, especially when they mirror energetic action, are apt to be dominated by skips; while those of a more contemplative type tend toward stepwise movement.

Ex. 5:11   Mazurka, Op. 7 No. 1 (Bars 1–6). Chopin.

Capacities of voices and the various instruments also condition the type of melody a composer can write for them. A vocal line, for instance, will have more conjunct motion, especially if it is intended for choral or congregational performance, since the use of frequent and irregular leaps is liable to render the line unsingable. A bugle call such as the familiar "Taps," on the other hand, is of necessity based solely on chordal skips since they are the only notes the instrument can produce. Trumpet melodies, such as the one Verdi writes for his "Grand March" in *Aida,* still preserve something of this military character even though modern valve mechanisms make stepwise movement possible.

The range of voices and instruments is still another factor in melodic writing. The average human voice, for instance, seldom extends more than an octave plus a fifth (the range of the *Star-Spangled Banner*), while the piano has over seven octaves. Individual instruments in the orchestra likewise have their limitations, but one member of the same family can continue a line where another leaves off. Mozart, as seen in Example 5:12, writes a widely spaced melody at the beginning of his *Haffner* Symphony but keeps it within the violin range.

Ex. 5:12   Symphony No. 35 (*Haffner*). First Movement (Bars 1–5). Mozart.

Melodic statements, just as in the case of those in spoken or written language, must assume some definite form and follow in certain sequences in order to be intelligible. As words in prose and poetry are grouped into phrases, clauses, sentences, and paragraphs, so tones in a melody are grouped into half phrases, phrases, and sections. The terms *period* or *sentence* are borrowed from language studies to describe certain units of musical forms in which two phrases are joined together much as two independent clauses combine grammatically into a single compound sentence. Melodies also have occasional pauses in their progress that approximate those after commas, semicolons, and periods. Such musical punctuation points, occurring as they do at the ends of phrases and sections, become convenient breaks for breathing and bowing; and by dividing a long line into shorter segments, they also serve to clarify complex statements and thus act as aids to the understanding.

Inflection in melody is also somewhat analogous to that in speech, although a writer has no such definite control over the pitch relationships of his readers as does a composer. A question in speech, for instance, is usually accompanied by an indefinite rising inflection, while with an answer it drops. When a half phrase in music shows a similar rise, it is often called a question, while the succeeding complementary half phrase constitutes the answer, as the following fugue subject will show (Ex. 5:13).

Ex. 5:13   Fugue No. 8, Book I, *Well-Tempered Clavier* (Bars 1–3). Bach.

Emphasis in a complex speech or soliloquy usually calls for a progressive raising of the voice in order to make each point more impressive than the last. At the ends of sentences and paragraphs, however, the voice will fall to a greater or less degree. Similarly, a melody achieves its climaxes by successive waves toward high points after which it declines at the cadences.

Formal units that are peculiar to melody and for which there are no exact equivalents in language are motives, themes, subjects, figures, and the overall aspects of structure. A *motive,* for instance, is a group of tones that is capable of being developed in a number of different contexts. Motives of this type that come immediately to mind are the three or four tones that open Beethoven's Fifth, and Brahms' Second and Third Symphonies. These brief fragments, which may have just as important rhythmic as melodic implications, are the germ cells that grow into larger musical organisms. A *theme,* by contrast, refers to a short melodic statement such as the theme for a set of variations that is not necessarily complete in itself (Ex. 5:6 shows two typical instances). A fugue subject, such as Example 5:13, is a theme, and as such it constitutes the kind of musical subject matter that Aaron Copland meant when he remarked, "The melody is generally what the piece is about." A *figure* is a recognizable and detachable part of a melody which can be segmented from it for purposes of repetition, variation, recollection, or development as in a sonata or fugue (as, for example, the first three notes of Mozart's Symphony No. 40 as shown in Ex. 10:1). Melodies, furthermore, expand by such processes as direct repetition or sequence, the latter a kind of dynamic repetition that gives a repeated figure a sense of progress. Moreover, some formal pattern must be devised for the repetition of a melody's parts in the interest of unity and variety. If regularity is in order, the melody can be made symmetrical and graceful; if irregularity prevails, it can become unbalanced and awkward. The overall structural patterns such as binary and ternary organizations of melody will be treated in Part II, under musical forms. Finally, it must be remembered that any melody worthy of the name is always much more than a collection of tones, motives, themes, and phrases; and that the whole will therefore always exceed the sum of its parts.

Thus, while melodies are primarily products of a composer's creative imagination, a number of rational procedures must come into play as his material is molded into shape and given spatial as well as temporal organization. A composer, in this case, is consciously aware that he is manipulating lines as they go upward and downward in direction, as well as forward in time. As his moving material acquires momentum, it must continue in some direction until it reaches its destination or encounters some obstacle in its path. Whether these linear goals are points of high tension or those of relative repose, moments of comparative excitement or of calm, the composer must exercise his control so as to give his melody a sense of purpose as well as direction. He is also aware of the power of his moving lines to communicate meaning—whether tangible or intangible, definite or indefinite, literal or symbolic—since they are connected with such universal human experiences as the inflections of speech, linear imagery, muscular memory, and emotional tension. He also knows that his lines move through the temporal dimension where they are free from the usual gravitational limitations and can thus give expression to some of the soaring aspirations of the human spirit. As a composer readies his melody for presentation to the listener, he must take into consideration such factors as some scale or harmonic system, the steps and skips of his intervallic stretches, the limitations and possibilities of the various voices and instruments, and the logical place of his melody in the overall structure he is creating. A melody, furthermore, can appear alone, in the contrapuntal company of other melodies, or against a harmonic background. And since it must always be sung or played either singly or in concert with other voices or instruments, it can take on an individual coloration, which can vary from the plaintive sound of a solitary voice to the surging power of the entire string section of a full symphony orchestra. In such ways as these, therefore, a composer can control his melodic lines, shape them in significant directions, and command his moving material so as to achieve his expressive ends.

The Harmonic
Complex

Chapter 6

U_P to this point the qualitative, rhythmic, dynamic, and melodic materials at the composer's command have been treated in the main as elements. Detaching them for separate consideration has been for purposes of clarity and convenience. As elements, however, they can never exist in isolation, but only in combination with one another in various complexes and textures. A melody, for instance, can never appear apart from the presence of some rhythmic pattern, nor can it be heard except through some vocal or instrumental medium. Each of these separate elements may also admit of complexes within its own sphere; for example, a complex of several instrumental qualities leads inevitably to the subject of instrumentation and orchestration, a complex of different metrical units to a polymetrical organization, and a complex of various rhythms to a polyrhythm. To go one step farther, melodies are rarely heard apart from some simultaneous sounds such as an accompanying chordal progression or in combination with one or more other melodies. These combinations are usually described as complexes or textures—in one case harmonic and the other contrapuntal.

It should be observed at this point that words such as "complex" and "texture" are not too precisely defined in music criticism. The term "complex" is used here in its ordinary or objective sense of a multiplicity of elements of the same kind, or of different kinds, as they appear in relationship to one another. "Texture," on the other hand, is a more subjective term referring to the quality of the given complex. The word itself is borrowed from the sense of touch to describe a quality in the sense of hearing in the same way a painter appropriates the word "tone" to describe the quality of his color complex. It is description by analogy and, of course, it can be illustrated by playing musical passages with different textures far more readily that it can be defined on the printed page.

INTERVALS

Harmony is a vast, all-encompassing field, concerned with nothing less than the study of the rational relationships that can exist within a complex of sounds. A mastery of it is essential to any composer, and an understanding of some of its underlying theoretical concepts can be of great value to the listener. Technical terminology is, of necessity, indispensable in a study of this sort, and a number of such terms will be encountered in this chapter. At all points, however, an effort will be made to discuss the concept before providing the technical word which composers use for it. Any precise description, whether in the field of science or art, always involves the making of measurements, and a commonly agreed upon measuring standard (no matter how arbitrary) becomes a necessary precondition for coherence. Since music is an art that exists in time, it was necessary to discuss the durational, temporal, and metrical measurement of tone in the chapter on rhythm. If the organization of any melody whatsoever is examined, the most obvious fact that emerges is that some of the notes are higher and others lower in pitch. They are therefore said to rise and fall, to go up and down. The moment that this is the case, a series of approximate measurements has been made. It is quite understandable, then, that musicians would want to state these measurements of pitch fluctuations more precisely.

The successive pitches that make up the linear designs of the melodies and the simultaneous sounds of harmony do not represent mere random choices on the part of composers but are related according to some system that orients them in space and time. "To compose," Stravinsky once remarked, "means for me to command sounds by looking for the center towards which they must converge." The intervals between the successive tones will therefore be found to conform to some harmonic plan. The separate tones of any melody are always based on some division of the octave. All peoples, even the most primitive, sing the octave, and it is also the most easily produced interval on stringed instruments. How it is divided so as to produce modal and scale systems points up geographical and temporal differences that reveal varying phases of civilization, ancient and modern practices, and the contrasting musical attitudes of East and West. The scales on which Oriental melodies are constructed, for instance, vary from the pentatonic (the fivefold division corresponding to the black keys on the piano) to those of a more complex nature involving quarter tones. Western music, however, divides the octave into twelve equal half tones, with most melodies falling into the seven-tone division (corresponding to the white keys on the piano) that forms the modes, including the familiar major and minor.

An *interval* in music, thus, is simply the distance between any two notes, whether these notes be sounded simultaneously or in succession. The system of measuring intervals is, to begin with, a relatively simple one. If one wants to know the interval between C and the G above it, or between A and the F above it, or between B and the D above it, then one can simply write out:

C D E F G

A B C D E F

B C D

In the first instance, there is a compass of five notes; hence the interval from C to the G above it is called a *fifth*. In the second case, there is a span of six notes, and the interval is called a *sixth*. In the third example, the interval is a *third*. If the G should be below the C, then the series is written in reverse (C B A G) in which case the compass is four tones and the interval is called a *fourth*. If two instruments are playing the same pitch (say, middle C) this interval is called a *unison*. If the interval spans the range of eight notes (for example, C D E F G A B C), then the interval is called the *octave* and the two C's are said to be an octave apart.

The above, however, are merely gross measurements. While the distance from C to G, C to G sharp, and C to G flat is in every case an interval of a fifth, the distances in each case are slightly but significantly different. The quality of the kind of fifth therefore becomes important. The standard against which such fine distinctions are measured in the present instance is the major scale. One simply assumes the lower note of the interval as the tonic (or starting note) of a major scale. In measuring C to the G above it, C to G sharp (G♯) above, or C to G flat (G♭) above, the major scale starting on C is assumed. Since G (unmodified by either a sharp or flat) is the note that normally occurs in the C-major scale, then the fifth from C to G is called a perfect fifth. But C to G♯ is the perfect fifth enlarged by raising the G a half step; hence it is called an augmented fifth. In the interval C to G♭, the fifth has been decreased by lowering the G to G♭, and hence it is called a diminished fifth. Intervals of the unison, fourth, fifth, and octave are, in their natural form, called *perfect*. When raised or lowered by a half step, they are called *augmented* and *diminished,* respectively.

Intervals of a second, third, sixth or seventh are, in their fundamental form, called *major*. When raised by a half step they become *augmented,* but when decreased by a half step, they are referred to as *minor*. Only when reduced by two half steps is a *major* interval called diminished. In measuring the distance from C to E, the lower tone is assumed to be the beginning of a major scale. Since E, unmodified by a sharp or flat, normally occurs in C major, then the distance is a major third; C to E♯ then becomes an augmented third; C to E♭, a minor third; C to E double flat (E♭♭), a diminished third; and similarly for the other major intervals. In theory, of course, all intervals can be doubly, triply, etc., augmented and diminished, but this has very limited application to common musical practice. Even the diminished third, C to E♭♭, is more usually written as a major second, C to D, since with tempered tuning in the case of an instrument such as the piano, the sound is the same. The two intervals (major second and diminished third) by contrast are not quite the same on a stringed instrument. The difference is so small, however, that it is but rarely observed. Many such rationalizations are carried over from the tempered tuning of the piano into music generally. Thus C to G♯ is an augmented fifth, and C to A♭ is a minor sixth. Apart from their differences in function, they are actually two different, even if minutely different, distances. Yet on the piano keyboard they are exactly the same distance, for G♯ and A♭ are the same note, while on a stringed instrument they are not. The word for this interchangeability of tones that sound the same but are written differently is *enharmonic* (B♭ and A♯, D♯ and E♭, G♯ and A♭, C♯ and D♭, etc., are called enharmonic tones). This will have consequences later in the discussion of modulation and key relationships.

At this point a table of interval measurements from the unison through the octave may serve as a summary. Intervals larger than the octave can be reduced to their equivalent within the octave; thus, ninths are measured as seconds, tenths as thirds, and so on. The basis in the following table is the C-major scale:

C	D	E	F	G	A	B	C
1	2	3	4	5	6	7	8

	Perfect	Major	Minor	Diminished	Augmented
Unison	C-C (same pitch)				C-C♯
Second		C-D	C-D♭	C-D♭♭	C-D♯
Third		C-E	C-E♭	C-E♭♭	C-E♯
Fourth	C-F			C-F♭	C-F♯
Fifth	C-G			C-G♭	C-G♯
Sixth		C-A	C-A♭	C-A♭♭	C-A♯
Seventh		C-B	C-B♭	C-B♭♭	C-B♯
Octave	C-C			C-C♭	C-C♯

The reasons for outlining this material in such technical detail should be clear. The purpose has been primarily to illustrate the fact that, if pitch distances must of necessity be measured, musicians do so in a fashion that is systematic and reasonable. While these measurements are not absolutely precise, they are to all intents and purposes precise enough for most practical uses. More to the point than memorizing the above table, is the listener's cognizance that differences in intervallic structure are differences in quality and hence of feeling. The composer understands (or at any rate, should understand) the *personality* of intervals and of intervallic complexes. And the listener, even if unable to identify the complex by name, can still be aware of these intervallic personalities and of the quality of feeling each communicates.

European and American ears have been largely conditioned, for better or worse, by a certain community of listening experience which most listeners share. The scalewise progression up to a perfect fourth and back again—C D E F, F E D C—surely sounds rather ordinary. Contrast this to the slight but definite strangeness introduced by raising the F to F♯ and increasing the distance of the progression to an augmented fourth— C D E F♯, F♯ E D C. Again, notice the quasi-Middle-Eastern quality introduced by retaining the distance of the augmented fourth (C to F♯), but changing the E-F♯ (a major second) to E♭-F♯ (an augmented second) — C D E♭ F♯, F♯ E♭ D C.

These intervals, or temporal stretches between tones, have varying degrees of tensile strength as they are spun out in a line so that each acquires a force of character and a certain individuality of its own. The degree of tension attached to particular intervals varies, of course, from period to period, from composer to composer, and from listener to listener. While exact agreement is therefore neither possible nor even desirable, a few general observations can nevertheless be made. Some, such as the perfect intervals with their close mathematical ratios, tend to be relatively static. The primes, fourths, fifths, and octaves that fall into this classification have a certain solidity and power that increases as they widen. A series of primes, as seen in the top notes of Examples 3:2 or 13:1, is completely stationary. However, the upward leap of the fourth, as Handel uses it in the aria "I know that my Redeemer liveth" from the *Messiah* (Ex. 6:1a), immediately arrests the attention. It is also the interval often heard at the

Ex. 6:1   "I know that my Redeemer liveth" from the *Messiah* (Bars 39–46).
        Handel.

beginning of marches including Wagner's "Wedding March" from *Lohengrin* as well as the French and Danish national anthems. The fifth is also a sturdy interval as Handel uses it in the same aria (Ex. 6:1b). In this instance it has a firm declarative power as it expresses the very essence of the word *stand,* which is then held for several measures over a moving accompaniment as if to symbolize a fixed force in a changing world. A bold octave leap, such as that used by Richard Strauss in one of the themes of his symphonic poem *Don Juan* (Ex. 6:2), proclaims in this context a challenge to do battle.

Ex. 6:2   Theme from *Don Juan.* Richard Strauss.

Imperfect intervals vary even more widely in character. The stepwise movement of seconds, proceeding along the neighboring tones of the scale as in Example 5:9, gives a smooth, even bland, effect. Thirds and sixths are likewise low in intervallic tension, especially when heard in parallel progression as, for instance, in Example 6:9. They are felt as pleasant consonances and hence not particularly eventful. Sevenths and ninths, on the other hand, set up dissonances by creating a demand for further action. Tchaikovsky's song *None but the Lonely Heart* (Ex. 6:3a) opens with

Ex. 6:3   (a) *None but the Lonely Heart* (Bars 1–2). Tchaikovsky. (b) "O terra addio" from *Aida.* Verdi.

both the downward and upward movement of the minor seventh thus creating the feeling of longing that calls for fulfillment. Verdi's startling use of the rising major seventh in "O terra addio," the final duet of *Aida,* (Ex. 6:3b) creates an almost unbearable tension that perfectly expresses the infinite longing of the doomed lovers on the brink of eternity as they bid farewell to the earth.

CHORDS

In a primitive, rather arbitrary way, a *chord* may be considered as any collection of notes piled one on top of another. A little more precisely, and perhaps more usefully, a chord can be defined as any combination of two or more intervals sounded simultaneously. Later a still more refined and specialized definition will be offered. When taken out of context and listened to as an isolated cohesion of sound, the quality or character of a chord is determined, among other things, by the kind of intervals that compose it. Consider, for example, the quite ordinary sound of a chord composed of 2 thirds, such as the notes C-E-G sounded simultaneously. Then compare it with the challenging character of a chord composed of 2 fourths: the notes C-F-B sounded together. Here the concern is with generalized measurements, that is, thirds and fourths. Returning to the ordinary chord C-E-G, it can be seen that it is composed of 2 thirds, one on top of the other, and more precisely, 2 thirds of different kinds. The first third, C to E, is a major third; while the second, E to G, is a minor third. It is known as a *major triad:* a triad being any chord of just three tones, and a major triad being a triad in which the first or lower third is major and the second or upper third is minor. Suppose now, the order is reversed, and the minor is the third placed below with the major third on top of it. The triad now reads C-E♭-G, and the difference in character, if no longer too astonishing, is surely still considerable. This is a *minor triad.* One can construct a minor triad on any starting note by superimposing a major third on top of a minor third. The qualitative difference between a major and a minor triad is thus achieved by reversing the order of the thirds. If two major thirds are combined (C-E-G♯), the resulting chord has the characteristic, arresting sound of an *augmented triad.* If two minor thirds are combined (C-E♭-G♭), the striking change may remind the listener of one of the favored uses of the diminished triad in romantic harmony—that of suggesting a sense or feeling of incipient tragedy.

SCALES

In the discussion so far, the reader may have noted that while some terms have been defined, others, such as *major scale,* have been used without explanation, and still others, such as *chord* and *tonic,* have been given only limited treatment. This was temporarily unavoidable; but it points to a deep contradiction that exists in attempts at exact discussion between a rooted faith in the togetherness of things on the one hand, and the human necessity of saying things piecemeal, one sentence at a time, on the other. To be brief, it seems natural to understand things in context. But we achieve this context, this system, this overall togetherness statement by statement. And to the degree that we do not understand the totality of a context, we rely upon our intuition of its existence. Historically, in a field as practical as music, the specific kind of togetherness of sounds which fall upon our ears as meaningful constitutes a harmonic system which evolved bit by bit, with generation after generation contributing its mite. The harmonic system to which our Western ears have been accustomed is not the only one that has ever existed, nor the only one now in existence, nor indeed the only one that can be conceived of as rational and useful. It is, however, the only one which we assume involuntarily in listening to Western music of the seventeenth, eighteenth, and nineteenth centuries; and, with modifications, it accounts for many things in the music of the sixteenth and twentieth centuries as well. For practical listening purposes, it is a harmonic system worthy of our close attention.

This is a system which confines itself to twelve tones within the octave. There are many twelve-number systems (hours, months, astrologer's charts, etc.) and our Western music is one of them. What this means is that the span of an octave is divided into twelve tones, each tone separated by a half-step interval from its neighbor (a half step is also called a semitone and is equal to a minor second). Starting on C, the twelve notes, with some of the more common enharmonic equivalents, are the following: C, C♯ (or D♭), D, D♯ (or E♭), E, F, F♯ (or G♭), G, G♯ (or A♭), A, A♯ (or B♭), and B. However, in traditional harmony (this excludes systems such as that of Arnold Schoenberg and his disciples) the twelve tones are divided into two groups of seven and five each. Seven tones are selected and are held to define a more specific system, the eighth note needed to complete the octave being a repetition at the octave of the first note in the series. These seven notes which lie within the system are called the *diatonic notes;* chords based exclusively on these notes are called *diatonic chords;* harmonies comprised mainly of such chords are called *diatonic harmonies;* and a music mainly confined to such tones, a *diatonic music.* The remaining five notes that lie outside the diatonic system are peripheral to it, and when introduced within the diatonic system, create frictions and tensions that require further clarification in the ensuing measures of the music. They are called *chromatic notes;* chords involving their use are called *chromatic chords;* a harmony heavily saturated with chromatic chords is a *chromatic harmony;* and a music overgrown with chromaticisms, a *chromatic music.*

When the seven notes are arranged in ascending order from lowest note to highest, this is called a *diatonic scale* (from the Italian *scala,* a ladder, hence a ladderlike arrangement of notes). When the twelve notes are so arranged, it is called a *chromatic scale.* A *major scale* exists whenever the ladder of diatonic tones is so constructed that a half step (or minor second) occurs between the third and fourth tones, and between the seventh and eighth, and where all other intervals between adjacent tones are whole steps (or major seconds). Thus, starting on C, a major scale would read as follows (the minor seconds are indicated by slurs):

$$1 \quad 2 \quad \overset{\frown}{3 \quad 4} \quad 5 \quad 6 \quad \overset{\frown}{7 \quad 8}$$

$$C \quad D \quad \overset{\frown}{E \quad F} \quad G \quad A \quad \overset{\frown}{B \quad C}$$

If the major scale is to be constructed on another note, A or B♭, for example, then modifications must be introduced to maintain the above-noted relationships of full and half steps. As seen in the table given below, a note may be *diatonic* in one scale and *chromatic* in another. It is the context that determines its quality. The note C is thus diatonic in C major and in B♭ major, but chromatic in A major.

1	2	3	4	5	6	7	8
A	B	C♯	D	E	F♯	G♯	A
B♭	C	D	E♭	F	G	A	B♭

Minor scales are somewhat more complex, with three varieties commonly encountered. First is the so-called *natural minor,* which, if one starts on A, reads:

1	2	3	4	5	6	7	8
A	B	C	D	E	F	G	A

It is not uncommon to find this form of the minor scale in folk music. The more prevalent variety of minor, that in which the seventh degree of the scale is raised a half step, is called the *harmonic minor* because of the harmonic strength of the major dominant chord (that chord based on the fifth degree of the scale) which results from this alteration. Starting on A the scale reads:

1	2	3	4	5	6	7	8
A	B	C	D	E	F	G♯	A

For the effect obtained in altering the G natural to G sharp, compare Example 6:4*a* (natural minor) with Example 6:4*b* (harmonic minor).

Ex. 6:4

When the harmonic minor is used as the basis for melody, the large interval (the augmented second), which occurs between the sixth and seventh degrees, may be quite effective in some melodic passages, but overly emphatic in cases where the context requires smoothness of line. A third species of minor scale, the *melodic minor,* smooths over this diffi-

culty by raising both the sixth and seventh degrees when ascending. However, the melodic minor when descending is the same as the natural minor:

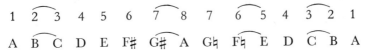

1 2 3 4 5 6 7 8 7 6 5 4 3 2 1

A B C D E F♯ G♯ A G♮ F♮ E D C B A

In the examples given below (Ex. 6:5), the same phrase is written in three
varieties of minor: (a) natural, (b) harmonic, and (c) melodic. Each, it
will be observed, has its own special quality.

Ex. 6:5

(a) Natural   (b) Harmonic   (c) Melodic

KEYS

The terms *scale* and *key* are sometimes needlessly confused.
Key is a more inclusive concept. By way of illustration, the C-major *scale*
is simply a convenient formula for naming in succession the notes that
are diatonic to the key of C major. But these tones, when found in a
C-major melody, are arranged in many other intervallic sequences; sometimes chromatic tones are interpolated; and, in any case, in chord progressions the tones are sounded simultaneously rather than in succession. The
key of C major, on the other hand, is the sum of all the relationships,
either melodic or chordal, that exist between the diatonic notes in that
key; plus the sum of all the relationships between the diatonic and chromatic notes, either in melodies or in chord structures; plus all the relationships between C major and all other analagous key structures, both major
and minor. This is much too involved to be of use here. In short, the sum
total of all these relationships is expressed as the key of C major. Stated
another way, the key of C major is a *system* of relationships. The scale of
C major, then, is simply one of the many relationships that exist within
the key of C major. Theoretically, the number of keys is unlimited. In
practical compositions, however, few composers have found need to go
beyond a set of fifteen major keys and an equal number of minor keys.
Even in this limited number, there are a few keys that are enharmonically
interchangeable.

These divisions of the octave, whether spread out sequentially in a
melodic line or sounded together in a harmonic progression, are felt to
group themselves around a tonal center which sets up a kind of musical
law of gravity known as *tonality* or key feeling. This *tonic*, as it is called,
functions as a place of rest or home base, and acts as a point of departure

and return. From it, excursions can be made upward to such related places
as the supertonic, mediant, and dominant; or downward to the subtonic
(leading tone), submediant, and subdominant. The process can be visualized by thinking of the tonic as the hub of a wheel around which the other
tones revolve axially (Ex. 6:6).

Ex. 6:6

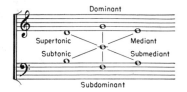

The concept of a key as a complex system of relationships requires that
some of these relationships be examined. As seen in the above diagram,
the point of orientation or *tonal center* is called the *tonic*. The note that
serves in this capacity is the *tonic note;* and the chord that is built up from
it is the *tonic chord* (or *tonic triad* when just three tones are used). When
a composition involves the use of several keys, the key that serves as orientation is the *tonic key*. Movement away from and toward the tonic can be
direct or devious, or it can be unencumbered or strewn with obstacles, depending upon the effect intended. More often than not, a sense of tonic
is very quickly and emphatically established for the listener; and in the
more simple types of popular melody, the tonic is often the first accented
note, the final note, and also a frequently recurring note. Movement away
from and toward the tonic tends to be direct and unencumbered. The
qualities of the other diatonic tones are evaluated in relation to the tonic.
For example, the second strongest tone in a key is the fifth degree of the
scale, and is called the dominant. Movement from dominant to tonic is
especially strong and emphatic. In the following examples all of these
points are illustrated. In Example 6:7*a* (C major), C is the tonic and G
the dominant; in Example 6:7*b* (F major), F is the tonic and C the
dominant.

Ex. 6:7a *Dixie*. American Folk Song.

Ex. 6:7b *Yankee Doodle*. American Folk Song.

In Example 6:7*b* the E F progression marked by an asterisk illustrates still another of the tonal relationships so strongly marked in simple melodies. Some tones in the key tend to depend upon others and to gravitate toward them. The most marked of these dependencies is the pull of the seventh degree of the scale (in this case E) to the tonic (F). The reader can easily verify this by pausing on the E, under which the asterisk is placed, and then testing out the possibilities of concluding the phrase by some note other than the tonic F. No other note will seem nearly so satisfactory. Because of the manner in which the seventh degree leads to the tonic, this seventh degree of the scale is called the *leading tone*. A similar pull—not nearly so strong, however, as from leading tone to tonic—also exists from the fourth degree down to the third. It is not uncommon, and the following (Ex. 6:8) is one of the many possible illustrations. The key in this instance is G minor.

Ex. 6:8 *If 'tis sorrow so to love thee*. Spanish Folk Song.

It is a rather melancholy Spanish love song, and its peculiar character derives from the avoidance of the tonic note (G), and from an avoidance of such strong, positive, emphatic pulls as dominant to tonic and leading tone to tonic. In place of a strong tonic repetition, the tonic is only implied and the next strongest note, the dominant (D), occurs most frequently. In place of the very strong progression from leading tone to tonic, the melody shows the weaker downward attraction of the fourth degree of the scale (C) to the third (B♭). This is entirely appropriate in view of the text, "If 'tis sorrow so to love thee." The folk usage here reflects a musical wis-

Ex. 6:9 *La Ricciolella*. Italian Folk Song.

dom at once instinctive and profound, in that it stresses the weaker rather than the stronger relationships between tones.

In Example 6:9, notice the pleasant interpolation of chromatic tones (the C♯ and A♯ marked by an asterisk) in the smooth flowing 6/8 melody. Only once in this Italian folk tune (*La Ricciolella*) do the chromatic tones occur on an accented beat, and then just before the close. The tones in the bass staff outline the simple tonic-dominant chord basis over which the melody flows so easily.

CHORD PROGRESSIONS

In a chordal sequence the tonic chord is always the strongest, and it is the base from which the qualities of other chords in the key are evaluated. The statement of the tonic cannot be overly frequent, for the chord tends too strongly to impose either a sense of complete finality, or too much stability and repose to phrase endings. To conclude every phrase on the tonic induces a static dullness. This sense of finality is called *cadence;* and since finality is a quality, a matter of degree, there are different kinds of cadences reflecting various degrees of stability or finality or repose. Example 6:10 shows three commonly encountered types of cadence.

Ex. 6:10

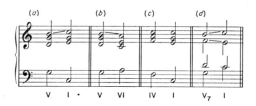

The first (Ex. 6:10*a*) is the strongest, for the movement is toward the tonic from the next most powerful chord, the dominant. It is called a *full* or *authentic cadence*. Much of its strength derives from the leading tone to tonic (B to C) movement in the top notes. This cadence is often strengthened (see Ex. 6:10*d*) by adding a seventh to the dominant chord. In this case the seventh is an F: for in the key of C major, G is the dominant, and to the triad on G (G B D) the seventh above G is added. This is called the *dominant-seventh chord,* or V_7 as it appears in abbreviated form. This chord is remarkably unstable since it contains both the seventh and the fourth degrees of the scale. In the C major of the illustration, B is the leading tone and F the fourth. Both tones are strongly dependent ones, with the seventh gravitating up to the tonic (B to C) and the fourth tending downward toward the third (F to E). As a result, the dominant seventh contains two tones that are not at rest, but demand, as musicians say, *resolution.*

A full cadence, dominant to tonic (V to I) or dominant seventh to tonic (V_7 to I), is usually reserved for the close of main sections and for the very end of a composition. Its tone, however, is too positive to be serviceable for all purposes. A progression from the subdominant (a chord built on the fourth degree of the scale) to the tonic is final enough without being aggressively or triumphantly so. This progression (IV to I, illustrated in Ex. 6:10c) is commonly used as the so-called *Amen* cadence heard at the end of most hymns, and it is also known as the *plagal cadence*. Sometimes, at an intermediate stage of a composition, a composer will avoid the finality of an authentic cadence by following the dominant chord (V) not with the tonic but with a substitute for it, a chord on the sixth degree of the scale (VI). It is a comparatively weak chord, and the cadence of V to VI is often valuable for the surprise achieved by the substitution. It is illustrated in Example 6:10b, and it will be noticed that the leading tone B resolves not, as one expects it to, upward to the tonic C, but downward to A. Hence, it is called a *deceptive cadence*.

The term "cadence," derived as it is from the Latin word *cadere* meaning "to fall," is associated with vocal inflections such as the drop of the voice at the end of a sentence and the moment of relaxation upon arrival at a destination. However, while Newton's law took it for granted that everything that moves up must come down, this is not necessarily true of a musical line, since a melody can come to rest an octave or more above or below the point from which it started. Cadences also, while usually implying a falling linear inflection and coming to a point of harmonic rest, can do just the opposite. Beethoven, for instance, ends a sonata movement on an ascending arpeggio, which seems to soar indefinitely upward and

Ex. 6:11   Piano Sonata, Op. 79 (last 3 bars). Beethoven.

Ex. 6:12   *Grand Rondeau,* Op. 107 (last 6 bars). Schubert.

then to continue even beyond the limits of physical hearing (Ex. 6:11). In the case of one of Schubert's cadences (Ex 6:12), he proceeds upward, while at the same time accelerating his rhythmic motion from the prevailing duple to triple meter, then to the indefinite speed of a trill, thus creating the impression of continuous accelerated motion upward into infinity.

In the nineteenth century, composers sometimes ended a piece on an unresolved seventh chord. Chopin, for instance, concludes his Prelude, Op. 28 No. 23, on a tonic-seventh chord, as did Schumann in "The Entreating Child" from his *Scenes from Childhood*. In both cases the poetic implication is one of incompleteness or unfulfilled desire. In the "Child Falling Asleep," also from the *Scenes from Childhood,* the line breaks off suddenly on a minor subdominant chord, and by deliberately avoiding a cadence, the composer creates the effect of suspending his piece in mid-air, leaving its completion to the imagination of the listener. In modern harmonic practice the numbers of unresolved and dissonant cadences are, of course, legion.

It is clear that the above discussion deals with a system of harmony in which chords are related to one another. These chords function with respect to one another, and each chord has its functions within the total system. At this stage, therefore, it is no longer sufficient to define a chord solely in terms of the intervals comprising it. Each chord must now be understood in terms of its functions. Some of the more obvious functions of a tonic or a dominant chord have just been indicated. Imagination in the discovery of subtle varieties of chord function is one of the strongest assets of a composer. The system of harmony here outlined is sometimes referred to as *functional harmony,* for the chord structures comprising it are understood in terms of function within the system.

Ex. 6:13   Symphony No. 5 (*From the New World*). Second Movement (Bars 1–10). Dvořák.

The difference between chromatic and diatonic chord progressions is illustrated by the opening measures in the slow movement of Dvořák's Symphony No. 5 in E Minor, *From the New World* (Ex. 6:13). The first four measures are chromatic, and the next six measures diatonic. The listener can hardly fail to notice the simple and effective sense of stability and clarity achieved with the emergence of a clear tonic (D-flat major) chord in measure four. Once the tonic is achieved, after three measures of harmonic drift, the melody emerges "in focus," so to speak. The contrast is thus between the chromatic ambiguities of the introductory measures, and the diatonic clarity that follows.

Mozart and Beethoven are rather partial to devoting the opening measures of a large-scale movement to establishing a firm sense of tonic. Formula subjects are especially suitable for this, and many of their major works open with such "tonic formulas." The opening of Mozart's Concerto No. 5 in A Major for Violin and Orchestra (K.219) is simply a rising progression on the notes of the tonic triad in A major.

Ex. 6:14 Violin Concerto No. 5 (K. 219). First Movement (Bars 1–5). Mozart.

The opening measures of Beethoven's Concerto No. 3 in C Minor for Piano and Orchestra, Op. 37, are likewise a unison and octave outline of the tonic triad of C minor, followed by a harmonized answering phrase on the dominant.

Ex. 6:15 Piano Concerto No. 3. First Movement (Bars 1–7). Beethoven.

Contrast the sense of straightforward, clear-cut definition in the above examples with the deliberate ambiguities in the opening measures of the Prelude to Wagner's *Tristan and Isolde* (Ex. 6:16). This is an opera of soul states, of passionate yearnings—a tragedy of thwarted lovers and longings unfulfilled. The "mood" opening is a chromatic evasion of direct key orientation; it is an avoidance of simple dominant-tonic statement of key. Each phrase ends with a chord requiring resolution. The resolution is explicitly avoided, and silence reigns when the unresolved chord ceases.

Ex. 6:16 Prelude to *Tristan and Isolde* (Bars 1–7). Wagner.

Nothing would so thoroughly and mercilessly destroy the sense of this passage as to resolve the final chord in each phrase. To establish a clear tonic here would be to define and hence obliterate the unresolved yearnings communicated so eloquently through the evasions of chromaticism and silence.

MODULATION

If, for most purposes, a clear tonic key orientation is desirable, it is equally desirable during the course of the composition to move away from the tonic. Key monotony is as deadening as any other kind of monotony. Movement from one key center to another is called *modulation,* and it is a process in which some composers have been inexhaustibly creative. The complex of key relationships may perhaps be clarified by analogy.

If each key is thought of as a tonal territory, and the complex of keys as a tonal geography, then a map may be drawn showing which keys are adjacent to one another, sharing a common border, and which keys lie far apart. The analogy is also to some extent psychologically apt, for tonal distance (that is, the distance between keys) is a verifiable psychological phenomenon, and composers such as Beethoven, Mozart, and Schubert assume an intuitive awareness of it on the part of the listener. A map showing key relationships, and hence the tonal geography which is the frame of reference for composer and listener, may be drawn as two concentric circles, the outer circle representing the major keys, and the inner circle the minor keys. The major and minor keys lying opposite to each other are called *relative* keys. For example, *A minor* and *C major* lie opposite one another. In this case A minor is the *relative minor* of C major; and vice versa, C major is the *relative major* of A minor. Modulations to adjacent keys, like stepping over the border to an adjacent territory, involve less of a sense of traveling than modulations to distant keys. This spanning of tonal distance is one of the primary mechanisms at work in large-scale constructions. (Further amplification of this point will be made in the section on sonata form; see Chap. 10.) It will suffice here to offer a few examples of near and distant modulations taken from Beethoven's scores.

The first (Ex. 6:17) is an example of a modulation from G major to C major. As the circular diagram shows, these are adjacent keys. (In the example given below, the measures are numbered so that a chord reduction can be apprended for each measure.)

Ex. 6:17   Piano Sonata, Op. 2 No. 3. First Movement (Bars 56–63). Beethoven.

The second illustration (Ex. 6:18) is of a modulation from C major to D minor, two keys still fairly close, although not adjacent.

Ex. 6:18 Symphony No. 1. First Movement (Bars 14–19). Beethoven.

The third illustration (Ex. 6:19) shows the effect of wide sweeping modulations (C minor to C-sharp minor to D minor) covering a vast tonal distance at each leap.

Ex. 6:19 Symphony No. 3 (*Eroica*). First Movement (Bars 78–87). Beethoven.

The next instance (Ex. 6:20) is a singular one indeed, for the modulations are built into the contour of the melody itself. Many things could be noted clinically as contributing to the character of this wonderful melody; but in the first instance, its unique profile derives from the modulations which control its contours.

Ex. 6:20 Piano Concerto No. 4. First Movement (Bars 29–40). Beethoven.

CONSONANCE AND DISSONANCE

One last consideration involved in the concept of a tonal system is the notion of *consonance* and *dissonance*. All too often these terms are mistakenly understood as equivalents for agreeable and disagreeable,

good music and bad music, easy to listen to and hard to listen to, or classical music and modern music. Actually, once any tonal system is defined,
there are tones that belong within it and tones that do not. For example,
a tonic triad in the key of C major is defined as C-E-G. These tones are
consonant to the triad because they belong to it. Our subjective psychological impression that this chord is a consonant one depends upon the
fact that all the tones one hears (C-E-G) belong to the same chord. If a
B natural is superimposed upon this chord, a note has been added that
does not belong. It creates a *dissonance*—a point of friction which demands explanation, or a point of tension requiring resolution. Hold the
C-E-G triad, superimpose the B natural, and then follow it by a C. A dissonance has been introduced and resolved. Consider the dissonances
(marked by asterisks) in the Example 6:21. In Example 6:21a, a C-major

Ex. 6:21   Ex. 6:22

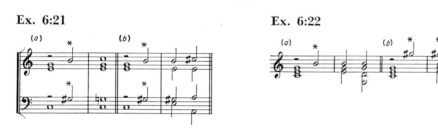

tonic chord is posited. Two dissonant tones are then added, a B natural
and a G sharp. Neither note belongs to the chord (C-E-G), and, in addition, the G sharp would be dissonant to any diatonic chord in the key of
C major (Ex. 6:22b), whereas B natural is dissonant to some chords in that
key but not to others (Ex. 6:22a).

In Example 6:21a the dissonances (the tones which do not belong)
have been resolved by leading them to tones that do belong. However,
should the composer insist upon these dissonant tones, then the remainder
of the system may be altered until these tones become consonant to the
system in which they find themselves. In Example 6:22a, the B natural is
reiterated. However, the chords underneath it are altered to such chords
as will admit the B natural as a consonance. As Example 6:22b indicates,
no diatonic chord sequence in the key of C major will admit G sharp as
consonant. Insisting upon it demands a rather radical alteration of harmonic context—a substitution of A major for C major, or, in the terminology already explained above, a modulation from C major to A major.
This is illustrated in Example 6:21b.

In every case, the esthetic principle illustrated is simply this: that a
dissonance is a point of harmonic tension, compelling the listener to focus
upon the next moment in time, when either the dissonant tone will be
succeeded by one that is consonant to the established harmonic context,

or the context itself will be altered so that the dissonant tone will now be a consonant one. A judiciously placed dissonance cannot be ignored. It compels explanation from the composer and anticipation of this explanation on the part of the listener. In short, it forces the continuity of the music from one moment in time to the next. Nothing in music is so utterly fatal as notes that follow each other in time for no reason other than that the performer is playing them one after the other. Music must create its own sense of the flow of time, a sense of the necessity, and the inevitability of the next instant. It must move through time as if by an inner momentum, and the art of well-placed dissonance is, in this respect, an invaluable and irreplaceable resource. The first chord that opens the last movement of Beethoven's Ninth Symphony is a dissonance violent enough to generate the momentum that carries through the next seven measures. This is a dramatic instance of the value of dissonance in imparting to music a propulsive movement through time. A quieter example is the following from Pergolesi's *Stabat Mater:*

Ex. 6:23 From *Stabat Mater*. Pergolesi.

Here, over a steadily moving bass progression, the upper parts are inwardly forced forward from one beat to the next, by a point of friction (dissonance). Every strong beat is marked by a dissonance, every weak beat that follows is its resolution.

Esthetic principles here are rooted in common sense. Dissonances are as necessary to music as problems requiring resolution are to a sense of achievement in life. One can overindulge in either, and composers are as humanly liable to a dislocation of values in this respect as anyone else. Likewise, consonance, agreement, stability, and repose are all qualities that neither life nor art can afford to disregard. And yet common sense cautions that a music unalleviated in the stability and restfulness of its consonances will close with that sense of futile fatigue known best to people who have been resting carefully all of their lives.

The Contrapuntal Complex

Chapter 7

In the actuality of its creation and of its performance, a musical composition is the focus of a remarkably subtle and often deeply moving interplay of human experience, expression, and communication. If, for a moment, these inevitable human involvements are set aside; if the music, as such, is abstracted from any possible human condition, then it may be said that it is simply an arrangement of sounds in time. In a fundamental sense then, music is essentially linear; for the tones, by their very succession, constitute what may be called a musical line. The line acquires contour when the tones are differentiated in duration and pitch, and color when they are performed on an instrument or sung.

A musical line is an essentially horizontal arrangement, just as a chord is an essentially vertical one. However, they are only essentially, not absolutely, so. A chord progression is given contour at the very least by the bass line of the progression; and conversely, a melodic line is composed of intervals—that is, measurable distances between successive higher and lower pitches. The nature of chords and the manner in which intervals contribute to the profile of a line of melody have been discussed in the foregoing chapter. Among other things, the study of harmony is concerned with the controls that may be exercized over these essentially vertical aspects of music. Analogously, the study of *counterpoint* is devoted to the

83

disciplines that are pertinent to the juxtaposition of two or more lines or
levels of music sounding simultaneously.

Literally, the word counterpoint refers to the process of setting against
each note on a given melodic line, a note corresponding to it on another
melodic line. However, this note against note, or point-counter-point, is a
primitive realization of the concept. Literally, the word *polyphony* means
music for many voices (or parts). It is the opposite of *monophony,* or music
for one voice. In common usage, however, polyphony and counterpoint
are interchangeable terms, as are their adjectival forms *polyphonic* and
contrapuntal. Such terms designate the kind of complex where several
lines (or layers, or levels) of music are in progress simultaneously. Each
line is an individual one and must be sufficiently distinguishable as such.
Yet all lines must be woven together so that, with no essential sacrifice of
individuality, all cohere as a single entity. Harmonic considerations are
always involved to one degree or another in the most rigorously contrapuntal music; but they are used primarily as an aid to the clarity and
coherence of the polyphonic complex.

Harmony and counterpoint are related, if often opposite, views of the
same musical situation. Consider for example the chordal view where the
sense of a progression of verticals is paramount:

Ex. 7:1

Compare this with the contrapuntal view of the same situation as Bach sees
it in the G-minor Fugue from Book I of the *Well-Tempered Clavier.*

Ex. 7:2   Fugue No. 16, Book I, *Well-Tempered Clavier* (Bars 5–6). Bach.

A chord is a homogeneous oneness of sound, and is heard essentially as
such. However, in Example 7:2, the sense for the chord is very much weakened, and each note tends to be heard primarily as a component of the
horizontal line to which it belongs.

Assiduous application to contrapuntal music is one of the most bene-
ficial disciplines available to the serious listener. An ear trained to follow

the inner clarity and complexity of well-written counterpoint will be sensitive to subtlety of detail and to the refinements of workmanship contained in every major musical masterpiece. The following discussion will be focused on those processes that show a strong tendency to set up horizontal levels within the musical complex. Some are quasi-contrapuntal, others more fully so. The distinction is based on the premise that linearity is never absolute and never entirely absent. In short, there are degrees to which a complex is contrapuntal.

PART WRITING

In a choral composition or a work for an ensemble of instruments, a passage conceived chordally is often somewhat contrapuntalized. For example, a hymn tune may be harmonized for an ensemble of sopranos, altos, tenors, and basses as follows:

Ex. 7:3

The setting is essentially vertical, a chord succession supporting the chorale melody. Each chord, however, is composed of four separate voice parts (soprano, alto, tenor, and bass), each part sustaining a note in the vertical alignment. Since the soprano part contains the chorale tune, it is usually left unaltered. For the remaining voices, sustaining a note in a supporting harmony is not always entirely interesting to the composer, to the singer, or to the listener. Since each note in the chord belongs to a "part," these parts can be made more interesting by introducing additional, in-between or passing notes. The effect is to linearize the parts, to give each part the sense of being, within limits, a line. To an extent, the chord progression is somewhat de-emphasized, and the texture, by virtue of its *part writing*, becomes quasi-contrapuntal. The following is the result of a contrapuntalized part-writing treatment accorded the above example by Bach.

Ex. 7:4   Chorale (Bars 1–2). Bach.

OSTINATO

The word *ostinato* means literally "obstinate" and refers to the process of repeating a musical figure over and over again. Often it is a purely rhythmical device, and as such, it makes its appearance quite frequently in the work of composers like Stravinsky and Bartók. Thus in Stravinsky's *Rite of Spring,* the section entitled "Dance of the Adolescents" owes much of its effectiveness to the persistence of a four-note ostinato. By the very obstinacy of its reiteration, the figure sets up a level within the music, and against this ostinato level other rhythms are played off in a rhythmic counterpoint.

Ex. 7:5 "Dance of the Adolescents" from *Rite of Spring.* Stravinsky.

Usually the ostinato figure is a melodic motive or line and customarily it is located in the bass. This obstinate bass (*basso ostinato*) can take any form the composer finds suitable to his purposes. In English usage, a basso ostinato is often called a *ground.* To the degree that reiteration tends to provide emphasis, a ground bass becomes a level apart from whatever may be going on above it. Implicitly, there is always a contrapuntal relationship, an interplay between distinguishable levels, whenever a ground bass is in operation. Sometimes the ground is a short one-measure motive, sometimes an extended eight-measure phrase. Brahms, for example, was fond of passages constructed over short ground-bass motives. The following, from the Finale of his First Symphony, is one of several examples that may be extracted from his orchestral music. The passage is extensive, but only the first four measures are given here.

Ex. 7:6 Symphony No. 1. Fourth Movement (Bars 118–122). Brahms.

Monteverdi's treatment of a motivic ground in his madrigal, *Lamento della Ninfa (Non havea Febo ancora)*, is more explicitly contrapuntal, for the ground is instrumental while the other parts are vocal. Moreover, the ground functions as a vital unifying element in a dramatically disjunct situation. The soprano laments her sad fate, while the men's voices offer commiserating commentary. The duality is unified, and the freedom of the voice parts firmly anchored, by the implacable obstinacy of the instrumental bass.

More extended ground-bass figures may be found in the works of Purcell and Bach. In the "Crucifixus" of his B-minor Mass (Ex. 5:4), Bach uses an ostinato reiteration of a chromatically descending four-measure phrase. Such slow, chromatically descending phrases, when used by baroque composers as ostinato lines, often connote states of deep emotional distress too ultimate for agitation. The irrevocable persistence of the slow descending line is in itself a level of commentary on, or interpretation of, a dramatic situation. However mystical or impassioned the music above it, it maintains its slow inevitable course with grief-laden deliberation. In the Bach setting of the "Crucifixus," the voice parts wander along lost in the mystical eternity of the scene, while the instrumental bass, by its reiteration, emphasizes the inevitability of the moment. Purcell uses an analogous ostinato figure (a slow chromatic descent) for the final aria in his opera *Dido and Aeneas*. Here too, the tragedy (Dido's impending death) is conceived as inevitable. But over the implacable ground, Purcell provides his heroine with a magnificently impassioned death aria. (The Bach bass will be found on p. 56, Ex. 5:4; the Purcell ostinato aria on pp. 294–296, Ex. 20.7.) Dido's first aria in the Purcell opera is also an ostinato composition, and a fine example of a tormented aria-line carefully unsynchronized with the phrasing of the reiterated bass. In Example 7:7 it is understood that the bass is to be repeated under each line of the aria.

Ex. 7:7 "Ah, Belinda" from *Dido and Aeneas*. Purcell.

Ostinato basses are also common in instrumental music. A rather free ostinato may be found in the slow movement of the Bach E-major Violin Concerto No. 2. The ostinato is free in the sense that the bass figure is altered in the course of its repetitions, although the ostinato pattern remains recognizable as such.

There are two types of variation design associated with the ostinato principle: the *passacaglia* and the *chaconne*. Rather than add to the considerable and unrewarding literature already accumulated in the attempt to offer universal and uninterchangeable distinctions between the two, discussion will be confined to two opposing concepts illustrated by a Bach passacaglia and a Bach chaconne. Both are continuous variations; that is, there is a continuous evolution of fresh musical material—in the *passacaglia* mainly *over* an ostinato bass line, in the *chaconne* mainly *out of* a basic harmonic progression. The ostinato bass in the Bach Passacaglia in C Minor for Organ is first stated unaccompanied.

Ex. 7:8   Passacaglia in C Minor for Organ (Bars 1–8) . Bach.

Over each of its reiterations Bach evolves continually varied counterpoints in the upper parts. In the Bach Chaconne from his Sonata No. 4 in D Minor for Unaccompanied Violin, the first four measures outline, not an ostinato line, but a harmonic progression; the ensuing variations then evolve out of this progression, which is used as a reference point. A similar chaconne construction may be found in Beethoven's Thirty-two Variations in C minor for solo piano.

In essence, the passacaglia principle entails a contrapuntal relationship between the ostinato bass line and the part or parts over it. Even where the upper parts are temporarily chordal in character, the distinction in levels is at least implicitly contrapuntal. However, the chaconne principle is one of continuous harmonic orientation. A variation in the Beethoven C-minor set is contrapuntal to the degree that Beethoven chooses momentarily to make it so. But unlike a passacaglia, nothing in the chaconne principle entails an automatically contrapuntal juxtaposition of discrete and distinguishable levels within the music.

CONTINUO

Continuo is a contrapuntal concept analogous to the basso ostinato and like it, favored by baroque composers. It too is located in the bass, and its full name is *basso continuo* (continuous bass) . As the name implies, it is a continuous bass line, defined sharply enough to function as a clearly distinguishable level within the musical complex. Actually it both supports and liberates the line or lines above it, because of the secure foundation its steady, seamless, easy flowing continuity imparts to the ensemble. The relationship between a basso ostinato and a basso continuo is simply this: a basso ostinato may be designed as a continuo, and in baroque music it usually is. However, not all continuos are ostinatos.

One of the common effects in continuo writing is the polarization that tends to be set up between the continuo part in the bass and the remaining upper parts. The number of parts that can be found over a continuo varies. In a baroque sonata for violin and continuo, for example, there is at least one main line over the continuo. In the middle movement of the Bach *Brandenburg* Concerto No. 2 in F Major, there are three such contrapuntal lines over the continuo. Listening to the Bach example will illustrate how the upper parts (violin, oboe, and flute) tend to be bound together against the continuo in the bass. The favorite medium for chamber music among baroque composers was the *trio sonata,* an instrumental composition in several movements composed in three separate contrapuntal parts, although not necessarily for three separate instruments. (A trio sonata is sometimes written for organ, because all three lines can be clearly rendered on an instrument like the organ, equipped as it is with two manual keyboards and a pedal board.) In a baroque trio sonata, the two upper parts tend to be bound together, as a contrapuntal duet, over the continuo. The favorite instrumentation is for two violins and continuo. There are, of course, variations from the norm: either two matched soprano instruments, such as two flutes over continuo; or two unmatched soprano instruments, such as violin and flute over continuo; or two instruments of unmatched ranges, like violin and viola over continuo. Any of the trio sonatas by Bach, Handel, Purcell, Corelli, etc., will serve as an illustration.

Trio sonata is as much then a texture, or a specific kind of counterpoint, as it is a musical form. And as a type of contrapuntal texture it is employed in works of many different kinds. In the Corelli *Christmas* Concerto, a concerto grosso, the concertino part is an example of a trio-sonata style of counterpoint (see p. 133, Ex. 11:1). And the opening chorus of Pergolesi's *Stabat Mater* is a similar example. The continuo part is instrumental in the Pergolesi, while the two upper parts are vocal. As in a trio sonata, the two vocal parts are bound together in a contrapuntal duet over the continuo (see p. 82, Ex. 6:23).[1]

---

[1] A trio sonata normally involves four instruments. The continuo is played on a keyboard, its bass line supported usually by a cello, while the upper keyboard part supplies harmonies. Thus the continuo has harmonic as well as contrapuntal functions.

CANON

   The point in the foregoing discussion has been to make clear that the presence of a continuo tends to polarize the contrapuntal complex. As soon as the continuo occupies the bass level with its steady seamless progress, the remaining voices tend to group themselves together in a contrapuntal complex of their own, operating as a unit above the continuo level and, to a degree, apart from it. (Exceptional measures can be taken to weaken this duality within the complex, but the point is emphasized by the fact that such measures are exceptional.) Now if a polarized counterpoint exists, there is, by implication, a nonpolarized counterpoint in which all voices are bound together in a homogeneity of texture. The homogeneous counterpoint practiced by the Renaissance masters of the fifteenth and sixteenth century was as remarkable for its purity as for its complexity; and the music of Ockeghem, Obrecht, Josquin des Prez, Palestrina, and Lassus affords ample illustration of the wonders of this art. Continuo counterpoint was a development in seventeenth-century composition closely allied to the growing sense of the harmonic importance of the bass, and the increasing interest in the dramatic implications of polarized textures of all kinds (see Chap. 20, p. 282). While continuo counterpoint lingered on well past the middle of the eighteenth century, homogeneous counterpoint remained alive by undergoing transformations that took into account new concepts in harmonic logic. In ways specific to a Bach or a Handel, it is as strong in their work as in Josquin or Palestrina.

 Among the procedures that tend to secure homogeneity of contrapuntal texture, the canonic is still the most useful for a mastery of fundamentals. The diversity of techniques possible in the construction of canons is less to the point here than the principle to which such diversity may be reduced. In essence, a *canon* is a composition in which all parts are realized out of one. For example, if the canon is in four parts, the second, third, and fourth are derived by imitation of the first. A canon, then, is based on the principle of *imitation,* and is still the prime example of *imitative counterpoint.* What is indeed marvelous to contemplate is the astonishing ingenuity shown in the contriving of imitations; there is perhaps no other area of musical composition where their use has been so prolific. A great many canons are hardly more than compositional pleasantries. Yet for some composers (Bach, in particular) the canon proved an apt vehicle for the stimulation of a searching musical intelligence, and often a profoundly human means of expression. Examples of Bach's canonic art may be found in his *Goldberg* Variations, in his Canonic Variations on the chorale *Vom Himmel hoch da komm ich her* (From Heaven high to earth I come), and in his *Musical Offering.*

The variety of canon with which most laymen are acquainted is the *round*. Examples like *Three Blind Mice* and *Row, Row, Row Your Boat* are familiar enough. The procedure in a round is simple. Each voice, as it enters in its turn on the unison or the octave, imitates literally what the foregoing voice has already sung. Lest the familiar examples be misleading, the following example by Haydn is given in evidence that rounds are not necessarily diversions fit for use mainly at picnics, sorority sings, and in kindergartens. The Haydn round is a moving piece of music set to a solemn text: "Death is a longer sleep, sleep is a shorter death." Rounds rarely offer latitude for expressive text setting, but Haydn has contrived his so that the word *langer* (longer) is mirrored in notes of long duration, and the word *kurzer* (shorter) in notes of shorter duration. Moreover, the affecting dissonances grow in intensity as the number of voices increases. The maximum of harmonic tension is achieved when all four voices are heard, and subsides as the voices drop out one by one. The contrivances of the round are used here to mirror the implications of the text, and the structure of the contrivances is simultaneously the structure of the emotion they are employed to convey.

Ex. 7:9 Canon, *Tod ist ein langer Schlaf.* Haydn.

The example is to be read as follows:

> When first voice reaches line 2, second voice enters on line 1;
> When first voice reaches line 3, third voice enters on line 1;
> When first voice reaches line 4, fourth voice enters on line 1.
> Each voice is exactly three measures behind its predecessor, and each voice, after it enters, sings the entire melody through.

A round, however, is a rather limiting type of canon, for several specific conditions are necessary to its existence. One such, for example, is the condition that all voices enter at the unison (or, where provision is made, at the octave). Canons equally strict can be written with the successive voices duplicating the first, but starting on a different degree of the scale.

For example, if the first voice were to begin on the note C, and if the second voice were to duplicate the first but starting on the note D, then this would be called a canon at the second. The following example illustrates several points.

Ex. 7:10 *Goldberg* Variations (Bars 1–4 of Variation 18). Bach.

The two upper parts are in canon at the sixth, and the canon proceeds over a free bass line which, although coordinated with the canon, still stands apart. If the canon in the right hand is played alone, it will be noticed that the texture is distinctly more homogeneous than when the canon is played over the free bass line. This serves to emphasize canon as a device for obtaining a smooth contrapuntal texture; and it also suggests the inventiveness that can be brought into play in the modification of this kind of texture through the addition of free contrapuntal parts.

There are a variety of imitative devices which provide, at minimum, an exacting exercise of ingenuity, but which may result in interesting and expressive modifications of the original voice. Thus the imitation may proceed by *inversion* or contrary motion; that is, where the original voice goes up, the imitating voice goes down an equivalent distance, and vice versa. Or the imitation may proceed by *augmentation* or *diminution;* that is, in augmentation the imitating voice renders each note of the original in double its time value (notes twice as long in duration), and in diminution at one half its time value (notes half as long in duration). Or the imitating voice may repeat the original in reverse order, starting at the last note of the original and ending with the first (a procedure called *retrograde, cancrizans,* or *crab*). In the Bach *Musical Offering,* the ten canons are divided in the Hans T. David edition into two groups of five. Bach founded the entire work on a theme proposed to him by Frederick the Great. In the first set of five canons, the royal theme is itself not treated canonically, but accompanies each canon as a free voice. In the second group of five, the royal theme is itself subjected to canonic imitation. Among the canons in the *Musical Offering* will be found examples of canon in contrary motion (inversion), canon in retrograde (crab), canon in contrary motion and augmentation (the two devices employed simultaneously), a modulating canon, and a canonic fugue (see Chap. 20 pp. 303–306 for a more thorough discussion of this work).

The foregoing is by no means a complete description of useful canonic procedures, but all such procedures reduce to the derivation (by imitation) of two or more parts from one. Despite differences in line that result from inversions, augmentations, and diminutions, all parts tend to reveal similarities which are as deep as they are subtle. Because of this origin in a common source, all parts in a canon seem intrinsically related, and the counterpoint that results from their interplay tends toward a marked homogencity of texture.

FUGUE

In all fairness to the reader, it should be said that discussion of fugue is strongly conditioned by the point of view from which one regards it. There are several plausible viewpoints, with a degree of merit in each. The assumption here will be that fugue is a type of contrapuntal process, its flexible and fundamental nature evident in the bewildering variety of specific fugue forms to which it has given rise. Several excellent manuals are in print offering detailed analytical commentary on each of the forty-eight fugues in the two volumes of Bach's *Well-Tempered Clavier,* as well as on each of the fugues in his monumental *Art of the Fugue.* The need to examine each fugue separately points to a high degree of structural individuality in any given Bach fugue, and underlines the value of abstracting from this maze of formal variables the ground source of their proliferation.

Customarily one desires to know at least two things about any process: what is in process, and how the process operates. What is in process is a musical entity called a *fugue subject,* and its nature is determined by the principle that underlies the techniques by which the process is maintained. The fugue process may be described as developmental; its counterpoint as a developmental counterpoint; and its structure, in general, as evolutionary, in that what happens at later points in a fugue design represents an evolution or a development of the original material. The nature of a fugue subject is, in general, then, predetermined. It must be a subject capable of polyphonic development. Since polyphony involves the interplay of simultaneously sounding lines of music, a fugue subject must be intrinsically amenable to simultaneous combinations. It should be capable of combining with itself (a technique called *stretto,* which points to an analogy between canon and certain aspects of fugue) . More particularly, the fugue subject should also be capable of combining with subjects other than itself. The technical expression for these "other subjects" is *countersubjects* when they appear in direct conjunction with the fugue subject. When a subject subsequently appears free of any direct relationship to the fugue subject or countersubjects, then it may be regarded as free episodic material. In a fugue *episodes* are interpolations between appearances of the fugue subject. They are prone to occur at nearly any stage of the design, and most often are compounded out of motives that have been derived from either the fugue subject or the countersubjects, or from both.

The fugue subject itself is apt to be short, clear in profile, and with certain characteristic intervallic and rhythmic features that help to identify it rather readily wherever it may appear in the contrapuntal fabric. A lyrical, songlike melody, too self-sufficient and too indrawn to tolerate much more than discrete chordal accompaniment, will scarcely function as a fugue subject. For it is the essence of a fugue subject to serve as an effective building material; to become a resource for development; to exercise upon its reappearances a certain assertive force within the fabric; and even to generate and sustain the rhythmic momentum of the music. The countersubject must be capable of maintaining a dual function simultaneously, for it is a continuation of the fugue subject at the very moment that it is in combination with it.

Ex. 7:11   Fugue No. 2, Book I, *Well-Tempered Clavier* (Bars 1–4). Bach.

As Example 7:11 shows, the first appearance of the fugue subject is unaccompanied. This is the statement on the tonic. The second appearance, or answer, is made on the dominant and in combination with the first of several countersubjects. In the first portion of the fugue, called the *exposition,* there are as many entrances of the fugue subject as there are parts to be involved in the contrapuntal complex. This particular fugue is in three parts; hence a third entrance, again on the tonic, is to be expected. Bach chooses to delay the third entrance by providing a two-measure episode in which the opening motive from the fugue subject is developed in combination with a new free subject. Via this episode, Bach modulates back to the tonic C-minor key, in which tonal area the third entry of the fugue subject occurs in combination with two countersubjects. In this instance, the third entry completes the exposition.

The exposition of a fugue may be summarized as follows: The fugue subject appears as many times, and on as many separate levels, as there are to be contrapuntal parts. With each entry, a line of counterpoint is set in motion. If there are three entries in the exposition, with the third entry all three lines of counterpoint are in operation. Key sense is established by alternate entries on the tonic and dominant. The presence of episodes within the exposition, as well as their duration, are optional.

Thereafter, fugue designs show a high degree of developmental freedom. Sooner or later there may be a recurrence of fugue-subject re-entrances, either first on the dominant and then on the tonic, or in a wider range of key relationships. The fugue may culminate in stretto reappearances of the subject, the effect being a kind of piling up of the subject on itself, level on level. Or the fugue may close with an essentially nonpolyphonic coda. The most vital point to grasp is that beyond the close of the exposition, formal consistency from one fugue to another is hardly likely. And this for the reason that in a developmental process the total design always depends upon the specific nature of the primary materials (subject and countersubjects) , and upon the specific nature of the musical occurrences to which this material gives rise and in which it often finds itself adventurously involved.

Devices already discussed under canon—such as inversion, diminution, augmentation—may also become operative in fugue. The complexity of fugue design may be further increased by adding to the number of fugue subjects. The above discussion has been confined to comparatively simple fugues with just one subject. The number of separate fugue subjects is sometimes increased to two, three, and four (double, triple, and quadruple fugues) . Furthermore, there are stretto fugues, ricercare fugues, chorale fugues, and many another variety.

Aspects of the fugue process are often adaptable to other types of musical structure, and in the works of Mozart, Haydn, and Beethoven these may be encountered as components of thematic developments and even of theme presentation in sonata-form structures, rondos, and variation movements. Convenient examples may be found in the slow movement of the Beethoven *Eroica* Symphony, the Andante of his First Symphony, the Finale of Mozart's G-major String Quartet (K.387) , the Finale of his *Jupiter* Symphony, and the Overture to the *Magic Flute*. There is general agreement that these instances are not fugues; but to say of them carefully that they are "in fugue" or fugal, is not only to describe them accurately, but to illuminate the nature of fugue as process.

PART II

The Composer
and His Product

Principles of
Organization

Chapter 8

A COMPOSER, literally, is one who puts musical materials together, and his product is aptly referred to as a composition. At a minimum, this is what a piece of music is and must be. With due respect for whatever else must exist before the music is "significant," "meaningful," "moving," or "expressive," it is scarcely possible (except on an essentially primitive level) for the music to make any sort of sense or to communicate anything at all, unless a manifest principle of coherence governs the relationship of the parts making up the whole. The *form* in a piece of music is the rational ordering of its component sections. It is also the totality or oneness that emerges out of the coherence of its component sections both within themselves and in their relationship to one another. *Formal devices,* so called, are such devices as a composer may use to make clear the relationship between one section and another. Form is not equivalent to symmetry, although it is equivalent to an adjustment of balances. For many listeners form is perceived intuitively. In such familiar masterpieces as the First Movement of the Beethoven Fifth Symphony or in the opening movement of the Mozart Symphony No. 40 in G Minor, form is the sense of the togetherness of the movement.

Prejudices rooted largely in personal temperament may becloud what is, in essence, not too complicated a matter. It is sometimes said, dogmatically and with much indignation, that cold form in music is meaningless. It would be interesting if the temperature of an abstraction could be determined, but the question is really quite irrelevant. It is not difficult, however, to show that form, as a logic of relationships, because of its abstractness, has meaning of an especially basic kind. The abstract form of an argument can make sense quite apart from the specific content that may be given it. The form of an argument, for instance, may run: if a is contained in b, and b is contained in c, then a is contained in c. One can claim, if one cares to, that this is cold, but it would be futile to insist that it is meaningless. As a logic of the relationships between the component sections of a composition, form is a level of meaning as basic to music as the abstract algebraic statement of relationships is to logic.

An occasional composer or listener may profess himself completely content with just the level of meaning expressed by the purely formal coherence of musical components, and much sensibility and imagination may well be poured into the contriving or the perceiving of such formal relationships. Most composers and listeners will, probably, out of their own experiences, find this an unnecessary limitation of the multiplicity of levels upon which a piece of music can effectively be meaningful. Yet even for the vast majority who would deny that formal organization is an end in itself, it is evident that a coherence of precisely this sort is mandatory if the work is to be understood on any level. Whatever it is that the composer wants his music to express, the fact remains that it is the music that does the expressing, and it is the music which serves as the mechanism of communication; and much of music's power to communicate and express effectively is dependent upon its inner coherence. Some grasp of the inner logic of a composition's organization and its coherence in its own terms, no matter how intuitive, is always a necessary, although not always a sufficient, condition for an understanding of the piece of music.

Because the form of a piece of music—that is to say, the order of its component sections—can often be represented in simple, neutral, algebraic fashion, there is a risk of oversimplification, and of an essential falsification. With some justice, textbook accounts of musical form, and the very term itself, are sometimes regarded with a degree of suspicion. In truth, if used injudiciously, the term "musical form" can encourage a number of singularly uncreative notions about the nature of the musical process. Inadvertently, the unwary may be left with the impression that musical forms are containers of standardized specifications, that there are a set number of these, and that composing consists in pouring musical content into such ready-made molds and allowing it to set. Sonatas, of course, are not made like cupcakes, and the notion of a "set form" is mainly a misleading one in music. Equally so, and also attendant upon the notion of the fixity of forms is the concept that musical composition is a kind of ancient and esoteric game, the rules for which are, in some mysterious manner, part of the absolute and inalienable order of the universe. Skill in composition consists in more than just the cleverness with which one complies with or circumvents the rules. To be accurate about it (and this distinguishes the composer from the composition student), there are no mandatory "rules" as such; only broad, flexible principles out of which rules are sometimes devised for student use. For example, there is no rule to the effect that every piece must begin in the tonic. There is, however, a broad, flexible principle to the effect that a point of orientation ought to be clearly established fairly early in the composition, unless one has a clear purpose in doing otherwise. Harmonic orientation has proved to be a singularly useful application of this principle, and beginning in the tonic key is the clearest and quickest way of establishing such an orientation. No composer is under obligation to observe this as a "rule"; but it is available to him as a most serious recommendation, for it carries with it the weight of conspicuous success in the work of prior masters, great and small. Forms, then, are not rules for proper musical behavior, nor intractable molds to contain such behavior. They are the specific expressions of general principle. The composer relies not upon rule, but upon good judgment and extensive technical experience when he relates one section of a piece of music to another; and upon imagination and genius (if he is so blessed) in making these formal relationships seem not only cogent but important, not only coherent but urgently and inevitably so.

Actually, then, the heart of the matter is in the simple, but basic, distinction between the general and the particular: that is, between a general principle of construction and a particular form which illustrates one of the ways in which the principle can be sensibly applied. Many of the things we call musical forms—rondo, theme and variations, and the like—are not really "forms" at all, but general principles of construction, basic ideas as to how the component sections of a work can be related to one another. The specific way in which, for example, the rondo principle is applied in a given work becomes the "form" of that particular rondo. Not only can there be, but there actually is a multiplicity of rondo forms; and while the number of such rondo forms is theoretically unlimited, experience and common sense indicate that some are more feasible than others. Varieties of formal type are often rooted (as is so much else in music) in such factors as differences in historical development, in personal temperament, and in the nature of the performing medium. A good example of all three may be found in comparing the formal structures of the first movement of a Beethoven symphony and the first movement of one of Mozart's later piano concertos. As divergent as the two movements are in form, both are nevertheless applications of the same general principles of sonata-form construction.

Since the subject is, in essence, one of general principles, the ultimate question is dictated by common sense. To wit: considering the nature of music, what general principles are likely to be most helpful in achieving coherence in a work comprising several sections?

Music, of course, is an art that quite literally exists in time. At the barest minimum, any principle of order in music must operate on the basis of the organization of sound in time. In this respect, music is profoundly different from either painting or sculpture. If an analogy is sought, perhaps the reading of a novel might come the closest to the experience of listening to an extended piece of music. Both entail the perception of unity over the period of time it takes either to read the novel or to listen to the symphony, and it is precisely here that the difference between the two is most instructive. If the reader has grown inattentive, or failed to finish the novel in one sitting, or for any reason lost the thread of the novel's development, he can go back and reread. If an earlier incident, character presentation, or locale is subsequently referred to, and the reader is not sure that he remembers the original detail well enough to appreciate the value of the later reference, he can always turn to an earlier chapter to refresh his memory. Similar situations in an extended piece of music would leave the listener helpless, frustrated, and inevitably confused. If he has lost the thread, or forgotten the main musical idea, he can scarcely rise from his seat and request a replaying of the first thirty-two measures. And while a composer may legitimately expect sustained and concentrated attention from his audience (although actually he does so at his peril), he cannot legitimately count on total recall.

Obviously then, musical construction cannot entail the perpetual accumulation of fresh incident. Periodically, during the course of the composition, the composer must find time to refresh his listener's memory, to keep him in touch with home base, to keep him tactfully but firmly reminded of the main argument. In short, the first principle in an extended work is the principle of repetition, and a dangerous one it is indeed; for if there is anything more irritating musically than the sensitive wanderer in the deep woods who forgets where he started from, where he is going to, or what he is doing there in the first place, it is the conscientious monomaniac who pauses every ten seconds for station identification.

There are no rules about repetitions beyond the self-evident one that they are necessary in some degree. When and where they occur in a work is completely at the composer's discretion. It is an act of judgment, and very personal judgment, to determine at what point structurally and psychologically the repetition of an opening subject or section is most valuable; and, as in all acts of judgment, experience, imagination, and inspiration count for a good deal. Likewise there can be no rule about how much is repeated or the particular manner of the repetition. Sometimes, in the composer's discretion, a full section must be repeated literally, sometimes he is content with a brief reference, or even with a mere suggestion if he thinks this sufficient to make the point. Repetitions are fruitful when they are either obvious to the listener or of the kind which he absorbs without being aware of it. In either case, if the listener's attention has in the process been redirected so that the composer can proceed with clarity, the main purpose has been accomplished. Recurrences of well-defined melody will tend to mark out rather obviously the main sections of a musical structure. After extended digressions from it, the recurrence of the tonic tonality (the harmonic home base) will tend to be taken by the listener more or less in stride, and it will probably register quite effectively without his being especially aware that it has occurred.

Recurrences, of course, are made necessary by the existence of contrasting material which has intervened between the points of recurrence. The amount of contrasting material and its significance in the total work depend upon the degree to which the composer feels that the work needs to be enlivened, or upon the range of ideas and emotions that he intends it to contain. A contrast may be minimal, it may be introduced as an easing of tension, or else simply to avoid monotony. Quite often, contrasting sections in themselves are strong statements of great intrinsic value. In such cases they bring with them a new range of emotionality and a new level of excitement. Regardless of the subtleties that may complicate any given instance, the general principles of musical construction derive from the reasonable, and usually fairly obvious, ways in which a sectional treatment of contrasts and repetitions can be organized.

A final word about the nature of form in general, and musical form in particular is now in order. Much unnecessary damage has been done to the appreciation of entire epochs of music history (for example, the Northern Renaissance of the fifteenth century, the classicism of the late eighteenth, and the romanticism of the nineteenth century) by a misleading dichotomy between form and content. These terms are two ways of talking about the same thing.

Any number of specific and opposing meanings can be read into a work like the opening movement of the Beethoven Symphony No. 5 in C Minor. For Berlioz, it was "the expression of the disordered sentiments which pervade a great soul when a prey to despair." Yet during World War II, equally sensitive people accepted the opening notes of this movement as a victory motive, a musical symbol that stood for confidence in ultimate triumph during a time of bitter struggle. The notion of its pre-

cise content, of its specific emotional quality, has undergone transformation in the hundred years between the despair of Berlioz and the hope of
the Allied cause. Yet both are agreed, and all other interpretations bear
out this agreement, that the movement is an impassioned one, and that a
quality of heroism, whether despairing or hopeful, is contained within it.
Likewise all musicians are agreed that the movement is an astounding
exhibition of sheer formal control. The two kinds of agreement—as to its
heroic content and as to the discipline of its form—are not really as separate as they may seem to be. The two agreements can be condensed into
one, and the specific quality of this movement attributed to the fact that
it proceeds from a supremely rationalistic control of a heroic passion. It
is simultaneously the product of an imagination powerful enough to conceive such magnificent ideas and of a patience untiring in the search for
the most remote and esoteric coherences in musical structure to contain
and clarify them. The severity of its structural discipline is the logical
urgency, the unencumbered coherence of pure heroism. Intensity of emotion and intensity of formal discipline become one and the same, and we
know one only in terms of the other.

Structure is then not only the structure of tones, but the structure of
the emotions they motivate within us. In a profound sense, to know the
music is to know ourselves, and therein lies the verifiable magic of that
moment of identity between the inner life of the music and the inner life
of the listener.

Principle of Recurrence

Chapter 9

SIMPLE SECTIONAL STRUCTURES

Simple sectional forms such as three-part (ternary or A-B-A) and two-part (binary or A-B) designs are elementary musical structures readily observable in simple tunes. Enlarged in dimension and more richly provisioned with subsidiary complexities, the elementary song forms are transformed for use in large-scale vocal and instrumental composition. For example, the English folk tune *The Keys of Canterbury* opens with a four-bar phrase A which is then repeated; a four-measure contrasting phrase B follows, and then the first phrase A is repeated.

Ex. 9:1 *The Keys of Canterbury.* English Folk Song.

This simple A-B-A structure can be varied in many different ways. In the example above, the entire melody is in the tonic key. In the following example, a popular Russian song in which Gregory is enjoined not to betake himself to dances lest he wind up married to a widow, the first section A is in the tonic minor, and the contrasting episode B is in the relative major.

Ex. 9:2 *Gregory*. Russian Folk Song.

The A-B-A song form is then simply: statement, contrast, and repetition of initial statement (or statement-departure-return). The same principle underlies two such instrumental works as the Brahms Romanze Op. 118, No. 5, and the same composer's Intermezzo, Op. 118, No. 6. In neither case is the opening section repeated either literally or in its entirety at the end. In both instances Brahms abbreviates the final A in the A-B-A design. Such famous arias as the tenor solo, "If with all your hearts ye truly seek me," from Mendelssohn's *Elijah,* or the alto aria, "It is fulfilled" (*Es ist vollbracht*) from Bach's *St. John Passion,* are also examples of A-B-A design. In each case, the relationship between sections is organized differently, and while the A-B-A design is as obvious in one as in the other, the Bach example is the more complex. Yet each of Bach's complexities underlines, rather than obscures, the clarity of the design. Mendelssohn is content to differentiate the B episode from the main A sections primarily by a shift from major to minor. A diagram for his aria would read: A (major), B (minor), A (major). Unity of tempo and of texture is maintained throughout. In Bach these elements are also contrasted, and the diagram for his aria is necessarily more detailed:

  A: Minor key, slow tempo, contrapuntal texture
  B: Relative-major key, fast tempo, harmonic texture
  A: Abbreviated reference to the melody in the key, tempo, and texture of the first section

The differences in the application of the A-B-A principle in the two arias could be a subject for a fruitful and extensive essay on the personal temperament of the two composers; on the musical styles of the periods in which they composed; and on the suggestions for setting offered both by the texts and by the larger dramatic situation within which the arias function.

The minuet and trio movements found in the symphonies, chamber music, and piano music of Haydn, Mozart, and Beethoven are amplifications of an A-B-A principle of design. The minuet is the A section, the trio the contrasting B section, and then the minuet is repeated (in the score the term *da capo,* meaning return to the beginning, appears at the end of the trio) . However, since each section is now considerably enlarged, each shows a highly organized interior structure which may be diagrammed as follows:

A $\left\{ \begin{array}{l} \text{Minuet: A (then A repeated)} \\ \qquad\quad \text{B-A (then B-A repeated)} \end{array} \right.$

B $\left\{ \begin{array}{l} \text{Trio: The melodies of the trio are different from the melodies} \\ \qquad\quad \text{in the minuet, but their formal organization is the same.} \\ \qquad\quad \text{A and B now representing new melodies, the trio diagram} \\ \qquad\quad \text{is as above:} \\ \qquad\qquad\quad \text{A (then A repeated)} \\ \qquad\qquad\quad \text{B-A (then B-A repeated)} \end{array} \right.$

A { Minuet: A-B-A (no repetitions)

The very simplicity of A-B-A structure shows the fundamental nature of the formal process which it exemplifies. Its extension is the *rondo,* and its apotheosis, the complex process called *sonata form.*

Curiously enough, two-part, or binary, forms (represented as A-B) are less obvious in structural principle than the three-part, or ternary, A-B-A idea. A strong contrast between A and B—for example, a contrast as strong as that existing between the A and B sections of the Bach aria discussed above—could be used only at the risk of an unrectified imbalance between sections. Inevitably there is a strong tendency to weaken the contrast and to suggest resemblances between the two sections, so that they may cohere more forceably as a unity. Sometimes—and this one encounters often in movements from Bach suites—the B section comprises much the same type of material as is found in the A section, but in a new key, and with a somewhat different configuration in melodic outline. The following tune, nicknamed *The Harmonious Blacksmith,* which Handel used as the basis for a set of variations, is short enough to quote in its entirety as an example

Ex. 9:3   *The Harmonious Blacksmith* Variations. Handel.

of two-part construction. The A and the B sections differ sufficiently for the distinction between them to be entirely clear. Yet the relationship between the two sections is never in doubt, even though Handel is rather tactful in his treatment of the family resemblances. (In the example, these resemblances are indicated by corresponding letters; that is, *x, y* in one section and *x, y* in the other.)

A rather fine distinction ought perhaps to be observed here. The two sections may be described as different versions of the same type of musical material. But one section is not a variation on the other. Further examples of this kind of binary form may be found in such movements from the Bach orchestral suites as the *Menuet* and *Badinerie* from the Suite No. 2 in B Minor, and the famous *Air* from the Suite No. 3 in D Major. As in the Handel example, each section is repeated. The Overture to Mozart's *Marriage of Figaro* is an example of a binary movement by default. Actually it is the beginning and the end (exposition and recapitulation) of a sonata-form movement, with the middle development left out. Hence in the two sections the same material is viewed and reviewed in the key relationships that establish the A section as a sonata exposition and the B section as its recapitulation (not repetition). A coda then rounds out the design.

THE VARIATION IDEA

The *variation* of a theme is simultaneously a reminder of, and a contrast to the theme, although in any given instance it may be more one than the other. Apart from the specific musical technicalities that can be brought to bear upon the variation of a theme, the ground principles of variation in music are very like those that would be involved anywhere else. What, for example, would be the ways of varying the appearance of a table? It might be decorated or embellished with a vase of flowers. It could be placed in another part of the room, or left where it is and the surroundings altered. In all cases the appearance is changed, varied, given a new tone, or literally, a new look. More drastically, the table could be cut into and its structure organically redesigned without altering its fundamental function as a table. Or, at an extreme, the structure can be altered to the point where it is no longer a table, but some other object that has emerged from the transformation. Essentially the same things can be done to a theme. It can be embellished with grace notes or figurations (decorative variation). It can be transported to another region of the orchestra (instrumental variation), or its harmonic surroundings can be altered (harmonic variation). It can be organically reconstructed so as to appear as a new musical personality capable of undertaking new functions (structural variation) ; for example, a lyrical melody can be transformed into a fugue subject.

The third movement (Andante cantabile) of the Beethoven String Quartet in A Major, Op. 18, No. 5, may be taken as a convenient example. The movement is in the key of D major and the theme may be characterized as somewhat lyrical in nature (*cantabile*, meaning songful). The theme is also quite simple in construction in that it follows a downward scale progression from tonic to dominant (Bars 1–2) , followed by an upward scale progression from the dominant back to the tonic (Bars 2 and 3 to 4) . This is not the entirety of the theme, but only its first four measures. Actually the theme is constructed in two eight-measure groups, each of which is repeated. The first four measures of the first group of eight are given here as a sufficient basis for grasping the variation techniques that Beethoven employs throughout the movement. In the musical quotations, the notes marked by a plus (+) are the notes of the theme.

Variations I and II may look much alike in that the notes of the theme seem tucked away in a new line of music as internal supports for this new line, much as bones are tucked within the human body for purposes of support. Yet the two variations are very different from one another. The second variation is a purely decorative line (a violinistic figuration) derived from the theme and supported by it; whereas Variation I represents an organic transformation, a lyrical tune becoming a disciplined fugue subject which each instrument takes up in turn. (The first variation is not a fugue, but the subject is treated in a sequence of fuguelike entrances. The order of entry on the subject in Variation I is first the cello, then the viola, the second violin, and first violin.) In Variations III and IV, the theme seems to be left relatively undisturbed. The viola and cello divide the presentation of the first four measures between them. Apart from the new tone coloring given the theme by the lower instruments, the buzzing thirty-second-note figuration in the upper strings is a variation in the theme's surroundings. In Variation IV, the measures quoted are identical with the theme, except for one note (A sharp) , but this identity is deceptive. During the first two measures the harmony is enriched in comparison with the initial harmonization of the theme, and from Bar 3 on (starting with the A sharp) the harmony is actually altered. It is the harmonic alteration which requires the sharp in place of the natural, and this variation may be best described as a harmonic variation. In Variation V, the theme is filled out by interpolating a little decoration between the successive notes of the theme. The coda begins with a literal presentation of the first two measures of the theme, but now it is transposed to a new key (B-flat major) and the journey back to the tonic (D major) serves to complete the composition.

These techniques lie on the surface and tell us little of the esthetic unity to which they contribute. It is perhaps most usual for the first few variations in a set to modify the theme only slightly, either with decorative additions or by a simple change in the surroundings of the theme; more drastic alterations and transformations usually emerge later in the proceedings. In this quartet movement, however, Beethoven elects to proceed directly from a simple theme to a radical transformation of it (Variation I) and then to backtrack (Variation II) to a decorative or figural variation. In Variations IV and V, the apparent changes are deceptively slight. The new richness of harmonic texture and the quiet restrained tone of Variation IV are in strong contrast to the boisterous circus-parade style of Variation V. As in any good set of variations, there is a unified variety of mood as well as an engaging diversity of techniques.

Ex. 9:4   String Quartet, Op. 18 No. 5. Third Movement. Beethoven.

Types of variations are as many and diverse as there are compositional procedures. Handel's *Harmonious Blacksmith* Variations, for instance, are of the rhythmical type known as "divisions on a ground"; that is, the initial note values are progressively shortened to give a sense of accelerated movement. Mozart's Piano Sonata in A Major (K.331), on the other hand, opens with a set of melodic variations in which the principal interest lies in the embellishments of the theme. Haydn's *Emperor* Quartet in C Major,

Op. 76, No. 3 (second movement), is a set of variations in which the melody remains intact while the other instruments supply obbligato adornments. Sets of coloristic variations can be found in Schubert's *Trout* Quintet in A Major, Op. 114 (fourth movement) and his *Death and the Maiden* Quartet No. 14 in D Minor (second movement), in which each instrument in the ensemble is spotlighted in turn. Mozart writes a set of double variations for the Finale of his Piano Concerto in C Minor (K.491), in which the two parts of the theme are varied alternately. Large sets of orchestral variations will be found in Brahms' *Variations on a Theme by Haydn,* Op. 56a, and the Finale to his Fourth Symphony.

IDEA OF MULTIPLE RECURRENCES: RONDO

A *rondo* is a multisectional structure based upon the recurrence of a well-defined principal section. Between recurrences of the principal section A, contrasting sections B and C are interpolated. The Purcell song, "I attempt from love's sickness to fly," is a simple example of the rondo idea. The principal section A remains constant both in text and music, while the contrasting sections B and C vary in text and music.

Ex. 9:5 "I attempt from love's sickness to fly" from *Indian Queen*. Purcell.

A (G major) : I attempt from love's sickness to fly . . .
B (E minor) : No more now . . .
A (G major) : I attempt from . . .
C (A minor–D major) : For love has more pow'r . . .
A (G major) : I attempt from . . .

The rondo principle was a favorite with classical composers such as Haydn, Mozart, and Beethoven, especially for fast movements at the conclusion of sonatas or symphonies. The rondo Finale of the Haydn Sonata No. 37 in D Major is a larger structure than Purcell's song, yet when the relationships between the sections of the Haydn movement are analyzed, the analogy between it and the Purcell song becomes obvious. Haydn begins the movement with a well-defined and self-enclosed section in the tonic key of D major. This principal section for purposes of convenience is called A.

Ex. 9:6   Sonata No. 37 in D Major. Third Movement. Haydn.

This is followed by the first contrasting section (B) which is in the key of D minor. Then comes the recurrence of the principal section A once again in the tonic key, and this in turn is succeeded by a second contrasting section C in G major. The concluding A section is somewhat extended, and since this recurrence is the final one, it concludes not only this single movement but the entire sonata. The diagram of the sections of this movement, A-B-A-C-A, shows that the principle governing the relationship between sections is the same as in the Purcell song.

Still another example is the slow movement (Adagio cantabile) of the Beethoven Sonata *Pathétique*. As the quotations show, the design is somewhat amplified, but its essential rondo structure remains clear.

1. {A   in A-flat major
2. {A₁ with melody repeated an octave higher
3.   B   beginning in F minor and closing in E-flat major
         (The importance of the E-flat major key is that it is the dominant

Ex. 9:7   Sonata *Pathetique*. Second Movement. Beethoven.

of A-flat major, and hence a natural harmonic basis from which
to move back to the principal section in A-flat major.)

4.   (X)   Transition from B to A   (E-flat major to A-flat major)
5.   A   in A-flat major
6.   C   in A-flat minor
7.   ⎰A   in A-flat major
8.   ⎱A₁ with melody repeated an octave higher
9.   Coda in A-flat major containing a figure related to C

These are relatively simple rondo designs. Matters become somewhat
more complex when the number of sections is enlarged (an A-B-A-C-
A-B-A rondo structure is often encountered), and when an additional
principle of composition, such as the idea of sonata development or con-

certolike polarity, is set in operation simultaneously with the rondo concept. The last movement of the Beethoven Violin Concerto in D Major, Op. 61 (Ex. 9:8), is a rondo treated in terms of a concerto relationship between solo violin and orchestra, and expanded to an A-B-A-C-A-B-A design.

The principal section A is designed as a threefold presentation of the main subject, with a little divider between presentations; a codetta to complete the entire section; punctuation chords to mark the point of completion; and a springboard from which the violinist can plunge directly into the next contrast section B. The principal subject, shown in Example 9:8a,

Ex. 9:8a   Violin Concerto, Op. 61. First Movement (Bars 1–8). Beethoven.

is an enclosed type of melody so typical of classical rondo finales. The little divider X appended to it

Ex. 9:8b   (Bars 9–10).

is derived from the theme and, since it is on the dominant, creates that sense of expectancy which is fulfilled by the reappearance of the theme in the tonic. The first statement of the theme A_1 was low in the violin's register; the second statement A_2 lies two octaves higher on the violin. The little divider X then follows, recreating the sense of expectancy which this time is resolved by the orchestral restatement of the theme A_3 in a register midway between the low A_1 and the high A_2 of the violin.

Ex. 9:8c   (Bars 11, 19, and 21).

This subject has now been heard three times in three different registers—twice on the violin and once in the orchestra—and with a divider X helping to spotlight each restatement. It remains then to bring the section to a close. As can be seen from Example 9:8d, the concluding passage (codetta) is based on an energetic descending scale formula which eventually reaches its point of completion with a few strong cadence chords. These chords are effective punctuation marks, and are followed by a springboard motive which generates again a sense of expectancy.

Ex. 9:8d   (Bars 32–33 and 40–42).

The violin now appears on the springboard that the orchestra has just constructed, and with its balance assured, it leaps directly to the first contrast section B. This section divides into three parts. From its springboard, the violin leaps to its high register while the horns outline a characteristic horn-call theme below.

Ex. 9:8e   (Bars 46–49).

This is the first portion B₁ of the contrast section and it opens in the tonic D major. The second portion B₂ is a vigorous, antiphonal statement and counterstatement subject divided between violin and orchestra.

Ex. 9:8f   (Bars 59–62).

It is in the dominant key of A major, and the last portion of this contrast section now consists of preparations for the return to A. First a decorative variation on the horn motive is heard (see B₁ in Ex. 9:8e),

Ex. 9:8g   (Bars 68–70).

followed by a marked harmonic change

Ex. 9:8*h* (Bars 73–75).

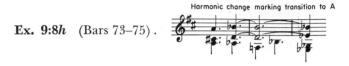

and the reappearance of a short motive from A

Ex. 9:8*i* (Bar 82).

repeated in the orchestra as signals to alert the listener for the recurrence of A. As in the opening of the movement, the principal subject is given out first by the violin in its low register (A₁ as in Ex. 9:8*a*); then the divider (X as in Ex. *b*); followed by the principal subject in the violin's high register (A₂ as in Ex. *c*); the divider once more (X as in Ex. *c*); and finally the principal subject in the orchestra (A₃ as in Ex. *c*). A new spring-board now emerges

Ex. 9:8*j* (Bars 125–126).

upon which the violin is momentarily poised, before moving gracefully on to the second contrast section C.

Ex. 9:8*k* (Bars 127–130).

    This is the midpoint of the movement. Thus far an A-B-A grouping has been encompassed, and it is shortly to be encountered again. Placed between these two A-B-A groupings, the C or second contrasting section now becomes the central portion of the design. It happens not infrequently in such rondo structures—A-B-A-C-A-B-A where C is in a central position —that an exceptional effort will be made at this point. The composer may elect, for example, to convert C into an extended development of A, in which case a rondo with sonata development would result. This alternative will be discussed below. In this instance Beethoven's choice is not for a sonata-style development, but simply for a section more strongly contrasted to A than B had been. Here the C section is in G minor, a contrast in both key and mode; and of the two contrasts, the change in mode (major to minor) is perhaps the more striking, for it implements the change from the cavorting gaiety of the principal subject to the rather tender lyricism of the G-minor melody; from the robust, extrovert manner of the movement thus far, to the intimate, introspective duet between violin and bassoon. The reappearance of a motive from the principal subject, reiterated by the orchestra and punctuated by violinistic flurries

Ex. 9:8*l*   (Bars 167–169).

Motive from A repeated as signals to prepare for return to A

serves as an alert signal for the return to the main section A. Once again we are taken through A_1, low on the violin (Ex. 9:8*a*); the divider (X as in Ex. *b*); the theme high on the violin (A_2 as in Ex. *c*); the divider again (X as in Ex. *c*); leading to the theme in the orchestra (A_3 as in Ex. *c*). The codetta passage based on a descending-scale formula (Ex. *d*) culminates in the expected punctuation chords (Ex. *d*), and the springboard (Ex. *d*) once more serves to catapult the violin on to a repetition of B. Note that the violin's appearance with the springboard motive now involves a tone-color variation: plucked strings (*pizzicato*) for the springboard motive, and the use of the bow the moment the horns enter (Ex. *e*, except that the violin is now an octave lower). The second part of B appears in due course (Ex. *f*), followed in turn by the violin's variation on the horn motive (Ex. *g*), the harmonic change (Ex. *h*), and the orchestral signals on the principal motive (Ex. *i*) to mark the final return to A. The expected return is, however, delayed, for the horn motive (from Ex. *e*) now builds up in the full orchestra, and, following a prolonged chord, the violin enters upon its cadenza. The orchestral signals on the principal motive eventually intrude upon the close of the cadenza, and a brilliant variation on the principal melody A now ensues. A literal repetition of the principal section A would scarcely do at this point, for this final return must not only complete the rondo design itself, but it must complete the movement and, be it remembered, also the entire concerto (of which this rondo movement is the finale). Recasting the return is a matter of sound musical logic. The verve and gaiety which seem to register unfailingly upon all listeners are, however, pure inspiration.

Further examples of rondo construction may be found in works widely diversified in style and in form. The rondo is a principle of sectional structure—a way of establishing relationships between the sections of a design. Any rondo will hinge upon the clear projection of its opening section, for this is the recurring unit, or the unit of orientation. Specific rondos will differ from one another, however, in the ways these recurrences are treated; in the number of contrasting episodes; in the specific relationships established between a contrasting episode in one part of the rondo and a similar episode in another; or in the overall balance struck between the recurrent principal section and the contrasting episodes.

In addition to the compositions already analyzed, the following will enlarge the listener's understanding of the range of rondo design. In the Bach Partita No. 6 in E Major (also referred to as Suite or Sonata No. 6) for unaccompanied violin, the last movement is entitled "Gavotte en Rondeau." This rondo is based on the folk principle of a recurring refrain with a new stanza between every recurrence. The refrain becomes the principal A section and is given first. It comprises the first eight measures of the piece and is promptly repeated. Four different couplets or episodes (B-C-D-E) ensue, each followed by a literal repetition of the opening eight measures (the refrain). The design of this rondo may be expressed as follows:

Refrain	A
Couplet No. 1	B
Refrain	A
Couplet No. 2	C
Refrain	A
Couplet No. 3	D
Refrain	A
Couplet No. 4	E
Refrain	A

The relationship here between a musical structure and a verse form is evident, and historically accurate. This type of design may also be found in rondo movements in the harpsichord suites of Couperin and Rameau. A rather free version of this general idea appears again in Schumann's *Faschingsschwank aus Wien* (Carnival Pranks of Vienna), where the recurrence of the initial section is used less for structural purposes than as a breather between a succession of episodes. Each episode is new, and in essence each is a piece in itself. Here rondo is less a principle than simply a device for tying together into one movement a collection of charming little pieces.

Still another type of rondo may be found in the last movement of Beethoven's Sonata for Piano in G Major, Op. 31, No. 1. The movement may be described as *rondo quasi sonata form*. Seemingly, the structure is one already discussed: A-B-A-C-A-B-A and coda. However, the second episode C, instead of presenting new material, is designed as an extended de-

velopment of the principle subject A. In this it resembles quite strongly
the development section of a sonata-form movement (see Chap. 10).
The influence of sonata-form development on rondo structure is likewise
evident in the lovely second movement of Beethoven's Sonata in E Minor,
Op. 90.

This combination of sonata and rondo is often referred to as *sonata-
rondo form*. The use of the word *form* here can be misleading. Actually
it is more nearly accurate to think of it as an idea for the production of
hybrid structures. As an idea, it can be applied in different ways. Hence
a number of *forms* are possible from the cross breeding of sonata and
rondo, and Beethoven, for one, seems to have been aware of all of the
feasible ones.

Principle of Development: Sonata Form

Chapter 10

I⊤ is necessary, unfortunately, to preface any discussion of the so-called sonata form by an attempt to straighten out a considerable confusion in terminology. Composers are often not responsible for the words used in descriptions of their music. Where they do share in the responsibility, it is more to the point for their music to be clear than for their descriptive vocabulary to be free of confusion. In the first place, the single movement whose structural principles are variously described as being in "sonata form," "sonata-allegro form," or "first-movement form" must be distinguished from the work in several movements which is also called "a sonata." In the latter instance, the word *sonata* refers very generally to an *instrumental* work in several movements; just as, analogously, a *cantata,* in an equally general way, refers to a *vocal* work in several movements. In the latter half of the eighteenth and during the first decades of the nineteenth centuries, a set of structural principles emerged most often in the first movement of a large-scale work such as a symphony, a concerto, a sonata, or a string quartet, and it became customary to refer to a movement so constructed as being in "sonata form." (Although these structural principles were sometimes operative in other movements of the work as well, their customary association with the first movement, usually an *allegro,* led to the designation of this first-movement structure as "sonata-allegro form.") It is perhaps unfortunate that the word "form" should inadvertently receive so much stress, and it is well to warn that an identification of the formal divisions of a sonata structure is not equivalent either to a full, or even to an essential, account of how such a movement is musically motivated and coordinated. However, the formal divisions are there, and it is just as well to identify them from the outset.

These divisions are general in nature and are identifiable by their position and by their function. To begin with, there is the *exposition* section: quite literally, that section where the musical materials of the movement are presented, set forth, or "exposed." (A repeat of the exposition section is customary.) Then follows the *development* section, concerned, as the word "development" (or working out) implies, with the ramifications of the musical ideas already presented, with an exploration of their possibilities, and with a realization of their potentials. Since this inevitably carries the composer rather far afield, a return to home base is naturally in order, from which point a *recapitulation*, or re-presentation, of the opening then unfolds. These three formal divisions—exposition, development, and recapitulation—are, at least in an essential degree, always present. Since they are constants, they are useful both to the composer and to his audience as points of orientation. Most often a sonata-form movement is confined to just this threefold division. Upon occasion, however, in sonata-allegro movements, the composer may elect to precede the exposition by a section in a slow tempo, the exposition proper beginning with the allegro tempo (for example, the Haydn Symphonies Nos. 102 and 104, and the Beethoven Symphonies Nos. 1, 2, 4, and 7).

Thus far only generalities have been mentioned, and advisedly so, for the moment the specifics of each section are considered everything depends on bearing firmly in mind a truism no less vital for being obvious: to wit, that a given work of art, like a given person, is a very particular entity. However similar to others of the same species the work of art may be, if it is to be sufficiently alive and distinguished to engage our enduring attention, it must be so as an individual with a specific personality. In short, like a human being, it must be true to itself. Certain common sense procedures will, to be sure, guide anyone engaged in the initial presentation or "exposition" of his subject to a large audience, be he a concert-hall symphonist, an essayist, or a responsible public speaker. Yet it stands to reason that exactly how the exposition proceeds must in significant measure be conditioned by the specific nature of the material itself, as well as by the possibilities for later development and ultimate restatement that the composer envisions (either consciously or intuitively) for his material. In like manner, while techniques of development sometimes tend to become standardized, any given development section must be conditioned by the particular exposition it came from, and by the relationship which the composer foresees between the development section and what is yet to follow. The development may be half the length or twice the length of the exposition; every detail of the exposition may be systematically probed in the development, or just one unit may be chosen and subjected to an intensive exploration of its potential. Development, as such, is fundamentally a challenge to the composer's imagination, and when certain developmental procedures become typical, they often constitute clues either to the composer's personal temperament or to the habits of his generation.

However varied a development section may be, a sense of return to the initial starting point will usually occur at its close. How marked the moment when the return begins, or how direct or devious, brief or prolonged the return itself may be, will vary necessarily from case to case. But the point at which the return to home base is achieved and the original subject of the movement reappears in the tonic key is almost always kept clearly and cleanly in focus by the composer. For it marks the beginning of the recapitulation or final portion of the movement, and from this point on the musical forces must be regathered and regrouped either for a drive to a climax, or else, if the high point has already been achieved in the development, for an orderly relaxation of tensions. After its first function of achieving and re-establishing the tonic key has been accomplished, procedures in the recapitulation section are conditioned primarily by the "psychological" structure of the movement. Is this last section to be on a "higher" or "lower" emotional level than the development? Does the movement now require, psychologically, succinct summarization, or are new developments needed to bring into complete perspective certain aspects of the exposition that had previously been neglected? Clearly the answers are particular to the case in point. As a general rule, however, a recapitulation will rarely be a literal repetition of the exposition. If it were, it could at best function only as a way of achieving a symmetrical, formal, balanced design. The danger in a literal recapitulation lies in its psychological falsification or dramatic untruth. If, in the last chapter of a novel, the major characters appear exactly as they were in the first chapter, one would seriously question the meaning and the value, either to the characters or to the reader, of the cycle of experience to which both have been subjected in the course of the intervening pages. A literal recapitulation implies that nothing really has happened to alter one's perspective with respect to the original presentation. In this view, the development may well become an irrelevance, a mere formal obligation.

So much then for the formal divisions of a sonata form and the function of these divisions within the unity that is the movement. It remains to get at the heart of the matter, and to seek for those principles that govern the movement from beginning to end. The answers are implicit in what has already been outlined, for what underlies and coordinates the structure is the development idea. Sonata form, for instance, is sometimes described as an "evolutionary" design or a strategy of key relationships. The latter is dictated by the necessity for a firm point of orientation (home base, so to speak) , from which and toward which the music can be directed. Especially in a large-scale structure must an orientation of this sort be clearly established. A theme, as such, can hardly accomplish this, for in the course of a sonata structure a theme will undergo fragmentation and expansion, variation and transformation. Nor is it usually feasible for all other themes to be orientated with reference to just one, so that everything evolves from and returns toward a single thematic source. (This, of course, is a possible though not a usual way to write a sonata-form movement.) Usually a duality or opposition of themes is more serviceable in a sonata structure which, since it is developmental, is also likely to be in essence dramatic. As has been demonstrated in an earlier chapter (pp. 72–77) , the sense of tonic or harmonic home base can be quickly and, if need be, even unobtrusively established for the listener. Furthermore key relationships, such as modulations from one key to another, are singularly adaptable to long-range planning. By the latter part of the eighteenth century the harmonic distances between keys and the location of keys with respect to one another had already a history long enough and rich enough for concepts such as tonal distance, tonal direction, and tonal geography to be more than fanciful metaphors. In a large-scale developmental structure, locating musical events in different keys, one of which is established as tonic, makes possible a sense of proximity or remoteness between events, a sense of rational direction in moving from one stage of the design to another, and a sense of a coordinated tonal geography as a framework for the unfolding of musical eventualities. With this in mind, an approximate account of the generalities of sonata-form construction may be rendered as follows:

EXPOSITION

First subject:

The dual purpose here is to establish the tonic key center, or home base, and to announce a leading subject. The word "subject" is preferred to such designations as theme, group, etc., because its connotation is general. The subject may be a full melody, a melodic line, a theme, a motivic fragment, a melodic outline of a chord, a complex or group of several melodies or motives, or the like. To be strict about it, at this stage one must refer to it only as the *first* subject. Whether it will turn out to be the *main* subject, or simply the first of several subjects of equal importance, remains to be seen. A position of prominence is, however, assured to it by virtue of its prior position, and by its association with the tonic. For example, later on its reappearance in the tonic at the outset of the recapitulation will necessarily constitute an event of major importance in the movement.

To this first subject a second is to be juxtaposed in a key other than the tonic. Hence, following the completion of the first subject, a passage ensues that carries the listener toward the key of the second subject. This is variously referred to as: *a transition, bridge, episode, run-on passage, etc.*

One or another of the above terms may be appropriate in any given instance. In any case, the point here is to lead into new tonal territory, and a vigorous sense of progressive harmonic direction is not uncommon in such a passage.

Second subject:

There are two decisions the composer must make at this point: one, as to the personality of the new subject, and the other, the choice of the new key center. Since this is still an early stage of the movement, the strongest tendency is to move to a nearby (closely related) key. Excursions into remote tonal territory are with reason reserved for a later portion of the design. The keys most commonly selected for the second subject are those of the dominant or the relative major (or minor). As for the personality of the second subject itself, inspection will show an astonishing range of variation from a polar opposition to the first subject to a virtual identity with it.

A transitional passage, however brief, will often occur after the second subject has been presented. It leads to the *closing subject* (also variously referred to as the *concluding section, closing group,* or *codetta*).

Closing section:

Sometimes new melodic material is used for this concluding section. Often recollections of the first subject serve to give the exposition a sense of unity, and a variety of "closing formulas" a sense of conclusion.

Usually a repeat of the whole exposition is stipulated in the score by the composer, though in the case of familiar classics it is often omitted in performance.

DEVELOPMENT

The possible techniques are too numerous to detail one by one. Customarily a process of thematic fragmentation is employed. Material selected from the exposition is broken down into its smaller components, and the inner resources of the material made explicit by working with these smaller units or motives. Upon occasion new thematic material may be introduced in the course of a development—as in the first movements of Beethoven's *Eroica* Symphony and Mendelssohn's *Italian* Symphony—but such instances are indeed exceptional. The range and variety of keys are considerably extended, for tonal distance and strong tonal direction are valuable as dramatic agents. Contrapuntal techniques are likewise dramatically useful, the tightness of a polyphonic texture and the strong linear directions within it often contributing a sense of controlled intensity to the development of the motives.

Return back to the tonic:

The degree to which this return is marked as a clear concluding section of the development varies considerably, as does its length, its directness, its level of intensity, etc.

RECAPITULATION

The recapitulation is marked by the reappearance of the first subject in the tonic key as in the outset of the exposition. This is not at all a mere mechanical formality, but a vital moment in the psychological design. If the arrival of the subject in the tonic does not carry with it a sense of a secure arrival back home and at just precisely the right moment, its function as a point of orientation is lost. Sometimes a "false recapitulation" (the right theme in the wrong key, as in the first movement of Beethoven's *Eroica*) serves to heighten expectation and focus the listener's attention. Devices to mark this moment are literally legion.

Once re-established, the tonic key strongly dominates the recapitulation. While new developments may occur to take care of whatever has been neglected in the development—a process that may involve further key changes—in the main the material tends to be reviewed on home ground. The second subject customarily reappears in the tonic and this necessitates alteration in the transition that originally led to it. The reasons for the varied character of sonata-form recapitulations, and for the avoidance of a literal repeat of the exposition, have already been discussed. It remains to add one further consideration.

Closing section and coda:

The closing section must now sound like the close of a whole movement, not (as originally) the close of just one portion of a movement. Some redesigning is usually in order. A few additional measures may be sufficient, although an expansion into a large and vastly enriched *coda* that sometimes assumes the proportions of a terminal development is sometimes necessary. There are instances where the *coda* approximates in size one of the three preceding main sections.

The illustration for a particular but typical sonata-form movement will be the opening one of the Mozart Symphony No. 40 in G Minor (K.550).

Three beats in Bar 1 precede the appearance of the first subject on beat four which is given to the violins. These first three beats may be just audible, but they serve to set the tonic (G minor) and to bring the melody into focus.

Ex. 10:1a   Symphony No. 40. First Movement (Bars 1–19). Mozart.

In this instance, the musical sentence that constitutes the first subject is a full melody. To set it off as a clear unit, Mozart concludes the sentence with a series of strong chords which serve as punctuation marks (in Ex. 10:1a, note the rhythmic figure in the lower part, a reiterated D, that is marked as X), and duplicate the rhythmic structure of the melody. A repetition of the melody is begun, but not completed for, after a few measures, it turns suddenly in a new direction. The moment is marked by a new

Ex. 10:1b   (Bars 28–33).

subject, exceedingly vigorous in nature; and by the momentum it achieves, the music drives swiftly and clearly toward new tonal territory. The appearance of this new subject thus marks the beginning of the transition. The second subject proper (Ex. 10:1c, below) is to be in the relative major (B flat). Hence the transition (Ex. 10:1b), arrived at with the F-major chord which is the dominant of B flat, terminates in two sharp chords and a measure of silence. The second subject (B-flat major) is modest to the

Ex. 10:1c   (Bars 44–47).

point of being a trifle unobtrusive, but attention to it is assured both
by the dominant of the new key and by the pause of one measure that precedes it. The pause acts as a clear divider. Having reached the border of
the new key, one is invited, so to speak, to step over into B-flat major,
which one does with the new subject. The first subject (Ex. 10:1*a*) had
been given to the strings. The second subject (Ex. 10:1*c*) is divided between strings and winds upon its first presentation, and contrariwise, between winds and strings upon its repetition. The last measure of the repeat of Example *c* is altered and, with this alteration, a new tentativeness
emerges in the music.

Ex. 10:1*d* (Bars 58–59).

This is the transition from the second subject to the closing subject. A
sense of expectancy swiftly and surely grows and, implemented by a crescendo, reaches its climax and resolution with the first of the closing
subjects.

Ex. 10:1*e* (Bars 66–72).

This is effectively a formula subject, a variation on a type often encountered in such passages. What underlies it is the formula of a scale line
going up, balanced by a scale line going down. Mozart dramatized the
formula by taking the upward progression by chromatic half steps up to
the A flat, then proceeding to the high G by abrupt leaps, and coming
down the scale this time diatonically. It is followed by the reappearance
of a fragment from the first subject (Ex. 10:1*a*), with clarinet, bassoon,
violins, violas, and cellos all contributing to the reminiscence of that half-
step motive which is perhaps its salient characteristic (Ex. 10:1*f*).

Ex. 10:1*f* (Bars 73–74).

This reaches its climax with a transformation of the first melody momentarily into a heroic subject (Ex. 10:1g).

Ex. 10:1g   (Bars 77–80).

The closing section (codetta) is then terminated by another formula subject which is, in effect, an extended punctuation mark—a formally emphatic way of declaring the exposition over (Ex. 10:1h).

Ex. 10:1h   (Bars 88–91).

The entire exposition is now repeated, and if any ambiguity exists for the listener in the first hearing, the second should clear it up.

Before proceeding with the development, however, it is worth pausing for a moment to take stock of the materials thus far presented. Technical analysis may be relatively unambiguous and hence quite safe. But if one assumes (and one has every right to do so) that this movement is, for the composer, the projection of human experience and, for the listener, a receiving of such experience, then it is possible to rephrase the technical commentary in human or psychological terms. In addition to noting the key of a subject and its instrumentation, one must be aware of its specific personality. To describe experience expressed in music in terms of experience expressed in words is to court the irritation of the fastidious reader. If musical experience could be accurately converted into an exact literary equivalent, then there would be no need for the two separate arts of literature and music. Approximations, then, are the best one can hope for. Apart from being approximate and hence to a degree necessarily both ambiguous and inaccurate, a description of personality, musical or otherwise, is in itself largely a personal matter. Any such characterization made here is open to such exceptions as any listener may care to make, since each listener must perforce receive the music in terms of his own musical and cultural conditioning and his own state of mind. This said, it is still most vital that the listener become aware of the personality of each subject in the exposition. With all due caution then, and in all due modesty, the reader-listener is invited to consider the flowing, lyrical nature of the first subject (Ex. 10:1a), the undercurrent of melancholy that pervades it and, curiously, the lilt that it preserves with such ease. It is neither depressing in its melancholy nor liltingly joyous; nor is it as yet a heroically commanding subject, although, for a brief moment in the closing section, it appears in that guise. (The difficulties in this sort of verbal characterization should already be apparent, and it is quite possible that the reader will already have a list of phrases to which he takes exception.) Contrast the lyrical character of the first subject (Ex. 10:1a) to the innocent lyricism of the second (Ex. 10:1c), an innocence bordering very nearly on the innocuous. Curiously enough, the most vigorous subject appears in the transition from the first to the second themes (see Ex. 10:1b). The muscular energy and the commanding manner of this passage are in the sharpest contrast to the gentleness of the two principal themes. And this energetic tone reappears in the formula subjects that conclude the exposition. Whatever quarrel is bound to arise with the specifics of this description, it must at least be granted that there is a pattern of personality or psychological contrast set forth. In other words, the two principals (Exs. 10:1a and c), while psychologically different from one another, are related in personality; and, on the opposite end of the psychological scale, a similar tie relates the first transition (Ex. 10:1b) to the concluding section (Exs. 10:1e, g, and h). If, for the sake of argument, it can be agreed that the personality antithesis may be approximately characterized as a polarity between the gentle and lyrical on the one hand (Exs. 10:a and c), and the energetic and commanding on the other (Exs. 10:1c, e, g, and h), then something emerges concerning the first subject which is of profound importance to the psychological design of the total movement: to wit (a) the first subject appears on both levels (Exs. 10:1a and g), and (b) it is the only subject to do so. The consequences of the startling range of personality shown by this first subject can be traced in every succeeding portion of the movement. For one thing, once established as intrinsically the richest of the subjects in inner resource, it emerges as the one most intensively exploited. For another, lacking the personality limitation of all other components of the exposition, it becomes the one element that can relate to all levels of the design, and hence, far more so than any other subject, it is the one most continually before the listener. For reasons of this sort one chooses to call it not only the *first* subject (an objective description), but the *main* subject (a value judgment).

The pacing of musical events in the exposition has been rather leisurely: each section is carefully defined for the listener, and the whole is then repeated. A sharp change of pace now occurs. The development is surprisingly short, and the dramatic nature of the events that transpire therein is much accentuated by the brevity of each event and the pace with which they are piled swiftly one upon the other.

The development is concerned exclusively with the first and main sub-

ject (Ex. 10:1*a*). Two chords (full orchestra) and a descending progression (winds) set the stage for the main subject which is carried through a
sequence of modulations into remote keys. The sense of tonal distance and
the feeling for tonal geography are nowhere more dramatic than at this
point, where the music seems to expand outward and to achieve, with
every modulation, a new frontier. The subject descends into the bass and
promptly above it a strong line of counterpoint rises. At its height it becomes the first subject, and now down in the bass the line of counterpoint
rises sharply against the subject. The dramatic fervor drains away and one
is left with the initial motive for Example 10:1*a* in the violins. Flute and
clarinet are then joined together in a dialogue with the violins on this
motive. It would seem from the tone of the dialogue that the high point
of the development has now passed, and the direction is toward home.
However, this draining away of dramatic energy is momentary, for as suddenly as it appears, just as suddenly does the whole orchestra rise to attack
the motive in a renewal of dramatic energy. This attack is, however, the
last, and the return now proceeds in a quiet but inexorable descent toward the tonic. Note that the return is based wholly upon the initial three-
note motive of the main subject, and that the subject itself appears while
the harmonies are still in transition. The harmonic movement reaches
home base (the tonic) just in time to catch the last notes in the first unit
of the main subject (Ex. 10:1*i*).

Ex. 10:1*i*   (Bars 160–166).

This dovetailing is not one beat too soon, for the moment it is achieved
(marked by an asterisk in Ex. 10:1*i*) the recapitulation is under way.

Although this development represents an enormous raising of the level
of dramatic intensity, the composer's decision, in this instance, is not to
regard it as the high-water mark of the movement. Hence, if the recapitulation is not to recede away from this level, the composer cannot be content simply to maintain it, for this would be emotionally (psychologically)
static. There is only one other alternative, and that is to conceive this particular recapitulation on a still more intense and (since this is the concluding stage of the drama) climactic level of emotionality. A summary
type of recapitulation is not in order, for more still remains to be said than

to be summarized. From a structural point of view, materials are needed
for constructing this new and climactic level. The first subject (Ex. 10:1a)
has already monopolized the development, and has become thereby the
dramatic centerpiece of the design. What remains is to see the other materials of the exposition (thus far unexploited) in a new and more dramatic
light. Following the restatement of the first subject in the tonic (note the
familiar punctuation chords heard at this point in the exposition), and
the partial repetition of the subject, the transitional passage (Ex. 10:1b) is
now given concentrated attention. Actually, a transition in a modulatory
sense is no longer a necessity for the second subject is to reappear in the
tonic; and while this intervening section is dramatic in its harmonic movement, it is now a movement both away from and back to the tonic. The
muscular energy that characterized Example 10:1b when it first appeared
(in the exposition) has already been emphasized as well as the curious
contrast it posed to the gentleness of the two principal subjects. All of its
vitality and drive are now summoned and exploited, and its restatement
is prolonged into a powerful development. As the full dramatic potential
of this subject (Ex. 10:1b) is realized, the music progresses to a still higher
level of intensity. The one measure of silence that precedes the second subject (Ex. 10:1c) is now reached, whereupon perhaps the most poignant
passage in the symphony occurs. Upon its first appearance, the melody of
the second subject had been modest and reserved to the point of appearing
innocuous. Melodies of this sort were routine among Mozart's minor contemporaries, and since, after its first appearance this melody had disap-
peared completely from the movement, one might have been misled into
supposing that its function was the purely formal one of marking the new
key. But it now reappears unaltered save in one particular. It is in the
tonic—a minor key—instead of in the major as originally; and this change
in mode, by its very simplicity and understatement, is a telling reflection
of the emotional vicissitudes that have engulfed this movement in its absence. The overt drama in the development of Example 10:1b is balanced
and perhaps intensified by the quiet pathos of Example 10:1c. The transition from the second subject to the concluding section (Ex. 10:1d) is
now somewhat expanded to permit not merely a restatement, but an intensified restatement. And the concluding section—now with all of the
increased intensity that a minor key can give to such vigorous formulas—
brings the movement to its climax and its conclusion. Also, this concluding section is necessarily somewhat amplified, for more emphasis and
more room for the accumulation of musical and emotional energy are now
needed to bring to a conclusion the total movement, and not merely (as
originally) the exposition section.

Principle of Polarity: Concerto

Chapter 11

THE broad principle that underlies concerto construction is one of a predetermined polarity of instrumental forces. Two contrasted tonal bodies are opposed to one another, either a solo instrument and an orchestra in the case of a solo concerto, or a small ensemble against a larger one in that of the concerto grosso. This opposition of unequal forces requires a continuous rectification of what, on the face of it, is a precarious state of imbalance. Intrinsic to a successful concerto is a mobility of interplay and a potential for drama, which is a challenge both to the composer's imagination and to his mastery of musical resources.

CONCERTO GROSSO

In a *concerto grosso,* the orchestra is divided asymmetrically into two disparate ensembles, large and small. The Corelli *Christmas Concerto* is useful as an initial example, for Corelli's application of the concerto-grosso principle is both modest and strict. The large ensemble called the *grosso* (large) or *ripieno* (full) here comprises the main body of orchestral strings. It is in four parts: two violin sections, a viola section, and a continuo. And since it is the large orchestral group, there are several performers per part. (In baroque instrumental music, the *continuo* is the bass complex comprising, at a minimum, a harpsichord and a low string instrument which doubles the bass part in the left-hand harpsichord line. The right-hand keyboard part was usually left for the performer to realize and improvise.) Set against the grosso is a small ensemble, the *concertino* of three parts in this case—two violins and continuo—with one performer for each violin part and a cello and harpsichord joined together to form the continuo. The Corelli example is modest in that only strings are used, and it is strict in the observance of the duality between the instrumental choirs and in the integrity of each ensemble within itself. Both grosso and concertino are treated as units. The components of the concertino, for example, are not detached from the ensemble and permitted to operate as individual solos. On the contrary, each instrument in the concertino is confined within the cohesion of the ensemble.

Ex. 11:1   Christmas Concerto. First Allegro (Bars 1–5) . Corelli.

Example 11:1 shows Corelli's penchant for a strict duality of instrumental choirs. The effect is one of a terraced dynamics, an automatic juxtaposition of piano and forte levels, a musical chiaroscuro of dark and light, a grounding of the litheness and agility of the concertino in the denser and heavier mass of grosso sound.

Freer applications of the concerto-grosso principle may proceed along several different lines. In his second *Brandenburg* Concerto, for example, Bach's choice of concertino instruments is the flute, oboe, violin, and trumpet. Apart from its expansion from a trio to a quartet, this concertino is remarkable in that it is intrinsically a rather unstable aggregate that rarely operates as a concerted unit. More frequently it disintegrates into individual solos or into a varying assortment of duets and trios. In addition to this more flexible treatment of the concertino, Bach also enriches the grosso through the simple expedient of adding the solo quartet with its colorful wind instruments to the orchestral strings. In his fourth *Brandenburg* Concerto, Bach crossbreeds two kinds of concerto: a concerto grosso and a solo concerto. At times, in this work, two flutes and a violin cooperate as a concertino unit against the main body of grosso strings. Sometimes, however, the violin is detached and treated as if it were the featured soloist in a solo concerto. Bach's third *Brandenburg* Concerto is one of his most unusual and flexible applications of the concerto-grosso idea. It is scored for three violins, three violas, three cellos, and a continuo of cembalo (keyboard instrument) and double bass. Each unit (violin, viola, and cello) is a group of three. The three either perform together in unison,

Ex. 11:2*a*   Brandenburg Concerto, No. 3. First Movement (Bars 1–2). Bach.

thus constituting a single massed violin or viola or cello line, or the massed group splits into three separate solo lines. Potentially, at the extremes, there are either nine solo lines (three concertino units) or one three-part grosso. Actually, the singular mobility of this concerto consists in the opposition set up between the process of splitting up into solos and the process of reforming into a unison mass. The process of dispersion never occurs simultaneously in all groups. Hence as one group breaks up into three solo parts (thus becoming a concertino), another group, already operating in this fashion, reforms into a unison line (grosso) to oppose it. A perpetually varied string texture is the result.

SOLO CONCERTO

The concerto idea as a principle differs from the wide variety of forms in which concerto movements may be cast. Where more than one compositional principle is at work, the formal structure may well

Ex. 11:2b Brandenburg Concerto, No. 3. First Movement. Bach.

tend toward a high degree of complexity. A Beethoven movement has already been examined (see pp. 114–117) in which a sectional ronda structure is worked out as concerto duality between solo violin and orchestra (last movement of the Beethoven Violin Concerto).

Structures of even greater complexity result from elaborating a developmental sonata structure via a concerto duality. In terms of general procedure there are two main traditions in such sonata-form concerto movements: the so-called classical tradition of Mozart and Beethoven and the romantic tradition of Mendelssohn, Liszt, and Tchaikovsky. The terms *classical* and *romantic* are far from rigorous. A romantic composer like Brahms preferred the classical concerto structure on principle, while an archromantic like Chopin adhered somewhat routinely to its main formulas for no apparent reason other than a temperamental disinclination to tinker overly much with large-scale structures. Needless to say, even in respect to general procedure, there are many works that stand apart from either tradition. As for the specifics of formal procedure, each of the traditions are sturdy enough to encompass a wide range of variation. As an example of a sonata-form movement in a classical concerto, the opening movement of the Mozart Concerto in D Minor for Piano and Orchestra (K. 446) will serve as an illustration.

Since this is a sectional structure, there are two kinds of sections that can be differentiated: one, in which the solo instrument is engaged with the orchestra, either in opposition to it, or in dialogue with it, or in a foreground-background relationship; and the other, where the soloist is silent and the orchestra proceeds alone. The latter type (for orchestra alone) is called the *ritornel,* or *ritornello,* an orchestral section that returns at intervals throughout the movement. As noted earlier (see p. 124), in the classical sonata-form design a repeat of the exposition is called for, so that, in a sense, there are two expositions, the second a literal duplicate of the first. The application of this to the classical concerto involves the retention of the two expositions, but with a strong distinction made between them, so that, actually, there are *two* expositions, rather than one that is heard twice. The first exposition is for orchestra alone; or, said another way, the opening ritornel is the first exposition. The second exposition involves the solo with orchestra.

Thus far the discussion has dealt in generalities in which composers as different as Mozart and Beethoven will show agreement. However, as one looks more closely into particulars, differences of importance become apparent. Mozart preferred to differentiate solo exposition from the ritornel by reserving certain themes for the solo instrument. The opening ritornel, therefore, is not a complete exposition. A common body of themes is shared by ritornel and solo exposition, but a few themes are specific to the latter.

Beethoven, on the contrary, in some of his concertos (for example, the Third Piano Concerto, and the Violin Concerto) preferred both sections to be full expositions. In these instances the opening ritornel, as a full exposition, outlines all themes to be heard in the second exposition for solo and orchestra. There are similar differences in each man's preference for the range of tonalities in the first ritornel, Beethoven preferring a more extensive modulation range (especially for the second subject area), Mozart a more restrictive one. Furthermore, any given concerto is a specific work of art with structural features peculiar to it. A comparative examination of a group of concertos by Mozart or a group by Beethoven will show variations in procedural detail even within the orbit of the composer's preferences. Such composers are far too creative to convert a generalized structural principle, or even a personal preference, into a compulsive ritual to which they are obligated at all costs. If one master is shrewd enough not to imitate another, he is also wise enough not to imitate himself. As in any other creative pursuit, general principles and personal preferences are valuable to the composer only to the extent that, within the context of the particulars of a given work, he can use them with firmness and with flexibility. The selected example (Ex. 11:3 from the Mozart D-minor Piano Concerto, K.466) is a norm neither for the classical concerto, nor even for all of Mozart. However, many of the procedures in it do occur in his other concertos, and some occur in all classical concertos. Like many another masterpiece, it is both typical and unique.

The first thirty-two measures of the ritornel comprise a group of themes which together constitute the first subject in the tonic D minor. Actually, the first subject here is the tonic area within which a number of distinctive motives make their appearance. The first such is a rising figure in the cellos and basses under a cover of syncopated chords in the upper strings (Ex. 11:3a).

Ex. 11:3a   Piano Concerto in D Minor. First Movement (Bars 1–5). Mozart.

The extension of this figure (A from Ex. 11:3b) leads to another distinctive motive (B from Ex. b) which in turn is followed by a rising sequence of syncopations leading to a duet between violins and oboes (C from Ex. b). The tonic group culminates in a strong closing formula: dominant-tonic cadence chords over a line progression in the bass (D from Ex. b). The last chord falls on the first beat of the measure. For the remaining

Ex. 11:3*b*   (Bars 17–32) .

three beats the orchestra is silent, and when it resumes, we are in the
second subject area of F major (the relative major of D minor) . A woodwind dialogue outlines an F-major melody (Ex. 11:3*c*) which appears to

Ex. 11:3*c*   (Bars 33–36) .

be the second subject. It is indeed just that, but it is not the entirety of it.
An important addition to it is reserved for the solo piano in the second
exposition. A transitional duet between the two violin sections (Ex. 11:3*d*)

Ex. 11:3*d*   (Bars 39–42) .

carries us back to the storm and stress of the tonic D minor and to a dramatic subject (Ex. 11:3*e*) which recalls features of the first theme group.
The opening measure of Example 11:3*e* is rhythmically the same as B in
Example *b,* and the motive marked as A in Example *e,* is very nearly as
close as it can be to the motive marked A in Example *b* without actually
being identical with it. Despite its evident passion, the subject (Ex. *e*) has
a formality which marks it as a closing subject. It is followed by a second

Ex. 11:3e (Bars 44–51).

closing subject in a much more tender vein (Ex. 11:3f) which prepares the ground for the expressive entry of the solo piano.

Ex. 11:3f (Bars 71–73).

In summary, this first ritornel, in comparison with the first-movement exposition section of Mozart's Symphony in G Minor (see pp. 125–129), shows an analogous exposition structure: tonic-minor area (first subject), relative-major area (second subject), and closing section (here anchored firmly in the tonic minor, whereas in the symphony, the analogous section had been organized primarily in the relative major).

The piano enters solo and its first subject (tonic D minor) is a new one especially reserved for it (Ex. 11:3g). Although the tempo is strict,

Ex. 11:3g (Bars 77–81).

the effect is improvisational. The piano line culminates in a coloratura flourish leading to the orchestral re-presentation of Example 11:3a. The orchestra is alone for four measures before the piano joins it in completing and extending the restatement of Example a. Of the remaining ritornel motives in the first subject group, all but the last are omitted, and following Example a, piano and orchestra proceed directly to D from Example b, the dominant-tonic sequence that concludes the first theme group in the tonic minor. Once again, as in the first ritornel, the last chord is on the first beat of the measure. There is a pause for the remainder of the measure, and then the woodwinds and piano resume their dialogue on Example *c*, the second subject which is in the relative major. To this, the piano appends another F-major melody which the wind instruments in

Ex. 11:3*h* (Bars 128–131) .

turn take up. The group of ideas that form the second subject is now complete (Ex. *c* plus Ex. *h*) , and an extended virtuosolike section featuring the soloist now ensues. Effectively this is the end of the second exposition. In summary, a few themes from the first ritornel have been reused (Ex. *a*, D from Ex. *b* and Ex. *c*) and two new solo subjects have been added (Exs. *g* and *h*) . A closing section is still lacking. In its place Mozart substitutes an eighteen-measure ritornel as a brief, but dramatically effective, section standing between the second exposition and the development. The material for this second ritornel is, as may perhaps be anticipated, the ritornel motives that have been omitted from the second exposition. The omission was purposeful, for he draws upon them here as a useful reserve. Heard one after the other are A and B from Example *b*, the duet between violins and oboes (C from Ex. *b*) , leading immediately to the last motive from the concluding section (Ex. *f*) . The ritornel motives (Ex. *a*, and D from Ex. *b*) are omitted here because they have already been used in the solo exposition. Only part of the concluding section is used here (Ex. *f*) , and part of it (Ex. *e*) is still held in reserve.

The re-entry of the solo instrument marks the beginning of the development. The polarization of piano and orchestra is now sharpened by an equivalent polarization of thematic material. Each adheres doggedly to its main theme: the piano to Example 11:3*g*, the subject on which it had made its entry into the concerto; and the orchestra to Example *a*, the brooding, restless figure with which it had opened the movement. The range of keys is considerably extended as one would expect in a development. Toward the close of the development, the piano breaks free of Example *g*, storms through an agitated sequence of figurations (the orchestra insisting meanwhile on Ex. *a*) , and ultimately arrives at a two-measure phrase in its low register reminiscent of B in Example *b*. Two more measures follow, as a rather stark final gesture by the solo piano, and the orchestra resumes with Example *a* in the tonic D minor to mark the beginning of the recapitulation.

The recapitulation constitutes a marshalling and review of the total subject matter of the movement with the exception of Example 11:3*g*. It alone is omitted from the recapitulation, presumably since its potential had been so thoroughly exploited in the development. At first the orchestra carries the burden of Example *a* alone, but the piano soon joins in the restatement. It drops out while the orchestra reviews A and B, from Example *b* and reappears to offer a decorative commentary upon the duet between oboes and violins (C from Ex. *b*). Piano and orchestra and then orchestra alone restate D from Example *b*, the cadence formula for the first thematic group. The second subject group (Ex. *c* plus Ex. *h*) now follows. Piano and winds are in dialogue on Example *c* which is still given (as originally) in F major; but Example *h* is reviewed in the tonic D minor, first by the piano, and then by the oboe with piano commentary. As in the solo exposition, so here, an extended virtuosolike section ensues featuring the solo instrument. At its close, a ritornel section follows, restricted to ten measures and to motives A and B from Example *b*. The final chord of this ritornel is a formula chord commonly encountered at this point in a classical concerto. Technically it is called a tonic six-four chord (I_6^4) — that is, a tonic chord with the fifth in the bass. The listener is bound to recognize it, for it has a rather distinctive sound and is heard at precisely this point in many a concerto. On this chord the ritornel comes to rest, and the soloist takes off on an unaccompanied improvisation called a cadenza.

Originally the solo *cadenza* was frequently improvised, and served to display the performer's creative musicianship as well as his digital dexterity. Mozart and Beethoven were themselves famous as improvisers. The practice gradually fell into disuse, and written-out cadenzas became the norm. However, even a written-out cadenza tends to carry some of the improvisational flavor which was originally its essence. There are a few written-out cadenzas by Mozart and Beethoven. However, the cadenzas used today for Mozart and Beethoven concertos have been supplied by other composers. Curiously enough, Beethoven was sufficiently fond of this particular Mozart concerto to provide written-out cadenzas for it. While the cadenza is free, its last measure is predetermined, so that when the soloist, in his own good time, arrives at this measure, this automatically signals the orchestra to be ready to resume.

In this instance, the ritornel is resumed very dramatically with Example 11:3*e*, the one subject that has been avoided ever since its first appearance. Mozart withheld it as a reserve for just this moment, and a more effective moment for its reappearance would be difficult to imagine. It now marks, most dramatically, the closing section of the movement. When the second closing subject (Ex. *f*) enters, it brings with it that peculiarly wistful quality that has marked it throughout. It resolves into reiterations of Example *a*, and on this motive (Ex. *a*) the movement concludes as restlessly and as somberly as it had begun.

In summary, the sonata structure of the movement may be outlined as follows:

Ritornel: First exposition.

> Tonic minor: First subject group (Ex. *a*, and A, B, C, and D from Ex. *b*).
>
> Relative major: Second subject incomplete (Ex. *c*).
>
> Tonic minor: Closing section (Exs. *e, f*).

Solo Exposition: Second exposition for piano and orchestra.

> Tonic minor: New subject for solo piano (Ex. *g*).
>
> > Then Ex. *a*, and only D from Ex. *b*.
>
> Relative major: Second subject group completed.
>
> > Ex. *c* plus a new subject (Ex. *h*) introduced by the piano.
>
> Virtuosolike passage-work section featuring soloist, culminating in return of orchestral ritornel.

Ritornel: On Ex. A, B, and C from Ex. *b*, and Ex. *f*.

Development Section: Soloist on Ex. *g*, orchestra on Ex. *a*.

> Extended key range.

Recapitulation: Tonic minor: First subject group.

> > Ex. *a* (orchestra and then with piano).
> >
> > A, B from Ex. *b* (orchestra).
> >
> > C from Ex. *b* (orchestra with piano commentary).
> >
> > D from Ex. *b* (piano and then orchestra).
>
> Second subject group:
>
> > Ex. *c* Relative major (piano and winds).
> >
> > Ex. *h* Tonic minor (piano then winds).
> >
> > Virtuosolike passage-work section featuring soloist, culminating in return of orchestral ritornel.

Ritornel: Ex. A, B from *b* coming to rest on tonic six-four chord.

Cadenza: Piano solo.

Ritornel: Closing section (or coda).

> Ex. *e*, Ex. *f*, Ex. *a*.

There is a variant of this structure associated with the romantic period which, in essence, consists in the elimination of the opening ritornel. The sonata-form first movement begins then with the solo exposition. The shortening of the design to just one exposition may or may not be accompanied by other structural alterations. Mendelssohn, in his violin concerto, not only wrote out the cadenza in full, but transposed it to a point in the movement where it serves functionally as a transition from development

to recapitulation. Also the three movements, while still separate, are linked together so that the music is continuous from the beginning of the concerto to the end. Beethoven had already experimented with the linking of the separate concerto movements to one another in his fourth and fifth piano concertos. Mendelssohn and Liszt continued this line of experiment. It was Liszt, in particular, who achieved in his second piano concerto a genuine one-movement concerto design. In place of a conventional three-movement structure (the first in sonata form), Liszt arrived at a one-movement design comprising a continuity of related sections. One basic subject runs throughout the composition with a few additional themes added by way of contrast.

The variety of forms in which a concerto polarization can be expressed is by no means exhausted in the foregoing discussion. As a principle of compositional procedure it is too fundamental to be limited by anything other than the capacity of the human mind to invent and to discover.

PART III

The Composer
and the Allied Arts

Music and the Other Arts

Chapter 12

───────────────────────────────────────

Music, from the mists of prehistory to the present time, has always been found in the company of its sister arts. The very word *music*, as coined by the ancient Greeks, included all the arts cultivated under the patronage of the Muses, those mythical maidens who presided over the destinies of poetry, drama, the dance, and other media of expression. Today, as well as in the past, the vast preponderance of musical output is accounted for by such combinations as the union of word and tone in solo and choral song; the coordination of step, gesture, and sound in the dance and ballet; the fusion of liturgy and music in solemn church ceremonials; as well as the conjunction of dramatic and tonal elements in opera and oratorio, incidental music to plays, and background music to films and television productions. In addition to its obvious affinity for poetry and the dance, music joins with the visual arts in religious rites, where it animates the spirits of the worshipers and predisposes their minds and hearts to profounder contemplation; architecture, meanwhile, supplies the setting, while sculpture and painting attract the eye, and crafts such as metalwork, tapestry, and embroidery add the decorative element. Opera, too, incorporates most of the other arts since, in addition to ensemble and solo singing, instrumental overtures and interludes, there is also dramatic action, dancing, painted scenery, stage decor, costumes, and

147

the like. Also since music is so closely associated with the social occasions at which it is performed, it follows that architectural and acoustical surroundings will play their part in the process. Hence whether music is intended for performance in public or private, outdoors or indoors, in church or chamber, concert hall or salon, opera house or living room, there is always a relationship between the type of music and its setting. Only in the last three centuries, in fact, has instrumental music evolved such relatively self-sufficient forms as the concerto and symphony that made possible its emergence as an independent art. Even so, there are still the songs without words, as well as the dramatic overtures and symphonic poems that come under the heading of programme music in which music is connected either overtly or by implication with the visual and literary arts.

This union of music with the other arts is rooted deeply in the history and experience of the human race. Long before any of the arts rose to independent status, they existed side by side in tribal festivals, war dances, work songs, magic rites, ceremonial processions, and the like. Here the shouting, stamping, clapping, and miming expressed the individual and group emotions of a society. The war whoops, battle cries, love calls, shouts of joy, and outbursts of grief eventually give rise to epic chants, heroic ballads, love songs, and laments. Out of the rhythms of group effort associated with hunting, harvesting, threshing, and mowing come the work songs and dances that relieve the tension and tedium of labor. The emotional responses to the milestones of family life—birth, childhood, maturity, marriage, and death—crystallize into lullabies, children's songs, love songs, courtship dances, and the like. Out of the magic incantations and ceremonial rites for the propitiation of the gods emerges the religious music of a given time and place. Thus music and the other arts are always united in the desire to commemorate great events, in the need for collective effort, and for purposes of secular sociability and religious observances.

Song represents the merging of the arts of poetry and music in a marriage of word and tone. In Western culture, religious chants go all the way back to the early Middle Ages and possibly earlier, when the body of church music grew through the diligent efforts of a vast number of musicians known and unknown. Many folk songs are of considerable though uncertain antiquity; also they were the products of anonymous creators and were passed down orally from generation to generation. Secular art songs, consciously composed and committed to paper by poets and musicians, date back to the medieval days of the minstrels, troubadours, and minnesingers. All involve a simultaneous presentation of a literary text and a musical setting.

The dance in all its forms represents the union of physical movement and music. Gesture, mimicry, and pantomime are visual languages that men often call upon when words fail to convey sufficient meaning. Like song, there are folk dances of indeterminate origin as well as art dances that go all the way back to ancient Greek drama. Later the dance is found at all social levels from the jugglers and tumblers of the medieval market places and village fairs to the stylized, courtly balls. In each case man dances for his own delight, to lighten the burden of his work, and to promote social companionship. By the conscious organization of choreography, the dance is raised to the level of an art through which man seeks to communicate with an audience by means of spectacle. Choreography can thus be traced all the way from primitive religious rituals and war dances to the modern abstract studies in free form and motion in the ballet. Finally, in addition to these actual dances, there are the forms of dance movements written for instruments alone and in which the dancing takes place in the imagination of the listener. Thus whether participating physically in the dance, watching a ballet performance in a theater, or conjuring up images of movement in the mind's eye at a concert, the dance in all its multifarious forms is always closely associated with the musical process.

Music also joins with all the arts in divine worship where it promotes the unity of a congregation, inspires the spirit of prayer and praise, and intensifies the feeling of mystical communion with the Deity. Out of temple, synagogue, and church have come the sacred services, masses, and cantatas that have contributed so much to the art of music through the ages. From the psalm singing in ancient Jewish synagogues, through the plainsong chants, sequences, and motets of the medieval Christian Church, to the chorales, hymns, and anthems of Protestantism, the forms of sacred music are a significant branch of musical literature.

Music and drama have always enjoyed a close working relationship through the course of their histories. Though the music of ancient Greek drama is no longer extant, it is well known that the tonal art played an important part in every presentation. The surviving terminology is enough to illustrate the point. A *melodrama,* for instance, originally meant a drama with melody. The circular space in front of the proscenium of the Greek theater was called the *orchestra,* and it served as the place where the *chorus* performed their round dances with step and song. In all dramatic productions, as Aristotle notes in his *Poetics,* "Melody holds the chief place among embellishments." This association of the two arts continues through the medieval miracle and mystery plays as performed by itinerant musicians and strolling players in castle and market place. The plays of such great dramatists as Shakespeare, Calderon, and Molière often made liberal use of musical sequences; and today no drama, moving picture, or television production would be complete without music. The differences become apparent in the degree of importance allotted to music. In a film, for instance, it may be only minor background material to provide atmospheric effects and intensify moods at certain times. On the other hand music may assume considerable importance, as evidenced in such additions to the concert repertory as Prokofieff's *Lieutenant Kijé Suite, Alexander Nevsky Cantata,* Copland's *Our Town,* and Virgil Thomson's *The River,* all of which were originally composed as film scores. The role of music in spoken drama mounts in importance to the point where composers provide complete overtures, music between each act, intermezzos between scenes, as well as instrumental interludes and lyrical song settings. The scale then tips its balance in the case of Italian *opera buffa,* French *opéra comique,* German *Singspiel* (song-play), English *ballad opera* and *operetta* of the Gilbert-and-Sullivan type, as well as American *musical comedy,* where the emphasis is on the music interspersed with spoken dialogue. The saturation point is finally reached with full-scale, through-composed opera and music drama in which every word is set to music.

Music and architecture also share an often-overlooked relationship. Whether intended for performance in the hypostyle halls of an Egyptian temple, an outdoor arena in ancient Rome, a vaulted medieval cathedral, an open-air fete at the Versailles Palace, an intimate aristocratic salon, or a modern concert hall, music always goes hand in hand with its acoustical and architectural setting. Finally, even though instrumental music exists today as a nominally independent art, divorced from song, dance, liturgy, and drama, it nevertheless retains forms which imply its age-old union with the other arts. A composer may write a song without words for piano or violin, a gavotte or minuet for a string quartet, a solemn, hymnlike slow movement for instrumental ensemble, or a dramatic overture for full orchestra. Such instrumental songs, orchestral operas, and symphonic poems, generally coming under the heading of programme music, are in reality simply abstract versions of music's more concrete connections with the other arts. The difference is one of degree not of kind, and as such it is based on a scale of progressive symbolization, ranging from the basic forms of musical communication to more abstract and universal types of expression.

Finally, when a composer writes a song, he is setting a poetic text to music; when he addresses himself to religious music, he is concerned with its place in the liturgy of temple or church; when he collaborates with a choreographer or playwright on a ballet or incidental music to a play, he must think in terms of the theater; and when he conceives a symphonic poem, he usually arranges his episodes and modifies his moods according to some literary plan. The musical isolationists who proclaim that music is a completely independent art concerned only with the abstract play of sound do so to their own peril and confusion. Thus from spontaneous folk songs to sophisticated song cycles, from artless group singing to mighty choral symphonies, from folk-dance festivals to courtly classical ballets, from primitive religious rites to stylized masses and oratorios, from simple hymn tunes sung by lay congregations to complex polyphonic choruses performed by professional choirs, from rural narrative ballads to cosmopolitan grand operas, and from the bone whistles of Cro-Magnon caves to modern symphony orchestras in concert halls, music is almost always associated either explicitly or implicitly with one or more of the other arts.

Union of Word
and Tone: Song

Chapter 13

THE art of song embraces the simultaneous presentation of a literary text and a musical setting. Both poetry and melody have separate existences and independent expressive capacities. Song, however, represents a compromise in which each supplements the other, while together they are brought into a balance in which neither art dominates completely. As closely related arts, poetry and music share such common elements as melody, meter, rhythm, accentuation, tone color, rhyme structure, and strophic organization. They also meet on common ground in matters of phrasing, articulation, and punctuation. Expressively, each or both together can be lyrical, epical, or dramatic as the poet or composer wills; and the entire emotional gamut is mirrored in poetic and song literature from the longing of tender love lyrics to the recounting of the doughty deeds of rugged warriors in the epic chants of ancient bards.

Any complete discussion of song would of necessity have to go very far afield, and as such it would strain the covers of a large volume in itself. Historically it would have to trace the development of sacred song from ancient psalm singing and early Christian canticles all the way to various contemporary religious expressions; and in the case of secular song, from the medieval troubadours to the practices of modern recitalists. Socially it would have to extend from rural folk song to sophisticated urban art songs. Ethnographically it would have to dwell upon national differences in such varied forms as the Italian frottola, the French chanson, the English catch and carol, and the like. Linguistically it would have to take into account the diverse speech patterns of various countries and such factors as the German declamation of Schubert and Brahms, the French inflections of Fauré and Debussy, and the accented English of Purcell and Sullivan. It also could not neglect a variety of media from solo songs with lute accompaniment to such ensemble forms of vocal chamber music as madrigals and rounds. Stylistically the discussion would have to range from types of recitative to operatic arias, and from concrete song settings to abstract songs without words. The present discussion therefore will have to be confined to the processes involved when a composer undertakes the setting of a literary text to music, plus some of the principal styles that are normally encountered in contemporary musical life.

PROSODY

The marriage of word and tone gives birth to *prosody,* that problem child of poet and composer alike whose artistic conflicts are deeply rooted in such matters as the inflections of the language, stressed and unstressed syllables, rhythmic accentuation, metrical patterns, and versification. A musical melody in some instances may be a simple straight-forward line that follows the natural inflections of language thus allowing the word-melody to come to the fore. On the other hand, the musical-melody can become a complex stylized affair such as an intricate coloratura aria in which the word-melody is completely obliterated. Normally, whether the poem is read or sung, the poetic and melodic accents coincide on syllables that are either stressed dynamically or prolonged lyrically. The composer, however, has more alternatives at his command than has the poet. Since the singing voice possesses greater sustaining power, the accented syllable in a song can be prolonged to a much greater extent than in speech. The composer can also spread a syllable out melismatically over several notes as Purcell, for instance, does with the exclamation "Ah" in "When I am laid in earth" (Ex. 20:7). In a musical setting, furthermore, it is often very effective to place the melodic accent on a syllable that is unaccented in the poem. Accentuation thus plays an important role in both speaking and singing. What is said is, of course, important; but how it is said is often even more important. In ordinary speech the meaning of a sentence can be drastically altered, depending on the point where the accent is placed. A poem or melody, for instance, suffers no basic change when taken at a faster or slower tempo, or when rendered a little louder or softer. But if the emphasis on certain syllables is changed, or the phras-

ing or the punctuation altered, the melody will present an entirely different aspect, even though the notes remain the same.

In matters of rhythm poets divide their lines into metrical feet in a
manner closely resembling the way composers fit their phrases into musical
measures. Verbal rhythms, however, are often quite at variance with musical rhythms, and the differences between poetic and musical practices are
numerous. For a detailed discussion of meter the reader is referred to
Chapter 3 on Rhythm. The formal aspects of poetry also have much in
common with music. Both, for instance, make use of rhyme, the refrain
principle, rondolike repetitions of lines, and the like. Much of the song
literature, particularly in periods dominated by poetry, such as the Elizabethan era, follows verse forms. Musical designs, however, by their very
nature usually require more repetition than literary forms. Here again is
a source of friction between poets and composers. Tennyson, for instance,
complained bitterly that musicians made him say a thing twice when he
had said it only once.

This marriage of poetry and music is not without its conflicts, and one
or the other partner usually dominates. In some instances the words are
most prominent, in others the melody. In the recitatives of Mozartian opera,
for example, the text is most important, the musical line secondary. In the
arias, on the other hand, the situation is reversed and the words are subservient to the melody. The stronger the poem, the less easily it yields to a
musical setting, a fact which accounts for the relatively few successful songs
written to Shakespearean texts. In a selection by the bard such as "She
never told her love," the text remains dominant in spite of the ministra-
tions of a composer of Haydn's stature. On the other hand such a ballad
as the *Erlking* is so completely engulfed in Schubert's setting that the poem
has hardly led a separate existence since—something that caused the poet
Goethe considerable misgivings.

Since, in actual practice, a song usually begins with a poem that inspires
a musical setting, the composer is generally the dominant personality in
the process; and the poet, whether he is aware of it or not, is the one who
must yield the right of way. Exceptions to this rule occur when a poet is
his own composer and vice versa, as was the case with such celebrated
Elizabethan figures as Thomas Campian and John Dowland. Still other
instances are found in the practice of fitting new words to familiar hymn
tunes; or in setting a patriotic poem like the *Star-Spangled Banner* to the
popular eighteenth-century English melody, *Anacreon in Heaven;* or when
writing the song *Goin' Home* to the pre-existing melody of the slow movement of Dvořák's *New World* Symphony. Poets themselves, since theirs is
an independent art, quite rightly contend that a good poem justifies its
own existence and stands in no need of music. The burden of proof, then,

falls on the composer, who must justify his setting of a poem by providing a musical frame to enclose the poetic picture, giving perspective to the poem through the added dimension of music, placing the poetic text in a new light, intensifying the moods and projecting the emotions of the poetry more powerfully, and in general by producing a satisfactory compromise between the often opposing demands of poetry and music.

TYPES OF SONG

Songs—folk, popular, or art type—are usually classified as *strophic* or *through-composed* (the latter term deriving from the German *durchkomponiert* meaning composed throughout) according to whether the several stanzas are sung to a single melody, or whether the melody and accompaniment are adapted in each successive stanza to the different meaning of each verse. Most folk, popular, and patriotic songs— such as those of Stephen Foster, *My Country 'Tis of Thee*, and so on—are of the strophic type; while most art songs—such as those of Schumann, Brahms, and Debussy—are through-composed. Strophic songs are built up by an additive process in which the melody is repeated over and over to the different stanzas of the poem. Through-composed songs, contrariwise, are treated with considerable freedom in which successive phrases and sections may be the same or different, symmetrical or asymmetrical, or altered according to the shifts of mood and dramatic necessity. Modified strophic forms occasionally occur, such as in Schubert's *Serenade* and *Margaret at the Spinning Wheel*, in which the melody is the same for each verse; but minor changes are made at the points of climax to produce the effect of an unexpected turn or to point up places of emphasis. In a strophic song the variety lies in the different verses of the poem, while unity is provided by the repeated melody. In a through-composed song the variety manifests itself in both the words and melody, while composers solve the problem of unity through a number of sophisticated practices such as recurring rhythmic figures in the accompaniment, repeating melodic fragments and phrases, developing motives and the like. Strophic songs are better adapted to simple forthright poetic statements, while those of the through-composed type serve more fully the needs of narration where a sense of progress is maintained as the text unfolds, and for dramatic poetry where building toward moments of climax is of overriding importance.

Art songs, as opposed to folk songs on the one side and concert or operatic arias on the other, are lyrical or dramatic expressions of slender proportions for one or two voices with instrumental accompaniment. Surviving examples of art songs by known composers can be traced all the way back to the twelfth-century troubadours and the songfests of the medieval courts of love. All the great secular composers of the Renaissance contributed liberally to the literature of Italian canzoni, and French chansons and many of the Elizabethan lute airs are often sung today. By far the largest segment of the literature that the modern listener is likely to encounter goes back no further than the late eighteenth century, when such songs were a species of house music and vocal chamber music. Sung traditionally in the home rather than in public, their style was simple rather than grand, conversational rather than oratorical. They stood in relation to elaborate arias scaled to the proportions of the operatic stage, as did small character pieces for solo piano to concertos, or sonatas for violin and piano to works for full orchestra. Even though these art songs are now sung mostly in public, something of this special intimate character associated with their origin still clings to them, and they resist their transplantation from the intimacy of the salon and drawing room to the arena of the large concert hall.

Art songs, representing as they do the union of word and tone, also reflect national color according to the language in which the lines were originally written, the special character of the poetry, and the type of musical setting. Songs, of course, differ as widely as the languages and literatures of the various countries, and the individual approach of the composers who write them. For example, there are the songs in German by Schubert, Mendelssohn, and Mahler; in Russian by Moussorgsky, Tchaikovsky and Rachmaninoff; in French by Berlioz, Fauré, and Debussy; and in English there are those by Arthur Sullivan, Edward Elgar, and Vaughan Williams in England, or by Stephen Foster, Edward MacDowell, and Charles Ives in America.

Comparisons of various settings of the same poetic text by different composers can be an illuminating experience in listening. Both Schubert and Loewe, for instance, were independently inspired to write songs on Goethe's *Erlking* at approximately the same time. Loewe, however, sets the poem as a strophic ballad closely akin to folk balladry, while Schubert, in spite of the stanzaic organization of the poem itself, devises different melodic lines for the more impersonal narrator, the anxious father, the frightened child, and the phantom Erlking. The unity of his song is in the pulsating figuration and rhythmic drive of the piano part. Loewe, Schubert, and Brahms each made settings of the old Scottish ballad, *Edward*. Goethe's "Knowest Thou the Land" has a setting by Beethoven, several by Schubert, and still others by Schumann, Liszt and Thomas. Another lyric from Goethe's novel, *Wilhelm Meister,* "None but the Lonely Heart," boasts no less than four settings by Beethoven, as well as others by Schubert, Liszt, and Tchaikovsky. Beethoven, Berlioz, and Moussorgsky, as well as most of the composers who dealt with Goethe's *Faust,* all made versions of the "Song of the Flea." It is also rewarding to compare vocal and instrumental settings of the same melody. Schubert's song *The Trout,* for example, becomes the subject of a set of variations in his *Trout* Quintet. His *Sei Mir Gegrüsst* appears also in his C-major *Fantaisie,* Op. 159, a duo for violin and piano. And Brahms' *Immer leiser wird mein Schlummer* becomes the melody for the lyrical slow movement of his B-flat-major Piano Concerto.

THE GERMAN LIED

Out of these various regional art songs, the German *Lied* (pl., *Lieder*) was lifted to the status of a style that transcended national boundaries by a remarkable chain of circumstances. The rising popularity of romantic poetry, the perfection and general acceptance of the pianoforte as the favored household instrument, and the birth of a number of men of genius, all conspired in the early years of the nineteenth century to bring about the flowering of this special lyrical art. The poetry of Burns, Scott, and Byron, as well as that of Goethe, Schiller, and Heine, was transformed in settings by such composers as Loewe, Schubert, and Schumann into intensely expressive little songs whose artistic and human importance loomed as large as the medium itself was small. These diminutive musical dramas for voice and piano fulfilled the romantic ideal of personal individualism, freedom of form, intimate atmosphere, and the outpouring of subjective emotion.

In these miniature music dramas the singer as protagonist must declaim the often impassioned lines with an eye on the poetic picture he is presenting, an ear for the melodic nuances, a mind alert to the subtle shades of meaning in the text, so as to transform these little lyrical and dramatic designs into engrossing musical and human events. The piano parts, moreover, are raised from the subservient status of mere accompaniments to full equality with the voice. These songs are, as Hugo Wolf designated them on the title pages of his published lieder, "for voice and piano," and not songs with piano accompaniment. Both voice and instrument join in service to the text in a true ensemble sense, and both share the responsibility for its interpretive projection. In practice the piano parts may vary —according to the differing demands of the poetry and the conceptions of the composer—from a comparatively minor role with the piano lending rhythmic and harmonic support to the melody, all the way to the point where it bears the full weight of lyrical responsibility with the vocal part becoming an obbligato. At the turn of the nineteenth century the more objective and impersonal harpsichord, on which the emphasis had been clarity of line, neatly terraced dynamics, and black and white contrasts of registration, was replaced by the pianoforte. With its ability to make dramatic dynamic shifts in crescendos and diminuendos, its capacity for mixing harmonies by means of the sostenuto pedal, and its sustaining power in melodic passages, the piano lent itself well to the expressive demands of the then new romantic poetry. As such, it was admirably adapted to enact scenes, create atmospheric effects, and reflect the poetic imagery of the text in an instrumental mirror. In prologues the piano could project the mood before the entrance of the voice, while in epilogues it could continue the meaning well beyond the point where the text leaves off. And in these preludes, interludes, and postludes, the piano part could provide the framework for the poetic verses, make occasional commentaries on the text, carry on a running dialogue with the voice on equal terms, and complete the formal design.

The principal barrier to the listener's full enjoyment of these songs is encountered when they are written and sung in languages other than his own. It is just as important to understand the text as it is to know the music, and for complete comprehension the poetry has to be understood in its own linguistic medium. German romantic poetry, as well as that of the French symbolists and impressionists, makes special use of the element of word color, which in turn blends with the vocal quality, the word projection, and the instrumental timbre. This so-called onomatopoetic element, moreover, usually defies translation and often disappears entirely in another language. Some of this verbal color, however, approaches the conditions of the music itself and, when the vowel sounds are treated purely for their color effect, something of this quality comes through even though it is heard in a foreign language. In the "Brook's Lullaby," for example, at the conclusion of Schubert's song cycle *Die Schöne Müllerin* (The Fair Maid of the Mill), the poem by Wilhelm Müller employs a series of "oo" sounds intended to produce the drowsy effect that lulls one to sleep. The expressive and soothing tone quality of the German words in this instance comes through in spite of the language barrier.

> *Gute Ruh', gute Ruh', thu' die Augen zu,*
> *gute Ruh', gute Ruh', thu' die Augen zu!*
> *Wand'rer, du müder, du bist zu Haus.*

Schubert, who built his songs on the models provided by his eighteenth-century predecessors—in particular, on the strophic examples of Reichardt and Zelter and on the ballads of Zumsteeg—was perhaps responsible more than any other single figure for raising the rank of the German lied to universal significance; and he provided the literature with more than 600 noble examples from his own inexhaustible creative imagination. Schubert's setting of Matthias Claudius' short poem, *Death and the*

Ex. 13:1 *Death and the Maiden.* Schubert.

Maiden (Ex. 13:1), will illustrate his approach to this particular creative problem as well as the solution he devised for it. The little drama is crowded into four poetic lines, shared equally by the two *dramatis per-sonnae*—the Maiden and Death. The poetic form likewise falls into the two parts allotted to these contrasting characters and the content reveals a corresponding duality of viewpoint, mood, word, melody, and tempo. If he had started with the Maiden's cry of fear at the entrance of the skeletal form of Death, it would have burst upon the ear too suddenly for its full impact to be felt. To prepare the listener, as well as to round out the form, Schubert therefore opens with the piano part by sounding a sustained choralelike procession of chords in slow march rhythm to warn of the somber inexorable approach of Death. At one stroke this sets the stage, creates the necessary sinister atmosphere, leads up to the Maiden's cry, and, more technically, allows for the symmetry of the A-B-A form whereby the beginning statement is followed by a departure in the middle and a return at the end.

The terror of the Maiden, too young to yield to Death's embrace, is inherent in the shrill, high-pitched melody; and her illness is apparent in the panting, breathless, broken line irregularly interspersed with gasping rests, and reinforced by an agitated piano figure that palpitates in sympathy with her wildly beating heart. The short transition in Bars 20 and 21 signifies her resignation and leads to Death's monotonous melody, which now takes on a soothing aspect as Death solemnly intones his reassuring words in a line as stiff as rigor mortis itself—that he comes not to punish but to allow her to sleep peacefully in his arms. The final modulation to the major key confirms that all is well. Thus in one short page, and in less than two minutes of time, Schubert is able to pack an entire drama of life and death, of youth and the desire to live, of pain and deliverance. Further shades of meaning contained in the song can be discovered in the slow movement of Schubert's String Quartet in D Minor, where an instrumental version of the song is expanded into a set of variations.

THE SONG CYCLE

With the development of the lied comes the rise of the *song cycle*, a group or series of songs sharing a common thought, theme, or musical treatment, and intended to be sung consecutively. By placing a number of lieder within a larger context, composers such as Beethoven, Schubert, and Schumann found a more expansive form than that afforded by the more isolated inspirations of single songs; and they thus achieved a degree of unity in song composition that compared favorably with the longer instrumental designs of the suite and sonata. Texts for such song cycles were usually selected by composers from the works of poets with an eye toward narrative continuity, dramatic balladry, retrospective contemplation, or the exploration of an all-pervading mood. Sometimes the poets themselves grouped their lyrics together for publication around some central idea, thus suggesting the idea of a cycle; or the composer could make a selection from the works of several different poets for his purpose. In the settings the composers, while allowing themselves ample elbow room for formal freedom, nevertheless sought for a semblance of unity in the presentation through such technical devices as sequential key relationships, common thematic substance, recurring motivic material, smooth modulatory transitions from song to song, and the like. In the course of a song cycle, an entire drama can thus be presented in a series of lyrical moments. Performancewise, they resemble one-man operas in which the dramatic interest is implied rather than overtly acted out, and the emotional content is inwardly rather than outwardly oriented. Many, in fact, exhibit such a high degree of individualism and are so personal and subjective, that they seem to be almost autobiographical.

The earliest song cycles to make their appearance are also excellent examples of contrasting types. In his *An die ferne Geliebte* (To the Distant Beloved, 1816), Beethoven set a series of six lyrics by A. Jeitteles. Poetically, as the title implies, they express the longing of a lover for his distant beloved. In the setting Beethoven employs marked contrasts of meter and tempo, key and mode, to correspond with the different moods. The unifying factor is found in the modulatory passages between each song, as well as in the return of the opening theme for the final song in the manner of a recapitulation. Schubert's first essay in the form, *Die Schöne Müllerin* (The Fair Maid of the Mill, 1823) is of the narrative type that tells a tale in a series of episodes; while the second, *Winterreise* (Winter's Journey, 1827) is more contemplative in style. In both cycles the composer allows the individual songs a more independent existence within the whole. Unlike Beethoven's, each has its own beginning and end, and consequently may be lifted out of its cyclical context and sung separately. A detailed discussion of Schubert's cycles may be found in Chapter 22, pages 335–337.

Robert Schumann, synthesizing the practices of his two illustrious predecessors, enriched the literature with numerous lieder and some song cycles of his own. The *Dichterliebe* (Poet's Love, 1840) is a particularly happy example of a composer finding his true poetic counterpart; and in Heinrich Heine, Schumann found a poet for whose verses he had a real affinity. Selecting sixteen poems from the sixty-five Heine had published under the title of *Lyrisches Intermezzo* (Lyrical Intermezzo), later to be included in the larger *Buch der Lieder* (Book of Songs), Schumann combines both the narrative and contemplative types of approach. In the manner of an intimate personal confession the cycle explores a gamut of emotions ranging from youthful rapture to pathos, morbid feeling to airy fantasy, and from romantic irony to grim humor. Musically the settings are equally multidimensional, and in them one recognizes a variety of types. There are purely lyrical evocations such as "All in the magic month of May" (No. 1), "Out of my tears" (2), "I will baptize my spirit" (5), "And were it known to the flowers" (8), "I hear an echo singing" (10), and "On a radiant summer morning" (12); folklike songs such as "A young man loves a maiden" (11), and "From ancient fairy stories" (15); dramatic ballads such as "I will not mourn" (7), "Beloved, in dreams" (14), and "The songs, so old and bitter" (16); dance songs such as "The rose and the lily" (3), and "The violins are shrilling" (9); and quasi-operatic recitatives such as "Whene'er I look into your eyes" (4) and "I wept as I lay dreaming" (13).

One of the most interesting is the sixth, "In the Rhine," composed in the spirit of Bach, the musician whom Schumann as well as most of his fellow romanticists admired above all composers. Like one of the master's organ chorale-preludes, the austere vocal melody is reinforced by resounding octaves in the bass register of the piano, while over it a precipitously descending obbligato figure in a majestic baroque dotted rhythm reflects the imagery of the text:

> In the Rhine, that stream of wonder,
> The great, the holy Cologne
> Is mirrored, and there under
> The waves the Cathedral is shown.

Somewhat less lean and angular is the setting for the second verse describing the interior of the cathedral. Rich organlike chromatic harmonies then fill the widely spaced unison intervals to give a warmer and more personal tone to the third and final verse:

> Mid flowers and angels she stands there
> Our Lady we bow before.
> But the eyes and the lips and the hands there
> Are those of the one I adore!

The piano part then takes over in an extensive postlude, and the song ends as austerely and starkly as it began.

Collectively the *Dichterliebe* has more continuity and organic unity than either of Schubert's essays in the form. Whereas the latter had preserved a perfect classical balance between the vocal and instrumental part, Schumann leans heavily on the piano and allows the voice to function often as a mere obbligato. This procedure, however, always has a clearly apparent poetic purpose, as for instance, in the ninth song, which describes the scene of the heroine's wedding to another. Instrumentally the "accompaniment" is a complete piano piece in its own right, while the voice part proceeds independently. The general impression is that of the lover looking at the scene from the outside, and a more effective means to show him and his beloved going their separate ways could hardly be imagined.

Ex. 13:2 *Dichterliebe* (Poet's Love). Schumann.

(a) I, Bars 9-12 and 20-23.

(b) V, Bars 17-20.

(c) VI, Bars 4-9.

(d) VIII, Bars 30-33.

(e) IX, Bars 25-31 and 59-65.

(f) X, Bars 26-28.

(g) XII, Bars 23-26.

(h) XV, Bars 1-2 and 9-10.

(i) XVI, Bars 16-19.

(j) XVI, Bars 53-56.

Schumann also integrates the songs of the *Dichterliebe* by the use of a recurring motive consisting of a simple four-note scalewise figure. This germinal motive appears first in the opening song in ascending order (Ex. 13:2a); later it evolves through a series of mutations beginning with the inverted order in songs No. V and No. VI (Ex. 13:2b and c); a chromatic variant appears in song VIII (Ex. 13:2d); and a sequential figure occurs in songs IX and X (Ex. 13:2e and f). Toward the end the motive

is restored to its original ascending form, as in the close of song XII
(Ex. 13:2g), and in the accompaniment figures of songs XV and XVI
(Ex. 13:2h and i); and finally it reaches its apotheosis in the piano post-
lude of the cycle (Ex. 13:2j).

Interestingly enough, Schumann also arranged various series of short
pieces for piano—such as the *Papillons,* Op. 2, the *Carnaval,* Op. 9, and the
Fantasy Pieces, Op. 12—into sets that combine certain features derived
from older keyboard dance suites and the poetic possibilities of mood and
fantasy of the song cycle. The song cycle since Schumann's time has attracted the attention of an increasing number of composers. Some have
gone beyond the confines of the original solo-voice-and-piano combination
as, for instance, Vaughan Williams' *On Wenlock Edge,* which is scored
for voice and string quartet. In his *Das Lied von der Erde* (Song of the
Earth, 1908), Mahler fuses the form with that of the symphony and scores
it for tenor, alto, and full orchestra; while Schoenberg in his *Gurrelieder*
(Songs of Gurre, 1911) adds elements of the secular cantata to those of
the song cycle and scores the work for orchestra, several choruses, vocal
soloists, and narrator.

Each of the post-romantic musical styles and literary movements has
its quota of examples in song form. Realism and naturalism, for instance,
are represented by Moussorgsky's *The Nursery* (1868–72); symbolism and
impressionism by Debussy's many settings of the poems of Mallarmé,
Baudelaire, and Verlaine; dadaism and surrealism are reflected in the
songs of Satie, as well as in Francis Poulenc's "profane cantata" *Le Bal
Masque* based on poems by Max Jacob. Neoprimitivism can be found
in Villa Lobos' *Song of the Ox-cart Driver;* neomedievalism in Hindemith's song cycle, *The Life of Mary* (Das Marienleben); and neoclassicism in the songs of Stravinsky, Ravel, and others; while expressionism receives a full exploration in the songs of Richard Strauss, Schoenberg, and
Alban Berg.

Contemporary experimentalism is likewise well represented by many
novel uses of the speaking voice, such as spoken roles for narrator and
musical ensemble as well as that hybrid between song and speech known
in German as *Sprechgesang.* A notable example of the latter is found in
Schoenberg's cycle, *Pierrot Lunaire,* in which the vocal inflections are de-
limited above and below in the score but not defined in precise notation.
Sirenlike, the voice moves upward and downward in vocal glissandos,
soaring and swooping as if over lunar landscapes. Stravinsky in his *Les
Noces* (The Wedding), *Persephone,* and *Oedipus Rex* makes some interesting experiments in prosody, some of which were later taken up by the
contemporary German composer, Carl Orff. Many recent instrumental
works include roles for narrator, as, for instance, in the popular orchestral

fairy tale by Prokofieff, *Peter and the Wolf*. The direct collaboration of poetess Edith Sitwell and composer William Walton resulted in *Facade*, a fascinating series of imagistic poems recited to satirical instrumental dances. In the words of her brother Osbert Sitwell, their intentions were in the nature of "Inquiries into the effect on rhythm, on speed, and on color of the use of rhymes, assonances, dissonances" and the like, so as to discover "an abstract method of presenting poetry to an audience."

Union of Body
Movement and Tone:
Dance and Ballet

Chapter 14

T<small>HE</small> dance—whether performed as a manifestation of emotion, group expression, religious exercise, or theatrical spectacle—is indissolubly associated with music. Even when musical instruments as such are absent, the human body itself takes over and functions percussively with rhythmic stamping of feet, clapping of hands, snapping of fingers, and also melodically with shouting, crying, or singing. Since both dancing and music-making have a common source in the rhythmic impulse as well as in the natural enthusiasm of the human spirit, dance rhythms and musical rhythms have always gone hand in hand. Functionally, of course, the musical rhythms serve to keep the participants in step; while psychologically they suggest appropriate moods and emotional states. Such rhythms, whether danced in actuality on the ballroom floor or in imagination at a concert, pervade all aspects of music from the dance tunes heard at folk festivals to those ballets for ears alone known as instrumental suites.

Just as the union of word and tone in the song results in all the complex forms of vocal music, the joining of measured body movement and sound in the dance leads to a host of forms, ranging from simple folk ex-

166

pressions to the sophisticated commentaries on the dance heard in sonatas and symphonies. It would, then, be quite impossible to overestimate the influence of the dance on the course of music; and whether a composer uses a primitive tribal war chant or an aristocratic minuet as his subject matter, the dance is always one of the principal resources of instrumental music. Such music thus accounts for a considerable segment of the concert repertory, and unless a listener can establish some historical, social, national, religious, or expressive frame of reference, much of its significance will escape him.

At present, as in the past, actual dances intended for active participation are found in all countries and at all social levels. Such dances are continuously cultivated in the countries of their origin, and often are performed by touring troupes that bring, for example, the flash and fire of Spain or the dash and color of some central European country to audiences internationally. In refined forms these ethnic dances find their way into operas, ballets, and concerts, where such music as Chopin's mazurkas, polonaises, and waltzes, Liszt's Hungarian rhapsodies, Dvořák's Slavonic dances, and Bartók's Romanian dances all reflect the exuberant spirit of the folk dance. Contemporary composers find such material useful and often liven up their scores with waltzes, fox trots, and jazz rhythms in various guises and disguises, just as Haydn, Mozart, and Beethoven had included and transformed in their works the popular dance tunes of their time. Surveying the contemporary scene one finds modern composers supplying music with liberal dance sequences for musical comedies and revues; incidental music for plays, motion pictures and television productions; music for operettas and grand operas, as well as for classical ballets and modern-dance productions. Much of it eventually finds its way into the concert hall in the form of instrumental suites, just as did the overtures and incidental music of their predecessors before them. A glance at the principal sources of such music—in the courtly entertainments of princely ballrooms, in theaters, as well as in opera and ballet houses—will reveal the importance of this partnership of the dance and music in both the past and present time.

THE DANCE SUITE

The fountainhead of the instrumental suite and the ballet is found in the aristocratic ballrooms of the Renaissance and baroque eras. Here, by a long process of refinement and courtly practice, the formulation of the steps, rhythms, gestures, and group patterns took place. Such dances, however, seldom originated in these rarefied social surroundings; and most, if not all, received their initial impetus in the energetic expressions of the common people. The chaconne, passacaglia, and sarabande, for instance, seem to have originated in the West Indies and Central America, from where they were brought to Spain by the sailors, traders, and colonists who followed in the wake of Columbus' voyages. In the process of acclimating themselves to Spanish soil, their crudities were discarded; and they then rose on the social scale until they were accepted in Spanish and French courtly circles and placed in the hands of the composers who supplied the music for their entertainment.

The Irish jig, in similar fashion, started life humbly as a vigorous folk dance, then rose in the world to the place where it was adapted to courtly life under Queen Elizabeth I. From there it went to glory in France at the court of Louis XIV under the spelling of "gigue." The minuet likewise began as a provincial French peasant dance of Poitou, and it gradually lost its rustic angularity while working its way up the social ladder to the point where it arrived in princely palaces and became the epitome of courtly decorum and ceremonial dignity. Goethe tells of its further transition from active dance to observed spectacle in a description of the old dances at the turn of the nineteenth century. "The minuet in particular," he says, "is regarded as a work of art and is performed by only a few couples. Such a couple is surrounded by the rest of the company in circles, admired and applauded at the end." In the hands of composers and choreographers these dances have been carried one step further and reached the pinnacle where participation is through listening to them in concert versions or viewing them as stage productions. The cycle from rustic folk dance to achieved work of art is thus complete.

Dances in instrumental form were played indoors on lutes, keyboard instruments, and string ensembles both as dinner music and as chamber music, and outdoors by wind bands as background music for social occasions. When such instrumental versions of dances were written by composers of stature, they underwent still further phases of sophistication, and the simple regular meters needed for actual dancing yielded to complicated commentaries on such rhythmic patterns. Such instrumental forms as the suite, partita, sonata da camera (chamber sonata), and the later eighteenth-century serenades and divertimentos are thus an outgrowth of the practices that began in princely ballrooms. Even the Viennese sonatas and symphonies retained a basic identification with the suite by the inclusion of such movements as minuets and rondos. Dance rhythms in disguise also found their way into the rhythmic backgrounds and textures of fugues and operatic arias. The dance thus pervades virtually all musical manifestations, whether presented for actual participation in ballrooms or merely felt as a presence in the imaginary dances heard in various instrumental and vocal forms.

These suites of dances gradually crystallized around four principal forms that were presented in sequence—the *allemande, courante, sarabande,* and *gigue.* This relatively stable core could be prefixed at the composer's discretion by a prelude or fantasia; and between the sarabande and final gigue, room was made to insert a group of the so-called gallant dances—musettes, minuets, bourrées, and gavottes. As written for instrumental solo and for various ensemble combinations, including the orchestra, these baroque dances in the hands of composers of the caliber of Corelli, Purcell, Handel, and Bach became models of terse, tidy musical statement and abstract tonal design. A typical Bach suite, whether scored for keyboard, solo violin, or cello, therefore, will consist of an *allemande,* a sturdy, energetic dance in moderate tempo and 4/4 time; a *courante,* a rapid, running patter of eighth notes in triple meter, occasionally complicated with cross rhythms; a *sarabande,* a slow, stately measured dance in 3/2 meter with emphasis on its dotted second beat. At this point comes the *galanterie*—usually a group of tuneful dances in the lighter rococo vein, such as the lively *gavotte* in 4/4 time, or an elegant *minuet* in 3/4. The finale of the suite is almost always the traditional *gigue,* a highly spirited dance in triple meter.

BALLET

Ballet, the most consciously creative and highly organized form of the dance, is a composite art combining elements drawn from drama, music, and the various visual arts. Like the drama, the dance exists at once in both space and time; poetry and music on the one side veer more toward time, and architecture and sculpture, on the other, more toward space. Like the drama, ballet can represent plot in episodes of action and narrative sequence; it can mirror human conflict and resolution; and it can portray comedy and tragedy, as well as project such emotional reactions as ecstasy and despair, passion and anger, confidence and fear. It communicates, however, principally through the visual language of gesture and pantomime rather than that of the spoken word. With music the dance shares the rhythmical patterns of motion, the lyricism of linear movement, and spatialized forms of flowing melodic line. The dance is allied with architecture in the three-dimensional framework of stage sets that create illusions of location, perspectives of foreground and background, and scenic spectacle. Dancers—either singly or in groups, in action or in repose—occupy space with much of sculpture's clean definition and plastic molding of space. The material of the dance, however, is the living human body rather than stone or metal. Like painting, the ballet presents pictures with all the refinement of line, shading, and color. Painting, however, can only suggest motion by means of poised human figures, while the dance uses movement directly as one of its foremost materials.

The *choreographer* is to the ballet what the composer is to the opera or symphony. A choreographer's inspirations come in patterns of movement, his inventions in types of motion, while his instruments are the individual soloists and ensemble groups of dancers. In designing a ballet he puts his dancers in action gliding through space to musical rhythms; he coordinates their movements and arranges them in various configurations, deploying them about the stage and preparing their entries and exits; and thus he gives definition and organization to the dance forms as they unfold in the spatial and temporal dimension. Choreography is at once as old as the social organization of the human race and as modern as today's ballet. Its beginnings can be traced from the primitive religious rites, in which tribal medicine men and temple priests were the choreographers, all the way to modern abstract studies in free form and motion. The *Old Testament,* for example, mentions Miriam the prophetess dancing with her maidens in celebration of the safe passage of the Israelites through the Red Sea (Exodus 15:20), as well as David dancing "before the Lord with all his might" (II Sam. 6:14) on the recovery of the ark of the covenant. Liturgies of all religions, as well as folk festivals and courtly ceremonials, are ballets whose choreographies are dictated by ancient usages, social customs, and historical tradition. In modern parlance, however, the term designates the organized pageants and dance spectacles that are found in theaters rather than temples or palaces.

The earliest surviving ballet music by a known choreographer dates only from the late Renaissance. Appended to this *Ballet Comique de la Reine* (Comedy Ballet of the Queen), which was performed at the French court in the year 1581, is a limited, but nonetheless accurate, definition of the ballet as "A geometrical arrangement of numerous people dancing together under a diverse harmony of many instruments." Thereafter, the development of the French court ballet, or *ballet de cour* as it is technically called, proceeded apace and eventually became a favored form of courtly entertainment. Because of the lavish scale on which they were produced and the attendant expense, they were generally performed on special occasions only, such as at princely weddings or coronations. The *ballet de cour* and its English equivalent, the court *masque* or mask, consisted of a casual combination of pageantry, poetic recitation, dancing, mummery, pantomime, costumes, scenic architecture, solo and choral song, and instrumental interludes strung loosely together along the lines of some mythological or allegorical plot.

In England these presentations were the cause of some of the most notable artistic collaborations in history. The *Masque of Blackness,* for instance, was performed at the court of James I at Whitehall in 1605. Shakespeare's younger contemporary, Ben Jonson, wrote the dialogue and poetry; the famous architect Inigo Jones designed the "scenes and machines," the latter being no less than the first use of movable scenery that changed before the eyes of the audience instead of remaining stationary in the manner of the stylized temple facades of Renaissance theaters. And the principal dancers were none other than James I's queen and her ladies. Perhaps the most famous of all masques was Milton's *Comus* with music by Henry Lawes, which was written for a performance at Ludlow Castle in 1634. Still another instance, though the original music is now lost, is the masque contained in the first scene of the Fourth Act of *The Tempest,* where Shakespeare, needing a festive note to celebrate the forthcoming nuptials of Miranda and Ferdinand, conjures up a mythological vision of Juno and Ceres joining in dance and song with nymphs and reapers. The ballet de cour and masque were both carried over into the seventeenth-century baroque style and thus became the common ancestral forms of opera as well as ballet. With the exception of the fact that the literary element is reduced to a pantomimed plot or dumb show, the modern ballet is quite close to the masque. Some modern composers—Falla in his *El Amor Brujo* (Love the Magician, 1915), and Stravinsky in his *Renard* (1916) and Les Noces (The Wedding, 1917), to cite three examples—have experimented with the reintroduction of the speaking and singing voice in their ballets.

No less notable were the collaborations at the court of Louis XIV in France. Lully, who was a ballet master and producer as well as composer, supplied abundant dance music for the theater pieces Racine called *tragédies-lyrique,* and Molière called *comédie-ballets.* The best known of the latter genre is the perennial favorite, the *Bourgeois Gentilhomme* (The Bourgeois Gentleman) of 1670. A *tragédie-ballet* called *Psyché* was staged in 1671 with Lully contributing the music, Corneille and Molière the spoken verses, and Quinault the prose for the recitatives. All these hybrid examples were transitional forms on the way to the later independent ballets and operas. Ever since this time, the ballet enjoyed a favored place among the arts in France; and classical ballet, even to this day, still employs a vocabulary dominated by such terms as *corps de ballet* (ballet company), *pirouette* (a turn while poised on the point of the toes of one foot), *pas de deux* (a dance duet), and so on.

Ballet likewise has always occupied a position of prominence in opera in France as well as elsewhere. Most operatic ballets, however, have little connection with the plot or dramatic action and are generally just an excuse for the introduction of some pageantry or eye-filling spectacle. At best their advent is prepared by some occasion in the plot that calls for general rejoicing such as a feast or betrothal, or general sorrowing such as a death or lamentation. The dances have, however, followed the changing trends of the time, and in the eighteenth century the ballets were stylized suites of dances including a procession of chaconnes, gavottes, minuets, and the like.

In the nineteenth century, national and local color entered the operatic ballet in such ethnic dances as the Bohemian waltzes in Weber's *Der Freischütz,* the rustic laendler in Humperdinck's *Hansel and Gretel,* the vigorous polkas in Smetana's *Bartered Bride,* the barbaric Polovetsian dances in Borodin's *Prince Igor,* the brilliant polonaise in Moussorgsky's *Boris Godounov,* and the spirited Parisian quadrilles and cancans in Offenbach's operettas. Significant reforms were carried out by Gluck and his successors in an effort to bring the dance sequences into a closer relation with the plot. Instead of momentarily interrupting the dramatic action while a troupe of dancers came tripping out of the stage wings in order to go through their routines, Gluck in his *Orfeo* wove the dances right into the musical and dramatic context. Mozart likewise never pushed the plot aside just to sandwich in a ballet, and consequently the dances in his *Marriage of Figaro* and *Don Giovanni* are models of dramatic continuity. Wagner also did not write ballets per se, and dancing is completely absent from his *Ring* cycle and *Tristan and Isolde.* On the other hand, ballets fit completely naturally into his *Meistersinger* and *Parsifal.* Wagner's *Tannhäuser* was rejected for production in Paris because it had no ballet. One of the conventions of French grand opera is the inclusion of a ballet, customarily placed in the fourth act. Anxious for the prestige of a Paris performance, Wagner made one of his rare compromises by writing a ballet, but he put it right after the Overture, of which it is in effect an extension, and he thereby preserved the continuity of his opera.

Thus out of such Italian Renaissance entertainments as the carnival pageant, comedy of masks, harlequinade, and intermezzo, out of the French court ballet and ballet-opera, out of the English masque, out of the incidental ballets performed as divertissements and between-the-act interludes, and out of the operatic ballet (whether integrated with or extraneous to the plot and dramatic action), the ballet gradually emerged in the relatively independent form in which it is now known. It still, however, retains its close alliance with music.

Ballets can be classified into general types, and they also follow the trends of their respective historical style periods. The dramatic ballet employs pantomime and mimetic characterization to carry out a story line, while the *abstract ballet* is concerned more with formal elements than with plot and confines itself principally to the composition and grouping of dancers and dance movements. The *folk ballet,* to cite still another type, uses ethnic dances as a principal ingredient and can employ plot or not as the choreographer and composer choose. Needless to say, these classifications represent dominant tendencies rather than fixed rules, and many examples in the repertory fall somewhere in between. It is also usual to classify ballets in style categories such as the *classical ballet,* which follows the formal dances and stylized steps and gestures stemming out of the traditions established in the seventeenth and eighteenth centuries. *Romantic ballets* and *modern ballets,* on the other hand, are based on the dominant styles of the nineteenth and twentieth centuries, respectively.

The dramatic ballet, also called the "mimed" ballet, leans heavily on the age-old art of pantomime. The word was coined by the ancient Greeks to mean "all-imitating," and it was used in those times to denote a means of telling a story through gestures: acting out a myth in sign language and symbolic suggestion, presenting tragic or comic situations with mimicry, and communicating with an audience through mimetic dance. In addition to its cultivation in the ballet, the art also survives in the antics of circus clowns and puppet shows, and recently flourished in the days of the silent film. Gesture has always been an eloquent visual language, and styles of acting in the theater and opera owe much to the art of the mime. A shrug of the shoulders or a wave of the hand often tells more than words. There is also an entire vocabulary of bodily movements, varying from those associated with work and occupations to obscure symbolic and allegorical gestures designed to convey meaning only to the initiated. The emotional spectrum encompassed by this visual language is tremendous, ranging all the way from the soaring aspiration expressed by an upward leap to the blackness of despair inferred by sinking earthward.

The first real, dramatic ballet is Gluck's *Don Juan* (1761), which he subtitled "Pantomime Ballet in the Manner of the Ancients." Presented apart from any theatrical or operatic context, the dance here emerged as an independent art form capable of commanding full attention in its own right as a dramatic spectacle with music. Replacing the poetic texts and song elements of the court ballets and ballet-operas, Gluck and his choreographer tell of the licentious lover on his way to perdition. The story unfolds through a combination of dumb show, expressive gestures, stylized and mimetic dances, and above all through the musical score, which now assumed primary importance. Like the Greek chorus of old, the orchestra became the prime emotional interpreter of the dramatic action. Continuing through the nineteenth century with such works as Beethoven's *Creatures of Prometheus* and Delibes' *Coppelia* and *Sylvia,* the dramatic ballet began to take on the color of romanticism, and the plots became fanciful fairy tales liberally populated with assorted mermaids, ondines, elves, and sylphs. Such was the background for Tchaikovsky's essays in the form, and his ballets—*Swan Lake* (part of which is also known as *Aurora's Wedding*), *Sleeping Beauty,* and the *Nutcracker*—are still, either in whole or in part, staples in the current repertory.

The dramatic ballet received its greatest impetus in the twentieth century from an offshoot of the Imperial Russian Ballet that established itself in Paris in 1909, under the guiding spirit of Serge Diaghilev (1872–1929). With rare discernment and creative imagination this genius among impresarios gathered about him choreographers of the caliber of Michel Fokine (creator of *Les Sylphides*), and Leonide Massine (*Pulcinella*), and George Ballanchine (*Orpheus*); composers of the stature of Ravel, Albeniz, Poulenc, and Stravinsky; scenic designers of the mastery of Bakst, Derain, and Picasso; and dancers of such legendary reputations as Nijinsky and Karsavina. The collaboration of these patrons, composers, choreographers, scenic designers, and dancers reflected all the movements that were stirring the world of art at the time—impressionism, neoclassicism, the mechanical style, to name but three—and lead to the creation of such enduring modern ballets as *The Firebird* (Stravinsky), *Three-Cornered Hat* (Falla), *Daphnis and Chloe* (Ravel), and many more. As a result of their labors, the ballet, formerly an art cultivated for the discriminating few, became a truly popular art with wide appeal for the many.

The scores Igor Stravinsky composed for the Diaghilev company just prior to World War I made musical as well as ballet history. In a crescendo of creative activity, the *Firebird* (1910), with its lush and colorful orchestration, continued the romantic fairy-tale tradition of Tchaikovsky and Rimsky-Korsakoff; *Petrouchka* (1911), with its tragic-comic situations and pantomime plot, became a dance drama that re-established the dramatic ballet as a genre among contemporary theater pieces. The *Rite of Spring* (1913) then brought about a revolution that changed the entire course of contemporary music. In this solemn evocation of pagan religious rites, Stravinsky's primitive polyrhythms and savage dissonances created such unforgettable images of brute force and primeval power that the entire rhythmic outlook of the twentieth century was re-evaluated and revitalized.

Petrouchka, subtitled "Burlesque Scenes in Four Tableaux," takes place against a kaleidoscopic cross section of life at a fair in old St. Petersburg at carnival time. The rise of the curtain reveals the hustle and bustle of the carnival crowds milling about amid the merry-go-rounds, booths, and stalls of the fairgrounds. The previously regular rhythmic pulse yields at this point to a polymetrical series of measures (Bars 69 to 77) consisting of such irregular units as 3/4, 2/4, 3/8, 4/8, and 5/8—a highly effective device to describe the irregular movements of the jostling crowds as they go this way then that, as well as to create contrast for the succession of bizarre dances that momentarily command their attention. Stravinsky's orchestra, meanwhile, functions like a gigantic accordion giving out a flood of blatantly raucous but festive music.

In the First Tableau a barrel-organ grinder plays banal hurdy-gurdy tunes while a dancer pivots and pirouettes on the tips of her toes. The piquant instrumentation here simulates the barrel organ by combining the piccolo, two flutes, three clarinets, bass clarinet, and triangle. Some competing entertainers on the other side of the stage then distract the fickle attention of the crowds with a music box. Next the Charlatan, a somewhat sinister-appearing showman whom the people regard with superstitious awe, appears before his puppet theater and draws an audience around him with an ingratiating melody on the flute. With a flourish he pulls up the curtain to reveal three marionettes with limp bodies and masklike faces—the Ballerina in the center, with Petrouchka and the Moor on either side. As the strings tighten, their inert, sawdust-filled bodies jerk to attention for the performance of the "Russian Dance." This masterpiece of calculated mechanical rhythms and percussive brittle sounds is well adapted for the automaton's dance, but an occasional lyric phrase suggests that even such inanimate creatures are capable of animate longings. There is also a rugged peasant vigor in this dance that has nationalistic overtones, as is the case also with many of the dances that follow.

The Second Tableau takes us behind the scenes and, beginning with Petrouchka, introduces each puppet individually. Petrouchka is the Russian counterpart of the Punch in Punch-and-Judy shows, whom Stravinsky himself has characterized as the "immortal and unhappy hero of every fair in all countries . . . the poor, funny, ugly, sentimental, and misguided creature, constantly shaken with rebellious rage, whether justified or not, who is known in France as Pierrot, in Germany as Kasperl, and in Russia as Petrouchka." Here he also resembles the lovelorn Pierrot of the Italian *commedia dell' arte*, pining for the fickle affections of the flirtatious Ballerina, who for her part is infatuated with the sinister Moor. "Petrouchka's Dance," with its sharp angular movements and harsh dissonant harmonies, expresses the despair of an ardent soul imprisoned in the body of a clown whom no one will take seriously. His dual nature is well symbolized in the bitonal chord that accompanies him—a C-major triad followed by or superimposed with an F-sharp-major "shadow." Interestingly enough, the whole ballet had its inception in Stravinsky's mind with this dance. At first it occurred to him as a piano concerto; but it eventually shaped up, as the composer himself relates in his memoirs, as a picture of a "puppet, suddenly endowed with life, exasperating the patience of the orchestra with diabolical cascades of arpeggios. The orchestra in turn retaliates with menacing trumpet blasts. The outcome is a terrific noise which reaches its climax and ends in the sorrowful and querulous collapse of the poor puppet. . . ."

The Third Tableau is in the Moor's room, and the mysterious, slightly menacing music Stravinsky writes for his dance is at once exotic and evil. He is interrupted by the Ballerina who enters to the roll of a snare drum and a flourish on the cornet. Mad with jealousy, Petrouchka bursts in and quarrels with the Moor. The fourth and final Tableau returns to the crowded market place where toward evening the hurly-burly of the crowds and kaleidoscopic glimpses of their revelry continues. The "Dance of the Nursemaids," based on an old Russian folk tune, is followed by the entrance of a peasant with a trained bear, whose grotesque movements are characterized by an awkward tuba solo sounding against some opaque chords in the lower string register. In turn, there are gypsy dances to the accompaniment of a simulated orchestral accordion, the "Dance of the Coachmen and Grooms," and finally the appearance of some masqueraders dressed in devil and animal costumes. As the revelry approaches its height the scene is interrupted by the entrance of Petrouchka wildly pursued by the Moor. The Ballerina vainly tries to restrain him, but he frees himself and stabs Petrouchka. For the brief death scene Stravinsky devises some remarkably poignant sounds. A melody that recalls "Petrouchka's Dance," with the symbolic bitonal chord as its motive, is carried in turn by the clarinet, violin, bassoon, and piccolo playing solo against the tremolo of muted violins and the harmonics of the violas.

The Charlatan arrives in time to reassure the bystanders that it is all dumb-show and make-believe. He picks up the limp body of Petrouchka, now bleeding with sawdust, in order to throw him behind the scenes. While the motley crowd disperses, however, the spirit of Petrouchka reappears above the puppet stage in a kind of mock apotheosis. He makes grimaces at the showman while the orchestra plays a shrieking dissonance and the curtain is rung down. Many philosophical, political, and allegorical interpretations have been attempted, and certainly the satire and subtlety of the score do not invite a literal conception. Since none of these is in any sense definitive, it is just as well to be content with the fruitful results of Stravinsky's fertile rhythmic and harmonic invention and let the eloquent score speak for itself.

From this point onward Stravinsky's creative work moved constantly toward greater economy of means and increasingly abstract tonal designs. The transitional phase is found in his choreographic cantata *The Wedding* (1917) and the mimed play *Soldier's Tale* (1918), in both of which the growing prominence of the music itself is symbolized by his placing the instruments on the stage where the movements of the players are integrated with the ballet action. As Stravinsky points out, "The sight of the gesture and movement of the different parts of the body that produce it (the music) are essential to seizing it in all its breadth." In the *History of the Soldier* there is a spoken part for narrator, while three characters—the Soldier, the Princess, and the Devil—mime the action to the accompaniment of a seven-piece instrumental ensemble. Combining qualities of intensity and intimacy, this is a bitter but beautiful modern version of an ancient fairy tale.

While the three great early ballets as well as those of the transitional period are nationalistic and folkloristic in orientation, Stravinsky's later efforts moved into the international orbit of neoclassicism. The early Stravinsky still is capable of making subjective personal statements, but in the later years all is objectively detached. More and more he speaks about "construction" and "achieved order" as his creative ideals; and in regard to the ballet he professes to see in classical dancing the "triumph of studied conception over vagueness, of the rule over the arbitrary, of order over the haphazard." In works such as *Pulcinella* (1920) , he recreates the eighteenth century in a score that becomes a contemporary commentary on the music of Pergolesi; while *Oedipus Rex* (1927) , *Apollo* (1928) , *Persephone* (1934) , and *Orpheus* (1948) are all obviously Greek in inspiration. One of his most recent works—*Agon, A Ballet for Twelve Solo Dancers* (1957) —is simply a series of stylized dance movements, all modeled on seventeenth-century and eighteenth-century French forms such as the musette, branle, and sarabande. For all their cool detachment and formal purity, such dance sequences are nevertheless an outgrowth of what has gone before and are thus oriented stylistically in space and time; and, no matter how restricted and refined, they still mirror some aspects of basic human attitudes and emotions. Whatever the creative problem Stravinsky sets for himself, it is always carried out with the customary Stravinsian conciseness and consummate sense of craftsmanship.

Some modern choreographers have tried to move away from what they call the "tyranny of the plot," just as modern painters such as Kandinski have broken with subject matter as well as representation and constructed their pictures with freely moving lines and splotches of color in the so-called nonobjective style. The abstract ballet is thus not so much concerned with narrative elements as it is with pure dance invention, as well as rhythmic, plastic, and formal movement for its own sake. As such, the dances tend toward the abstract aspects of the musical scores that accompany them, and they thus become a species of visible music. Balanchine's ballet called *Concerto Barocco,* by way of example, is a choreographic version of Bach's Concerto for Two Violins and Orchestra. In it, two dancers are the visual equivalent of the concerting solo violins; the rhythmic pulsations correspond to the changes in meter and tempo; the entrances and exits are regulated by the thematic entries; the visual lines are coordinated with the contours of the melodic phrases; and the grouping of figures is synchronized with the tuttis and solos, textural contrasts, and dynamic fluctuations of the score.

Other aspects of the modern dance have struck out on paths that lead away from all formal restrictions and restraints. Unimpeded by the tradition of the classical ballet, they allow the body to move in any direction, limited only by the basic laws of anatomy. The expressionistic dances of Isadora Duncan, Mary Wigman, and Martha Graham, for instance, are thus able by means of the human body to develop a vocabulary of symbolic gestures and movements designed to give plastic shape to the secret longings, hidden fears, dark passions, and all the wild dreams that emanate from the psychological subconscious. In all these modern phases music continues its age-old partnership with the dance, and all the choreographic experiments in new rhythmic, dynamic, coloristic, and formal approaches are paralleled by corresponding developments in the scores that composers provide for the ballet.

Union of Music and Drama: Opera and Oratorio

Chapter 15

OPERA

THE notion that an opera is a play with music contains enough apparent truth to be seriously misleading. To be sure, in an opera there is a play and there is also music; but there are plays with music like Shakespeare's *Merchant of Venice* or *Richard II* which are hardly operas, although the music, when called for, is an important component of the drama. Nor is opera necessarily the kind of play where all the words, or nearly all, are sung; for Mozart's *Magic Flute* is an opera, although much of the text is spoken.

The tangle of misconceptions can be avoided by recognizing to begin with that opera is theater, and that a concert performance of the music, however gratifying, robs the music of its function on stage and hence destroys it as opera. Opera, then, is a special kind of theater. Yet, however particular it may be unto itself, it shares certain fundamentals with drama of every type. It is concerned, as theater must necessarily be, with the projection of character on stage; with the complex of relationships between

179

characters; with the situations in which these relationships develop; with the reactions to and solutions of situations; and with motivations for such reactions and solutions. In summary, opera is concerned with the total complex of character and situation, which is called plot.

Yet for character and situation to be realized on stage, there must be a complex of dramatizing media through which such a realization is effected. Many kinds of theater operate on the basis not of one, but of several coordinated dramatic mechanisms—a complex, for example, of word, song, gesture, physical movement, etc. Essentially what differentiates one type of theater from another is the choice of that mechanism in the complex which is to function as the central dramatic agent, the fundamental medium to which all other media are related in the projection and probing of character and situation. An ill-conceived relationship or an unimaginative coordination may well produce results that are distracting or dull. Too often, for example, no distinction is made between a motion picture and a filmed play; and the camera (which should come into its own as a strategic dramatic mechanism in a motion picture) is often reduced to the boring business of "filming" the characters as they close and open doors. In an unimaginative transference of a play onto film, the camera is used to record rather than to comment upon. As a result its value as a dramatizing agent is overlooked, and its role is reduced to mere routine. Where a genuine translation is made from a play into a film, the camera (after all, the one dramatic mechanism which makes a film different from any other type of theater) is given a truly imaginative dramatic role. In the Laurence Olivier production of Shakespeare's *Henry V,* for example, the impact of Henry's soliloquy on the eve of battle is enormously heightened by the camera as it moves around the camp; Shakespeare's poetry (spoken off stage as it were) now functions as a profoundly human commentary on the scenes the camera selects for the viewer's inspection. It is the role of the camera, then, which makes this a motion picture of *Henry V* rather than a film record of the play.

Ballet is still another kind of theater. In this case, the most primitive and potentially the most moving of dramatic media—human gesture and the movement of the human body—is the central fact, with the music functioning as an indispensable adjunct, helping in the control, the coordination, the outlining, and the underlining of movement and gesture. Here it is the choreographer who is the dramatist, not the composer or the author of the scenario; for it is the choreographer who, with his understanding of the expressive potential of the human body, must conceive and plan the evolving pattern of movement and gesture, which is the drama in ballet. A fine musical score is most welcome, but it cannot in itself guarantee the success of the ballet as effective theater.

In comparable fashion, opera is that type of theater where music is the central dramatic agent, and where, through music, character is made understandable. The heroine is, dramatically speaking, the music she sings; and it is through music that the situation is interpreted. No justification of opera would be necessary in Italy where, for several centuries, it has been the national form of theater. This is hardly the case in England, although in this country the species of opera (or lyric theater) which is called musical comedy has some claim to the status of indigenous theater. Unfortunately, the peculiar snobbery of the Anglo-American theater holds as "legitimate" only that species of stage where character and situation are projected through the spoken word. By implication, theater centered around another dramatic mechanism is presumed disreputable in parentage, foreign in nature, and suspect in social status. The mechanisms of opera require no defense in moral terms, but simply explanation as theater. Regardless of legitimacy, in opera it is the composer who is the dramatist, and the world stage is the richer for possessing Mozart and Verdi, as well as Shakespeare and Shaw.

To repeat: Opera is that type of theater where music is the central dramatic agent. A good play is certainly a help, although it is no guarantee that it, in itself, can ensure the opera's success. Further, what constitutes a good *libretto* for opera is often much different from what constitutes a good play. Usually a play must first be converted into a libretto before the composer can use it, just as it must first be reconstituted as a scenario or script before a motion picture can be made of it. An opera libretto or a film script cannot be judged independently as literature, since neither was ever intended to have esthetic meaning or merit apart from the opera or the film for which it was designed. The objection that a play is ruined when it is reworked as an opera libretto is as senseless as the objection that stone is spoiled when it is cut for use in a building. To hold that opera involves inferior literature is as pertinent as to observe that a stone building involves desecrated geology. A mediocre play like Victorien Sardou's *La Tosca* is not automatically fatal to an opera, for the libretto which Luigi Illica and Giuseppe Giacosa made of it is, purely as a libretto, first rate. Puccini, it should be remembered, worked with the libretto, not with the play. On the contrary, a bad libretto (regardless of its source) is always an inconvenience. If it is bad enough, it is a catastrophe, for it can defeat opera composers as courageous as Schubert and as cunning as Rossini.

In opera, music is composed in terms of the stage, and its function as theater is paramount. Where the composer lacks an infallible instinct for the stage or a true sense for theater (as was the case often with Schubert and seldom with Puccini), or where the conventions that govern a particular type of theater have, in a later age, grown so obsolete or so remote from current practice as to render the work pointless and difficult to relate to as theater (as has happened with the operas of Handel or Spontini), then the opera loses its viability as theater. The excellence of the music alone, regarded for its own sake, is not sufficient to maintain the opera on the stage. The music, as music, can be rescued by excerpting the best portions of it for concert use, but under such circumstances it is no longer opera.

It happens sometimes that large stretches of music, enormously exciting on the stage and fully understandable only in the actuality of performance in the theater, may seem undirected or downright dull when transposed to the concert hall or excerpted for inclusion in a record album. There are pages of this kind in the operas of Puccini. This music is unrewarding only in the wrong context, just as a grand piano is unrewarding if one uses it to sleep in. But it can also be true—and operas like Mozart's *Marriage of Figaro* or *Don Giovanni* are excellent examples—that the music, superbly conceived in terms of character and situation and functioning naturally and profoundly on the stage, can then be detached from the theater, and yet remain, simply as music, completely comprehensible and completely captivating. However, when we listen to it as music, for its own sake, we are not listening to it as theater. Two different levels of listening are involved. It is possible to keep them separate from one another and to "appreciate" the music in each case for different reasons. Or, if one is skillful enough and knowledgeable enough in the listening process, the two levels can be combined in a more complex unity of comprehension and enjoyment.

That music provides the basic dramatic mechanisms in opera is understandable enough. But what may cause discomfort are the conventions that have grown up around these mechanisms and which condition their use. There are few things seemingly as funny, or as offensive to what is generally considered common sense, as conventions that evolve from an unfamiliar context. And at no point is criticism of opera more replete with irrelevancies than that sector of it that deals with a supposedly common-sense criticism of its conventions. Now conventions are useful things, and it is quite doubtful that society could get along without them. They are founded sometimes in reason and always in expediency. In art, as in any other aspect of life, a convention is simply an agreement to do certain things in certain ways. In all forms of art, and in particular those addressed to a large public, conventions are a great convenience for they ensure ease and intelligibility of communication from artist to audience. As in life, so in art, a convention can become constrictive when construed in too absolute a sense, when held as holy and hence as unchangeable, or when permitted to condition a course of action too literally and too completely.

Forms of art that are both public and expensive, like opera, church architecture, or the motion picture, are especially susceptible to the degenera-
tion of once meaningful conventions into esthetically meaningless clichés.
The reform of accepted practice in these fields is never easy. One has only
to witness the literary wars that have been fought over the "reform of
opera" in the cases of Gluck or Wagner; the bewilderment of a community
when confronted with a new concept of what a neighborhood church
ought to look like; the caution of a low budget for a film production that
risks even a modest deviation from those conventions of character and
situation that have been sanctified by financial success.

However, conventions change even in opera. In any given opera some
of the conventions may be time-bound—that is, specific to the period when
the opera was composed—yet still viable when treated with understanding
on the stage. One simply needs a proper esthetic perspective as well as a
sense for the type of stage upon which a particular operatic convention
such as the aria, for example, can function with ease. Once the function
of an aria in a drama is understood, it is, as a convention, no more artificial
than conventions usually are, and no sillier than conventions which are
accepted as sensible in other types of theater.

Take, for instance, the convention of an aria in an opera. An aria is a
self-contained musical number. Within itself it possesses a formal integrity
which often invites excision from the opera and transplantation to the
concert platform as an independent solo piece. Since in the operas of
Wagner a continuous chain of music is posited as the basic convention,
formal, self-contained arias are rare. Actually the aria belongs to the type
of opera which is called *number opera*. (The type is often strongly modified and varied, but any opera with self-contained musical numbers is, to
a degree at least, a number opera.) The designation "number opera" is a
tautology, since *opera*, as the plural of *opus*, means in this connection a
drama conceived as a sequence of musical "numbers." Since Wagner substituted a continuous chain of music for a sequence of self-contained musical numbers, he insisted that his work was not *opera* but *music drama*.
There is less here than meets the eye, for opera is also music drama, albeit
music drama with non-Wagnerian conventions.

Among the many functions of an aria in one or another species of
number opera, the following facts are frequently encountered. In the
course of the action on stage, the composer decides—and as dramatist it is
his choice—that the moment has come for the events to be understood in
terms of an individual participating in them. Action is reduced to a minimum and effectively frozen for the moment; the stage becomes in a physical sense relatively static; and a character, the heroine let us say, steps forward for an aria. The music sung at this point by the heroine *is* the her-

and her relationship to the situation thus far unfolded. This personalized emotional record, this inner history, is needed at this point, if the drama is to be a drama of human beings rather than of puppets. This convention is artificial to be sure; but opera is not on this account a species of prolonged affectation or a form of unnatural idiocy. As a convention, the aria is no more and no less artificial or profound than the comparable convention of a soliloquy in a Shakespeare play. It can be abused, and the abuse derives from a peculiarity of grand opera to which the composer may willingly or involuntarily fall victim. Opera is a public and expensive art form. The leading roles in it are necessarily taken by people who, on the one hand, are characters in a play and, on the other, famous singers. There is a duality here which the composer, as a dramatist, would like to suppress, concentrating exclusively upon aria as the projection of a character in a drama, rather than aria as the projection of the vocal talents of a particular singer. There is, unfortunately, a species of commercialized box-office opera where the leading role is meant to be performed by a famous prima donna, where the audience has come as much to hear her sing as to witness a drama, and where, in consequence, the composer may feel prevailed upon to interrupt the drama for no other purpose than to offer the star an opportunity to display her vocal elegance and dexterity. Box-office conventions of this sort occur, and sometimes rather crudely, in operas by Bellini and Donizetti. Mozart, however, had a singular ability to maneuver through such difficult moments, usually without making significant compromises, for he had an uncommon instinct for conceiving even a coloratura passage as a display of character.

Perversions of the dramatic meaning of an operatic convention do exist, just as violations of traffic conventions are not uncommon. But if an argument is to be made, it must be directed against the commercialized abuse of a convention, rather than against the convention per se. To hold that, even in its best use, an aria is unnatural is to confuse life and art. If men, exhausted and near death, do not customarily arise to sing heroic arias in voices strong enough to fill an opera house, then by like token men do not, Hamletlike, sit on curbstones declaiming to arrested traffic their convictions on happiness and the hereafter. Nothing is as natural as nature, or as true to life as life itself. A work of art is, as the word itself implies, an artifice, a construct of a man's imagination. It does not duplicate the world and the people in it, but rather it interprets them. And an aria is an interpretation, through music, of a human being. By convention, the aria isolates him, indeed insulates him, momentarily from the context of circumstance (the action on stage). This, to probe him more deeply and project him more profoundly as a human being, before restoring him to the continuum of the drama.

It is possible to make a catalogue of operatic conventions and append a generalized critical justification of each. However, since the validity of a convention must derive from its function at a particular moment in a drama, it seems more feasible to focus the discussion in a more practical and particular way. Mozart's *Don Giovanni* will be used for illustrative purposes here. Mozart is a master dramatist, and his *Don Giovanni* provides illustrations worth the closest study.

MOZART'S DON GIOVANNI

The opera *Don Giovanni* is based on the legend of Don Juan. During the seventeenth and eighteenth centuries in Italy, Spain, France, England, and Germany, the legend served as the source for numerous theatrical productions (plays, plays with music, puppet plays, and operas). In 1761, Gluck and Noverre used it for a famous ballet, and for a dozen years prior to the premier of the Mozart-Da Ponte version (October 1787 in Prague) it was a subject common enough on the Italian opera stage. Its popularity with theater audiences was, no doubt, a factor that figured in its choice by Mozart and Da Ponte for their opera. Certain conventions in the telling of the story were known and expected ahead of time by Mozart's audiences. For example, there were two aspects to the Don Juan legend: the Don as the fabulous lover, and the Don as a sinner who is carried off to hell for his transgressions. The theater-going sophisticate of Mozart's day could relish the comedy of the Don's amorous adventures, the loose talk, and the astounding heroism of the Don in defying the terrors of the supernatural as well as his refusal to repent even on the brink of eternal damnation; and he could also tolerate (with some amusement, no doubt) the sop to the sanctimonious tacked on to the close of the opera, where all remaining characters assemble on stage following the heroic death of the Don and enjoin the audience to ponder well whether they are heaven-bound or, like Don Giovanni, headed straight for hell. The supernatural agency invoked for the moral part of the story is the stone guest, a graveyard statue of Donna Anna's father, the Commendatore, whom the Don had slain in a duel early in the opera. That the stone guest would appear and the Don go to his doom, were foregone conclusions for Mozart's audiences.

That an overture to an opera as full of life and laughter as *Don Giovanni* should begin in a glowering and fateful fashion was a cause for neither dismay nor mystification. It is the stone-guest music, and a reminder before the curtain goes up of the doom which awaits the Don, and it is heard again toward the close of the opera. The *overture,* as an operatic convention, has a number of possible uses. Sometimes it is a completely detachable orchestral composition bearing a minimum of relationship to the opera which is to follow. One suspects from the lively, festive fashion in which nothing of importance either musically or dramatically is said in some of these overtures, that the composer intended them as background music for saying hello to your neighbor, waving to a friend, and settling down before the opera begins. The overture, however, often has a relationship to the drama. It may set the mood for the first act; it may even preview important melodies to be heard later on in a more specific dramatic context. Some overtures are thus detachable and may be used as concert pieces, while others lead without interruption directly into the opera.

The Overture to *Don Giovanni* is, in the main, bound to the drama. The slow, dramatic introduction is a preview of the stone-guest music and the fate of the Don. The main body of the Overture, however, is a bright allegro movement, its high spirits setting the tone for much of the opera to follow. It is not detachable but leads directly to the first scene. The key relationships make this clear. The slow introduction is in D minor (Mozart's "storm-and-stress" key), while the main bulk of the Overture (allegro) is in D major. But the Overture closes in C major, and the reason for closing away from the tonic (D major) is that Leporello's first number is in F major. C is the dominant of F, and hence the strongest base from which a transition to F can be made. Without pause then, the key relationship carries us from the Overture into the opera proper. What intervenes necessarily is the raising of the curtain, and this too is on signal from the music.

Ex. 15:1   Overture to *Don Giovanni* (Bars 282–292). Mozart.

Mozart is thorough and meticulous in observing the stage function of his music. The last seven measures of the Overture (Ex. 15:1) mark the raising of the curtain. They do not conclude the Overture, but lift the curtain on Leporello, the Don's manservant, pacing back and forth in front of the residence of the Commendatore and his daughter, Donna Anna.

It is night. The Don has stolen into the house under cover of darkness to force his attentions (which, no doubt, he assumes will be welcome) upon Donna Anna, leaving his servant, Leporello, on sentry duty outside. There are three principal ingredients to the little aria which Leporello sings, and each has its function. The first (Ex. 15:2) is a pacing motive announced by the orchestra, which literally paces him back and forth on the stage. The orchestra even turns him forcibly around and sets him pacing the other way (asterisk in Ex. 15:2).

Ex. 15:2   Act I, Scene I, *Don Giovanni* (Bars 1–4). Mozart.

Leporello takes up this pacing motive and to it outlines the sad lot of a servant who slaves night and day, eating poorly and seldom sleeping. A gentleman is what he would like to be. And for this line of text his music flows in a lordly legato, while the violins accompany with the trills and the graces characteristic of the gallant, aristocratic music of Mozart's day. (The *gallant* was one of the primary styles in late eighteenth-century music, and Mozart's audiences would recognize almost intuitively even a fleeting reference to it.)

Ex. 15:3   Act I, Scene I, *Don Giovanni* (Bars 20–23). Mozart.

The third component restores Leporello to reality and to his role as the comic, complaining servant. It is a "patter" motive, so often encountered in comic characterizations. It is heard, for instance, when he protests that he is sick of being a servant (Ex. 15:4) and again when, in a spate of

Ex. 15:4   Act I, Scene I, *Don Giovanni* (Bars 28–32). Mozart.

Ex. 15:5 Act I, Scene I, *Don Giovanni* (Bars 61–62). Mozart.

che ven-ga gen-te; non mi vo-glio far sen-tir,
(I hear people coming I'd rather not stay around)

words, he babbles about his fear of discovery (Ex. 15:5), for on his back
often fall the blows paid out for his master's misbehavior.

Noises are heard within, Leporello hides, and Don Giovanni and
Donna Anna enter. However, they do not simply rush on stage. The music,
as always, is the principal agent in this drama and, just as the orchestra
had previously signaled the raising of the curtain, so here it literally
sweeps the two antagonists onto the stage, communicating in five short
measures of crescendo their state of comic frenzy before either has had a
line of text to sing.

Ex. 15:6 Act I, Scene I, *Don Giovanni* (Bars 70–73). Mozart.

What follows now is one of the conventions, peculiar to the opera,
which composers like Mozart, Rossini, and Verdi often exploit with singular dramatic felicity. It is the *ensemble*. Several characters are gathered on
stage, and they all talk at once. While Mozart's purpose at this point is
comedy, the ensemble is adaptable to many moods and a wide diversity
of dramatic purposes. In a play without music, everybody talking at the
same time produces confusion. It is a serviceable device if the playwright
desires to mirror the confusion and astonishment caused by a surprise
announcement, or if his purpose is simply to create a comic uproar. An
ensemble in music can likewise create such effects; but since it operates on
a principle intrinsic to singing and not to speech, it can do much more.
Three people talking at the same time tend to nullify one another. Three
people singing at the same time can be heard, if the composer is careful to
control the part writing, on two different levels simultaneously: together
as a single unit (a trio) and, despite their togetherness, as individual components within the trio. Both the unity and the parts that comprise it can
thus be heard at one and the same time. All counterpoint is based on this
duality in listening. In an opera, moreover, since the separate voice parts
emanate from different people on the stage, it is not tremendously difficult to hear this separateness and togetherness simultaneously. The sense

of what each is saying can be safeguarded by the clarity with which the musical lines are interwoven, even though some of the words may get lost.

Like any other operatic convention, the ensemble can be abused. There used to be a type of box-office opera which lured customers by advertising an all-star cast—four or six famous singers instead of one. At a point in the plot where they would all be found together on stage, the composer would oblige with a set ensemble piece such as a quartet or sextet. The piece, to be sure, could be sung with a decent regard for the blending of parts into an overall unity. But it did happen (and there are old 78 rpm records to prove it) that some in the all-star cast were ready to rend the music limb from limb, each endeavoring, for the edification of the audience and the utter despair of the composer, to outscream his companions. In such a box-office ensemble piece, the composer was sometimes content with only the minimum relevance between the music and the dramatic context in which it was presumably to function. The famous sextet from Donizetti's *Lucia da Lammermoor* is, certainly, a fine bit of ensemble writing. But it would take a most generous appreciation, and a rather easy-going set of dramatic standards, to find in its pleasant, charming, and rather sentimental tunefulness much that accords with either the extravagantly melodramatic situation or with the horrendous nature of its text. The equally famous quartet from Verdi's *Rigoletto* is, to the contrary, a most responsible (that is, dramatically functional) example of ensemble. Every voice in the ensemble is kept in focus as belonging to a particular character in a particular situation. Each voice contributes to the ensemble a line of melody completely in character with the individual singing it, and completely consonant with how each character might reasonably react to the situation at hand. The unity of the ensemble is built out of the dramatic juxtaposition of four divergent points of view expressed simultaneously: the Duke's elegant and licentious flattery, Maddelena's giggling, flirtatious small talk, Gilda's pathetic outcries as she watches while her beloved betrays her, and Rigoletto's solicitude for his daughter. The *Rigoletto* quartet is very nearly an ideal example of what an operatic ensemble ought to be: a counterpoint of dramatic characterizations as well as of voice parts.

To return now to *Don Giovanni*: The Don and Donna Anna are swept on stage (Ex. 15:6) in a high state of excitement. His attentions have been decidedly unwelcome; Donna Anna is determined to know the identity of her attacker, and the Don is equally determined to keep his face concealed. Leporello is convinced that none of this bodes him any good. The Commendatore, Donna Anna's father, arrives. She rushes indoors to fetch help. The Commendatore orders the Don to defend himself. At first the Don refuses, feeling it beneath his dignity to fight with an old man. But the Commendatore insists, and the Don, growing impatient, draws his sword. They fight a duel, and the Commendatore falls fatally wounded. The Commendatore calls for help while Don Giovanni and Leporello observe his last moments. He dies. Don Giovanni calls to Leporello and, after a brief dialogue, they leave.

This scene is worth examining in some detail for it is a splendid example of the composer's salient role as dramatist. The text for the scene is given in its entirety.

DONNA ANNA:	(*Clutching Don Giovanni's arm*) You'll not escape unless you kill me.	
DON GIOVANNI:	(*Trying to hide his face*) You're crazy! Screaming won't help. You'll never find out.	
DONNA A.:	You'll not escape, etc.	
DON G.:	You're crazy! etc.	*Together*
LEPORELLO:	What a racket! God, what screaming. My master's in another jam.	
DONNA A.:	Help! Help! Seize the traitor!	
DON G.:	Be quiet or you'll be sorry!	
DONNA A.:	Scoundrel!	
DON G.:	Lunatic!	
DONNA A.:	Scoundrel!	
DON G.:	Lunatic!	
LEP.:	It's plain this rascal will be my undoing.	*Together*
DONNA A.:	Help! Help!	(*This portion of*
DON G.:	Be quiet and beware!	*text and music*
DONNA A.:	Like a raging fury will I pursue you.	*repeated.*)
DON G.:	This raging fury wants to destroy me.	
LEP.:	What a racket! God, what screaming. It's plain this rascal will be my undoing.	
	(*The Commendatore arrives. Donna Anna, hearing her father's voice, releases Don Giovanni and hurries into the house.*)	*Orchestra* (*4 measures*)
COMM.:	Unhand her, wretch, and draw your sword.	
DON G.:	Come now! I can't duel with an old man.	
COMM.:	On this pretense you seek to escape me?	

LEP.:	I'd do anything to get out of here.	
DON G.:	Come now! I can't fight you. No!	
COMM.:	On this pretense you seek to escape me?	
LEP.:	I'd do anything, etc.	*Together*
DON G.:	Fool!	
COMM.	Fight!	
DON G.:	Fool!	
LEP.:	I'd do anything, etc.	

DON G.:   Miserable fool! On guard then, since you want to die.

	(They fight. The Commendatore falls fatally wounded.)	*Orchestra (9 measures)*

COMM.:	Ah, help me! I am betrayed! The assassin has run me through. From my throbbing breast I feel my soul take leave. *(Dies.)*	
DON G.:	Ah, the wretch has fallen. He draws his breath in agony. From his throbbing breast I see his soul take leave.	*Together (sotto voce)*
LEP.:	What a crime! A crime beyond reason! My heart is pounding in my breast. I don't know what to do or say.	

(Four measures for orchestra, after the Commendatore dies. Don Giovanni and Leporello remain silent.)

DON G.:	*(Whispering)* Leporello, where are you?	
LEP.:	I'm here, worse luck. And you?	
DON G.:	I'm here.	
LEP.:	Who's dead, you or the old man?	
DON G.:	What a stupid question! The old man.	
LEP.:	Congratulations! Two charming accomplishments! Rape the daughter and kill her father!	*Dialogue in recitativo secco*
DON G.:	His hard luck. He was hankering for it.	
LEP.:	And Donna Anna, what was she hankering for?	
DON G.:	Shut up, and don't bother me. Let's go. Unless you're hankering for something too. *(Threatens to strike him.)*	
LEP.:	No thank you master. I am happy with what I have. I'll say not another word. *(They leave).*	

Mozart has designed this scene, except for the concluding dialogue, as a sequence of ensemble trios. Throughout the scene, the stage is tremendously active. The scene is divided into several clearly marked sections: the comic uproar with the Don trying to pull himself loose from Donna Anna; the more serious exchange between the Commendatore and the Don, leading to the duel and the death of the Commendatore; and, finally, the brief dialogue serving as exit lines for Leporello and the Don. It is the composer who selects the lines to be repeated, and the composer who decides when a line will be sung unencumbered by interruption from another character and when several lines of text will be sung simultaneously. This balance must be viable on stage. The ensemble writing (where the three sing together) is not continuous, but is alternated with passages in which each character sings separately. This blend of clarity and deliberate confusion, projects, in the first trio, the uproar of voices arguing and babbling at cross purposes, without blurring the focus in which each character is set. Interestingly enough, in this first trio (Donna Anna, Don Giovanni, Leporello), the two male voices might be expected to pair together as more similar to one another in range and color than either could be to a soprano. Actually Mozart consistently pairs Donna Anna's and Don Giovanni's voices together, while Leporello's part is independent of either. This is dramatically exact, for the conflict is between Donna Anna and Don Giovanni. They are the primary characters in the action, while Leporello stands apart to observe and comment. The music thus makes this dramatic distinction clear (Ex. 15:7).

Ex. 15:7   Act I, Scene I, *Don Giovanni* (Bars 102–109). Mozart.

Four measures for orchestra take Donna Anna off stage and bring the Commendatore on. The music, appropriately styled to the circumstances, consistently takes care of this stage business of entrances and exits. The abrupt, declamatory manner of the cellos, violas, and bassoon, under a sustained woodwind harmony and a shuddering sixteenth-note repetition of a single tone high in the violins, prepares the entry of the Commendatore who is prone to a sobriety verging on the pompous, and to the striking of eminently honorable attitudes. In another context he might well have been the foil for Mozart's wit. But here he comes to challenge the Don and to go to his death, and Mozart provides a certain seriousness to the musical style of his declarations which subtly infects the entire scene. His challenge and the Don's refusal ring out clearly, for each is sung separately. Instantly the voices tangle in conflict, with Leporello adding his point of view. This, however, is brief, for patience is not part of the Don's character, nor is it germane to this heated scene. The last line, in which the Don tells the Commendatore to prepare to die, is placed shrewdly in a dramatic spotlight, for it is to lead to the tragedy. It is detached from the ensemble, sung without the encumbrance of other voices, and given weight as well as a certain gravity of emphasis, by the long note values to which the syllables are declaimed (Ex. 15:8).

Ex. 15:8   Act I, Scene I, *Don Giovanni* (Bars 160–166). Mozart.

mi – se – ro! at – ten – di,   se   vuoi   mo – rir!
(poor fool! on guard then,   since you want to die)

The duel is depicted in nine swift measures by the orchestra in music apt for the occasion. When the Commendatore falls, the ensemble that ensues answers a purpose much different from the two that preceded it. The scene that began as comedy ends with what must be, in any reasonably sensible drama, a tragedy: the death of a human being. The Commendatore is dying and Mozart seizes upon this as a moment of inwardness, a moment in which each character must evaluate the situation within himself. There are few scenes in opera more humanly moving than this trio, where Mozart has conceived each of the three men as alone within himself on the stage. In a play three short soliloquies, or asides, might be in order, with an appropriate verbal imagery to explicate and orchestrate the feelings of each. In opera, three separate arias would become necessary if one is to know what is happening within each man's soul. The time factor, however, is prohibitive; for these meditations on a static stage would wear out the audience's supply of sympathy if protracted into three separate arias. The three meditations, each from a separate point of view, are projected, in this case, simultaneously in ensemble, unified by that sobriety which falls upon all alike in the presence of the dying. And again, it is through the music that the inwardness of each man's feeling and the unity of mood are created and sustained.

The Commendatore dies. The Don and Leporello are no longer needed on stage. The crime which motivates the story has been accomplished, and thereafter the story is concerned with the pursuit of the Don, and his ultimate punishment. An exit aria for the Don would be redundant following the trio and, in any case, would rob the next scene of its dramatic purpose. Obviously the stage must be readied for the emotional scene which is to follow: the reappearance of Donna Anna, her discovery of her father's body, and the inevitable vow of vengeance. The Don takes Leporello off stage in a brief dialogue that is managed musically through an operatic convention called a "recitative."

A *recitative* is speech (or literally, recitation) on musical tones. Here the relationship between speaking and singing is much more direct than in an aria. The raw materials for recitative are the musical components inherent in speech: speech rhythms, speech melody or the pitch variations of the voice, and the weight, density, color, swiftness, or slowness of words when they are spoken. Recitative is, to use a rather barbarous word, speech "musicalized." In the Italian opera of Mozart's day, there were two kinds of recitative in common use. The first, called *recitativo secco* (dry recitative), was used primarily for quick entrances and exits, desultory conversations, the routine of messages, reading of letters, or instructions to a lady in waiting. It was the ordinary and necessary business of the stage that was largely transacted in this *secco* recitative. The orchestra remained silent, while the conductor, presiding at the keyboard instrument, provided a few chords in the manner of harmonic punctuation marks to ground the singers as they recited their text on musical tones. The word *secco* (dry) accurately describes this type of recitative.

The second type answered quite another purpose. Here the orchestra was involved, and hence this type was called *recitativo stromentato* (literally "instrumented recitative," or "orchestrally accompanied recitative," but usually referred to simply as "accompanied recitative"). The terminology is somewhat unfortunate, since *secco* recitative is not, strictly speaking, unaccompanied. This accompanied recitative, in which the orchestra punctuated the vocal phrases, was eminently useful for the striking of heroic poses, for strongly emotional declamations, or for the build-up that might reasonably precede a grand aria.

The Don takes Leporello off stage in a *secco* dialogue. Following directly upon the deeply moving trio, this has an unceremonious abruptness, a dry brutality, that accords well with the Don's character, and serves as a foil for Donna Anna's outpouring of emotion which is in the offing. Donna Anna and Don Ottavio, her betrothed, enter hurriedly. She is telling him, and her words are heard almost in midsentence, that her father was here just a moment ago. This too is the sort of conversational entrance fit for *secco* recitative. And hence the exit of one pair (the Don and Leporello) and the entrance of the other (Donna Anna and Don Ottavio) are both effected through the same device. This is better theater than the listener is liable to realize, for the continuity in the convention that takes one pair off and brings another on effects a seamless transition on stage from the completion of one level of action to the beginning of another (see Ex. 15:9).

The change from *secco* to accompanied recitative marks the moment when Donna Anna sees the body of her father; and again, since music is the vehicle for the essentials in the drama, the exclamatory half-step figure intrudes from the orchestra (see Ex. 15:9), recording and dramatizing her reaction before she does so herself. Her exclamatory outcries are treated not as *secco,* but as accompanied recitative. The interval distances between the notes in *secco* recitative are short, more approximate to speech, and often a reiterated note serves for several words of text. In accompanied recitative, on the other hand, the interval distances between notes are larger; that is, they leap upward and downward contributing (in addition to the orchestral interjections) a more declamatory and impassioned tone to the text so rendered.

The following (Ex. 15:9), from the conclusion of the Don's dialogue with Leporello through to Donna Anna's discovery of her father's body, illustrates the distinction between the two types of recitative.

The dialogue, in orchestrally accompanied recitative, between Donna Anna and Don Ottavio carries the action up to the point of climax. Donna Anna exclaims in horror, faints, and revives. Don Ottavio orders smelling salts, comments commiseratingly upon her affliction, and oversees the removal of the body of the Commendatore. Effectively, the scene now requires one last dramatic effort to conclude it and bring the curtain down. Since there are two characters on stage, the concluding number is a duet which falls into two sections partitioned by the interpolation of a few strategic measures of accompanied recitative. The first section begins wildly in D minor and projects Donna Anna's distraught state of mind as she demands that Don Ottavio remove himself and leave her to die. He comforts her and the music mirrors his gentle solicitude. She asks forgivness; Don Ottavio bids her find in him both husband and father. At this point a few measures of orchestrally accompanied recitative are interpolated. The heroic declamatory style, for which this type of recitative is so apt, is used to isolate for emphasis the two key lines of text where Donna

Ex. 15:9   Act I, Scene I, *Don Giovanni* (Bars 205–217) Mozart.

Anna demands, and Don Ottavio agrees to, an oath to avenge her father's murder. The last portion of the duet is perhaps redundant in text, for together they simply repeat that the oath is a sacred one. But it is fast in tempo and brilliant in vocal style, and the pairing of the voices adds to that special musical and dramatic excitement which, at its conclusion, inevitably brings the curtain down, and just as inevitably releases the audience (whose presence the composer-dramatist must always remember) in an outburst of applause.

At every point in this scene the music has been the central dramatic agent through which the stage and the characters on it are brought to life. The music signals the raising of the curtain and provides the excitement to which it can be rung down to applause. The music sweeps the characters on and off stage, provides the transition from one level of action to another, delineates character, and controls the pace of the action on the stage. Two of these particulars deserve some amplification: the pace of the stage action and character delineation.

There are few things that so subtly and profoundly challenge the imagination of the dramatist as the control of the pace of incident on stage, the acceleration and the slowing down in the succession and accumulation of occurrences, the balance between the relatively active and the relatively static moments, and the allocation, within the time span of the scene, of the right number of minutes and seconds to each of the events that comprise it. In his sense of timing and in his mastery of easy change of pace,

Mozart is among the very greatest of stage masters. Consider the scene just analyzed, which flows so easily on the stage, and Mozart's rather astonishing pacing of the events. From the entrance of Don Giovanni and Donna Anna, through the duel, the death of the Commendatore, and the exit dialogue of Don Giovanni and Leporello (approximately four minutes and thirty seconds of music), the elapsed time is no longer than that allocated for the scene in accompanied recitative between Donna Anna and Don Ottavio, and no longer than the final duet. In time measurement, these are three approximately equal sections. Yet there is a wide disparity in the amount of stage incident within each. The libretto-text tells us nothing of this vital matter. The timing of incident, so essential to effective theater, is wholly within the control of the composer.

As for characterization, the libretto will stipulate what the character is to say, but the music will establish the precise interpretation to be placed on the words. For example, following the first scene discussed above, the curtain rises on Don Giovanni and Leporello in conversation (*secco* recitative). They see a young lady approaching and conceal themselves the better to observe her. Donna Elvira enters in traveling costume and soon makes clear that she is on the trail of a seducer who betrayed her. It takes little acuity to realize that she is an infuriated relic of one of the Don's recent amorous escapades. Consider her text, which resounds with pathos, imprecation, and rage.

DONNA ELVIRA: Ah, who can direct me to that monster who scorned me, and whom I loved so shamelessly? Ah, if I find him, the scoundrel, and he will not return to me, I will kill him, I will tear his heart out!

This reads like high melodrama. Mozart chose to construe it as comedy. The orchestra alerts us to this conception, ushering Elvira on stage with a few mincing measures that are a travesty on her pretense to a grand passion (Ex. 15:10).

Ex. 15:10   Act I, Scene II, *Don Giovanni* (Bars 1–3). Mozart.

Elvira's vocal line is impassioned to be sure, but the orchestral remarks are utterly without seriousness or sympathy. The violins titter delicately and pointedly (Ex. 15:11) when Elvira declaims that the monster has

Ex. 15:11   Act I, Scene II, *Don Giovanni* (Bars 6–7). Mozart.

scorned her. And when she adds that she has loved him to her shame, violins, violas, and cellos toss around what is evidently a Mozartian snicker emphasized by sforzandos (*sf*) and syncopations (Ex. 15:12).

Ex. 15:12   Act I, Scene II, *Don Giovanni* (Bars 22–25). Mozart.

The essence of the characterization (Elvira can never be taken very seriously after this) lies in the duality of text and music; and, more specifically, in the duality, within the music, between that which Elvira is given to sing and the music the orchestra is given to play. For further examples of the function of music as the delineator of character, contrast the virility, the intoxicated love of pleasure, the enormous vitality of Don Giovanni's drinking song, *Finch 'han dal vino,* with the effeminate gentility of Don Ottavio's arias, *Dalla sua pace,* or *Il mio tesoro.* Once so characterized by the music he sings, one could never expect Don Ottavio to pick up a mandolin and accompany himself in a canzonet sung in a popular style. But no such refinements in Don Giovanni's music inhibit him from doing exactly this, especially since the lady to whom this popular music is addressed is none other than Elvira's maid (*Deh vieni alla finestra*).

The above has been an analysis of one type of opera only, the Italian "number" opera with its conventions of overture, recitatives, aria, and ensemble sections, together with their function as mechanisms within the lyric drama. Other operas of this type, both before and after Mozart's time, are discussed elsewhere in this book. Those of the baroque period will be found in Chapter 20—Monteverdi's *Orfeo* (pp. 284–285), Lully's *Alceste* (pp. 291–293), Purcell's *Dido and Aeneas* (pp. 294–296), and Handel's *Semele* (pp. 297–298); the Viennese classical period in Chapter 21, Gluck's *Orfeo ed Euridice* (pp. 321–324); the romantic period in Chapter 22, Weber's *Freischütz* (pp. 356–358), and Verdi's *La Traviata* (pp. 369–371). The distinction between the "number" opera and those in which the music moves along in unbroken continuity is an important one, and the reader would be well advised at this point to turn to Chapter 22, pages 371–375, in order to contrast an opera such as *Don Giovanni* with the conventions of Wagnerian music drama.

ORATORIO

Oratorio utilizes many of the conventions of opera, but the similarities between the two will be misconceived if oratorio is construed as unstaged opera. (A play is not an unfilmed motion picture any more

Union of Music and Drama: Opera and Oratorio

than a sailboat is a motorboat without a motor.) In an early phas
history, oratorio and sacred opera were indeed close; but a Hande
Mendelssohn concert oratorio is an art form whose esthetics are indepe
ent of, although not unrelated to, opera. Arias, recitatives, ensembl
choral numbers, and overtures are common to both. Oratorio, like opera
may also involve a full-scale plot and concern itself with strong characterizations of the individuals in the story. However, oratorio, unlike opera,
may sometimes be meditative and essentially nonnarrative. In this type of
oratorio there would be no story in the conventional sense and hence no
characterizations of individuals as such. Plot in this case must be construed
liberally as the complex of ideational relationships in the textual passages,
sacred or secular, out of which the composer operates. Oratorio, incidentally, while often sacred in text, may also be purely secular in this respect.
The *Messiah* of Handel is an example of this kind of meditative, essentially
nonnarrative oratorio. In it there are no personages requiring specific
characterization. Although the work has an overture, arias, recitatives, and
choral numbers, it lacks a conventional story plot and a specific cast of
characters. Since the *Messiah* is so remote from opera, Mendelssohn's
Elijah will serve better to illustrate the present discussion.

The *Elijah* is a narrative plot and character oratorio, performed from
the concert stage. On this type of stage, drama is projected in ways germane
to it, and as such it is necessarily different in essentials from the operatic
stage. It is here that the description of oratorio as "unstaged opera" can be
misleading, for if costuming and stage furniture are lacking, the sense of
stage is nevertheless important. The staging is not visible any more than
it is in a radio play, but the situation (sometimes even the locale in which
it is set), the individuals involved in it, and the continuity of occurrence
are nevertheless always before the listener.

A narrator is therefore a necessity in an oratorio. He may be a designated individual, one of the cast of characters, or someone who stands
apart—like the Evangelist in the Gospel story—intruding only when it is
necessary for him to set the scene, to identify the participants in the plot,
or to link the events one to another. (A *passion* is an oratorio based on one
of the four Gospel accounts of the suffering and death of Jesus. The narrator in such cases is the particular Evangelist whose account of the passion is
used: for example, the Bach *Passion According to St. Matthew*.) In seventeenth-century oratorio, the narrator was simply designated as *testo* (the
speaker of the text). The necessary intervention of the storyteller has als
been treated by depersonalizing the part and distributing it among varic
voices. In Carissimi's *Jepthe*, for example, the burden of the narratic
~red between a bass voice and an alto. Neither are principals j
elf, and hence simply identified in the score as bass and alt

ariwise the narration has also been distributed among specific character parts. In the Mendelssohn *Elijah,* for example, the narrational outline of situation is given sometimes to Elijah himself (the main character in the drama), sometimes to an Angel, and sometimes to the chorus of the afflicted folk. Recitative is the natural medium for the narrator.

Plot oratorio does not preclude the interpolation of meditative interpretation and commentary of a generalized, nonpersonal nature. This provides for an extension in the functions of an aria or a choral number beyond what has already been encountered in the discussion of opera. At one moment, an aria may serve (as in opera) for character projection, or for an emotionalizing of a high point in the plot. At another, however, an aria for alto, let us say (no character in the story specified, and hence an aria depersonalized but not dehumanized), will be interpolated as a generalized mediation appropriate to the dramatic situation, but not, in a story sense, part of that situation. Likewise, the chorus may be (as in an opera) a conglomeration of particular people—the mass of the "folk." However, whenever the composer deems it appropriate, he may detach the chorus from its role in the plot, and convert it (after the manner of a chorus in a Greek tragedy) into a neutral commentator upon the situation rather than a biased participant.

The treatment of a dramatic scene in *Elijah* involves its projection from three different, though integrated focal points—the outlining of situation, the enactment of the event, and the commentary upon it. Part I of this oratorio comprises four separate scenes with several musical numbers per scene. The first is essentially introductory and unresolved, depicting Israel in its state of affliction. In the three scenes that follow, dealing with the miracles wrought by the Lord in answer to the prayers of the prophet, each of the situations is presented at its point of crisis, and carried, in each case, to the point of resolution.

An outline of the musical and dramatic structure of the first scene follows.

ELIJAH (*Recitative*): "As God the Lord of Israel liveth."
 The prophet makes a short, but solemn pronouncement on the calamity that shall befall the land: There shall be neither dew nor rain, but according to God's word.
OVERTURE: This is not a self-contained orchestral number. It opens in a somber and agitated manner, and the climax of its mounting intensity coincides—the raising, so to speak, of an invisible curtain—with the anguished outcry of an afflicted folk. (The effect is operatic to be sure; very like, in point of fact, the opening of Verdi's opera *Nabucco,* where the outcry of an aded people bursts upon us at the moment of orchestral climax.)
 's OF THE PEOPLE: "Help! Lord! Wilt Thou quite destroy us?"

The invisible curtain has now risen on a scene actually present only in the listener's sympathetic imagination. What is visible is a concert stage, with orchestra and chorus, and soloists in evening dress flanking the conductor. The fact that the stage for the drama exists only in the imagination makes for an elasticity peculiar to oratorio. But the composer is still under obligation to control the logic of the invisible drama as rigorously as if it were actual to the eye. Musically, a scene is a sequence of musical "numbers," as in a "number" opera. However, unencumbered by the necessity for moving people around on a stage, the composer's focus may well sharpen on the psychological design of the scene—that is, the structure of emotional levels on which the sequence of occurrences is presented. This structure of emotional levels is realized as a sequence of musical numbers. Thus this choral number is a unit in a dramatic scheme. The emotional level on which it opens relates it to the two numbers preceding it, while the emotional level of its close relates it to the numbers that follow. The two preceding prologue numbers (recitative and overture) contribute to a rising state of tension, the climax of which is reached with the opening of this choral number. For all of the overwrought emotionality of the initial cry for help, the ultimate tone of this first chorus is one of exhaustion and despair. This recession—marked by a draining away of dynamic force from fortissimo to pianissimo, and by a descent from high to low vocal register—leads to the level on which the next two numbers are pitched.

CHORUS OF THE PEOPLE (*Recitative*):

The chorus is divided into its component sections (sopranos, altos, tenors, basses), each section of the folk in turn describing in unison recitative the afflictions that have befallen them. (Notice the schematic disposition of entrances from the sopranos down to the basses and up again to the sopranos, and the simple but effective text division.)

SOPRANOS: "The deep affords no water."
TENORS: "And the rivers are exhausted."
ALTOS: "The suckling's tongue now cleaveth for thirst to his mouth."
BASSES: "The infant children ask for bread."
TENORS: "The infant children ask for bread."
ALTOS: "And there is no one."
SOPRANOS: "And there is no one breaketh it to feed them."

DUET WITH CHORUS: "Lord, bow Thine ear to our prayer."

The emotional level has now receded considerably from the anguished outcry of the first chorus. With admirable instinct for the pathos of the situation, Mendelssohn continues his dramatization by distinguishing between individual sufferers and the community of the folk. Two women step forward (soprano and alto solos) to continue the lamentation in a more personal fashion—"Zion spreadeth her hands for aid, and there is neither help nor comfort"—while the chorus of the people, men's voices and women's voices alternating in unison, quietly implore, "Lord, bow thine ear to our prayer."

OBADIAH (*Recitative*):   "Ye people rend your hearts."

With the foregoing duet with chorus, the emotional recession reaches its ulti-

mate point for this scene. Since the drama has become individualized through
the emergence of solo voices, the next step is to personalize it by naming the
individual who next speaks. Obadiah's recitative is a stern admonition to the
people to rend their hearts and not their garments, to turn away from
the worship of idols, and once again, in their hearts, truly to seek the Lord.

Tenor Solo (*Aria*) : " 'If with all your hearts ye truly seek me, ye shall ever
surely find me.' Thus saith our God."

At this point, oratorio and opera divide sharply, for this aria is not sung by,
nor does it characterize, any particular participant in the drama. It is an
interpolated meditation, and for its duration the "plot action" is suspended.
Musically, the aria is a simple A-B-A structure, the two outlying sections in
major and the middle section in minor. But this abstract structure is related
to the context upon which the music is a commentary. Thus the opening
and closing sections in major are set to the same text, and the text (given
above) is nonpersonal in that it is God's saying and not man's. Enclosed
within God's injunction (in major) is the middle section which, in a minor
key, expresses a poignant personal longing to stand in the presence of the
Lord. "Oh! that I knew where I might find him, that I might even come before his presence."

Chorus of the People: "Yet doth the Lord see it not."

The emotional level has now risen from the quiet pleading of the duet with
chorus to the stern admonition of Obadiah and the exalted tone of the foregoing meditation. When the story is now resumed with this chorus, attention is turned back to the intensity of a folk's agony and outcry. The
tempo is a furious one (allegro vivace) , and the melody line steep in its
interval leaps: devices which dramatize the communal terror of God's wrath
which shall pursue the idolators to destruction. The pace is suddenly arrested
on an unresolved chord (the text: "Till He destroy us") . A protracted pause;
and when the chorus resumes (slow tempo) it is no longer the chorus of the
people.

Chorus: "For He, the Lord our God, He is a jealous God. . . . His mercies
on thousands fall."

Essentially, this first scene serves not to narrate a complete event, but to
establish the framework within which the subsequent events transpire. Now
that this has been accomplished, the chorus ceases to be a participant in the
drama and becomes the medium through which a generalized commentary
can be offered as an epilogue to the first scene. Such changes in chorus or
aria function are among the common conventions of oratorio. While in opera
such an epilogue to a dramatic opening scene would seem like gratuitous
moralizing, in oratorio it is integral to the drama for it is one of the several
points of focus through which the event is viewed.

If this were opera, the curtain would fall at this point and a scene change
would be effected for the next scene between Elijah and the widow. Here the
transition comprises a recitative (alto) in which an Angel sends Elijah forth,
a double quartet in which Elijah is assured that "He shall give His angels
charge over thee," and a second recitative (alto) in which the Angel sends

him to abide in Zerepath, where "The Lord hath commanded a widow woman there to sustain thee."

The ensuing scene between Elijah and the widow is treated, not in separate numbers, but as a continuity of juxtaposed recitatives and arialike passages. The widow's son is sick and she fears (recitative) that the prophet has come to call her sins into remembrance and to slay her son. In the arialike section that follows, she implores his aid: "Help me, man of God, my son is sick." The characterizations in this scene are sharply drawn: the distraught mother, and the prophet who implores the Lord so earnestly and so eloquently to "let the spirit of the child return, that he again may live." When the miracle is accomplished and the child revives, the widow and Elijah join in a brief duet. Without pause a choral commentary completes the scene, the text for the commentary opening with a repetition of the last words of the duet, "Blessed are the men who fear Him, they ever walk in the ways of peace."

The two remaining scenes in part one of the oratorio deal with further miracles wrought by God in answer to the prayers of the prophet (Elijah and the idolators of Baal, Elijah and the sign of the Lord's mercy). In each case, as in the scene with the widow, the situation is outlined, the event enacted, brought to a satisfactory resolution, and illuminated by commentary.

Union of Architecture and Music

Chapter 16

A<small>NY</small> adequate insight into the various types and styles of music must take into account the architectural setting for which the music was originally designed. Music in the past was conditioned to a considerable degree by the places where it was performed as well as by the occasions on which it was heard. Since music has often been designed with respect to some social function, it is quite naturally affected by its external environment. Chamber music was thus distinguished from concert music, theater music from church music, salon music from outdoor music, and so on. In former times when worldly music was in the process of emancipating itself from forms connected with religious worship, it was customary to attach the Italian term *da camera* to sonatas, concertos, and cantatas suitable for secular entertainment as opposed to *da chiesa*, meaning those intended for church performance. A *sonata da camera*, or chamber sonata, with its active, dancelike movements and its secular spirit generally was thus distinguished from a *sonata da chiesa*, or church sonata, with its more rigorously fugal textures and more contemplative character.

This adaption of musical means to environmental ends usually has to be made by the composer himself, who must take into consideration the size and purpose of the place where his music is to be heard. Haydn's early symphonies are stylistically distinguishable from the later ones by their dimensions, their instrumentation, and by their general character. Writing for a household orchestra in the Esterhazy salon, where he had to tread lightly with his horns and kettledrums, was one thing, while composing for the large-scale "Salomon Concerts" in London was quite another. Similarly with Mozart's works in this form, only the *Prague* Symphony and the great last three, including the famous G-minor Symphony, can be called symphonic in the public-concert sense, while the others remain in the aristocratic salon as a part of the social-music scene of the time. Beethoven, with a far wider choice of places of performance at his disposal, developed a correspondingly greater sensitivity to his architectural surroundings than was possible for his Viennese predecessors. As Hindemith has so aptly pointed out, Beethoven "had the finest feeling for the proportional relationship between space and compositional technique . . ."

Nowadays when slender eighteenth-century symphonies are performed with mechanical amplification in huge open-air amphitheaters and the mightiest of grand operas are heard via radio, television, and recordings in tiny living rooms, it is small wonder that so many misunderstandings about the nature, purpose, and character of musical works prevail. The confusion of musical uses and abuses in modern concert life is legion. In the concert industry an enterprising manager is more likely to be guided in his choice of halls by the number of tickets he hopes to sell than by the appropriateness of the medium of expression to the size of the setting. The transfer of music originally meant to be played in intimate circles to large public arenas is partially responsible for the transcription mania, which involves the transfer of music from one medium to another. Tampering with a composer's instrumentation by doubling and trebling the woodwind and brass parts in order to compensate for the greatly enlarged string sections of modern orchestras is a peccadillo indulged in by conductors ever since Wagner's time. But taking a small piece, such as a chaconne by Bach for violin alone, and then magnifying it into a gigantic set of variations for full symphony orchestra, complete with ponderous brass choirs, is symptomatic of the disease of tonal elephantiasis that afflicts all too many contemporary conductors and arrangers. The situation would be comparable to a modern artist taking a Rembrandt etching, blowing it up to dioramic proportions, and using it for a mural in a railroad station.

Even musical instruments suffer from some of these same sins. The great Stradivarius and Guarnerius violins, for instance, were made to be played in small rooms, but the violinists of today use them to perform in halls seating thousands. As a consequence bows are subjected to great pressure, gut strings are replaced with metallic ones, and performers hew and hack away at their fiddles in a frenzied effort to produce a tone that will reach the distant galleries. That such lamentable practices continue is attributable principally to a lack of discrimination between musical means and ends. In the past when a solo instrument was called upon to fill comparable architectural spaces, the choice would probably have fallen on an organ whose vibrations were capable of setting a vast cathedral in reverberation. Commenting on the prevailing lack of knowledge about the specific purposes and places for which the music of the past was composed, the noted historian Alfred Einstein wrote, "How barbarous our concert life has become is shown principally by the fact that we no longer feel such distinctions." The fact remains that most of the music of past centuries is comprehensible only when its specific purpose and original reason for existence is known and understood. Architectural settings must then be taken into account in any serious attempt to fathom the function the music was designed to fulfill.

Public speakers, when making addresses in huge halls, know that they must adjust both their subjects of discussion and their manner of delivery to the setting. Conventional sentiments, positive statements, and resounding declarations will make their effect, while subtle reasoning and equivocal conclusions would be out of place. Such a speaker also realizes that he must slow his pace and enunciate his words clearly to compensate for the reverberation and echo of a large auditorium. If similar sentiments and oratorical prowess were employed in the midst of a small gathering, his listeners might well ask each other why he does not hire a hall. When a composer "hires a hall," so to speak, his forms, subject matter, instrumentation, and general technical treatment are scaled accordingly. If his subject lends itself to a grandiose oratorical type of utterance, it will be built to symphonic specifications. But if he is concerned with confidential confessions and introspective thoughts, he will probably choose the solo or chamber music medium. A symphony, then, is heard to good effect in sizable surroundings with a good crowd in attendance, while chamber music is better adapted to an intimate atmosphere where it can be addressed to the connoisseur level and where its restrained understatements and formal refinements can better be appreciated. In one case heroic proportions, eloquence, and grandeur are to the point, in the other subtle inflections and delicate balances are in order. If the tables are turned and the symphonist indulges in too many harmonic and contrapuntal complexities, his overly subtle treatment will get lost in the shuffle; and if the string quartet composer tries to force his slender resources into the monumental mold, he will clearly be overstating his case.

Certain conditions and innovations of modern life are responsible for all manner of misconceptions in the minds of composers of church music as well as audiences. Each of the two greatest opera composers of the nineteenth century, for instance, tried his hand at writing religious music.

Verdi's *Requiem,* a setting of the Roman Catholic Mass for the Dead, reflects the increasing secular spirit of its time in both its dramatic treatment and theatrical grandiloquence. Designed for performance in concert halls rather than in churches, it has, with more truth than humor, been called his greatest "opera." Wagner, for his part, attempted to turn the opera house into a place of worship with his pseudo-Christian mystery drama, *Parsifal.* Audiences are still expected to maintain a reverent hush and refrain from applause when it is performed, though such a practice at an opera performance is a patent absurdity.

When an important contemporary composer like Stravinsky writes a mass or other religious music, more than likely it will be heard in a public hall rather than in a church. Consciously or unconsciously, therefore, he is addressing his sacred music to a secular gathering. Music in a church, of course, is an adjunct to divine worship; while in a concert hall or opera house it exists as an independent entity and constitutes its own reason for being. If such stylistic confusion is to be avoided when the great masses, cantatas, and oratorios of the past are heard today in concert halls, an act of the imagination on the part of the listener is required in order to reconstruct the original setting and occasion. Palestrina's masses and Bach's cantatas were written as integral parts of church services, while the more ambitious oratorios were conceived as festival offerings during the Advent and Lenten seasons. Today they are heard in public places where ladies appear attired in evening gowns and the gentlemen are resplendent in white ties and tails. The shades of those pious composers, as well as religious leaders of the past, must indeed have some uneasy moments in eternity.

Temples and churches were the scenes of large-scale musical activity long before public concert and opera houses came into being. The composers who wrote for these religious ceremonies were as sensitive to the acoustical possibilities of the buildings where the work was to be performed as they were to the appropriateness of the music for divine worship. While some of this early music is still effective in its original or similar settings, much of it does not survive transplantation from its native habitat. The elemental simplicity of Gregorian chant, for instance, is ideally adapted for intonation in the interiors of basilican churches where it acquires a vibrant and colorful quality uniquely its own. When removed from these architectural and liturgical surroundings and sung in concert halls or recording studios, much of its warmth and resilience is lost. When Perotin the Great conceived his grandiose choral music for the Cathedral of Notre Dame in Paris, he took the reverberations of its vast vaulted su⸍ faces into account. In such a Gothic edifice the tones and overtones enriched and prolonged as they echo through the cavernous interior sp⸍
⸍ the tones that precede mix with those that follow so that the

building resounds with their harmony. In other places the empty fifth and octave intervals are open and exposed and thus seem barren and hollow in comparison.

The unusual acoustical properties of St. Mark's in Venice provide another case in point, since they seem to have fostered the growth of an important musical style. This domed church with its two organ lofts, one on each side of the nave, suggested some musical experimentation to the choir masters of late Renaissance times that eventually led to the formation of the so-called polychoral and concerting style. By dividing the choral and instrumental forces into two or more groups so that they could answer each other antiphonally either in whole or in part, many new and fascinating possibilities were realized. The results of this interplay of sound permeated the entire baroque style and led directly to such forms as the concerto grosso and to such dynamic effects as the echo nuance.

Certain vocal and instrumental combinations as well as individual choices of instruments often provide not only the key to the character of a work but also a clue to its original setting. *A cappella* choirs, as their name suggests, are associated with chapels and churches where their pure polyphony is blended with the acoustical surroundings of Renaissance vaulted buildings. Antiphonal choruses and their instrumental counterpart, the concerto grosso, recall the Venetian polychoral style with all its accompanying spatial implications. Bach's keyboard works are written for three different instruments. Those for organ are expressly for church use; while those for the household clavichord are homelike and informal by comparison, since one does not declaim in oratorical tones in the bosom of the family. Those for harpsichord, accordingly, are more pompous and formal, in keeping with their palatial surroundings, since it would be considered improper to make personal confessions in public places. In each case the type of communication as well as the manner of delivery is conditioned by the place where the instrument is normally found.

In aristocratic circles music was also performed during the summer in the courtyards and gardens of palaces. Yet in all these times the music was specifically written and designed for the setting in which it was to be heard. When Lully, court composer to Louis XIV, scored his ballets and operas with the inner courts and garden pavilions of Versailles in mind, he added woodwinds and brasses to the usual indoor orchestra of twenty-four viols. Handel wrote his *Water Music* Suite for performance on a Thames River barge when his patron, George I, made his royal progress on London to Hampton Court. He also composed his *Fireworks Music* performance in one of London's public gardens where the strains of music formed a prelude to a later display of Roman candles and s rockets. In each case he chose his instruments—principally woodwinds and brasses—so that they would sound properly in their open-air surroundings.

Nowhere is this differentiation better illustrated than in that genial genre of eighteenth-century Viennese social music, consisting of those informal collections of marches and dances that are loosely designated as divertimentos, serenades, and cassations. A definite line of demarcation can be drawn on the basis of instrumentation, with those scored principally for strings pointing in an indoor direction and those with a preponderance of wind instruments moving toward the outdoors. Citing the serenades of Mozart as examples, the finely wrought *Eine Kleine Nachtmusik* (K. 525), a little nocturnal serenade as the German title implies, belongs inside, since it is written for strings only; while those of his divertimentos that are scored for pairs of wind instruments—oboes, horns, bassoons, and clarinets, when available—were clearly designed for open-air performance. According to contemporary accounts such ensembles were to be heard in the streets at almost any hour. No matter how late, as one report puts it, whenever the serenaders struck up, there were "people at their open windows and within a few minutes the musicians were surrounded by a crowd of listeners who rarely departed until the serenade had come to an end" (Vienna Theater almanac of 1794).

When Mozart wrote music for weddings, birthdays, garden parties, and the like, as he often did, he carefully worked within the intended setting and with the instruments that were available. His *Serenata Notturna* (K. 239), for instance, is scored for small stringed orchestra and timpani. The work is written in the concertante style with the ensemble divided into separate groups—one consisting of two solo violins, viola and bass; the other of a string quartet and drums. Such scoring suggests that the players might well have been seated separately, so they could answer each other antiphonally in such a way as to make an interesting interplay of sound and suggest spaciousness. His Serenade in D (K. 286), on the other hand, points in the direction of garden-party music. It is scored for four groups of instruments—designated as principal, first echo, second echo, and third echo orchestras, respectively—each of which contains first and second violins, viola, bass, and horns. Despite this designation of four orchestras, the effect is that of a single orchestra which is answered by the others in triple-echo fashion. In performance the first orchestra plays an entire phrase, the second repeats it exactly, the third plays only the last half of the phrase, and the fourth the last measure only. When the respective orchestras are deployed in the four corners of the garden, as seems indicated, an ingenious acoustical round-robin effect is obtained.

A vast amount of music, designated as "house music" or "chamber music," has been written for private performance in middle- and upper-class homes. In Elizabethan times in England as well as in the northern countries on the Continent, the cult of the home fostered this genial type of music-making by amateurs. In contrast to southern climates where much musical activity flourished in the open air, the social life of the English, Dutch, and German people was more strictly an indoor affair. In those days a well-equipped family reception room would be furnished with a keyboard instrument such as a spinet, clavichord, or harpsichord; some stringed instruments, such as lutes or a chest of viols; and in addition a small library of vocal and instrumental numbers. Groups of singers could then sit around a table to perform madrigals; singers together with instrumentalists could gather around the keyboard for group or solo songs; and string players could participate in ensemble numbers.

Chamber music, in this early sense, included madrigals and other secular music for voices in which the parts were not doubled; vocal and instrumental combinations of all kinds; as well as exclusively instrumental ensembles. The English historian, Dr. Burney, in 1776 still spoke of chamber music as, "Cantatas, single songs, solos, trios, quartets, concertos, and symphonies of a few parts." Later, after the turn of the nineteenth century, he came to define it as, " Compositions for a small concert room, a small band, and a small auditorium; opposed to music for the church, theater, or a public concert room." Full orchestral and choral music with liberal doubling of parts was thus excluded from the medium, as were solo works of various kinds. More and more, chamber music came to be dominantly instrumental, though voices in combination with instruments are still occasionally used.

Most of the lighter chamber music of the Viennese classical period was conceived and written for intimate entertainments in princely parlors. If this type of music is to be understood in its proper context, the limitations of its setting as well as those of the medium must be reckoned with. A poet in such surroundings would read some sonnets rather than his epical pronouncements; a painter would exhibit his miniatures rather than his murals; and a composer would choose his sonatas rather than his symphonies. Music, like the conversation in such elegant and aristocratic surroundings, can be witty but not heavy, energetic but not bombastic. It must seek to persuade rather than overwhelm, confide rather than pontificate, probe for philosophical profundities rather than rant and roar.

Because of the increasing intricacy of chamber-music writing from the eighteenth century on, it began to point more and more in the direction of professional musicians. Since the players and listeners are in such close proximity, however, and since the audience is more selective, such complexities are more readily understood than in larger halls where the auditors are farther away from the source of sound. Chamber music, by remaining the delight of the trained and talented amateur as well as that of the discerning listener, has managed to retain much of its original warmth and individual character. The particular distinction of the medium lies in its reduced proportions and in the equal right of each instrument within the ensemble. When the several parts, as in an orchestra or chorus, for instance, are performed by a multitude of players and singers, individual responsibility correspondingly declines. Each member of a performing duo, trio, or quartet, however, has his own sphere of influence and the power to make his particular contribution to the group. Chamber music is thus not for the entertainment of crowds, and its effectiveness in large halls is all too easily lost.

Today it seems to be taken for granted that music moves out of doors in the summer. Concerts and opera performances spring up in city parks and in assorted stadiums and bowls. Yet the repertory remains the same as that played indoors in winter but heard here under far less favorable circumstances. Outdoor concerts are, of course, as old as the history of public concert life. In London, where music-making for the general public dates from the seventeenth century, there were "garden" performances that achieved enormous popularity. The American colonies during the time of George Washington and Francis Hopkinson also had their share of outdoor performances at such places as the "Pennsylvania Tea Gardens" in Philadelphia and at the "Orange Garden" in Charleston, South Carolina. The confusion nowadays, however, comes from the fact that music originally written for indoors is played in settings where it was never intended to be performed. Conductors have to slow the pace of their fast movements to compensate for unwanted echoes and other acoustical peculiarities of the places where they are performing. Strange instrumental balances occur in which the wind and brass sections, playing in their natural element, overwhelm the strings and sometimes make familiar works seem like first-night novelties. Moveover the symphonies and concertos that are normally heard in these outdoor arenas were never intended by their composers for such surroundings. All the subtle features of their work disappears and only the blare and bombast remains. In such settings the music should have either a directness and simplicity, or else the festive quality and gigantic dimensions of such works as Tchaikovsky's *Overture, 1812*, Berlioz' *Requiem*, or Mahler's *Symphony of a Thousand*. Until the directors of these institutions choose their repertory accordingly, or emulate the good example of past periods and see fit to commission competent composers to write music appropriate for these places, the confusion is likely to continue.

The electronic revolution of the twentieth century, by which music became so readily available via the vacuum tube, recorded disk, film sound track, and magnetic tape, has turned every living room into a potential concert hall. While home listening has by no means replaced concert giving and concert going, a music lover's living room today is probably a busier scene of activity than Carnegie Hall ever was. In former times it took a princely purse to provide music even in palatial surroundings. Only an Esterhazy family could maintain a house orchestra for its enjoyment, and only a Baron von Swieten could enliven his Sunday mornings with chamber music matinees in which Mozart and Beethoven participated. Musical riches once at the call of kings are now within the reach of every one. Less than a century ago, a music room was simply a parlor with a piano, and the repertory heard there seldom went beyond simple songs and piano pieces. In today's music room, however, operas are seen and heard by means of the television set, symphony concerts are brought in by radio, and masterpieces of all periods can be experienced through recordings. A wider musical variety and range of styles are available to the modern listener than ever before. Owing to recordings many a neglected masterwork by such Renaissance and baroque composers as Josquin des Prez, Palestrina, Monteverdi, Purcell and others has been re-established in the current repertory, while vast new territories of musical literature still remain to be explored. What this music of the past loses in the intimate contact of composer, performer, and patron is perhaps compensated for by the expansion of the audience from a few hundreds into the millions. It has been estimated, for instance, that a greater number of people see a Shakespearean production in the course of a single nation-wide telecast than the sum total of all those who have attended Shakespearean performances in theaters since the play was written over three centuries ago.

The possession of such vast riches, however, provides no cause for complacency; rather it constitutes a challenge to the cultivation of a deeper sense of responsibility. If this musical abundance in the living room is to be more than an incitement to louder conversation, some discrimination as to style and type must be developed. Ephemeral dinner and conversation music, for instance, must be distinguished from the eternal truths uttered by the great masters, and each assigned to an appropriate place in a balanced musical life. With such a radical change in music's locale and such revolutionary new means of production, it is more imperative than ever for the listener's imagination to place works of various kinds in their proper context. It is also well to remember that in the broadcasting and recording processes many fundamental alterations take place. The climactic crescendos, for example, are toned down and the delicate pianissimos are amplified by the sound engineers in keeping with the capacities and limitations of their mechanical equipment. Hence much of the effect of these dynamic mountains and valleys of music are lost in the living room. In both broadcasts and recordings, moreover, the sound emanates from a single source (except in binaural broadcasts and on stereophonic tapes), while in an auditorium there is a more spacious distribution of sound reaching the ear from many different sources, both directly and from reflected surfaces. Antiphonal effects, echo nuances, and the building up of cumulative climaxes are correspondingly reduced in effectiveness as they leave larger halls and take up their abode in the living room. Furthermore no matter how high the fidelity of the reproduced sound, it is still never quite the same as the original. A recorded symphony, like a photographic portrait, can serve to recall the image of a familiar face, but can never replace the beaming countenance of a living person.

Thus music—whether for church or theater, home or concert hall, salon or open air—is indissolubly associated with its acoustical and social surroundings. Any competent composer is governed to a considerable extent in his choice of style, form, instrumentation, and even expressive content by the spatial environment in which his work is to be performed. A pavane or minuet, whether written by a musician at the time these dances were current or by a contemporary composer as a period piece, belongs (either in actuality or imagination) in a rarified courtly atmosphere, while a laendler is at home in country taverns. With the wholesale transfer of the music of the past from surroundings approximating those the composer had in mind, an awareness of the environment as well as occasions for which the work was originally intended is a necessary part of any complete insight into musical styles. Especially is this true at the present time when all types of music have become accessible by means of the modern mass media—motion pictures, television, radio, and recordings. Since confusion of form and function is so widespread, the only remedy is an act of the imagination by which the proper settings are conjured up mentally as a part of the listening process. Any serious attempt to fathom the function music was designed to fulfill must take such authentic architectural settings into account.

Union of Imagery
and Music:
Programme Music

Chapter 17

In addition to the synthesis of poetry and tone in solo and choral song, the merging of step and gesture with sound in all dance forms from the simplest folk expressions to the ballet, the union of drama and music ranging from the incidental music to plays to the through-composed operas, and the environmental influence of architectural settings for which the music was designed, one further bond of music and its sister arts remains to be explored—*programme music*. Before this kind of composition can be described with anything approaching precision, however, it becomes necessary to point out its origins, the musical materials that are employed, and the formal types that serve its purposes.

Programme music, in both a descriptive and narrative sense, is as old as the art of music itself. The ancient Roman poet Lucretius, writing in the first century B.C., ascribed the origin of music to the desire of men to imitate "with the mouth the liquid notes of birds." Then, he continues, "The whistling of the zephyr through the hollows of reeds first taught the men of the countryside to breathe into hollowed hemlock stalks. Then little by little they learned the sweet lament, which the pipe pours forth, stopped by the player's fingers, a lament discovered amid the pathless woods and forests and glades, among the desolate haunts of shepherds, and the divine places of their rest." Lucretius' theory, of course, is closely allied with the ancient esthetic doctrine that all the arts—verbal, visual, and musical alike—are based on the imitation of nature. Such imitative or descriptive effects as the cooing of turtledoves can be found in early medieval Gregorian chants, just as the sounds of modern engines are to be heard in Honegger's locomotive tone poem, *Pacific 231,* written in 1923.

The oldest reference to narrative programme music goes all the way back to ancient Greece in 586 B.C., when a piece representing the contest between Apollo and the dragon was performed by an aulos-player at the Pythian games. In the baroque period, Kuhnau, Bach's predecessor in Leipzig, wrote his *Bible Stories in Six Sonatas* for the keyboard, one of which depicts the "Combat between David and Goliath" and another, "David Curing Saul by Means of Music." Battle pieces were prime favorites with nineteenth-century audiences, while the narrative tone poems of Richard Strauss enjoy a secure place in the contemporary orchestral repertory. Programme music is, thus, far from a novelty and must be considered a recurring phase of one type of musical approach. However, while examples appear in the works of such composers as Corelli, Vivaldi, Bach, Haydn, and Mozart, they occupy no particularly preponderant place in their total musical output. In the work of Berlioz, Schumann, Liszt, Mahler, and Richard Strauss, on the other hand, programme music receives major attention.

All the arts depend for communication on some association of ideas. In the more abstract phases of any art this association is less explicit, and the art must rely for its unity more on form than on specific content. The story of programme music has to do with the tensions that arise between these polar extremes of form and content, and the extent to which one or the other of them is allowed to dominate. Music, in contrast to poetry and painting, cannot convey specific imagery with any particular precision. When a painter, for example, wants to represent a rock or a tree, he can draw it with considerable exactitude. When his art veers toward the abstract, it can never completely part company with nature. Even a so-called nonobjective picture, for instance, has colors, lines, angles, surface textures, and so on. While these may be quite unspecific, they are nevertheless concrete to some extent, since color, line, shape—at least in their unrefined state—are all present in nature. Music, contrariwise, is really not a representative art at all, and sounds of nature can never be imitated with any particular precision. A few sounds such as bells and hunting horns, to be sure, can be reproduced, but these are man-made and musical rather than natural in the first place. Rameau called one of his harpsichord pieces *La Poule* (The Hen) because it had a cackling theme. But lest the list-

miss the point, the composer found it necessary to inscribe above the notes the syllables "co-co-co-co-co-co- cocodai."

Only when music is coupled with words as in a song, with pantomime as in the dance, or with the drama as in the opera and oratorio does this associative process become clear and direct. The "word painting" of the so-called "representative style" as employed by the baroque composers is a case in point. In the aria "Every valley shall be exalted" from the *Messiah,* Handel uses a rising line for his mountains and a dipping line for the valleys. In his *Israel in Egypt* he depicts the plagues with instrumental effects describing frogs and flies as well as hailstones. Without a text, however, no one would know exactly what his intentions were. Such descriptive passages are also found in Schubert's song accompaniments such as the *Erlking* and *To Be Sung on the Water* (Exs. 3:10 and 3:11). Here again, without a text, the accompaniment patterns would be subject to a variety of interpretations. In the traditional shepherd plays a Sicilian dance rhythm (see page 42) gradually became associated with pastoral settings, so that when Bach and Handel interpolated an instrumental interlude at the point where the adoration of the shepherds comes in their Christmas stories, their audiences knew exactly what was intended whether the composers designated it a "pastoral symphony" or not.

Similarly a certain rhythm in the instrumental music of the eighteenth and nineteenth centuries was identified with cavalry marches (Ex. 3:6), and when Chopin wanted to suggest the battlefield in the middle section of his Polonaise in F-sharp Minor, Op. 44, his communicative symbols were perfectly intelligible. In general, however, the composer in such cases needs a title, text, or verbal description of some sort, if he wants to avoid obscurity and possible misinterpretation. Such simple sound imagery as described above, however, must be separated from programme music proper, even though programmatic writing relies rather heavily at times on such illustrative means to convey its message.

Programme music, as it took shape in the instrumental writing of the eighteenth and nineteenth centuries, freely borrowed descriptive images and dramatic devices that were traditionally associated with the opera and oratorio. Certain tonalities were associated with special moods and situations. The key of D minor was often a "storm and stress" or demonic key for Haydn and Mozart. It is heard, for instance, in Haydn's *Lamentation Symphony,* No. 26, and Mozart's Piano Concerto in D Minor (K. 466); and Mozart also uses the key in his opera *Don Giovanni* as well as for the fire-and-brimstone, doomsday imagery of the "Dies Irae" (Day of Judgment) section in his *Requiem.* The tonality of F major, by contrast, was a peaceful, pastoral key. Instrumental colors also carry symbolism as, for instance, the warlike trumpets, the foreboding trombones which were associated with solemn church festivals and funerals in Germany and Austria, the supple French horns for hunting scenes, and the pastoral woodwinds for bucolic country scenes and landscapes. Symbolism of both an obvious and obscure sort is sometimes found side by side. In Saint-Saëns' *Danse Macabre* (1874), for instance, a general Halloween atmosphere prevails with the harp and pizzicato strings striking the witching hour of midnight, xylophone passages imitating the dancing of skeletons, and the oboe sounding the cock's crow at dawn. The poem on which it is based describes the devil beating time with his heel on a gravestone, while he tunes his fiddle for the forthcoming infernal festivities. Here the composer calls for the violin to be retuned by lowering the E string one-half step. With the devil striking the perfect fifth (D and A) in alternation with the diminished fifth (A and E flat), all might seem fairly obvious; but there is a subtle allusion involved, since the latter is the tritone interval known in medieval times as the *diabolus in musica* (the devil in music).

A vocabulary of such symbols was common musical currency, and when Mendelssohn wrote a "song without words" intended as a spinning song, he had a ready-made figure at hand that had been used by Schubert before him and was to be employed by Wagner and others many times after him. Similarly, by taking a phrase (Ex. 21:1) such as Gluck had used to characterize Eurydice in his reform opera *Orfeo* in 1762, Berlioz was able to write an "opera without words" such as his *Harold in Italy* (1834). By identifying the protagonist of his wordless drama with a recurring melody, he then links his hero to a series of episodes freely associated with Byron's poem, *Childe Harold's Pilgrimage*. In the process he reveals his hero's melancholy musings by subjecting him to such situations as being alone in the mountains, meditating as a religious pilgrimage passes by, and being kidnaped by wild and lawless brigands.

The term *programme music,* then, can be said to refer principally to instrumental music based on a series of actions or sequence of episodes that are designed to make narrative or dramatic sense, and declared by the composer to be subject to some sort of literary, pictorial, or philosophical interpretation. A composer, if he chooses, may concoct his own programme as Berlioz did in his *Symphonie Fantastique,* turn to Dante as Tchaikovsky did in his *Francesca da Rimini,* or have a writer publish an "inspired" poem to serve as an authorized interpretation as Richard Strauss did with his *Death and Transfiguration*. Mendelssohn, when composing his incidental music to Shakespeare's *Midsummer Night's Dream,* clearly knew in advance what scenes he was setting. Spohr and Schumann, on the other hand, said that they gave titles and programmes to their pieces after they were written. In this event, as Tovey has observed, "The music throws far more light on the programme than the programme on the music." All the above cases, however, can properly be classified as programme music.

A work need not necessarily fall into one category exclusively. Beethoven's *Pastoral* Symphony, for instance, is a symphony first and "pastoral" afterwards; while Berlioz' *Symphonie Fantastique* may be said to be primarily "fantastic" and only secondarily a symphony. Beethoven, however, always knew where to draw the line, and in his own words his *Pastoral* Symphony was "more an expression of feeling than tone painting." It is not programmatic because of the composer's excursion into ornithology in the second movement at the place where he indicates that the flute, oboe, and clarinet parts are imitating the calls of the nightingale, quail, and cuckoo, respectively. This passage makes perfectly good sense, since it fills out a pause in the slow movement at a point where a cadenza for solo instruments seems to fit naturally. Also it is not necessarily programmatic because of a rustic band playing folk dances for the merrymaking of the third movement; Beethoven's design would have called for a scherzo movement at just this juncture in any case. It is, however, programmatic to the extent that the composer fits the movements into a series of episodes implied by his subtitle. "A recollection of country life," and individually labeled: "Cheerful feelings aroused on arrival at the countryside"; "By the brook"; "Merrymaking of country folk"; "Storm—Shepherd's song—Joy and thanksgiving after the storm."

Occasionally programmatic hints are found in such abstract works as Beethoven's String Quartet in A Minor, Op. 132, where the slow movement bears the superscription, "A hymn of thanks to the Deity by a convalescent on his recovery. Feeling of new strength and reawakened sensation." By this reference to a personal episode in his later life, Beethoven indicates to his listeners that he attaches more than ordinary significance to this work. Otherwise the quartet is free of overt programmatic suggestions. Beethoven, on the other hand, writes straight programme music in such works as the Third Overture to his opera *Leonore*. Because of its identification of context with the climactic scene of the opera as well as its dramatic treatment generally, it has been justly hailed as "the first and greatest of all symphonic poems." (See Chap. 5, page 51 for a more complete discussion of this work.)

Those opposed to this type of programmatic suggestion feel that music should be heard solely as music and should not be subjected to literary, pictorial, or philosophical interpretations. Since music cannot, in any case, convey any very specific imagery, so the argument runs, this fact should become the source of strength rather than the weakness of the art. The Viennese critic Hanslick, one of the most ardent champions of "pure" music, upheld the position that music was a self-contained art having no relation to anything outside itself. Commenting on the bleating of sheep in one of Strauss' *Don Quixote* variations, a practical-minded orchestra conductor once asked why a composer should indulge in the expensive realism of the dozen muted brass instruments which take ten rehearsals to accomplish what a flock of sheep can do quite naturally. The danger of such frank description, as most everyone would admit, is that it can all too quickly degenerate into mere sound effects or background music. The poet Goethe once said, "To imitate thunder in music is not art, but the musician who excites in me the feeling as if I had heard thunder would be very estimable." Ultimately, as most people would agree, music as a language must be understood in its own terms and is compatible with the other arts only to a certain extent. Just how broadly or narrowly these limits are to be defined is, of course, the crux of the question.

Any attempt to separate music into two opposing camps with one labeled "absolute" and the other "programme" is bound to fail. Some composers may put abstract considerations above concrete ones, formal outlines above emotional content, craftsmanship above communication; but fortunately these oppositions are not mutually exclusive, and the difference becomes mainly one of degree, not of kind. No composer writes without some image in mind. In one case it might be as generalized a notion as a series of tonalities in a sonata movement, in another as particular as a sequence of episodes in a drama; as indefinite as a fleeting mood, or as precise as a dance rhythm; as subtle as an isorhythm in a medieval motet, or as obvious as the thunderstorm in Rossini's Overture to *William Tell*. When such sounds of nature as birdcalls or gusts of wind do appear in music, they are reproduced as sound patterns rather than represented directly; hence they are always abstract to some degree. Furthermore all composers, those of the absolute and programmatic persuasion alike, must take cognizance of formal considerations and decide whether they are to be precise and predictable or fluid and free. Regardless of whether the parts are patterned on the principle of variation, recurrence, or development, or arranged according to adventures, episodes, or dramatic vicissitudes, they are always based on some aspect of human experience—either generalized or particularized, symbolic or actual. In fact, it is possible to say without the risk of too much exaggeration, that programme music is abstract music in which the composer saw fit to disclose his intentions, while absolute music is programme music in which the composer keeps his intentions to himself.

Since no clear-cut dividing line between musical form and content is possible, a compromise position is generally taken that seems more or less satisfactory to all concerned. No programme, it is conceded, can ever replace the intrinsic structural quality of the music or assure the listener's interest unless the work can be launched independently. A bad piece of music, like a leaky vessel at sea, will sink in any case and no literary S.O.S. will save it or keep it afloat. If, however, a composer wants to add a title or reveal some poetic or pictorial idea that he had in mind, it is his privilege as a creative artist to do so. It is also the listener's inalienable right to disregard a poetic programme if he so chooses. Just as an untitled sonata movement may mean more to one person if he imagines some programme of his own fancy with it, so a programmatic piece may give greater pleasure to another when he considers it as abstract music. Richard Strauss himself suggested just such a solution in one of his rare comments on his own works. A tone poem, he wrote, "must be ship-shape musically considered. Let him who likes look at it merely as a musical work of art. In *Don Quixote,* for instance, I show how a man goes mad over vain imaginings. But I do not wish to compel any listener to think of Don Quixote when he hears it. He may conceive of it as absolute music if it suits him."

A review of musical literature will reveal that programme music exists in every instrumental medium and in all combinations from solo instruments to full orchestra. Since by definition it seeks formal freedom, programmatic works will be found to bear a bewildering number and variety of titles. In addition to programme symphonies and symphonic poems, there are overtures to operas remembered and forgotten, existing and imaginary, finished and unfinished. There are suites for all instrumental combinations, fantasies for everything from organ to orchestra, and programmatic string quartets and concertos. If, however, programme music is properly considered as a type of musical approach, some of the confusion can be dispelled and a modicum of clarity established.

Since the literature is so vast, it is possible at this point to cite only some of the outstanding examples. J. S. Bach, for instance, made one of his rare excursions into programme music in an early work for keyboard called *Capriccio on the Departure of a Beloved Brother.* Much the same emotional approach is found in Beethoven's Piano Sonata, Op. 81a, subtitled *Les Adieux,* in which the individual movements are labeled "Farewell," "Absence," and "Return." Chamber music, which is normally associated with the more abstract sonata literature, has escaped some of the programmatic excesses associated with other media. Smetana, however, wrote his autobiographical string quartets under the title *From My Life;* and biographical elements are also to be found in the last movement of Tchaikovsky's Trio in A Minor for Violin, Cello, and Piano, a work dedicated to the memory of Nicholas Rubinstein. Another important example of programmatic chamber music can be heard in Schoenberg's *Verklaerte Nacht* (Transfigured Night) , a work based on a poem by Richard Dehmel and originally scored for string sextet. Occasional instances of programmatic concertos are also to be reckoned with. Vivaldi's four concertos for violin based on sonnets entitled *Spring, Summer, Autumn,* and *Winter* come to mind, as does Spohr's Eighth Violin Concerto, subtitled *Gesangszene,* which is written like an operatic scene though with general rather than specific content. There is also Liszt's *Dance of Death* (*Totentanz*), a set of variations for piano and orchestra thought to have been inspired by a late medieval fresco by Traini called *Triumph of Death.*

Two examples—Vivaldi's series of solo violin concertos entitled *The Four Seasons* and Moussorgsky's *Pictures at an Exhibition*—will illustrate the approach to programme music by a baroque and romantic composer, respectively. In *The Four Seasons* (part of a set of twelve concertos, Op. 8, that Vivaldi called collectively *The Strife between Harmony and Invention*), each concerto is set to a sonnet describing one of the seasons of the year; and the individual movements, as well as passages within each movement, are collated to specific lines of poetry which they are intended to suggest or imitate. Vivaldi was well aware of the musical alternatives between an acceptable evocation of mood, sentiment, or passion on the one side and that of an imitative naturalism in the manner of sound effects on the other. With an abandon bordering on innocence he uses both techniques. When called for in the text, Vivaldi describes quite literally the sounds of thunder, birdcalls, and the barking of dogs. But he also knew that there are things in nature—like the quality of summer heat, or the precise ambiguity of cloud formations—that can be rendered in music only as sentiments, mood suggestions, or soul states. In each case, however, Vivaldi possesses the gift for an aptly descriptive phrase, a trait that is most charmingly and candidly displayed in the *Seasons.* The texts of the sonnets (freely translated) follow with a running commentary on the musical setting:

Spring Concerto:

Spring comes joyously	A robust country tune for orchestra. This is the Spring motive.
Hailed by the birds in happy song. The Zephyr's breezes play on the fountains Which reply in murmuring sweet sounds.	Three solo violins. (A baroque version of "a twittering machine.") The Spring tune reappears and is followed by a "murmuring" figure.
Soon the sky darkens And Spring's heralds—lightning and thunder—come.	The Spring tune is briefly interpolated. Then thunder (*tremolo* for strings in unison and octaves) and lightning (rapid ascending scale run).

The storm subsides and the birds
Renew their enchanting song.

Spring tune, followed once again by three solo violins for a second song of the birds. Spring tune (orchestra), a passage for solo violin, and the spring tune again (orchestra) completes the movement.

On the verdant meadow
While the foliage rustles gently
The goatherd sleeps, his faithful dog
    beside him.

A gentle, sleepily undulating figure in the violins, and a wakeful repeated note for the violas (the faithful dog?) over which the solo violin sings as if entranced. (Slow movement.)

To rustic pipes and their festive
    sounds
Nymphs and shepherds dance
Adorned in the brilliance of Spring.

A lively dance in 12/8 time (finale).

Summer Concerto:
In the season of enervating heat
Man and beast and the trees alike all
    droop.

An exhausted drooping figure on the second and third beats of a 3/8 measure. (The first beat is silent, and then the sigh.)

The cuckoo's call is soon joined
By the song of the turtledove and the
    finch.

Solo violin and solo cello.
The turtledove melody is a wonderfully expressive one for solo violin. The finch is represented by a few measures of birdlike twittering in a high register for unaccompanied solo violin.

Sweet zephyrs are rudely driven
By contending northern winds.

A gentle figure for upper strings represents the sweet zephyrs, and an abrupt and stormy one for full orchestra the contentious northern winds.

The shepherd laments in dread
Of the havoc of the tempest.
He is weary and knows no rest
Assailed by lightning and thunder
And by swarms of infuriated flies.

The drooping summer motive reappears and gives way to the shepherd's soulful lament (solo violin). Again a furious outburst of orchestral energy. The lament continues in an expressive solo violin aria interrupted by thunder (orchestral *tremolos* in unison and octaves). Effectively this is the middle (slow) movement. The last movement is devoted to summer's impetuous climate, and largely to the ferocious buzzing of insects.

Autumn Concerto:

With song and dance, the peasants mark
The happy harvest time,
Drink deep from the cup of Bacchus
And end their joy in slumber.

Even more so than the Spring concerto, this is a rollicking affair. The Autumn tune is a broad-backed peasant dance. The drunkard (solo violin) like a clown on a high wire, staggers through a series of precisely executed virtuoso arabesques before departing in off-beat syncopations. The Autumn tune resumes, alternating with more bravura arabesques for solo violin. The drunkard finally sleeps, as befits his honest exertions, most lyrically, innocently, and tenderly. (An aria for solo violin.) The Autumn tune brings the section to a close.

Now one by one they cease their sport
The mild and temperate season
Inducing sleep in all.

A slow movement whose harmonies are slow moving, shifting chromatically down and up by half steps. A heavy, deep, and vaguely restless sleep following wine, and the exertions of the dance.

At dawn the hunter
With horn and hound
Flushes his prey. The chase is on.
The tiring and bewildered beast
Assailed by dogs and the din of guns
Falls fatigued, and wounded, dies.

The finale is a hunting movement, the rhythm of the chase the dominant figure. A brief passage for the guns and the dogs appears intermittently.

Winter Concerto:

Shivering amid mounds of snow

A reiterated eighth-note motive piling up from instrument to instrument. The harmony is somewhat strained.

Pierced by cruel winds

Rapid, high-register figurations for unaccompanied solo violin, with orchestral "shudders" interpolated.

We run and stamp our feet

Appropriate music for running and stamping.

And our teeth chatter from the cold.	The opening Winter motive recurs followed by rapid, high-register double stoppings for solo violin (chattering of teeth) .
We pass contented days by the fireside While those outside are drenched by rain.	A contented, lyrical melody for solo violin, with a rain-drop sound-effect accompaniment in the orchestral strings. This serves as the slow movement.
We walk on the ice	A sliding figure for the solo violin.
Gently and timorously.	Carefully paced progress in the upper strings.
We adventure more bravely	A more determined figure.
And fall to the ground.	An orchestral slide (unison and octaves) down an octave and a sixth.
But we get up and run again. The ice breaks, cracking wide open.	A display of bravura skating for solo violin, culminating in an abrupt unison-octave figure for orchestra (the ice cracking) .
From behind closed doors we hear The southeast wind, the north wind And all the winds at war. Such is winter, but it has its pleasures.	The southeast wind is represented by an undulating figure in the upper strings and an ascending viola line in counterpoint to it; the war of the winds, by shuddering orchestral tremolos, agitated figurations for solo violin, and an overall rhythmic drive.

Pictures at an Exhibition by Moussorgsky is an interesting instance of a composition that has made its mark both in the original piano version and in orchestral investitures by Ravel and others. The work can also claim distinction on the grounds that it is one of the few in the repertory that has successfully incorporated the visual arts as the basis of a poetic programme. It will also serve at this point as a good illustration of the manners and methods of programme music in general. The exhibit referred to in the title was a memorial showing of sketches, architectural drawings, and watercolors by the composer's friend Victor Hartmann, which was held in St. Petersburg (now Leningrad) in 1874 shortly after the artist's death. These drawings, most of which are now lost, are by no means to be reckoned among the imperishable masterpieces of art. They do reveal, however, that Russian architects such as Hartmann were searching for national sources of Russian art, just as Moussorgsky and his colleagues were looking for national idioms in musical expression. The coincidence of their ideas happily resulted in the present work.

To suggest the sauntering gait of a viewer in a gallery as he pauses now and then before a picture that happens to attract his attention, Moussorgsky opens with and later interpolates a recurring but variable section called "Promenade" (Ex. 3:7). This device is akin to a ritornel, such as those found in opera scenes between arias and choruses, and it functions in this case as a connecting link in the chain of musical pictures. To some it suggests the overall formal outline of a rondo with alternating episodes. The general design, however, seems more closely related to such suites of character pieces for piano as Schumann's *Carnaval*, with the promenades exerting a unifying force as they effect the transition from picture to picture.

"The Gnome" was originally a design for an ingenious little toy nutcracker intended as a Christmas-tree ornament. Hartmann's drawing is now lost except for Moussorgsky's musical version of it, which depicts the gnome as a figure out of Russian folklore waddling along on his bandy legs to an awkward grotesque rhythm. A variant of the "Promenade" then leads to "The Old Castle," which, according to the catalogue of the exhibit, portrayed a minstrel singing and strumming in front of a medieval castle. Another version of the "Promenade" introduces a pair of pictures— "Tuileries" (subtitled, "Children Quarreling after Play") and "Bydlo," a Polish ox-cart lumbering along across the landscape (Ex. 3:9). Over the rumbling wheels soars Moussorgsky's fine melodic representation of the driver's song, which is every bit as robust and stolid as the peasant who sings it.

The "Promenade" interlude now takes the listener to the "Ballet of the Unhatched Chicks" as they dance in their shells. The drawing in this case was a costume sketch for a fanciful ballet production, and the catalogue describes the costume as representing "canary chicks enclosed in eggs as in suits of armor" (Fig. 17:1). Next, "Samuel Goldenberg and Schmuyle," two Polish Jews, one rich and the other poor, haggle and quarrel in a humorous episode. The "Promenade" then changes the scene to France for a glimpse of the bustling "Market Place at Limoges" where the women are furiously disputing with one another, and for an eerie view of the "Roman Catacombs" in Paris by lantern light. A mysterious version of the "Promenade" follows, which bears a cryptic inscription from the composer's hand, "With the dead in a dead language." Baba-Yaga," the wicked witch of Russian fairy tales who lives in a hut that stood on chicken's legs, now puts in an appearance. Moussorgsky in this case is translating a design for a clock with medieval Russian decorative motives (Fig. 17.2) into a whimsical witch's dance, and at the end she takes off in the traditional manner on a broomstick. For his Finale Moussorgsky contrives a massive and majestic musical version of Hartmann's project for "The Great Gate of Kiev" (Fig. 17.3). The catalogue's description reads in part, "The archway rests on granite pillars, three quarters sunk in the ground. Its head is decorated with a huge headpiece of Russian carved designs with the Russian state eagle above the peak. To the right is a belfry in three stories with a cupola in the shape of a Slav helmet." Hartmann's design is built up by Moussorgsky to a truly monumental piece of musical architecture in which a pageantlike procession of chords, the solemn chanting of monks, and the ringing of bells are all heard in turn as on a festive occasion.

In the main it is the orchestra that carries the principal weight of programmatic output, since the development of the modern symphonic medium in the nineteenth century coincided so exactly with the growth in popularity of programme music. The constantly increasing numbers in the orchestral ranks and continuously expanding color possibilities during that time confirmed the orchestra as the ideal means for programmatic expression. Many of these orchestral works are classified as overtures, though to all intents and purposes they are the same as symphonic poems. Overtures in the beginning, of course, were simply "curtain raisers" for the purpose of preparing the audience for what was to follow, whether it was to be a play, a ballet, an oratorio, or an opera. As such they were orchestral compositions of a more or less formal type without any direct connection with the work as a whole. Beginning with Gluck's operatic reforms and carrying on with Mozart's contributions, however, overtures began to have a dramatic as well as thematic connection with the opera itself. Examples of this type are found in Mozart's Overture to *Don Giovanni* and Beethoven's Overtures to *Leonore,* and continue with all of Weber's overtures and Wagner's Overtures to the *Flying Dutchman* and *Tannhäuser.* Overtures to operas no longer in the current repertory, such as Weber's to *Euryanthe* and Wagner's to *Rienzi,* still appear on concert programs, but their full meaning can be garnered only from a knowledge of the lyric dramas with which they were once associated. Then there are the overtures to unfinished operas, such as Berlioz' to *Benvenuto Cellini* and *Beatrice and Benedict,* in which the listener should look to the projected stories for their full significance. Incidental music to plays, such as that for Goethe's *Egmont* by Beethoven and Shakespeare's *Midsummer Night's Dream* by Mendelssohn, usually included overtures which now survive in the concert repertory. Then there are the overtures written especially for concert performance, some of which are based on novels,

Fig. 17:1 *Chick in Shell* (Costume sketches for the ballet, *Trilbi*). Victor Hartmann (1834–1873). Institute of Literature, Leningrad.

Fig. 17:2 *Bronze Clock in the Form of Baba Yaga's Hut.* Victor Hartmann (1834–1873). From the magazine *Pchela,* No. 1, 1875.

Fig. 17:3 *Project for the City Gate of Kiev.* Victor Hartmann (1834–1873). Drawing in the Institute of Literature, Leningrad.

poems, plays, and sundry other sources that fired the composer's imagina-
tion. Examples of this type are Berlioz' Overtures to Walter Scott's novels
Waverly and *Rob Roy;* Mendelssohn's *Calm Sea and Prosperous Voyage*
and *Legend of the Lovely Melusina,* overtures on literary works by
Goethe; Wagner's *Faust Overture* (1840) on Goethe's drama; and Brahms'
Tragic Overture with only the title as a clue to its content.

In addition to the simple designation of "overture," there are a host
of hybrid and fanciful titles by various composers. Tchaikovsky called his
Romeo and Juliet (1840) an "overture-fantasy," and his *Hamlet* a
"fantasy-overture." These, together with his *Ouverture Solennelle, 1812*
(Solemn Overture, 1812) and his *Francesca da Rimini* (1873) called an
"orchestral fantasy," must be charged to the composer's whim since they
differ in no essential respect from other concert overtures. Even more
fanciful are some of Debussy's designations such as his *Afternoon of a
Faun* described as a "prelude"; his *Clouds, Fêtes,* and *Sirens* grouped together as "nocturnes"; and his *Gigues* and *Iberia* labeled as "images."

The suite, originally a series of dance movements, has also not escaped
the attention of composers of programme music. In this category come
orchestral suites extracted for concert purposes from ballets, such as Tchaikovsky's *Nutcracker* Suite (on a short story by E. T. A. Hoffmann), and
Stravinsky's *Firebird* and *Petrouchka* Suites (on choreographical ideas by
Fokine); suites compounded out of incidental music written for plays such
as Bizet's *Arlésienne* Suite, originally written for a play by Daudet, and
Grieg's *Peer Gynt* Suite for Ibsen's drama of that name; there are suites
written initially for piano and later arranged for orchestra by their composers such as Ravel's *Mother Goose* Suite; and those written expressly
for concert performance such as Rimsky-Korsakoff's *Scheherezade,* a suite
based on stories from the *Arabian Nights.*

After the middle of the nineteenth century, however, composers generally followed Liszt's lead, and "symphonic poem" or "tone poem" became the commonly adopted designation for these one-movement orchestral works. Their sources of inspiration, however, continued to be highly
varied. There were those with literary antecedents, such as Liszt's *The
Preludes,* after a poem by Lamartine (for a detailed discussion of this
work see Chap. 22, pages 366–367); Franck's *The Accursed Huntsman,*
on a ballad by Bürger; and Richard Strauss' *Don Juan* on Lenau's dramatic poem. Those based on pictorial sources include Liszt's *Battle of the
Huns,* suggested by Kaulbach's fresco; and Rachmaninoff's *Isle of the
Dead,* on the painting of that name by Böcklin. There are orchestral discourses on philosophy, such as Richard Strauss' *Also Sprach Zarathustra*
(Thus Spake Zarathustra) inspired by Nietzsche's book; Scriabin's *Poem
of Ecstasy,* which reflects the composer's mystical views on theosophy; and

Charles Ives' *Unanswered Question*. Examples fired by national sentiment and patriotism are Liszt's *Hungaria*, Smetana's series called *My Fatherland*, which includes the descriptive one on the Moldau River; and Sibelius' *Finlandia*. There are also those derived from general sources such as Moussorgsky's *Night on Bald Mountain*, a witches' sabbath with no definite literary source; Saint-Saëns' *Omphale's Spinning Wheel*, from mythology; Delius' *On Hearing the First Cuckoo in Spring*, subjective impressions and springtime moods; and Gershwin's *An American in Paris*, a jaunty, jazzy piece of musical tourism.

In addition there are the lengthier programme symphonies, which differ from symphonic poems in that they are somewhat larger in scope as well as comprising a cycle of separate movements grouped into a symphonic whole. The history of such symphonies can be traced to Haydn's series of three called *Morning, Afternoon,* and *Evening,* respectively, and, of course, Beethoven's *Pastoral* Symphony. The cornerstone in this category is Berlioz' *Symphonie Fantastique,* and its successors include Liszt's *Faust* Symphony with its several movements entitled "Faust," "Marguerite," and "Mephistopheles," as well as the same composer's *Dante* Symphony embracing movements entitled "Inferno," "Purgatory," and "Magnificat." A couple of the more recent works in this genre are Richard Strauss' *Sinfonia Domestica* and Hindemith's *Mathis der Maler* (Matthias the Painter). Then there are some less usual designations by which composers attempt to attach some special meaning to their programme symphonies, such as Tchaikovsky's *Manfred* (1885), which is subtitled a "Symphony in Four Tableaux"; Richard Strauss' *From Italy,* in reality a suite but entitled by the composer a "Symphonic Fantasia"; and Debussy's orchestral seascape *La Mer,* the movements of which are grouped by the composer under the title of "Three Symphonic Sketches."

Programme music, as it appears in the nineteenth century, is thus essentially dramatic music cast in instrumental forms. As such the composer could write songs and ballads without words as did Schumann and Brahms, and librettoless and singerless operas as did Berlioz and Liszt. With the humanization of musical instruments, a programme symphony or a symphonic poem becomes a kind of orchestral opera in which the dramatic action is implied in the poetic programme rather than explicitly acted out and sung. In a play, for instance, a person is first presented, then exposed to a series of situations in order to reveal his character by reactions to the various dramatic vicissitudes. Similarly in programme music, the motive or melody is substituted for a personality and eventually discloses its true nature by evolving through a sequence of qualitative changes. Far from being too concrete, as it is so often accused of being, programme music, by freeing the song from words and liberating opera from librettos, actually becomes the most abstract of all dramatic music.

PART IV

The Composer

and the World

Music in History

Chapter 18

MUSIC is essentially a social process—an art addressed to, performed with and enjoyed in the company of others. In all places and at all times music, as well as architecture and the other arts, has been, and still is, woven into some aspect of the fabric of community life. And just as a building is incomprehensible except in terms of its place and function, so also does a musical work resist understanding until its nature and purpose are known. The discovery that a particular edifice was a temple, a theater, or a dwelling place does not reveal everything about it, but it does say a good deal. Likewise the revelation that a piece of music was composed for a religious observation, a public spectacle, or a domestic gathering does not tell all, but it certainly tells much. Like architecture, music in society is a coordinating force. Its function may be as basic as a work song or as exalted as a symphony that celebrates the liberation of the human spirit. Music, then, is one of the experiences by which man realizes his humanity, and one of the ways he creates a meaning for his life.

Music has, for the most part, a direct relation to the various social occasions at which it is designed to be performed. Like the other arts, it is always addressed to some segment of society. Religious events, civic celebrations, and official functions all call for appropriate music; and, in times prior to the present, special music by contemporary composers was usually commissioned for such purposes. This situation immediately points to the problem of patronage. According to an old saying, he who pays the piper calls the tune. There are, of course, as many levels of enlightenment and discernment among patrons as there are levels of competency among composers or any other craftsmen. The application of the proverb by no means implies, then, that the tune will necessarily be either a good or bad one. Music, like all great forces in life, is a double-edged sword. It can ascend to the Olympian heights of great creative art, and it can descend to the depths of blatant propaganda and the cheap perversions of the "singing commercial." The important point, always, is whether its control rests in the hands of those who will ennoble the art or debase it.

Since music has so many functions to fulfill, the very diversity of the sources of patronage is one of its special protections. In periods such as the Middle Ages, the Church selected, educated, and encouraged the finest available talents. During the Renaissance, the musical direction pointed more toward courtly entertainment, and many a princely purse was opened for the training and support of outstanding musicians. In modern times, a vast and anonymous patron known as the "public" contributes or withholds its support via its patronage, not of the composer, but of the free market (that is, the concert hall and the opera house) where the composer's products are offered for inspection. As Romain Rolland has said, music "adapts itself to all conditions of society. It is a courtly art under Francis I and Charles IX; an art of faith and fighting with the Reformation; an art of affectation and princely pride under Louis XIV; an art of the salon in the eighteenth century. Then it becomes the lyric expression of revolutionaries; and it will be the voice of the democratic societies of the future, as it was the voice of the aristocratic societies of the past. No formula will hold it. It is the song of centuries and the flower of history; its growth pushes upward from the griefs as well as from the joys of humanity."

Besides being an organized whole, a piece of music (as well as every other work of art) is also a social and historical fact. Beethoven's Ninth Symphony—proclaiming as it does the ideals of liberty, equality, and the brotherhood of man—is as much a document of the revolutionary years as the Rights of Man, the Declaration of Independence, or the American Constitution. Thus the soaring aspirations of both individual and collective ideals can be expressed through music with its own special language of tonal symbols and auditory images just as through any other form of human expression. Like other works of art, a piece of music is a bridge between the world of inner experience and the world of external reality; and since it represents the crystallization of a moment in time, it is also a bridge between past and future. Upon this work of art and within this moment of time, the composer as its creator focuses all of his past experience, all his capacities of craftsmanship, and all of his present inspiration. The particular event known as the work of art, moreover, does not stand in isolation but is based upon the background of the sum total of experience, both individual and social. The more intense the inner life of the artist and the more vision he can concentrate into the given moment, the more meaningful will be the particular event that finds its expression in his art. Through the eyes and ears of their artists, then, societies can see and hear aspects of their world they never saw or heard before. By training his perceptions and sensitizing his eyes and ears, a new and richer world is revealed to the individual observer and listener. The insights of poets and musicians thus become part of a larger world outlook and part of a life more intrinsically satisfying.

A composer is as deeply sensitive to his environment as any of his fellow citizens. As Robert Schumann once wrote to his wife, "Everything touches me that goes on in the world—politics, literature, people. I think after my own fashion of everything that can express itself through music . . ." As articulate members of their respective communities, composers—whether their language is direct or indirect, abstract or concrete—are interpreters of the individual, human, and social issues of their times.

Music moves its mountains slowly, yet it shapes the soul of man as surely as any other force. This may not be open to proof or amenable to the same manner of adducing evidence that would satisfy an inquiry into the impact on human behavior of a mechanical invention like the cotton gin or power steering. But belief in the truth of the proposition is an article of faith that is found not only among musicians; both Bach and Shakespeare are agreed on it, likewise Monteverdi and Socrates, and Beethoven and the early fathers of the church. Shakespeare marks for suspicion the man whose soul does not respond to music. This a musician can readily understand. A melody communicates a level of experience more basic than language, for words do not obtrude to distract by their demand for translation. Bach, Purcell, and Verdi speak through the abstract inflections that underlie language, and hence their communications cross the borders of time and space, and are understood by all who listen attentively. To be deeply moved by the life experience of another is indeed a profound education for every human being.

In order to communicate meaning, the artist—whether he speaks in a verbal, visual, or tonal vocabulary—must do so in a system of symbols, images, and conventions that are, at least for the most part, understood by those to whom his works are addressed. The composer lives in the world of tone. Through his tonal perceptions he directs his moving materials, builds his sonorous masses, and creates his musical shapes. As he puts together the sounds that reflect his experiences and his reactions to his world, he must obviously do so in terms of a tonal language that his audience can understand. As in the case of his native tongue, the composer first learns the musical language of his cultural environment and more specifically the musical speech of his immediate predecessors. When he reaches maturity as craftsman and artist, he may have something new and unique to say which entails departures from past precedents. In the process of so doing he may find it necessary to add to the existing vocabulary, discover new grammatical syntaxes, and devise new musical symbols that correspond more exactly to his intentions. His inherited language, his personal usage of that system, the vocabulary he chooses, and the conventions he adds to the common currency all add up to his *style*. By definition, style, then, is the totality of the symbols, the entire esthetic system, by which a composer communicates his conceptions of order and meaning. It is thus through his style that he makes clear his attitudes and comments toward the world around and within him. When a musical style becomes socially established and universally accepted as it did, say, in the latter part of the eighteenth century, the demand for new works becomes such that composers can hardly keep up with it. Hence one witnesses with a sense of awe the unparalleled creative activity of a Haydn and a Mozart. During the period when they were composing, a common bond existed between composer and public, so that the music of churches, salons, concert and dance halls all spoke in essentially the same language. Even the street musicians of Vienna played the melodies of Gluck, Haydn, and Mozart. Yet within the framework of a common musical language, each composer speaks in accents that are his own.

Music is a many faceted art, and at various times it presents different aspects to the world. The notion of progress should be promptly dispelled. No one era such as the romantic period is necessarily better than any other, but it is certainly different. There is, in fact, no all-embracing art of music, but rather as many musics as there are social orders, historical periods, regional centers, and composers of strong individuality, each speaking a different language with a different syntax, vocabulary, and style. Musical systems rise and fall, come and go; and since there is nothing fixed or immutable about them, a historical and cultural context must be postulated. By a study of the history of these styles and their common conventions, the listener can master these languages of the musical past sufficiently to establish at least partial understanding. Interpreting the music of the past, of course, presents many problems. Some listeners will inevitably feel a closer kinship with one period than with another, but much will inescapably elude the contemporary ear. One cannot hear music from a period of pure melody, such as the early medieval music, with ears accustomed to lush orchestral sonorities and rich harmonic accompaniments. Much of its pure otherworldly beauty, however, is still discernible if the ear is reoriented to this earlier style. It is likewise impossible to hear the

music of Bach and Mozart with eighteenth-century ears. Although much
of its inner radiance transcends the centuries, some of its meaning is lost
unless it is understood as closely as possible within its original cultural
context.

The history of the arts is the record of the establishment of types of
order. Every individual and every society has a conception of the universal
environment and the position of the individual in the general order.
Within that society, the creative artist conceives that order in appropriate
symbols and images and gives articulate expression to it. His art may be
in essential agreement with the established system, be predicated on some
values of the past he seeks to preserve, or be dedicated to overthrowing the
existing order and bringing about a new era. In political life there are
those who seek to uphold traditional values, those content to swim along
with the tide of their times, and those who want to strike out in new directions. So also in music there are composers who represent various shades
of artistic opinion. J. S. Bach, for instance, was a staunch conservative who
sought to preserve the values of the grand universal polyphonic style in
the face of a movement toward harmonic writing and delicate personal
nuances of expression. Mozart, for his part, was quite content to speak in
the accents of his own time; and without fundamentally changing the established language, he contributed his many matchless masterpieces to
musical literature. Then there are the revolutionaries—Monteverdi, Wagner, Schoenberg, for instance—who formulated new theories and forged
new musics based on new concepts, and in the process awakened and
aroused their contemporaries.

Just as the visual arts can present the visage of a period through portraits, costumes, gestures, attitudes, and scenes from daily life, so music, by
dipping deep into the wellsprings of emotion, can yield understanding of
an age. The history of song reflects both the joys and sorrows, the fortunes
and misfortunes of the people who sang them. The history of the dance
reveals the inner rhythms as well as the outer steps and gestures that mirror
the strivings and goals of the individuals and groups who perform them.
The history of the lyric stage including opera can become a rich source of
commentary on the conceptions a society had of itself, its deeds, its manners, and its characteristic attitudes. The music of a period tells not only
of its harmonies but also of its conflicts. In epochs of oppression, music
represents the passionate outpouring of the human heart. In periods of
religious revival, it sings out with resounding declarations of faith. In
ages of reason, it reflects the logical processes of well-ordered minds. In
interludes of social upheaval, it rings with revolutionary anthems.

There are those who feel strongly that history is irrelevant to a particular piece of music, because the musical work as such is essentially a

personal document—a record of how one man felt. In this view all music
is self-expression; it is personal autobiography rather than social commentary. There is, to be sure, a measure of truth in this viewpoint. But
as Lincoln once said, no man can escape history; and a personal record
becomes universally meaningful when it reveals more than the man himself. Music history is a special kind of history. It is not a record of the
political reasons for a war, or of the points of doctrine underlying a religious dispute; but it is a record of how one human being felt during the
course of that war, or of one man's reaction to a religious controversy.
Some individuals are by nature more sensitive and more articulate than
others. When the depth of their feeling is transmitted through sound, it
becomes a measure of the emotions of many of their inarticulate contemporaries for whom they may be said to speak. Thus Beethoven as a composer may be considered a profounder spokesman for the ideals of his age
than either Napoleon or Metternich as statesmen. And Bach may well provide as deep an insight into the human ideals cherished by the Protestant
community as Luther does in his capacity as a theologian. As Romain
Rolland has so eloquently declared, "Yet the political life of a nation is
only a superficial part of its being; in order to learn its inner life—the
source of its actions—we must penetrate to its very soul by way of its
literature, its philosophy, and its art, where the ideas, the passions and the
dreams of its people are reflected."

Music must thus be accorded its rightful place in the history of ideas,
and when seen in the light of the larger rhythms of human history, its
levels of meaning acquire new horizons, new vistas, new dimensions. A
quotation from Romain Rolland's moving manifesto, "On the Place of
Music in General History," is as appropriate today as when it first appeared in the early years of this century. "The thought of the eternal
efflorescence of music," he comments, "is a comforting one, and comes like
a messenger of peace in the midst of universal disturbance. Political and
social history is a never-ending conflict, a thrusting of humanity forward
to a doubtful issue, with obstacles at every step, which have to be conquered one by one with desperate persistence. But from the history of art
we may disengage a character of fullness and peace. In art, progress is not
thought of; for, however far we look behind, we see that perfection has
already been attained; and that man is absurd who thinks the efforts of
the centuries have advanced one step nearer beauty since the days of St.
Gregory and Palestrina. There is nothing sad or humiliating in the idea;
on the contrary, art is humanity's dream—a dream of light and liberty and
quiet power. It is a dream whose thread is never broken, and there is no
fear for the future. In our anxiety and pride we tell ourselves that we have
reached the pinnacle of art and are on the eve of a decline. That has been

said since the beginning of the world. In every century people have sighed, 'All has been said; we have come too late.' Well, everything may have been said; yet everything is still to say. Art, like life, is inexhaustible; and nothing makes us feel the truth of this better than music's ever-welling spring, which has flowed through the centuries until it has become an ocean." [1]

[1] Romain Rolland. *Some Musicians of Former Days.* Translated by Mary Blaiklock. New York: Henry Holt and Co., 1915. This and the previous excerpts from Rolland's essay are quoted by permission of the publisher.

CLASSICAL, MEDIEVAL, AND RENAISSANCE CHRONOLOGY

Greek Philosophers

Pythagoras	c.582–c.507 B.C.
Socrates	469– 399 B.C.
Plato	427– 347 B.C.
Aristotle	384– 322 B.C.
Aristoxenus	c.350– ? B.C.
Euclid, active	c.300 B.C.

Greek Dramatists

Aeschylus	525–456 B.C.
Sophocles	496–406 B.C.
Euripides	480–406 B.C.

Church Fathers

Clement of Alexandria	A.D. c.160–	c.216
St. Basil	c.330–	c.378
St. Ambrose	340–	397
St. Jerome	c.342–	420
St. John Chrysostom	c.345–	407
St. Augustine	354–	430
Boethius	c.480–	524
Cassiodorus	c.485–	c.580
Isidore of Seville	c.570–	636
Gregory the Great	c.540–	604

Medieval Composers and Theorists

Notker Balbulus	c.840– 912
Hucbald of St. Amand	c.840– 930
Odo of Cluny, active	c.899– 942
Guido of Arezzo	c.995– 1050
Wipo of Burgundy	c.1000– 1050
Adam of St. Victor	c.1122– 1192
Leonin, active	c.1150–c.1180
Perotin, active	c.1183–c.1200
Wolfram von Eschenbach	c.1170–c.1220
Walther von der Vogelweide	c.1170–c.1230
Thomas of Celano	c.1200–c.1256
Thomas Aquinas	c.1225– 1274
Adam de la Hale	c.1237–c.1288
Franco of Cologne, active	c.1260
Jacopone da Todi	c.1230– 1306
Walter Odington, active	c.1280–c.1330

Renaissance Composers and Theorists

John Dunstable	c.1390– 1453
Guillaume Dufay	1400– 1474
Gilles Binchois	c.1400– 1460
Conrad Paumann	c.1410– 1473
Joannes Ockeghem	1430– 1495
Antonio Squarcialupi	1436– 1475
Alexander Agricola	c.1446– 1506
Jacob Obrecht	1450– 1505
Heinrich Isaac	c.1450– 1517
Loyset Compère	c.1455– 1518
Josquin des Prez	c.1460– 1521
Pierre de la Rue	? 1518
Johannes Tinctoris	1471– 1511
Clément Jannequin	c.1475–c.1560
Martin Luther	1483– 1546
Ludwig Senfl	? c.1555
Henricus Glareanus	1488– 1563
Adrian Willaert	c.1490– 1562
Johann Walther	1496– 1570
Luis Milan	c.1500–c.1562
Cristóbal Morales	c.1500– 1553
Jacob Arcadelt	c.1505–c.1567
Louis Bourgeois	c.1510–c.1561
Claude Goudimel	c.1510– 1572
Philippe de Monte	c.1521– 1603
Giovanni da Palestrina	c.1525– 1594
Guillaume Costeley	1531– 1606
Orlandus Lassus	c.1532– 1594
Giaches de Wert	1535– 1596
William Byrd	1543–c.1622
Tomás Luis de Victoria	c.1548– 1611
Luca Marenzio	1553– 1599
Thomas Morley	c.1557–c.1603
Francis Pilkington	c.1562– 1638
John Dowland	c.1563– 1626
Giles Farnaby	c.1565– 1640
Thomas Campian	1567– 1620
Thomas Weelkes	c.1570– 1623
Martin Peerson	c.1572– 1650
John Wilbye	1574– 1638
Orlando Gibbons	1583– 1625

Composers and Theorists of the *Ars Nova* (Fourteenth Century)

Philippe de Vitry	1291– 1361	Jean de Muris	c.1300–c.1351
Guillaume de Machaut	c.1295–c.1377	Jacob of Liége, active	c.1325–c.1350
Marchettus of Padua, active	1318	Francesco Landino	1325– 1397

Ancient, Medieval, and Renaissance Influences and Styles

Chapter **19**

THE GREEK HERITAGE

For over 2000 years, Western thought has periodically gravitated back toward ancient Greece. From time to time, philosophers find it necessary to speculate on the world views of Plato and Aristotle; men of letters reappraise and reinterpret Greek poetry and drama; architects and sculptors theorize on the measurements and meaning of the ancient monuments; and composers as well as musical historians find inspiration in the implications of Greek esthetic views and music theory. The actual body of ancient Greek music is reduced to about a dozen extant fragments. Knowledge about the art is therefore confined to these meager remains, various literary and philosophical commentaries, as well as some surviving theoretical and critical treatises. Since there is no sizable corpus of musical compositions comparable to the monuments of Greek architecture and sculpture, the body of Greek drama, or the writings of Plato and Aristotle, it is not possible to point to a Greek musical style as

241

one can, for instance, to a Renaissance, baroque, Viennese classical, or romantic style.

The musical legacy of Greece, since the actual musical examples are so few, is principally a legacy of ideas. Yet the authority of Greek musical thought persists. It is found, for instance, in the basic words of the musical vocabulary—*music, rhythm, melody, harmony, symphony, melodrama* (originally drama with melody) —which are Greek in derivation. Greek precedents are encountered in the practice of classical metrics both in poetry and in music; and they are ever present in the rational basis of Western musical theory which rests firmly on the mathematical relationships of the musical intervals and logical scale systems formulated by the Greeks.

The vitality of ancient Greek musical thought is attested to by its prominent place in all historical periods. When Boethius and Cassiodorus in the early sixth century discoursed on music, they relied on Greek authorities. So also did the authors of later medieval musical treatises. In formulating the principles underlying lyric drama, the Florentine Camerata group cited the precedents of ancient Greek drama for their innovations; so also did Monteverdi in his justifications of certain "modernisms" in his early seventeenth-century madrigals. The French baroque drama and opera were replete with ancient Greek characters, forms, and esthetic theories; and Gluck's operatic reforms of the late eighteenth century relied on a reinterpretation of Aristotle's *Poetics.* Such movements are customarily called neoclassical, and since all periods in Western art have interpreted Greek ideals in one way or another, there are almost as many neoclassicisms as there are styles in art or music. Whether it is the Renaissance, the baroque, the Viennese classical or the twentieth-century, in each style period there are individuals who come to terms in some way with Greek ideals, and either accept, modify, reject, or employ them as points of departure.

In actual practice Greek music was apparently purely melodic in character with no accompanying chordal harmonies and no part writing in the contrapuntal sense. While the Greeks did have a music for such stringed instruments as the lyre and cithara, and such wind instruments as the syrinx (panpipes) and aulos (an oboelike instrument with a pungent, penetrating sound) , it appears that by far the greater part of Greek music was vocal. As Plato explains it in the *Republic,* "Melody is composed of three things, the words, the harmony (by which is meant the relationship of the successive melodic intervals) , and the rhythm." This concept of a purely melodic music was general throughout the Mediterranean region, and it survives in modified forms to the present day in the practices of synagogal, Byzantine, and Gregorian chants.

From all available evidence, Greek music attained its highest and most complex form in conjunction with drama. The great Greek dramatists—Aeschylus, Sophocles, and Euripides—were, in addition to being playwrights and producers, also composers. There is fairly general agreement among scholars that Greek tragedy originated in the dithyramb—a choral hymn sung in honor of the god Dionysus. It was thus a union of poetry and music; and in the drama that grew out of it, this unity was closely maintained. In the developed form of the Greek drama, the *chorus,* immediately after the *prologue,* made its entrance while singing and dancing. Throughout the play the chorus remained in the *orchestra* (originally a dancing place), the circular area in front of the proscenium or raised stage. Its leader performed solo songs and dances, and the chorus itself performed either as a single unit or divided into two groups for antiphonal singing. The chorus could also perform while in motion or in a stationary position. One of the surviving examples of Greek music is a fragment of a chorus from Euripides' *Orestes* (B.C. 408). Since it is too fragmentary for any general conclusions, the metrical basis and something of the emotional tone of the choral choreography must be determined from the poetic text alone. The role of the chorus in the drama varied considerably. Its usual function was to make choral comments on the dramatic action. Sometimes, as in the later plays of Euripides, it simply provided lyrical interludes between scenes. At times a choral ode alternated with the plot scenes, or *episodes,* performed by the actors on the stage proper, and at others it was replaced by a lyrical song sung by one or more of the actors with chorus. But more often than not, the chorus was a vital element in the drama, and its music presumably functioned as a strategic resource, helping to project and to realize those moments in tragedy that are beyond the power of the unaided word. Greek drama was thus a spectacle that included elements of choral chanting and dancing, vocal and instrumental music, as well as dialogue and plot. As the literary historian W. T. Oates has remarked, the "dramatic synthesis" in Greek tragedy, "in many ways resembles the modern opera." While not an exact parallel, the analogy between Greek tragedy and opera is at least a helpful one.

Since the actual practice of Greek music is, for the most part, a lost art, the most influential contribution to Western musical tradition is the foundation of a rational basis for music theory. The momentous discovery of the mathematical relationships of the musical intervals is attributed to Pythagoras, a semilegendary figure. How much acoustical learning he acquired in his travels in Egypt, and how significant a role he himself played in acoustical experiments, is lost in obscurity. About 300 B.C., long after the death of Pythagoras, Euclid conducted the now-famous experiments on a calibrated one-stringed instrument called the monochord. By varying the length of the vibrating string and noting the resultant pitches, he established the mathematical measurements for the musical intervals (see Chap. 1, pp. 5–6). If half the string was allowed to vibrate, then the pitch produced was an octave higher than that of the full string; and the octave could therefore be reduced to a relationship of two numbers—that is, the ratio of 1:2. Similarly, the perfect fifth could be expressed by the ratio of 2:3, and the perfect fourth as 3:4; and thus all musical intervals were reducible to number relationships. These observations are still basic to the science of acoustics, and they still govern the playing of the violin— based on the vibration of the whole or parts of the strings—as well as the oboe or trombone, which are based on the vibration of lengthened or shortened columns of air.

Once these incontrovertible mathematical and acoustical truths were established, the followers of Pythagoras thought they had the keys that would unlock the secrets of the universe. When they discovered that number ratios could be sought for with success in the heavens as well as on earth, "They assumed," reported Aristotle of the early Pythagoreans, "that the elements of number were the elements of all things." The human soul, they theorized, was united with the body by a concord or harmony, and a healthy person had to be not only in harmony within himself, but also with his natural, social, and ultimately his cosmic environment as well. The latter state was described as being "in tune with the infinite." The Pythagoreans also postulated a harmony in the heavens, and music and astronomy were considered to be the "sister sciences." Since bodies on earth, much smaller and slower than the stars, produce sounds when in motion, they reasoned that each heavenly body must also produce a sound as it moves in its orbit through space. And since the courses of the celestial bodies could be expressed in number ratios like the intervals in music, a complex of related pitches must also be sounded when the stars revolved in their courses. "Assuming these things," remarked Aristotle, "they (the Pythagoreans) say that the sound of the stars moving in a circle becomes musical." This "music of the spheres," they considered, was an unheard music, for such sound was in the very structure of the universe, and could not be distinguished from silence.

These Pythagorean speculations have served for 2000 years as a poetic playground for the intellect and the imagination. The music of the spheres was a concept passed on to later European medieval thought via Boethius early in the sixth century A.D.; he called it *musica mundana* and used the term to designate one of his three basic classifications of music. As a poetic fancy, it persisted through the waning of the Middle Ages well into the eighteenth-century Enlightenment. (See, for example, poems as diverse as Chaucer's *The Parlement of Foules* and Addison's *Hymn on the*

Glories of Creation.) And as a blend of metaphor and metaphysics, it is found as an eloquent parable of the relationship between the earthly and the divine. Sir Thomas Browne (1605–1682) so used it in his *Religio Medici* (Part II, Section IX). "For there is a music," he wrote, "wherever there is a harmony, order, or proportion; and thus far we may maintain 'the music of the spheres': for these well-ordered motions, and regular paces, though they give no sound to the ear, yet to the understanding they strike a note most full of harmony." All earthly music, he continued, was an intimation of the divine, and even tavern music had "something in it of divinity more than the ear discovers," for a melody audible to the mortal ear was the "hieroglyphical and shadowed lesson of the whole world," and a "sensible fit of that harmony which intellectually sounds in the ears of God."

For music per se, more important than the music of the spheres, was the Pythagorean concept of the number basis of music. One finds it echoed continuously in medieval treatises. Thus in the early sixth century A.D., Cassiodorus defined music as "The discipline which treats of numbers in their relation to those things which are found in sounds." Several centuries later, a commentary (*Scholia enchiriadis*) to a ninth-century instruction manual in music contained the following exchange between disciple and master. The disciple asked, "What is music?" and the master replied, "The rational discipline of agreement and discrepancy in sounds according to numbers in their relation to those things which are found in sounds." The author (whose identity is disputed) of the *Scholia* had evidently read Cassiodorus, and via this source continued to provide a neo-Pythagorean basis for elementary musical instruction in the Middle Ages. Centuries later, this doctrine was still very much alive, for Walter Odington opens his treatise on music, *De Speculatione Musice* (c. 1300) with the flat assertion that music "is number related to sound." The measurement of interval ratios was still basic in sixteenth-century musical theory, and the broader concept of a mathematical basis of music is still a field for theoretical exploration today. An extended study by Joseph Schillinger entitled *The Mathematical Basis of the Arts,* for instance, was published as recently as 1948.

To return now to the Greeks—music was considered by all the major philosophers to possess the quality of *ethos*, or ethical character. Music, they felt, since it is based on the rational attunement of the strings in their just proportion, could also be a reflection of the divine order of the universe. Hence, if properly controlled, music could distill the essence of supreme orderliness, create the harmonious image of a moral universe, and become a melodious representation of truth and beauty. As a spiritual discipline, therefore, music should be used for its most noble purposes, and its undoubted power should be exploited only for human betterment. Socrates, Plato, and Aristotle all sanctioned the teaching of music to the young, and its study occupied an important and highly honored place in ancient education. The study of music, according to Plato in his *Symposium,* could instill the love of beautiful melodies. The love of beauty—whether found in nature, in a fair face or form, or in a work of art—led logically to fair thoughts, then to the relationship between one expression of beauty and another, and ultimately to the contemplation of the eternal verities—the good, the true, and the beautiful. "For from the love of the beautiful," says Plato, "has sprung every good in heaven and earth." With a more practical turn of mind, Aristotle allowed that music was usually studied mainly for the pleasure it afforded. But, as he counseled, it really should be pursued because it "is useful for the rational enjoyment of leisure," and hence it could contribute to moral character and living the good life.

More than any other figure in the ancient world, Aristoxenus of Tarentum comes closest to the modern conception of a scientific theory of music. He sought to coordinate all the data available to him in a systematic fashion, and his theory encompasses, in consequence, a psychology and an esthetic of music as well as an ordering of its inner mechanics. He was a pupil of Aristotle and may well have aspired to have succeeded his master as head of the famous Lyceum (Aristotle's school of philosophy). At an earlier stage he had studied with the Pythagoreans, but became convinced that their "numerical ratios and relative rates of vibrations" were, as he expressed it in his *Harmonic Elements,* "utterly extraneous to the subject." Aristoxenus consequently based his system on a relationship between sense perception and intellect. The Pythagoreans, he felt, were in fundamental error because they rejected sense data in music as inaccurate and untrustworthy, and because they substituted what he characterized as "fabricated rational principles" for the evidence of one's ears. Unlike the geometrician, who begins with the postulation of a straight line or a circle and leaves the sense perception and application of these figures to a carpenter, the student of music, Aristoxenus argued, cannot be content to postulate a musical interval. He must hear it, and further, he must train himself to hear it accurately. Deficiency in sense perception, for Aristoxenus, was fatal in any serious speculation about music.

However fundamental the sense data upon which the musician or listener must rely, the intellect must nevertheless also be engaged in making discriminating judgments vital to music as an art. This was a conclusion Aristoxenus drew from the following facts. A musical interval, or single pitch, was in one respect a constant and in another a variable. Thus the same half step, in two different musical situations, could function in two different ways, although the half step in itself remained literally the same. The interval remained constant, but its function changed. Accuracy in musical sense perception was necessary to grasp the constant interval, whereas the intellect was necessary to follow its change of function. "Our subject matter then being all melody, whether vocal or instrumental," he wrote, "our method rests in the last resort on an appeal to the two faculties of hearing and intellect. By the former we judge the magnitude of the intervals, by the latter we contemplate the function of the notes."

It is beyond the scope of the present discussion to follow Aristoxenus through all the ramifications of the inner technical mechanics of Greek music. Suffice it to say with Farrington in his book *Greek Science,* that the "achievement of Aristoxenus finds its nearest parallel in the *Poetics* of Aristotle where for the first time science had been successfully applied to the analysis of a great branch of art. With the *Poetics* of Aristotle and the *Harmonics* of Aristoxenus, the basis had been laid for an intelligent and conscious criticism of the nature and function of art. The human spirit had made immense gains in its consciousness of itself."

THE CHURCH FATHERS

The apparent hostility toward music encountered in the writings of the early churchmen—"Let her be deaf to the sound of the organ," advised St. Jerome on the subject of female education, "and not even know the uses of the pipe, the lyre, and the cithara"—may well be attributable not to an insensitivity to the art, but to an impressive regard for its power over the passions. Several of the Church fathers were aware of the strong associations which an instrument or a melody might have with a way of life from which the Church was eager to wean its members. Instruments were tied to the connotations of their traditional use in pagan rituals, or associated with worldly and corrupt customs. Efforts to rehabilitate the moral standing of an instrument took the form of symbolical or, as St. Augustine phrased it, "mystical" reinterpretations. "On the timbrel," he observed, "leather is stretched, on the psaltery gut is stretched; on either instrument the flesh is crucified."

While the use of instruments in early Christian music was rather rigidly circumscribed, vocal music was quite another matter. There were, of course, a host of worldly songs that exerted a corrupting influence. But many astute churchmen believed in fighting fire with fire; and with new words to old melodies, as well as the creation of new hymns, a distinctive body of Christian vocal music began to grow. Some of the Church fathers, however, still had many reservations about such concessions to the weaknesses of human nature, and they rationalized the use of song in many ingenious ways. "For when the Holy Spirit," wrote St. Basil, "saw that mankind was ill inclined toward virtue and that we were heedless of the righteous life because of our inclination toward pleasure, what did he do? He blended the delight of melody with doctrines in order that through the pleasantness and softness of the sound we might unawares receive what was useful in the words, according to the practice of wise physicians, who, when they give the more bitter draughts to the sick, often smear the rim of the cup with honey." St. John Chrysostom's account of the creation and use of sacred melody is essentially the same. "When God saw that many men were rather indolent," he wrote, "that they came unwillingly to Scriptural readings and did not endure the labor this involves, wishing to make the labor more grateful and to take away the sensation of it, He blended melody with prophecy in order that, delighted by the modulation of the chant, all might with great eagerness give forth sacred hymns to Him."

For the highly educated and deeply sensitive St. Augustine, who before his conversion was the product of the pagan Roman culture, the process of reconciling himself to music in the Church was an agonizing one. St. Augustine's acute critical faculties distinguished between the beauty of prayer expressed in song, and the loveliness of the song apart from the prayer. And since he frequently found himself engrossed in the seductive charms of music for its own sake, he was often in a state of contrition and even outright despair. "Whenas I am moved not with the singing, but with the thing sung . . ," wrote St. Augustine in his *Confessions,* "I then acknowledge the great good of this institution. Thus float I between peril of pleasure, and an approved profitable custom: inclined the more (though herein I pronounce no irrevocable opinion) to allow the old usage of singing in the Church; that so by the delight taken in at the ears, the weaker minds be roused up into some feeling of devotion. And yet again, so oft as it befalls me to be more moved with the voice than with the ditty, I confess myself to have grievously offended: at which time I wish rather not to have heard the music."

EARLY CHRISTIAN CHANT

In the early centuries of the spread of Christianity, the shaping of a new body of chant may well have involved the adaptation of musical traditions already existing in the localities where the Church had established itself. Developing as it did in the eastern provinces of the Roman Empire, the early Christian chant absorbed, in all probability, a commingling of Hebraic and Greek influences. In the Ordinary of the Mass, for instance, the Sanctus, the words of which come from the Book of

Isaiah (6:3), points strongly to Old Testament synagogue worship. The Kyrie (a prayer in Greek) is a reminder that Greek was at first the official language for Church ritual. However, if traces of synagogue song and even of Greek melody can be detected in later Christian chant, a variety of regional melodies and melodic types may well have found their way into Church use via the vernacular music of the locality.

A number of musical procedures seem to have been rooted in what must have been familiar synagogue and temple routine. Antiphonal singing (the alternation of separate choirs) seems to have been introduced into the monasteries of Syria and Palestine early in the fourth century, modeled after such practices in the Jewish communities in that area. And earlier, the cantillation of the Psalms, the singing of hymns, and the chanting of ecstatic jubilations such as the *Alleluia* (a Hebrew word) may well have been retained from the Jewish synagogue and temple worship. Owing to the paucity of actual examples, however, it is not possible to point with certainty to just which influence was the most decisive. Suffice it to say that early Christian chant was rooted in synagogue practices, modified by the various vernacular musical traditions of diverse localities, and shaped within the framework of an officially recognized Greco-Roman culture.

When Constantine the Great, Emperor of Rome, transferred the capital of the Roman Empire in A.D. 330 to the Eastern city of Byzantium and renamed it Constantinople, impetus was given to the growth of a body of Church song in that region, which is called *Byzantine* or *Eastern* chant. The Byzantine repertoire was greatly enlarged during the reign of the Emperor Justinian (sixth century A.D.), whose imperial Church of Holy Wisdom (Hagia Sophia) in Constantinople was serviced by a prodigious number of musicians. While both Eastern and Western (*Gregorian*) chant are related to each other and to ancient synagogue chant, they differ strongly in details of regional tradition, and even more importantly in the melodic styles that grow out of the different languages. (Byzantine chant is set to Greek texts, while Gregorian chant is in Latin.) Byzantine chant spread westward through the Balkans, across North Africa, and into Sicily and parts of Italy. St. Ambrose, who served for a time in Syria, presumably adapted aspects of Eastern practices for use in Milan, when he was later installed in that city as Bishop. This type is called *Ambrosian*, or *Milanese*, chant. The Church chant that developed on the Iberian peninsula is designated as *Mozarabic*, while the term *Gallican* refers to chant usage in Gaul. With Pope Gregory the Great, a movement was instigated to codify this diversity of practice into a single body of official Church chant. This *Gregorian*, or *Roman*, chant eventually replaced the Mozarabic, Gallican and other repertoires; and in so doing, helped greatly to establish a uniform and universal service throughout the Roman Catholic world. Byzan-time chant, however, remained within the orbit of the Greek Orthodox Church.

Gregorian melodies are grouped into modes. Each mode is character-ized by a scale progression (a division of the octave into whole and half steps) peculiar to it, by an octave range (called *ambitus*), a central tone (called *finalis*), and formulalike groupings of notes typical of the melodies in that mode. Several styles of matching text and music may be distin-guished in Gregorian melody: (a) *syllabic,* or one note for each syllable; (b) *neumatic,* where a *neum* (or musical symbol) representing a cluster of two, three, or even four notes is set under each syllable of text; and (c) *melismatic,* where an extended sequence of notes (similar to colora-tura passages) is set to selected syllables of the text. Syllabic settings were especially useful for chanting prayers with a considerable amount of text. Melismatic settings were particularly appropriate for ecstacy songs like the *Alleluia,* or for prayers with very short texts like the *Kyrie eleison* (Lord have mercy), where melismatic prolongations of the syllables give the prayer the proper proportion and gravity denied it in a brief syllabic set-ting of the words.

THE TROPE

If the development of medieval Church music is viewed from the com-poser's standpoint, then the key question is how one creates for a service in which the appropriate music (Gregorian) has already been authorita-tively established. All musical creativity must then develop within the framework of the Gregorian chant. In short, it must be composition oriented to Gregorian authority. This is less a restriction than may at first seem evident, for just as the acceptance of Church authority was instinc-tive to medieval man, so the assumption of a Gregorian basis for musical composition was instinctive to the medieval Church musician. In general, two broad principles may be found in the treatment of Gregorian melodies in the Middle Ages: (a) interpolations within the chant; and (b) addi-tions above and below the chant. Such modifications of the chant (either in text, in music, or in both) are called *tropes,* and *troping* is, in essence, the fundamental creative principle in medieval music.

The *sequence* is an *Alleluia* trope, and an example of a modification in the character of a Gregorian melisma. The traditional story of its in-vention, told by Notker Balbulus (a monk at the monastery of St. Gall who died in the year 912), is that the sequence arose from the problem of remembering the *jubilus,* which was the long, and often very elaborate, melisma that adorned the final vowel of the word *alleluia.* To facilitate memorization, new verses were set beneath the *jubilus* melisma, one note for every syllable of the new text. Thus a melismatic melody was transformed into a syllabic one. Inevitably, the notes themselves were at times altered (for one freedom begets another), and eventually new melodies were evolved for the new verses. Incidentally, the practice of so treating the *Alleluia* seems to have been known before Notker. Also, other texts were so treated (the *Kyrie eleison,* for example); but the word *sequence* is specifically reserved for the *Alleluia,* while analogous modifications in other chants are subsumed under the general heading of tropes.

The Council of Trent (1545–63) ruled that all tropes and sequences except four were to be eliminated from Church use. The four sequences that were retained are *Victimae paschali laudes,* an eleventh-century Easter sequence by Wipo of Burgundy; *Veni sancte spiritus,* the Golden Sequence, so-called, for Whitsunday, attributed to Innocent III (late twelfth century); *Lauda Sion* (*c.* 1261), the Corpus Christi sequence by Thomas Aquinas; and *Dies irae* (*c.* 1200), a sequence for the Requiem Mass, or Mass for the Dead, probably written by Thomas of Celano. A fifth sequence, the famous *Stabat mater dolorosa,* sung at the feast of the Seven Dolours, was probably written by Jacopone da Todi in the late thirteenth century, but was not accepted for liturgical use until 1727. Sequences in general are important to music history because of the large number of polyphonic settings to which they later gave rise. The sequence was also the source from which two important forms of medieval secular music— the *lai* and the *estampie*—were ostensibly derived. The *lai* is a form of thirteenth-century French troubadour poetry and music, with a musical structure basically the same as that of the sequence; while the *estampie,* whose musical structure is also analogous to the sequence, is the most important of the forms of instrumental music in the thirteenth and fourteenth centuries.

ORGANUM AND MOTET

Additions over or below the chant resulted in one or more lines of melody sounding simultaneously with the Gregorian melody. This elementary polyphony was called *organum.* (In medieval practice, *polyphony* simply refers to singing in two or more parts, as opposed to *monophony,* which is unaccompanied unison melody.) Several types of organum may be distinguished. The most elementary type, as given in the *Scholia enchiriadis,* a ninth-century manual on music, is called *parallel organum.* Here an added voice, called the *vox organalis,* runs exactly parallel to the Gregorian melody, or plainsong, which is called *vox principalis.* It does so, however, at an interval of either a perfect fourth or fifth below. A composite four-part parallel organum is arrived at by singing the same melody simultaneously on four separate starting tones.

Ex. 19:1   Parallel Organum from the *Scholia enchiriadis.*

Sit   glo - ri - a   Do - mi - ni   in   sae - cu - la:

Later, a *free organum* evolved with the chant (*vox principalis*) in the lower voice, and with the upper part (*vox organalis*) no longer parallel but in a combination of parallel and contrary motion with respect to the chant. This resulted in the coordination of two different melodic lines, each a unity within itself. Parallel organum involved the movement of solid blocks of sound all going in the same direction; free organum meant the intertwining of independent melodic lines. Free organum, examples of which were plentiful in the eleventh century, was still a matter of the co-ordination of note against note between the two lines of melody. (In medieval Latin the word for a note was *punctus* or point; and the phrase "note against note" is simply a modern way of rendering the Latin *punctus contra punctum*, or point counter point, which contracts in English usage to counterpoint.) By the twelfth century, in such centers as St. Martial at Limoges in southern France and in the Cathedral of Notre Dame in Paris, an elaborate style of melismatic organum had been developed. Here a few notes of the chant were held in the lower part, each note being considerably prolonged; while in the upper part, called the *duplum,* or second voice, an elaborately melismatic melody, moving quite freely and often with exquisite grace, evolved. The voice that sustained the notes of the traditional chant was called the *tenor* (from the Latin *tenere,* to hold). Later, when a third voice was added, it was called the *triplum.*

In the two-part organum compositions (also called *organum duplum*) by Leonin, a leading figure in the School of Notre Dame in Paris during the latter half of the twelfth century, an innovation of great importance is found. The music is organized into a strictly measured rhythm, the lines in consequence losing something of their free, unmeasured Gregorian flow, but gaining in rhythmic coordination and definition. Sometimes only the elaborate upper voice is measured into rhythmic units, while the Gregorian excerpt, held by the tenor in long sustained notes, still lacks rhythmic definition. Sometimes, however, the sustained-note technique in the tenor gives way to shorter note values, in which case the two parts—tenor and duplum—are rhythmically coordinated. Perotin, who succeeded

Leonin at Notre Dame in Paris, extended organum composition of this general type to three and even four parts. Leonin's cycle of two-part organa was called the *Magnus Liber,* and the decade of 1160–70 may be presumed as the date of its composition. A contemporary account by an anonymous Englishman reports that Perotin reworked portions of Leonin's great work.

Just as the sequence arose out of the addition of new text to a melismatic vocalization, so early in the thirteenth century an analogous development occurred. A new text was added to the melismatic duplum part. When words (*mots*) were added to the duplum, the texted duplum was called the *motetus.* Such, in effect, was the origin of the *motet* in the Middle Ages, and the use of the new poetic text served to strengthen the emerging principles of rhythmic organization. The vagaries of motet composition in the thirteenth century are too numerous to recount in detail. In some three-part motets, the tenor voice retained a fragment of a Gregorian melody, but the two upper parts, both the duplum and triplum, had new Latin texts added—a different text for each voice (a *poly-textual motet*). In others, one of the texts was in Latin and the other in French (*poly-lingual motets*). Sometimes both new texts sung over the Gregorian tenor were in the vernacular language (French). At others, the motet became completely secularized with two melodies sung to French texts over a freely invented secular tune in the tenor, which replaced that traditional Gregorian melody.

The *Historical Anthology of Music* (Vol. I) (Harvard University Press) provides complete written examples of all these motet types. No. 28 in the *Anthology,* for instance, shows the various transformations of the plain chant *Benedicamus Domino,* of which the following examples are brief excerpts.

The first excerpt is from the monophonic plainsong *Benedicamus Domino* (Ex. 19:2).

Ex. 19:2

A melismatic organum over the same *Benedicamus* chant is shown in Example 19:3.

Ex. 19:3

Example 19:4 shows a two-part melismatic organum (organum duplum) of the School of Notre Dame in Paris, in which the notes of the *Benedicamus*

chant are sustained in the tenor, and only the melisma in the upper voice is organized into measured rhythmic units:

Ex. 19:4

Be -

Next, both upper voice and tenor are coordinated into measured rhythmic units, the tenor on a fragment of the chant beginning on the word *Domino* (Ex. 19:5).

Ex. 19:5

(Soloists)

(Chorus)

Be - ne - di - ca - mus   Do -   [mino

Then a two-part motet appears in which the duplum voice becomes a motetus by the addition of a new Latin text (*Domino fidelium*) over the chant fragment on *Domino* in the tenor (Ex. 19:6).

Ex. 19:6

Do - mi - no fi -   de - li - um   Om - ni - um

Do -   [mino

This is followed by a three-part Latin motet with two new Latin texts (*Ecce ministerium* in the duplum, and *Dominator Domine* in the triplum) over the chant fragment on *Domino* in the tenor (Ex. 19:7).

Ex. 19:7

Do - mi - na - tor Do - mi - ne   Qui de vir - gi -   ne   Ma - tre

Ec - ce mi - ni - ste - ri - um   Pro - fert al - vus   vir - gi - nis

Do -   [mino

In Example 19:8, over the chant on *Domino* in the tenor, two new texts are sung, both in French (*Je lanquis* in the duplum and *Pucelete bele* in the triplum).

Ex. 19:8

Pu-ce-le-te bele et a-ve-nant   Jo-li-e-te, po-lie et plei-sant,

Je lan-guis des   maus d'a-mours   Mieux aim   as-sez

Do --   [mino

No. 32*b* in the *Anthology* provides an example of a Latin motet which becomes secularized as it becomes polylingual. The tenor carries the Gregorian melody (*Hec dies*); the duplum, a Latin poem to the Virgin of virgins (*Virgo virginum*); and the triplum, a second Latin poem (*O mitissima Virgo Maria*) appealing to the Virgin to intercede on behalf of those who need help. This triplum part, however, has as a variant text, a French love poem (*Quant voi revenir*), in which the singer sighs and weeps, when summer returns, for the fair maid Marion whom he so much desires. No. 33*b* in the *Anthology* is an example of a completely secular motet. All texts are in French. The triplum praises a life of ease with wine, capons, good companions, and the comforting ladies of Paris; the duplum enumerates how even poverty stricken men may enjoy themselves in Paris; and the tenor reiterates the street cries of a vendor of fresh strawberries and wild blackberries.

SECULAR MUSIC

The growing sense of the joys of this world, in contrast to the otherworldly orientation of the Church, is reflected in the surviving secular poetry and music of this period. The famous *Song of Roland* (a *chanson de geste,* or song of deeds) is significantly an epic poem in the vernacular French rather than the universal Latin. As an expression of eleventh-century feudalism, the period just before the Crusades, it sings of the doughty deeds of fighting men during the days of Charlemagne. The poetic text is intact, but the actual music to which it was sung is unfortunately lost. Such epics, however, were customarily performed by strolling musicians who sang while accompanying themselves on small harps or bowed viols. Between verses they apparently played or sang short refrains or cadence formulas much in the manner that *Alleluias* were chanted between verses of Psalms in the church practice of the period. These minstrels, or *jongleurs* as they were also called, were singing actors, or mimes, who illustrated the action of the poem with appropriate gestures. As the name "jongleur" suggests, they were also jugglers and general entertainers, the descendants of the *ioculatores* of old Roman days. Usually they wandered from town to town and from castle to castle along the pilgrimage routes, where they performed at gatherings, weddings, and festivities of all kinds. Sometimes, however, they were attached to castles as jesters, or court fools; and their colorfully costumed image with cap and bells still survives as the joker in packs of cards.

On the upper side of the social structure were the *troubadours* of southern France, the *trouvères* of northern France, and the *minnesingers* (love singers) of Germany, who flourished in the twelfth and thirteenth centuries. Unlike the jongleurs and minstrels who were a professional class of musicians drawn from the ranks of the people, the troubadours were of noble lineage. Theirs was a courtly art, the reflection of a knightly society. The words "troubadour" and "trouvère" are derived from the Latin "trovare," meaning "to invent" or "to discover"; and the troubadours were thus the "finders" or "inventors" of songs. The troubadour songs were the songs of chivalry, the ideals of knighthood, and the aspirations of the Crusaders. Chivalric love, placing womanhood on a high pedestal of perfection, was the secular counterpart of the religious cult of the Virgin Mary in the Gothic phase of medieval civilization. In addition to these courtly love songs, there were such types as historical ballads recounting the adventurous deeds of the Crusades, or the death of a hero in battle; dramatic songs, involving dialogue and several characters; dance songs like the *estampie* (or *stantipes*) , a stamping dance; pastourelles, or pastorals, that told of the love of a knight for a fair shepherdess; dawn songs, or serenades; and some lyrical expressions with overtones of political intrigue, particularly in those associated with the powerful court of Henry Plantagenet and his Queen, Eleanor of Aquitaine.

In the ranks of the German minnesingers there were many celebrated literary names including those of Wolfram von Eschenbach, author of the love epic *Parzifal;* Tannhäuser, whom Wagner made into the hero of his medieval-revival opera, the plot of which is woven around the songfest, or tournament of song, held at the Wartburg castle in 1209; and Walther von der Vogelweide, one of Germany's greatest lyric poets. Among the trouvères were Thibaut IV, King of Navarre; and the commoner Adam de la Hale, whose pastoral play *Jeu de Robin et Marion* (Play of Robin and Marion) is an early example of secular drama with music.

MIDDLE AGES TO RENAISSANCE (ARS NOVA)

The more complex organa of Leonin and Perotin, as well as the motets of the thirteenth century, are an art music bound to Gregorian chant. As with the earlier tropes, the union was unavoidable, since the body of Gregorian music could not be set aside in the Church service. As long as the chant was retained in some fashion or other, the organa and motets that evolved around it could find a place in the liturgy. "To creep into the liturgy," as Jacques Handschin remarked, "was for the new art the only chance to live, because the church was the foremost concert hall of the epoch." As popular as this new development undoubtedly was, a sector of Church authority opposed it on the grounds of impurity, and because it seemed to open a wide path by which secularization could stream into Church practice.

These objections were encountered during the course of the twelfth and thirteenth centuries; and in the year 1322, Pope John XXII, then in residence at Avignon, delivered a strongly worded denunciation of all aspects of the development. He took particular exception to the free melismas which were written, coloratura fashion, in notes of small time value (semibreves and minims). "The music of the divine offices," charged the Pope, "is now performed with semibreves and minims, and with these notes of small value every composition is pestered." A device known as the *hocket,* the breaking of a line into fragments or even into single notes

which are then dispersed in alternate voices (for example,),

found its way into the motet; and several church dignitaries found this chopping up of a vocal line most unseemly during prayer. Further, continued the Pope, the upper parts were often made out of secular songs; composers tended to lose sight of the Gregorian melodies, and to forget "the fundamental sources . . . upon which their superstructure is raised." It was Pope John's particular complaint that "the modest risings and the temperate descents of the plain chant" were obscured by "voices incessantly running to and fro, intoxicating the ear, not soothing it, while the performers themselves endeavor by their gestures to convey the sentiment of the music which they utter. In consequence, devotion, the true end of worship, is little regarded, and wantonness, which should be eschewed, increases."

Such methods were summarily banished from Church music by papal decree. But the impulses behind the creation of this music were too deeply rooted to be so simply eliminated. A historical process, deep within the art of music itself, was in motion; a process which, far from subsiding, grew apace during the course of the fourteenth century. The process is sometimes described as one of secularization, and equated to the emergence of Renaissance humanism in the fourteenth century and to its maturation during the fifteenth century. The concept of secularization in music is useful, if not interpreted too narrowly. Many of the musical techniques that attended the development of an increasingly complex art music were indeed secular in character. And outside the Church, centers of secular wealth and prestige became increasingly important as sources of patronage for a sophisticated art music. The deepest aspects of secularization, however, lay in the maturing of the historical process already noted during the Middle Ages—that is, the growing awareness of music not only as a handmaiden to worship, and of musical composition not merely as the application of techniques, but of music as an art governed by laws intrinsic to it. During the fourteenth century, a subtle shift in perspective took place, which grew to the level of conscious compositional procedure in the music of the early fifteenth century. This shift in perspective involved the composer's growing awareness of his primary obligation to music as an art; and, concomitantly, the composer's increasing consciousness of himself as a creative personality contributing, through his art, to society. In essence, this was part of the emerging humanism of the Renaissance which conceived art, regardless of its religious function, as an independent activity of man, worthwhile in itself and governed by its own esthetic laws. This emerging humanism was evidenced in music just as it was in painting, sculpture, and architecture; it appeared in the sacred music as well as in the secular; and it was just as basic to developments in northern Europe as it was in Italy.

The title of a famous early fourteenth-century treatise on music, *Ars Nova* (The New Art), is symptomatic of an implicit awareness that a new era was under way. Its author, Philippe de Vitry, significantly, was Bishop of Meaux; and the gulf that separates the *ars nova* innovators from their predecessors of the late thirteenth century may be measured by the term *ars antiqua* (the ancient art) that was applied to the music of the immediate past. De Vitry's treatise, similar to analogous ones by Marchettus of Padua, show that both in France and in Italy, there was a deep concern with a new art. But the concern was not philosophical, it was practical. Both writers were interested in the critical problem of a musical notation. This is as basic a problem as there can be in music; for the notes on the page are not music as such, but a system of symbols designed to represent the patterns of sound imagined by the composer. A crisis in notation arises only when the art is in so radical a process of transformation that the existing notational symbols can no longer convey the subtleties and complexities of the composer's imagination. For all their concern with technicalities, Philippe de Vitry and Marchettus of Padua offered deep insights into the ideals of the new art. Although their notational systems were different, both men were, in essence, interested in the accurate notation of small note values. And both were concerned with the duple or binary divisions encountered in secular and in popular music, as well as with the ternary or triple divisions sanctified by Church preference. These smaller time values yielded melodic lines of greater internal rhythmic complexity; and in polyphonic music, this leads to an enormous gain in the subtlety of the rhythmic relationships between parts. By the end of the century, there were composers wholly enraptured by the exquisite intellectual subtleties that were now realizable. The Example 19:9 by Magister Zacharias is an instance of the limits to which notational trickery and its attendant rhythmic complexities were pursued.

Ex. 19:9

While the above example is more extreme than anything in Vitry or the work of Guillaume de Machaut, it is evidence of the intense experimentation characteristic of much fourteenth-century music. In this the fourteenth century is not without parallels to the twentieth century. Then, as now, there was a self-conscious concern with "modernism," a strong penchant for experimentation, and the same context of a world in crisis. Curiously, with some of the "modern" composers in both centuries, there was also an equivalent nostalgia for what seemed the purer, quieter, and nobler art of the past. Admittedly, the quoted example is a rather freakish affair, but esthetic evaluation aside, it may be taken as the outer limit of a restless interest in the inner mechanics of the art.

Although the medieval world was in the process of dissolution during the fourteenth century, a nostalgia for certain of its traditions is evident in the work of France's great composer-poet Guillaume de Machaut. His chansons are in spirit a throwback to the chivalrous world of the trouvères, although his technical methods were wholly those of his own day. His Mass has won a place for itself in history as a complete setting of the Ordinary of the Mass written by one composer. The significance of this will be evident later.

In Italy, the importance of Florence as a center for the new style may perhaps be inferred from the names of several of the principal composers resident there. Jacopo de Bologna, Bartolino da Padua, and Vincenzo d'Arimino, as their names indicate, were musicians attracted to the secular wealth of Florence from cities such as Bologna, Padua, and Rimini.

The following generation shows a preponderance of native Florentine composers, and of this group the blind organist, composer, and poet,
Francesco Landino, was the most celebrated. The art of the Florentine
ars nova composers was secular in orientation. Examples of sacred music
from fourteenth-century Florence are meager, and in the main, inferior.
The best talent was attracted to the *madrigal* (not to be confused with the
later form) , the *ballata* (a type of song dance) and the *caccia* (literally a
hunting song, but in general a type of lively descriptive music in which,
as in a chase, the voices follow each other in canon) . The interludes in
Boccaccio's *Decameron* contain descriptions of the manner in which this
ars nova music functioned in the entertainments of well-to-do Florentines.
"The growing prosperity of the independent cities of northern Italy,"
writes Leonard Ellinwood in his study of Landino, "through their extensive commercial interests and their comparative freedom from the inter-
ference of the Holy Roman Empire, gave rise to a class of people who had
leisure time to devote to an interest in art, letters, and music . . . The
human emancipation, which was being expressed more and more in the
paintings of the early Renaissance, found an immediate expression in these
madrigals, *cacce,* and *ballate* of the Italian *ars nova."*

The music of Landino and his colleagues is a sophisticated secular art,
and completely Italian in its mellifluous flow of melody. By comparison,
French *ars nova* music seems often more nervous, and sometimes less attentive to a sensuous loveliness of sound. But, like Machaut, there is some
nostalgia in Landino for a vanishing culture. While Landino was a secular
musician of his own day, he looked back to the old aristocratic castle
culture, and the rate at which a popular art was proliferating on all sides
filled him with dismay. The text which he wrote for one of his madrigals
(*Musica son che me dolgo piangendo*) is the lament of a personification
of Music, who weeps to see intelligent people deserting art for popular
songs. Everybody now wants to write music (madrigals, catches, and ballads) , the text continues. Once, Music was prized by knights, barons, and
great lords, but now gentle hearts are corrupted. But, concludes Music, I
am not alone in my lament, for other virtues are also being neglected.
Yet Landino contributed to the popular forms, and his musical account
of a fishing scene is a lively setting with such lines as: "Isabella began
screaming, 'Oh, Oh!' 'What happened?' 'What's up?' 'I've been bitten in
the toe!' 'O Lisa, the fish is getting away!' " The style is that of the *caccia,*
although, since this is a fishing scene, the term *pescha* would perhaps be
more accurate.

The differences between French and Italian *ars nova* music bear witness to a clear emergence of national styles; and while this is especially
marked in the secular music, it can be noted in the Church music as well.

A regional song and dance tradition makes itself more immediately felt in a secular art music than in music composed for the Church; and moreover, the secular music was composed not to Latin texts, but to verses in the vernacular language. As the Florentine *ars nova* style demonstrates, patronage sources outside the Church were becoming increasingly important, and centers of secular wealth were rapidly replacing monasteries and bishoprics in the plans that a young composer might make for his future. The royal chapels which developed apace throughout Europe sought to rival the Papal Choir in the excellence of the music performed; and while court musicians wrote a great deal of church music for the court chapel, such an atmosphere necessarily encouraged interest in secular music as well.

THE RENAISSANCE

The settings of the Ordinary of the Mass which developed in the northern European centers show how greatly advanced was the humanistic emancipation of musical esthetics from the necessities of liturgical use. The Ordinary of the Mass comprises five principal sections (Kyrie, Gloria, Credo, Sanctus, and Agnus Dei) which, during the celebration of the Mass, are not actually sung in direct sequence, except for the Kyrie and Gloria. No liturgical necessity exists, therefore, for treating the Ordinary of the Mass as a musical unity, for such a unity would be nullified by the intervening portions of the service. As long as a composer's horizon was limited to what was necessary in Church usage, it was entirely satisfactory to write individual settings for the separate sections. A wholly adequate music for the Ordinary of the Mass could be assembled by selecting the separate movements from diverse sources. Signs, however, of a growing desire on the part of the composer to build an esthetically related structure of Mass movements, even though such a unity was liturgically unnecessary, first begins to be evident in the composition of paired movements such as Gloria-Credo, and Sanctus-Agnus Dei. The Mass by Machaut is, in this respect, a significant undertaking; for, even if it falls short of the ideal of a structurally unified cycle of Mass movements, all sections of the Ordinary were written by one man, and a closeness of personal style relates the movements esthetically to one another.

The full emancipation of musical esthetics from the limitations of liturgical function is evident in the Mass cycles of the fifteenth century. Dufay's setting of the Mass, *Se me face ay pale,* may serve as an example. All movements of the Mass are structurally coordinated by the presence of the same melody in the tenor part of each movement. This recurring melody is called the *cantus firmus,* and it provides a common point of orientation for all movements. Furthermore, there are structural balances between the movements, so that a given section in one movement is related proportionately to an equivalent section in another. A comparison of the abstract structure of two such distant sections as the Kyrie and the Agnus makes this clear. (The tenor melody is in three sections designated as A, B, and C.)

Kyrie I

Four-part setting ⎱ Tenor on **A**
(37 measures)   ⎰ and **B** portions
                of the cantus-
                firmus melody

Christe:
Duet: soprano and   ⎱
        counter-tenor   ⎮
Duet: counter-tenor   ⎮ No
        and bass   ⎬ cantus-
Duet: soprano and   ⎮ firmus
        bass   ⎮ melody
Trio: soprano, coun-   ⎮
        ter-tenor and   ⎮
        bass   ⎮
    (40 measures)   ⎰

Kyrie II
Four-part setting ⎱ Tenor on
(25 measures)   ⎰ C portion of
                cantus-firmus
                melody

Agnus I
Duet: soprano and   ⎱ No tenor
        counter-tenor ⎬ cantus firmus
    (6 measures)   ⎰

Four-part setting ⎱ Tenor on A
(37 measures)   ⎰ and B por-
                tions of the
                cantus-firmus
                melody

Agnus II
Duet: soprano and   ⎱
        counter-tenor   ⎮ No
Duet: soprano and   ⎬ cantus-
        bass   ⎮ firmus
Trio: soprano, counter-   ⎮ melody
        tenor and bass   ⎮
    (67 measures)   ⎰

Agnus III
Four-part setting ⎱ Tenor on
(25 measures)   ⎰ C portion of
                cantus-firmus
                melody

The parallels between the proportions of the Kyrie sections and the equivalent Agnus sections, between the disposition of the cantus-firmus melody in each movement, and (with variation) between the treatment accorded the duets and trios are all evident enough. Other movements show similar coordinations in abstract design. The motivation for structural unity of this sort, for the purely musical cohesion within a large-scale design, lies wholly within the composer himself. His horizon is now enlarged to encompass not only what is liturgically sufficient, but what he regards as esthetically necessary. And since this unity will be nullified or unnoticed when the movements are dispersed in actual use throughout the celebration of Mass, the concern with such structural unity betokens the existence for the composer of an authority more compelling than the limitations of traditional liturgical need. This authority, then, is his conscience as a composer, his obligation as an artist to himself and to his art.

The cyclic Mass, because of its large-scale, five-movement structure, became the vehicle for the most powerful creative imaginations in Renaissance music. It occupies a prime position in the work of Ockeghem, Obrecht, and the greatest of northern masters, Josquin des Prez. As Bukofzer has noted, "It held as dominating and as prominent a place in the hierarchy of musical values as the symphony did in the eighteenth and nineteenth centuries." The Dufay Mass cycle described above used for its tenor cantus firmus a secular love song, *Se me face ay pale* (If my face is pale). This type of secularization (the replacement of Church chant by secular songs) became fairly common in Renaissance music, and melodies such as *L'homme armé* and *O rosa bella* were used both for polyphonic settings of secular chansons as well as for tenor melodies in the cyclic Mass. In the northern courts where this practice was widespread, sacred and secular music thus developed in close relationship to one another.

The course of music history is marked, from time to time, by the emergence of a composer like Josquin des Prez in whom the ideals of an epoch are realized, not clamorously, but with quiet power. In Josquin's music, the most intricate and esoteric of contrapuntal procedures is always at the service of a deeply sensitive subjectivity. He was a master whose tenderness was the more eloquent for the austere disciplines of his technique. A music in which complexities unfold as if governed by the calm inevitability of a law of nature betokens a mastery which no man achieves unaided. Early in the fifteenth century, the Burgundian masters, foremost among whom were Guillaume Dufay and Gilles Binchois, succeeded in freeing themselves, in the main, from the nervous rhythms, the tension-ridden dissonances, and the intellectual intricacies of the late *ars nova* practice. And in the achievement of a more tender, more sensuously appealing music, the Burgundians acknowledged their indebtedness to the great English composer John Dunstable.

With the death of Dufay, leadership passed to the Flemish masters, Jacob Obrecht and Joannes Ockeghem. In the purity and serenity of his style, and in his careful treatment of contrapuntal detail, Obrecht points the way to Josquin. But more than any other composer, it was Ockeghem whose work provided the single most important source for the music of Josquin and his contemporaries. Thanks to Ockeghem's thoroughness in the exploitation of contrapuntal device, the formal complexities of counterpoint became an open book to the Renaissance composer; and with so secure an achieved mastery over the vast resources of polyphony, the independence of music, as an art of composition, was established on an unshakable foundation.

What Ockeghem meant to Renaissance music can still be felt in the moving lament, *La Déploration de Jehan Ockeghem,* which Josquin wrote upon the death of the master. Toward the end of the *Déploration,* the singers cry the great names in contemporary music—Josquin des Prez, Antoine Brumel, Pierre de la Rue (Pirchon), and Loyset Compère—as one by one they come forth to weep for the loss of their "good father." Significantly, Josquin's name is just one among his contemporaries; for this work is more than a personal tribute, it is the record of the grief of a generation. Curiously, while the tenor carries a versicle from the Roman Catholic Burial Service (*Requiem aeternam*), the other voices enjoin the nymphs of the woods and the streams to lament. This blend of Christianity and paganism is characteristic of the liberalism of Renaissance thought. Yet the essence of Renaissance humanism lies deeply ingrained in the very tone of the music; for Josquin's *Déploration* is a record of a profoundly moving relationship between human beings, between the "good father" Ockeghem and his spiritual children whom he had raised to maturity as composers.

The art of Ockeghem, Obrecht, and Josquin is characterized by an evenness of tone, an equality of contrapuntal parts, a homogeneity and transparency of choir texture, a seamless flow of sound, and an impeccable mastery of contrapuntal resource. To Josquin's successors it seemed an *ars perfecta* (perfect art), and since perfection is the limit of progress, there were some who feared that after Josquin's death the art of music must decline. Such predictions are a sign of crisis, and the course of sixteenth-century music after Josquin was indeed one of a deep conflict of directions.

In essence, the conflict may be simplified down to the retention and transformation of the involved counterpoint of the *ars perfecta,* on the one hand, and the search for new harmonic resources on the other. The problem was not only musical, but social, religious, and national as well. The stylistic orientation of a sophisticated, secular art music was not always compatible with tendencies apparent in popular dance and song; nor could the musical needs of a Lutheran Church service be satisfied by a style that functioned to perfection in the Vatican. Further, there were necessarily differences in temperament between an Italian and an English madrigalist, between a follower of Luther and a disciple of Calvin.

Far from being exhausted, the *ars perfecta* of the fifteenth-century Flemish masters took on new life as it spread, in the course of the sixteenth century, to every major center in Europe. A singularly malleable style, despite the abstract austerity of its counterpoint, it was transformed to suit the temperament of a series of strong personalities. It suited the conservatism of Giovanni da Palestrina who, working in Rome, brought to the style of Flemish church music an impressive dignity and, at times, a wonderfully ethereal quality. With a Spanish composer like Tomás Luis de Victoria, who was for a time a colleague of Palestrina in Rome, the Flemish style lost none of its austerity for being enriched harmonically. Yet with Victoria, the style acquired an atypical fervor, an urgent emotional tone, which betrayed a growing interest in more overt dramatic expression. This accent on more obvious emotionality is also evident in the magnificent *Penitential Psalms* of Orlandus Lassus, the last of a great school of Netherland composers. The *Penitential Psalms* are late works and reflect the complete mastery with which Lassus handled the Flemish idiom, both technically and expressively. Lassus was an eclectic and an internationalist, as much at home in secular music as in sacred, and as proficient in the Italian madrigal as in the German polyphonic lied or the French polyphonic chanson. A study of Lassus is very nearly a study of the sixteenth century; in many respects, he was the most universal of the great composers of the century. And finally, the Flemish style is still evident in the work of the greatest English composer of the era, William Byrd. In Byrd's church music a sensitive lyricism and a profound nobility of style are particularly evident, while in his secular music there is a warm and tender feeling for popular English melody.

An art capable of being transformed by four such powerful personalities was scarcely in its decline. Although the Flemish style was entrenched primarily as a vehicle for church music, this very fact gave it international currency, and further modifications of it can be encountered in the sophisticated polyphony of secular art music. The invention of printing also greatly facilitated the spread of musical styles, and raised to ever-increasing importance the role of the educated amateur as a musical consumer. The taste of the amateur was increasingly a factor in the musical market. Significantly, the first printed book of polyphonic chansons—the *Harmonice Musices Odhecaton* issued by Petrucci in 1501 in Venice—featured predominantly the work of northern composers such as Ockeghem, Alexander Agricola, Obrecht, Heinrich Isaac, and Josquin. Designed as a kind of "one-hundred famous pieces" collection to be disseminated to a wide public, the *Odhecaton* testifies to the great popularity of the Flemish style in the secular music of the early sixteenth century.

Much of the elaborate polyphonic technique characteristic of the Flemish style found its way, with appropriate modification, into the Italian madrigal and polyphonic French chanson of the sixteenth century. In the chansons of Guillaume Costeley, one of the most delightful of the French composers, polyphonic sections were alternated with harmonic passages. In his charming *Allon, gay, gay* (Come now, gay shepherds) the refrain is in brisk chordal harmonies, much like a choral dance, while the intervening stanzas are accorded the familiar contrapuntal treatment. The liveliness of the piece is much enhanced by this diversification of techniques.

The range of subject matter in sophisticated secular art music sometimes shows influences from popular sources. The educated gentleman's repertory consisted of pieces in which passionate shepherds make love polyphonically to languishing shepherdesses, and learned lovers sing of the agony of parting in the most exquisitely sophisticated counterpoint. A well-schooled Englishman like Thomas Morley contributed pretty little fa-la-la pieces, and an austere Netherlander like Lassus several chansons such as the one in which the counterpoint cleverly mimics a comic situation between a jealous and rather elderly husband and his young and high-spirited wife (*Quand mon mari,* or When my husband comes home). Programme polyphony of this sort became quite popular. Among the more famous examples of this invasion of the exalted domain of polyphony by lively naturalistic imitations, there is Jannequin's *La Bataille,* suggested by the battle of Marignano; his *Chant des Oiseaux* (Song of the Birds), in which a host of feathered creatures twitter and chirp their way through the counterpoint; and Ludwig Senfl's *Kling klang,* a clever contrapuntal simulation by the choir of the sound of bells.

The Italian madrigal was the product both of Flemish composers such as Jacob Arcadelt and Adrian Willaert who were resident in Italy, and native Italian musicians of lesser note. Although ultimately its cultivation devolved upon such great Italian masters as Luca Marenzio whose counterpoint is remarkable for the manner in which it subserves a strong emotional expressivity, the Italian madrigal continued to lay claim to the talents of northern composers like Lassus and Giaches de Wert. During the course of the sixteenth century, the northern dominance that had culminated in Josquin, gave way to a proliferation of powerful national and regional styles, one of the strongest of which was the Italian. The music of Italy was much admired in England and, before the close of the sixteenth century, several publications of Italian madrigals (appropriately "Englished," that is, the texts translated) were issued on English soil. No doubt such publications exerted a definite influence on English composers. But the musical style of the English madrigal was rooted too strongly in the metrical peculiarities as well as in the verbal music of English Elizabethan poetry to be, in the main, anything but itself.

In summary, despite the continued prevalence of the polyphonic style in both sacred and secular music, after Josquin's death the style was increasingly modified and differentiated in the church music of Palestrina, Victoria, Lassus, and Byrd. This is even more evident in sophisticated secular music, with the intensification of distinctively national traits in the Italian madrigal, the English madrigal, the French polyphonic chanson, and the German polyphonic lied. This process of style transformation was, however, accompanied by a more arresting development which was effectively a flat negation of the Flemish art as such. In this development, a simple and expressive melody is supported by clearly shaped chord structures, the harmonic complex now motivated by a well-defined rhythmic beat. The seamless flow of sound, the immaculate contrapuntal weaving of equal voices is totally eliminated. The music is now conceived vertically rather than horizontally, and in this sector of sixteenth-century music, the Flemish art is, to all intents and purposes, defunct.

This development is especially strong in instrumental dance music, in accompanied solo song, and in Protestant church chorales. Both in sacred and in secular music there was need for an art more popular than the sophistications of the madrigal or of the music for High Church ritual. The fashion for solo song with lute accompaniment was strong in France, Spain, and England. In France it was known as the *Air de cour* (Court song). In Spain, it was cultivated by a group of composers (Luis Milan, Alonso de Mudarra, Enriquez de Valderrábano) who were singularly gifted in the creation of noble and expressive melody. And in England, a diversity of styles was absorbed into the popular lute song. Along with the magnificent madrigals of John Wilbye, Thomas Weelkes, and Orlando Gibbons, the lute songs of John Dowland, Thomas Campian, and Francis Pilkington are among the treasures of Elizabethan culture.

The lute as a solo instrument, as well as an accompaniment to song, enjoyed a wide vogue throughout Europe. Since, intrinsically, the lute is more a chordal than a polyphonic instrument, the popularity of the instrument helped to strengthen interest in music that was conceived harmonically and with strong rhythmic beat. Such stylistic attributes are also intrinsic to instrumental dance music, and examples of a sharp decline of interest in contrapuntal complexity are plentiful in the large collection of dances for four- and five-part instrumental ensembles by Claude Gervaise, which date from the middle of the sixteenth century.

Keyboard instruments, on the contrary, are as feasible for contrapuntal purposes, as for a music conceived on a chordal basis. The remarkable collection of English keyboard music known as the *Fitzwilliam Virginal Book* shows how diverse were the styles that were considered adaptable to the keyboard. There are, of course, in this collection popular dances like the Pavan and Galliard, the Volta and the Morris dance. But at the opposite end of the stylistic spectrum, there is the overly long Fantasia by Peter Philips which may well serve as a model of contrapuntal learnedness. On the one hand, there is a set of variations by William Byrd on a popular tune known as the *Carman's Whistle;* while on the other, there are two keyboard settings of a Gregorian plain chant by the same composer (Byrd's two *Miserere* pieces). Perhaps the most attractive pieces in the collection (to judge by frequency of performance) are the delicately descriptive tone poems, such as *The Bells* by William Byrd and *The Primrose* and *The Fall of the Leaf* by Martin Peerson. In the latter piece, Peerson is more concerned with evocation of mood, than with literal description, although the depictive element is not neglected. This introspective quality is noteworthy, for it reappears in a set of three pieces by Giles Farnaby, entitled, respectively, *Giles Farnaby's Dreame, His Rest*, and *His Humour*, which are early examples of overt psychological autobiography.

The rise of keyboard music only partially diverted the attention of composers from counterpoint as the primary mechanism of musical expression. The Protestant Reformation, in stronger measure, reduced the emphasis on counterpoint. The ideology of the Reformation granted each man the right to address the Lord in prayer without intercession of priest or saints, and community prayer was once again restored to an important position in church ritual. Music was prayer made more eloquent; and a melody that a man could sing when alone, at home with his family, or in church as a member of the congregation had to be simple, foursquare, and unencumbered either by coloratura or by lines of counterpoint weaving around it. Luther encouraged the creation of a body of choral melody (hymn tunes) of this type, to which he himself contributed. The famous *Ein feste Burg ist unser Gott* (A mighty fortress is our God) is attributed to him. Four-part settings of such tunes were likely to be in simple chordal style, with full pauses at the end of phrases for the congregation to take breath before the next line.

Stylistic simplification in Calvinist centers was perhaps more pronounced than in the Lutheran; the Psalm settings of Louis Bourgeois, for example, were usually simple harmonic progressions, with a chord under each note of melody and one note for each syllable of text. Upon occasion, northern Protestant composers like Claude Goudimel (who perished in the St. Bartholomew's Day Massacre) were too deeply steeped in Flemish tradition to discard it casually. One finds for instance, alternate settings of the same Psalm by Goudimel reflecting varying degrees of contrapuntal complexity and harmonic simplification.

The Flemish tradition was too powerful to be quickly overthrown, and too wonderful purely as music for its disciplines ever to disappear completely. But during the course of the sixteenth century a re-evaluation was in process, marked not only by the maturing of other musical styles, but also by the maturing of the ideals upon which the new styles were based. By the turn of the seventeenth century, a deep contradiction in esthetic beliefs was mirrored not only by clamorous contradictions in musical

Fig. 19:1 Traini (?). *Triumph of Death,* detail. *c.* 1350. Figures in lower right illustrate an Italian *ars nova* ensemble of the type referred to in Boccaccio's *Decameron*. This painting was also the inspiration for Liszt's *Dance of Death*.

style, but in a series of urgent and sometimes acrimoniously polemical treatises on music written by composers and theoreticians alike. The dispute and its resolution mark the emergence of a new epoch in music history. It is a period called the *baroque,* an era which in many respects marks the beginning of modern music.

BAROQUE CHRONOLOGY

Venice

Adrian Willaert	c.1490–	1562
Andrea Gabrieli	c.1510–	1586
Cipriano de Rore	1516–	1565
Gioseffe Zarlino	1517–	1590
Claudio Merulo	1533–	1604
Giovanni Gabrieli	1557–	1612
Claudio Monteverdi	1567–	1643
Francesco Cavalli	c.1602–	1676
Orazio Benevoli	1602–	1672
Marcantonio Cesti	1623–	1669
Giovanni Legrenzi	c.1625–	1690
Alessandro		
Stradella	c.1645–	1682
Antonio Caldara	1670–	1736
Antonio Vivaldi	c.1675–c.1740	
Benedetto Marcello	1686–	1739

Rome

Filippo Neri	1515–1595
Emilio de' Cavalieri	c.1550–1602
Girolamo Frescobaldi	1583–1643
Luigi Rossi	1598–1653
Giacomo Carissimi	1604–1674
Arcangelo Corelli	1653–1713

Florence

Vincenzo Galilei	c.1533–	1591
Giulio Caccini	c.1550–	1618
Jacopo Peri	1561–	1633
Ottavio Rinuccini	1562–	1621
Marco da Gagliano	c.1575–	1642

Bologna

Giuseppe Torelli	c.1650–	1708
Arcangelo Corelli	1653–	1713
Francesco		
Germiniani	1674–	1762
Pietro Locatelli	1693–	1764
Padre Martini	1706–	1784

Padua

Giuseppe Tartini	1692–	1770

Mantua

Salomone Rossi	c.1565–c.1628	
Claudio Monteverdi	1567–	1643
Lodovico Viadana	1564–	1627

Naples

Carlo Gesualdo	1560–1613
Alessandro Scarlatti	1659–1725
Francesco Durante	1684–1755
Domenico Scarlatti	1685–1757
Leonardo Vinci	1690–1730
Giovanni Battista Pergolesi	1710–1736

Paris

Jehan Titelouze	1563–1633
Marin Mersenne	1588–1648
Jacques Chambonnières	c.1597–1672
Pierre Corneille	1606–1684
(Molière)	1622–1673
Robert Cambert	c.1628–1677
Jean B. Lully	c.1633–1687
Philippe Quinault	1635–1688
(Jean B. Racine)	1639–1699
François Couperin (Le Grand)	1668–1733
Jean P. Rameau	1683–1764

London

Henry Lawes	1596–1662
William Davenant	1606–1668
Matthew Locke	c.1630–1677
John Dryden	1631–1700
Pelham Humphrey	1647–1674
John Blow	1648–1708
Nahum Tate	1652–1715
Henry Purcell	c.1658–1695
John C. Pepusch	1667–1752
John Gay	1685–1732
George F. Handel	1685–1759

North Germany and Holland

(Martin Luther)	1483–1546
Johann Walther	1496–1570
Jan P. Sweelinck	1562–1621
Michael Praetorius	1571–1621
Jeinrich Schütz	1585–1672
Johann Schein	1586–1630
Samuel Scheidt	1587–1654
Heinrich Scheidemann	1596–1663
Johann Reinken	1623–1722
Dietrich Buxtehude	1637–1707
Johann Kuhnau	1660–1722
George F. Handel	1685–1759
Johann Sebastian Bach	1685–1750

South Germany and Austria

Leo Hassler	1564–1612
Johann J. Fux	1600–1641
A. Hammerschmidt	1611–1675
Johann J. Froberger	1616–1667
Georg Muffat	1645–1704
Johann Pachelbel	1653–1706
Ferdinand Fischer	c.1660–1738
Pietro Metastasio	1698–1782

The Baroque Styles

Chapter 20

THE STYLISTIC BACKGROUND

THE *baroque,* a term first associated with the visual arts, is now commonly applied to the corresponding style period in music history. Derived from *barocco,* Portuguese for a pearl of irregular shape, the word was originally used in a derogatory sense by partisans of the Renaissance ideal of symmetrical design in order to indicate their disapproval of buildings, statuary, and paintings that seemed in their eyes grotesquely extravagant, overly ornate, and excessively exuberant. The new music likewise sounded somewhat strange and aberrational to the ears of those accustomed to the balanced *a cappella* choral style of the Renaissance. None, however, were more conscious of the new spirit than the innovators themselves. Vincenzo Galilei, father of the famous astronomer, published in 1581 an argumentative little book entitled *Dialogue on Music, Ancient and Modern;* and his Florentine compatriot and fellow composer, Caccini, brought out in 1602 a collection of songs entitled *Nuove Musiche* (New Music). Its preface served as the manifesto of the new musical order and its title became the battle cry of the baroque.

Baroque art in all fields was, in fact, a new and progressive style, and as such it was the product of a period seeking new religious orientations, new philosophies of life, new geographical discoveries, new scientific knowledge, and new mechanical inventions. The period coincides with the time of the Reformation and Counter Reformation; with Descartes'

271

conception of the world as "matter in motion"; with the exploration of the vast new world of the Americas; with Copernicus' theory of a sun-centered solar system in which the earth was no longer static but whirling around through space; with Newton's speculation on the laws of gravitational attraction and repulsion; with such inventions as the balloon to probe the upper atmosphere, the diving bell to plumb the depths of the sea, as well as the telescope and microscope to open men's eyes to distant and minute regions of space. The Renaissance ideal of balance and repose, in short, was supplanted by a world in restless motion.

In architecture the love of lavish ornamentation was in the ascendancy over restraint and severity, and the angular symmetrical regularity and clear definition of Renaissance facades gave way to irregular unbalanced lines, undulating curves, and deep recesses. The sculptured figures of Bernini seemingly defied gravitational limitations as they floated freely in space on tons of marble clouds. Painters replaced the repose of vanishing-point perspective with restless diagonal accents and broken perspectives, and Rembrandt's dynamics of light and shade dissolved the sharply defined contours of Renaissance pictures. It is hardly cause for wonder, then, that musical theoreticians began speculating on new acoustical possibilities, new systems of tuning instruments, new concepts of key feeling and modulation between tonal centers; or that baroque music started to teem with new energy, that tempos were quickened, that complex ornamentation crept in, or that a new interplay between vocal and instrumental forces developed. "Music hath two ends," wrote one of the philosophers of the period, "first to please the sense, . . . and secondly to move the affections or excite passion."

The baroque period can be viewed from a number of different angles. Chronologically it extends from the transition time of the late sixteenth century, throughout the seventeenth, and on into the first half of the eighteenth century; or, to put it in human terms, from the three great early figures, Giovanni Gabrieli, Frescobaldi, and Monteverdi, through the time dominated by those twin titans, Bach and Handel. Geographically the style had its inception in such Italian centers as Venice, Florence, and Rome, and then moved outward into the wider aristocratic orbits of the Spanish crown; the French court of the Sun King, Louis XIV; and the English Restoration rule of Charles II and his successors William and Mary. It then went on to its consummation and close in Georgian London with Handel and in Protestant Leipzig with Bach. The new practices of the baroque quickly took on national and regional character. French opera, for instance, was distinguished from Italian opera, while in Italy itself local preferences in taste accounted for such distinctive types as the Florentine recitative opera, the Roman choral opera, and the Venetian and Neapolitan solo opera. Religious music in Catholic South Germany differed radically from that heard in Protestant North Germany. Composers everywhere wrote "French" or "Italian" overtures, and Bach composed keyboard pieces variously designated as *Italian* Concerto, *French* suite, and *English* suite.

Different sources of patronage account for such distinctions as Counter-Reformation, aristocratic, and Reformation aspects of the baroque. Counter-Reformation baroque, for instance, was the art and musical style fostered by the church militant. In a chapel in Rome called the Oratorio (literally, oratory, or a place for prayer), allegorical representations and spiritual dramas were set to music and performed, and the building gave its name to one of the important dramatic expressions of the period. Here such social workers as San Filippo de Neri discovered a way of making Biblical stories come to life so dramatically that the man in the street to whom these "dramas" were addressed was both entertained and edified. The aristocratic baroque, on the other hand, nurtured the type of dramatic presentation in the courts of Italian noblemen that made opera "the spectacle of princes." Politically the period was one of such great sovereigns as Philip II of Spain, Louis XIV of France, and the Stuarts of England, all of whom were striving to impress the world by their magnificent way of life. Elsewhere in the centers of the Reformation movement, greater frugality, austerity, and industry prevailed; but even in Calvinistic Holland organ music was sponsored by the city of Amsterdam and the Lutheran churches of North Germany all had their professional organists and choirmasters. Baroque composers themselves also distinguished music according to its function in such settings as church, chamber, or theater. Several types of music were thus composed for certain definite purposes on the orders of different patrons. Professional composers discriminated between the style of a concerto or sonata written for church use and one composed for chamber performance. This distinction was expressed in the titles *sonata da chiesa* (church sonata) and *sonata da camera* (chamber sonata). A similar differentiation was also made in the case of the concerto.

The baroque period was also marked by a new awareness of the expressive possibilities of various vocal and instrumental media. Renaissance composers, for instance, often merely indicated in their scores that certain passages were "to be sung or played"; and the choice of voices or instruments was left to the discretion and convenience of the performers. Whether an Elizabethan composer was writing for a group of voices or a "chest of viols," very little difference in the style of writing could be detected. With early baroque composers, however, the terms *cantata* and *sonata*, used in their basic sense indicating works to be sung or played, respectively, began to take on a special meaning. There was a definite awareness, for instance, of the different ways of handling small and large choruses, solo and choral situations, and vocal and instrumental combinations. The period was one in which the stringed instruments, especially violins, reached the high point in their construction at the celebrated North Italian center of Cremona, whence, from the workshops of the Amati, Stradivari, and Guarneri families, came the finest specimens of the violinmaker's art. The impetus for this development was doubtless inspired by the desire for an instrumental counterpart to the human voice; an instrument that would extend the voice's range and increase its dependability while at the same time retaining its sweet singing quality. Stringed instruments were thus established as the nucleus of chamber-music groups and the orchestra, as evidenced, for instance, in the rise of the trio sonata and the concerto grosso.

With the organists of St. Mark's Church in Venice, and Frescobaldi at St. Peter's in Rome, an idiomatic organ style gradually differentiated itself from the ways of writing for string and wind instruments; and later the distinction was made between idioms appropriate for organ music and those suitable for the clavichord and harpsichord. The *toccata,* for instance, literally means "touched," or a "touch piece" as an organist would finger the keys, rather than a piece intended to be played by bowing or blowing. The keyboard pieces called ricercare and canzone, while related in their early stages to the vocal motet and French chanson, respectively, definitely began to take on a special instrumental character.

Above all, however, the early representatives of the baroque were very style conscious, and stylistic rather than formal considerations prevailed in the products of the period. The books by Galilei and Caccini separating the old from the new music have already been mentioned. Specifically their criticism was directed against the polyphonic principles of Renaissance writing, which emphasized complex contrapuntal manipulations at the expense of projecting and clarifying the dramatic meaning of the text. Their experiments resulted in the formulation of a type of monodic, or single-voiced, form of vocal rhetoric with instrumental accompaniment that they called the *recitative style.* By intoning the lines of a dramatic text while intensifying the natural inflections of speech, they achieved a manner of declamation suitable for opera scenes that they designated as the *representative style.*

Another early evidence of change comes with the new polychoral practices of the Venetian composers. The breaking up of the unity of the Renaissance polyphony by opposing a full choir against a divided one, by contrasting a chorus with solo singers, and by pitting vocal groups against instrumental ensembles, led to the development of the *concerting style.* Monteverdi, while continuing to write church music in the Renaissance manner, injected a new note into his madrigals by emphasizing the dramatic meaning of the text. In the various prefaces to his publications he noted his departure from tradition by coining the term "second practice" as opposed to the older "first practice" of Renaissance polyphony. Putting his position into a neat epigram, he pointed out that in the first practice of the Renaissance "harmony is the master of the word," while in his second practice, "the word is the master of the harmony." Furthermore, within his second practice, he went on to make still finer distinctions, such as the "agitated style" (*stile concitato*). These new stylistic elements serve to emphasize that the baroque encompassed a wider emotional spectrum, one that went far beyond the simplicity and restraint of the Renaissance by including such extremes as agitation and joyful abandon.

All these early baroque practices that will be encountered and clarified later—recitative, concertato, concerto grosso, fugue, and the like—are principles or styles of writing rather than forms. Other terms—such as ritornel (principle of return), basso continuo (continuous bass), basso ostinato (ground bass), variation techniques, and so on—are to be considered as structural devices. The opera, oratorio, and cantata are free fusions or combinations of all prevailing vocal and instrumental styles, techniques, and structural devices within dramatic and liturgical contexts, rather than formal units capable of precise definitions as such. Only in the later phases of the period was there a crystallization of such sectional schemes as binary and da-capo arias and their instrumental opposite numbers within single movements. Also it was late in the period before cyclical structures were clarified into such relatively predictable series of units as those found in church sonatas (with four movements in slow-fast-slow-fast sequence, and chordal alternating with contrapuntal textures); chamber sonatas and dance suites with relatively fixed movements; French overtures (with a slow harmonic opening in dotted rhythm, then a faster fugal section, and usually a return to a shortened version of the opening slow section); Italian overture (with a triple division in fast-slow-fast sequence); the concerto design (with its late consolidation into a three-movement, fast-slow-fast organization); and such two-part combinations as the prelude and fugue, toccata and fugue, fantasy and fugue, and the like. Even in this late phase, however, it must be borne in mind that a very considerable latitude and formal freedom still prevailed.

VENICE AND THE CONCERTING STYLE

Venice, that unusual city built over the waters of the Adriatic Sea, was the scene of many of the most progressive developments of the early baroque period. A flourishing maritime trade brought this Most

Serene Republic a measure of prosperity unequalled at the time in any other world capital. Among its many enterprises were numbered the famous Aldine Press, that brought inexpensive editions of the classics within the reach of scholars and literate laymen, and Petrucci's early printing of musical anthologies, through which the most important composers of the day found a wider audience. As a cultural center Venice previously had seen the establishment of the first public library in modern Europe, and was to see the opening of the first public opera house in 1637. An unusual degree of liturgical freedom prevailed in Venice, since the secular authorities exercised considerable control in the appointments of church officials and clergy, including the organists and choirmasters of St. Mark's, which despite its size was not a cathedral but the "private chapel" of the doges. Thus while Rome remained the bastion of tradition, Venice became the center of progress that charted the course of the musical future.

St. Mark's, with a central plan that organized all architectural parts under the all-embracing unity of a dome, lent itself to a type of acoustical experimentation that led to the so-called *polychoral style*. Its ground plan resembled the equal-armed Greek cross; and instead of the usual long nave with all of the singers concentrated in a single section, the choir of St. Mark's was divided into two groups (hence the term *chori spezzati*, or broken choirs) and placed above the ground level in separate lofts on either side of the central area under the dome. Each choir was a complete four-part unit with its own organ and supporting instruments. When Adrian Willaert was appointed chapel master in 1527, he raised this polychoral practice to a high level of prestige that commanded the attention of the musical world.

Willaert, a Netherlander, was a practitioner of the "perfect art" of polyphony associated with his distinguished forebears—Ockeghem, Josquin des Prez, and Isaac—and he consistently worked within the contrapuntal techniques of the older style. By perceiving new potentialities in the acoustical conditions of St. Mark's, however, and by utilizing the opposing choral groups for spatial contrast, he made the first significant departures from the pure polyphony of his predecessors. Through Willaert, the Venetian school began to speak in new accents, while still retaining the traditional Renaissance contrapuntal vocabulary. In his motets, however, there is a noticeable breaking up of the unity of the chorus, as well as a new way of handling the bass parts almost as if they were conceived harmonically. While his vocal lines still flow smoothly in the Renaissance manner, there is an increased sense of verticality in contrapuntal writing. The dissolution of the unified flow of Renaissance polyphony is likewise seen in the tendency of Willaert and his successors, both in their choral and instrumental music, to separate the several sections of their works at certain cadential points. In the older counterpoint, the voice leading was managed so smoothly and the beginnings and ends of phrases overlapped one another so skillfully, that nothing impeded the continuous flow. The Venetian motets and madrigals, as well as the keyboard works of the time, thus definitely began to display a sectional character.

From Willaert through his colleagues and successors—Zarlino, de Rore, Merulo, to Andrea Gabrieli and his illustrious nephew Giovanni Gabrieli—the polychoral style progressed in a continuous line toward its climax. With the publication by the Gabrielis in 1587 of a book they called *Concerti . . . per voci e stromenti* (Concertos for Voices and Instruments), the new concerting idea, based on the principle of opposing tonal masses of unequal numbers, volume, and density, began to take more definite shape; and the culmination came with Giovanni Gabrieli's *Symphoniae Sacrae* (Sacred Symphonies), the first book of which was issued in 1597 and the second was published posthumously in 1615. The words *concertato* and *concerto* (both derived from *concertare*, meaning to compete with or strive against) were used at this time only in a general sense to indicate an interplay of contrasting elements such as an opposition of two or more choirs; part of one chorus sounding against another full chorus; solo voices against choral forces, vocal groups versus instrumental ensembles; as well as the setting up of polarities between high registers and low, polyphonic textures and homophonic, loud intensities and soft, string tone quality and that of wind instruments, and so on.

Giovanni Gabrieli, in the score of his polychoral motet *In ecclesiis,* calls for two four-part choirs (Chorus I to be used either as a whole, or with its soprano, alto, tenor, and bass sections singing separately; Chorus II to function always as a unit), vocal soloists, an organ, and an instrumental ensemble consisting of three cornetti (trumpets of wood), a viola, and two trombones. It is a nonliturgical motet of the processional type apparently intended for performance on some grand civic occasion such as that depicted in Gentile Bellini's picture *Procession in St. Mark's Square* (Fig. 20:1). The Venetian love of splendor here receives a musical realization equal to or even exceeding Bellini's visual pomp and pageantry.

In this motet the sopranos of Chorus I, accompanied by the organ, lead off with the first stanza of the psalmlike text (Bars 1–5), while Chorus II chimes in on the Alleluia (Bars 6–12), which functions as a recurring refrain between verses (Ex. 20:1). The tenors of Chorus I then proceed with the second verse, also with organ accompaniment (Bars 13–31), and the Alleluia follows once more. The choruses are then silenced for the instrumental Sinfonia (Bars 32–43) resembling that depicted in Figure 20:2, which enters with blazing, brassy sonorities and arresting, festive chordal progressions. The third verse is given to the altos and tenors of

Fig. 20:1 *Procession in St. Mark's Square.* Gentile Bellini. 1496. Academy, Venice (Anderson).

Fig. 20:2 Detail from *Procession in St. Mark's Square.* Gentile Bellini.

Ex. 20:1   *In ecclesiis* (Processional Motet). Gabrieli.

Chorus I, accompanied now by the six-part instrumental ensemble rather
than the organ. Fullness of sonority increases in the next Alleluia (Bars
93–99), when the entire Chorus I and organ join with the other forces.
The fifth and final verse brings in the soloists, the complete double choir,
the instrumental aggregate and organ, to make a total of fourteen inde-

pendent parts. The accumulation of tonal masses and volumes is then brought to a climax in the concluding Alleluia, in which all forces unite in a mighty cadence that projects the full color of the authentic Venetian sound in one huge tonal block, and at the same time revels in the wealth of grandiose sonorities for their own sake.

In ecclesiis is an excellent illustration of the *concertato* principle with its variety of contrasting elements brought together in a harmonious union of opposites. The slower and faster tempos, the polyphonic and homophonic sections, the solo and choral forces, the vocal and instrumental colors, the contrast of soft and loud dynamic levels, all contribute to the total effect. Moreover, a unity is created by the repetition of the Alleluia, as it alternates with the contrasts provided by the intervening sections. The larger body, represented by the Alleluia with its ritornel or refrain, contributes unity in its summarizations and repetitions, while the smaller groups are entrusted with the variety. Furthermore, the active progress of the parts or episodes, reinforced by the prevailing dynamic duple rhythm, can be perceived as moving against the more solid background of the whole with its more static triple rhythm. The throwing back and forth of the unequal tonal masses thus promotes the feeling of progress through time and space. *In ecclesiis,* to be sure, is a religious expression, but one of a particular kind with much sonorous excitement, rich textural contrasts, material splendor, all projected on an enormous spatial scale.

In Giovanni Gabrieli's *Sonata pian' e forte* the polychoral style and the concertato principle cross over into the realm of instrumental music. It is a sonata only in the sense that it is meant to be played rather than sung; and in it two unequal ensembles—one consisting of a cornetto and trombones I, II, and III, and the other of a violin and trombones IV, V, and VI—are set up in opposition to one another. The *piano* and *forte* announced in the title are true dynamic contrasts of soft and loud levels achieved by combining and separating the two instrumental choirs. Further contrasts are to be noted in this instance in the interplay of high and low registers and the string and wind colors. With one stroke, Gabrieli thus cleared the way for the transition of the concertato style to the instrumental medium, and with this work as the prototype the road was now open for the developments that led to the concerto grosso and solo concerto.

Concurrently with such experiments in instrumental ensemble writing, the Venetian composers, beginning with Andrea Gabrieli, developed several types of idiomatic solo pieces for the organ such as the intonation (*intonazione*) , toccata, fantasia, ricercare, and canzone. In each case the early examples were obviously written-out versions of the free improvisatory practices of the time. The *intonation,* as its name implies, was an introductory "warm-up" piece in which the organist, by running his fingers rapidly over the keys and coming to a definite chordal cadence, established the pitch and mode for the choir, and as such it was functionally a prelude to the singing of a motet. *Toccatas* and *fantasias* were usually longer and more elaborate, with the organist scampering and scurrying over the keyboard in cascades of scales, arpeggios, and broken chords, after which it was customary to settle down to a contrapuntal section in free fugal fashion. The *ricercare* began its history as an instrumental counterpart to the vocal motet. Deriving its name from the Italian verb meaning "to search" or "to seek again," the name clearly refers to the periodic recurrence of the first subject. As each subsequent subject or countersubject appears, it ushers in a new section in which contrapuntal imitations and rhythmic as well as melodic variation techniques are employed. The ricercare is the prototype of the later fugue. The *canzone* at first was an instrumental version of the secular French chanson. Compared to the ricercare it is lighter in texture, more dancelike in spirit, and less strict in its contrapuntal treatment. Both the ricercare and canzone could be played either at the keyboard or by an instrumental chamber ensemble. In the work of Girolamo Frescobaldi, organist of St. Peter's in Rome, these keyboard types took on a functional character in the liturgy. Such titles as *Toccata per il elevazione* (Toccata for the Elevation of the Host), and *Ricercar dopo il Credo* (Ricercare after the Creed) obviously indicate the points in the mass during which they were intended to be played.

THE CAMERATA

In Florence, meanwhile, a group of intellectuals and musical enthusiasts formed a literary and artistic circle they called the *Camerata*. Together they argued, with considerable heat and in the light of some scholarship, the need for saving "modern" music by a revival of Greek tragedy. Vincenzo Galilei, animated by the spirit of classical antiquity, enthusiastically attributed all musical excellences to the ancients. But while he and his Camerata colleagues were relatively well-informed on Greek philosophy, poetry, the texts of the extant dramas, and the legends attributing miraculous powers to music, their knowledge of Greek music was largely a figment of their lively imaginations. They were aware, however, that the Greek dramas were set to music, that the chorus sang and danced, and that the dialogue was intoned in songlike fashion; but beyond this, any actual "revival" of the music of antiquity was, on the face of it, a patent absurdity.

With the deaths of both Palestrina and Orlandus Lassus in 1594, the way was open for a full-fledged attack on the principles of Renaissance counterpoint. Polyphonic settings of poetic texts, the members of the Camerata felt, were overly concerned with contrapuntal manipulations that tended to obscure rather than illuminate the meaning of the text. Such overemphasis on the perfection of craftsmanship, in their view, limited music's expressive range and precluded concern with its moral and dramatic significance. In order to realize the full meaning of the text, each word and phrase, in their opinion, had to be projected with proper emphasis and sufficient force so as to communicate its full measure of human and dramatic power. This, they argued, could be done only with a single melodic line supported by appropriate instrumental accompaniment. Hence Galilei, Giulio Caccini, Jacopo Peri, and Marco da Gagliano composed and published books of secular solo songs they called *monodies*.

The most notable departure from Renaissance polyphony lay in eliminating the homogeneity of the contrapuntal texture. In baroque practice, the upper melodic line was isolated as a solo melody, and the lower voices were absorbed in a bass complex called the *basso continuo*. Where the continuo was a melodic line, the resultant counterpoint was *amphonic,* or polarized—that is, an upper and lower line moving against one another. The continuo line was played by the left hand of the harpsichordist or the organist, or both, and by a melody instrument like the viola da gamba, the modern equivalent of which is the cello. Other instruments might be added, for the continuo was a bass complex. Between the top and bottom lines (that is, between the melody and the continuo) filler parts were added improvisationally by the keyboard performer. Often numbers were placed beneath the continuo bass line to guide the keyboard player in realizing the filler parts. Such a figured-bass part was called, quite simply, a *figured bass.*

Sometimes the continuo part was not primarily a melody line, but simply the bass notes of vertical chords. Given the bass notes, the harpsichordist would then fill in the vertical chords to support the melody. Chords were often chosen coloristically, to "paint" the meaning of the text. According to Peri the vocal line should be maintained at the same pitch level until the meaning of the text called for a change upward or downward. The chord that supported the singer's pitch should also remain the same until the vocal line and mood dictated a change. Chords in the Camerata conception were thus not organized into harmonic progressions in the modern sense, but functioned more on a mood basis and were closely tied to a text.

The *recitative style,* or *stile recitativo* as the Camerata called it, was a new type of vocal declamation designed to imitate the natural inflections of speech. Galilei advised composers to concern themselves less with the intricacies of counterpoint and more with the ways people speak with one another. "Observe," he said, "when one quiet gentleman speaks with another, in what manner he speaks, how high or low his voice is pitched, with what volume of sound, with what sort of accents and gestures, and with what rapidity or slowness his words are uttered. Let them mark a little what difference obtains in all these things when one of them speaks with one of his servants, or one of these with another; let them observe the prince when he chances to be conversing with one of his subjects and vassals; when with the petitioner who is entreating his favor; how the man infuriated or excited speaks; the married woman, the girl, the mere child, the clever harlot, the lover speaking to his mistress as he seeks to persuade her to grant his wishes, the man who laments, the one who cries out, the timid man, and the man exultant with joy. From these variations of circumstance, if they observe them attentively and examine them with care, they will be able to select the norm of what is fitting for the expression of any other conception whatever that can call for their handling."

In the course of the Camerata experiments the principles of monodic melody with continuo accompaniment, the new musical rhetoric based on the natural inflection of speech (recitative), and the desire to imitate Greek tragedy (however fanciful its factual basis) were all combined and applied to the setting of complete dramatic texts. The poet and playwright Ottavio Rinuccini, the principal literary figure of the Camerata, collaborated with the various composing members on a number of these musical dramas. Peri's *Daphne* of 1594 chronologically came first, though its music is now lost; it was followed in 1600 by *Euridice,* which survives in settings by both Peri and Caccini; and still another setting of the *Daphne* was made in 1608 by Marco da Gagliano. These productions may be distinguished from the pastoral plays long established in Renaissance tradition. The distinction is correctly drawn, however, on the grounds of their being composed with continuous music throughout, rather than merely with intermittent musical interludes between the sequences of spoken dialogue. Thus in their zeal to recreate Greek tragedy, the Camerata had actually uncovered an entirely new formula; and the momentous result was nothing less than the foundation for the art of opera.

Furthermore, the very same year that saw the performance of Peri's *Euridice* in Florence also witnessed the production in Rome of a sacred counterpart—*The Story of the Soul and the Body* (*Rappresentazione di Anima e di Corpo*). Its composer, Emilio de' Cavalieri, whose extended period of residence in Florence coincided with the time of the Camerata, was thoroughly conversant with all the developments and devices employed by his colleagues there. The subject of his sacred representation, however, had nothing to do with classical antiquity; it was, rather, a religious morality play with such allegorical characters as Time, World,

Life, as well as the Soul and Body of the title. Its sacred character, its similarity in procedure to the early Camerata opera experiments, as well as its printed publication in 1600, gave it an influence out of all proportion to its actual musical importance. While it can certainly be considered one of the early prototypes of modern oratorio, that branch of musical drama had to await the coming of a more powerful and persuasive advocate than Cavalieri. This it found later in one Giacomo Carissimi who became the first great master of the oratorio style, just as Monteverdi was the genius who perceived the dramatic possibilities in the various experiments of his time and went on to become the first great master of the operatic stage.

MONTEVERDI AND EARLY OPERA

The musico-dramatic ideals, envisaged but far from realized by the Camerata, were translated into living action by Claudio Monteverdi. Early in his career this distinguished musician had not only mastered all the traditional musical techniques, but had also assimilated all the current experiments and important innovations of his time. Unlike the Camerata composers, Monteverdi was not so much interested in overthrowing Renaissance polyphony as he was in bringing the art of counterpoint up to date in a way that was more suitable to the spirit of his time. Seeing that the old and new styles could be made to operate side by side, he separated them partly on a functional basis, retaining the *a cappella* counterpoint of Palestrina for sacred purposes and calling it the *first practice*. The representative style and other promising experiments of his time he thought better adapted for secular music, especially in connection with dramatic presentations, and they therefore became the *second practice*.

The group of operas that Monteverdi produced at Mantua and Venice, as well as the series of nine books of madrigals that he published, quite literally created the basis of modern music. In 1607 with his first opera, *Orfeo,* Monteverdi in a single stroke determined the future course of lyric drama. In this opera Monteverdi combined all the styles, ideas, techniques, and devices known to him. The opening instrumental Sinfonia, the prototype of the future overture, is an orchestral toccata in the style of the Gabrielis; as such it would have been equally at home in Venice at St. Mark's. The Prologue, intoned by a personification of Music, is a strophic song with an instrumental ritornel separating the stanzas. Groups of nymphs and shepherds sing madrigal choruses, while the principals in the cast declaim their lines in a recitative style of deeply expressive character. Orpheus' love song, "Rose of Heaven" (*Rosa del ciel*) , and his lament, "Thou art departed" (*Tu se' morta*) , are cases in point. When Orpheus has to summon his most persuasive powers to pacify the infernal furies, he pleads with them in an eloquent aria *(Possente Spirito)*, a concerted dialogue in the Venetian concertato manner. In a series of strophic variations the voice contends with instruments that personify the shades of Hades, and the vocal part is opposed in turn by two violins, two cornetti, two harps; and, between the fourth and fifth stanzas, by trio combinations including the lower strings. As Orpheus is being rowed across the river Styx, the vast spaces of the underworld are suggested by the choral echo effects so typical of baroque dynamics. The score is also important for its primitive but powerful orchestration, since Monteverdi wrote independent parts for instruments instead of following the customary practice of letting them double the vocal lines. He selected the instrumental colors that were most in keeping with the character they accompanied and with the dramatic situation at hand. The choruses of shepherds, for instance, appropriately have a piping obbligato of piccolos and flutes, while the recitatives of the sepulchral boatman, Charon, are accompanied by lugubrious chords on the organ and spectral tones on the trombones. Thus by dramatically contrasting pastoral and infernal elements, by organizing entire scenes with recurrent choral and instrumental ritornels, as well as by combining all the various musical ideas at his command with those of the poetic text—plus scenery, gesture, acting, ballet sequences, and the like—Monteverdi succeeded in making opera effective in both the dramatic and theatrical sense.

Ex. 20:2 "Lament" from *Arianna*. Monteverdi.

The "Lament" (Ex. 20:2), a surviving fragment of Monteverdi's opera *Arianna* of 1608, is an eloquent instance of the way he focuses on moments of intense human emotion in order to reveal human character within a dramatic context. The story is that of Bacchus and Ariadne of classical mythology, and the situation is that in which Ariadne, realizing she has been abandoned by her lover Theseus, gives expression to her overwhelm-

ing grief. The downward plunge of the first half phrase from B flat to E
encompasses the daring melodic dissonance of the diminished fifth. Rising
emotional tension is portrayed in the chromatically ascending line in Bars
4 and 5, as well as the precipitous decline from the upper D to the octave
below (5–6). The second and contrasting phrase (Bars 7–14) gradually
mounts in a moving manner to the poignant climax of Bar 14. The exact
repetition of the opening phrase (Bars 15–19) makes this compact example the prototype of the three-part da-capo aria that was destined to
become one of the most important formal designs of the period. An interesting comparison can be made between this homophonic aria and the
polyphonic madrigal setting Monteverdi made of the same melody some
years later. His problem, of course, was to turn a free-flowing aria with a
melody that followed the natural speech rhythms into a contrapuntal
composition. In the process the melody does not change essentially, but
the style of counterpoint is adapted to it. The harmonic dissonances within
the counterpoint are geared to the meaning of the text, and the result is a
good example of the modern harmonic counterpoint that Monteverdi
called the "second practice."

Monteverdi's early operas, as well as the extant later ones he wrote for
Venice—*Return of Ulysses* (1641) and *Coronation of Poppea* (1642)—
were always conceived and executed in terms of the theater. He well understood the need for the text and music to be maintained in a certain
balanced relationship, but he also knew that in the final analysis the music
had to carry the real dramatic weight. The above "Lament," (Ex. 20:2)
for instance, occurs at a place where Ariadne prepares to bid farewell to
life itself, and as such it is the model for the great *addio* scenes of Italian
opera. For all its individual melodic excellence, however, it makes no real
dramatic sense except in terms of what precedes it and what is to follow.
In other words, the audience must be prepared by the previous hopes and
fulfillment so that everyone knows exactly to what the heroine is bidding
farewell. Thus the planning, preparing, and placing of scenes is the all-
important aspect of opera.

In his effort to widen the range of dramatic music, Monteverdi undertook a series of works in which he experimented with new rhythmic and
orchestral devices. Such devices, however, were used to project specific
emotional states. An analysis of such emotional states was therefore primary. Hence he prefaced his eighth book of madrigals (1638) with a fore-
word which begins as follows: "I have reflected that the principal passions
or affections of our mind are three, namely, anger, moderation, and hu-
mility or supplication; so the best philosophers declare, and the very nature of our voice indicates this in having high, low, and middle registers.
The art of music also points clearly to these three in its terms 'agitated,'
'soft,' and 'moderate.'"

The Italian for "agitated" is *concitato*. Reflecting that the soft and temperate styles were already well known, but that he had never encountered an example of the agitated or *concitato* style, Monteverdi undertook to rediscover it by following the precepts for it laid down by Plato. "Take that harmony," wrote Plato, "that would fittingly imitate the utterances and the accents of a brave man who is engaged in warfare." Monteverdi further observed, "that it is contraries which greatly move our mind," and hence his eighth book is suitably entitled *Madrigali guerriere ed amorosi* (Madrigals warlike and amorous).

The most arresting of his *concitati* works is a curious theater piece entitled *Il Combattimento di Tancredi e Clorinda* (The Combat of Tancred and Clorinda) and based on part of the twelfth canto of the famous *Gerussalemme liberata* (Jerusalem Delivered) by Torquato Tasso, one of the most impassioned of Italian baroque poets. In a preface to this work, Monteverdi asked the instrumentalists to observe the distinction between the *concitati* (agitated) passages and *molli* (soft) passages, and further urged that they interpret their parts "in imitation of the passions of the words." The narrator (*testo* or text part) was enjoined to sing his part clearly, with careful pronunciation of the words, and to forebear from the insertion of ornament except for the one instance where Monteverdi felt it allowable. The singing style likewise was to be "a simulation of the passions of the words."

From a technical point of view, the *Combattimento* is a compendium of the *concitato* style. Many rhythmic devices are used to mirror the text more realistically (like the figure that represents the galloping of horses). The most famous of the orchestral devices in this score are the *pizzicato* (plucking the strings rather than bowing) and the *tremolando*. The latter in particular was useful for states of excitement. In a *tremolando* a note is rapidly repeated many times in one measure, producing a shuddering effect. Monteverdi reported that musicians at first found his device "more ridiculous than praiseworthy," and in simplifying the passage by playing one note instead of sixteen to a measure, they destroyed "the resemblance to agitated speech" which he intended. He cautioned them to perform such passages in the "manner as written." Monteverdi's *tremolando* is now one of the clichés of modern orchestration, a stock-in-trade device to represent foreboding, uneasiness, mystery, agitation, or hypertension of any sort.

Both in his operas and in his madrigals Monteverdi contributed many of the melodic and rhythmic figures that quickly became an accepted part of the vocabulary of baroque operas, oratorios, and cantatas. Baroque psychology, one must remember, conceived the affections as states of mind in the sense of static mental and emotional attitudes, rather than as the more dynamic psychological moods of later times. Specific musical patterns were thus intended, through a process of psychological association, to produce certain emotional responses in audiences.

Monteverdi's rendering of the poetic imagery of the text is well illustrated by his setting of Rinuccini's sonnet "Return, O Zephyr" (*Zefiro torna*). Monteverdi invents an undulating melodic figure for the word "waves" (*l'onde*) Example 20:3a; still another for "murmuring" (*mormo-*

Ex. 20:3a *Zeffiro torna* (Return, O Zephyr). Monteverdi.

rando) Example 20:3b; and the scenic profile of the "mountains and val-

Ex. 20:3b

leys high and deep" (*da monti e da valli ime e profonde*) is appropriately described with mounting and dipping lines (Ex. 20:3c). For passages of

Ex. 20:3c

more intense personal expression Monteverdi rises to the occasion with telling harmonic shifts; and to convey the ardent lover's emotional dilemma—"As my fate wills it, now I weep, now I sing" (*Come vuol mia ventura hor piangio, hor canto*) —he employs such contrasts as the downward chromatic descending line and startling dissonance of tremendous intensity for "weep" (Ex. 20:3d), as well as a festive florid coloratura for

Ex. 20:3d

"sing" (Ex. 20:3e). This little chamber duet for two tenors and continuo

Ex. 20:3e

accompaniment can be described technically as a vocal chaconne with free strophic variations over a steadily repeated ground bass. Since the wealth of melodic and harmonic variety takes place over this insistent basso ostinato, the unity of the composition, despite the freedom of the vocal lines, remains serenely undisturbed. Monteverdi, as well as the later baroque composers, conceived of an emotion as a psychological disturbance that could be represented by a specific type of dissonance, and the ensuing state of rest could therefore be conveyed by an appropriate resolution and consonance. Melodic figurations could thus be made to correspond to figures of speech; and above all, there was a new concept of rhythm in which an agitated, a restless, or a calm emotional state could be represented with a particular rhythmic pattern.

THE BAROQUE AS AN INTERNATIONAL STYLE

While the various Italian centers were the proving grounds of the early baroque, the style was destined to reach its culmination in the great northern centers of Paris, London, Dresden, and Leipzig. The Venetian polychoral practice was represented by Gabrieli's gigantic choruses and moved into a stylistic phase known as the "colossal baroque." In its later manifestations this aspect of baroque style saw the number of choral parts expanded to unprecedented proportions in such works as Orazio Benevoli's Mass for the dedication of the Salzburg Cathedral (1628), in which the mighty assembly of musical forces adds up to a total of fifty-three parts—sixteen choral, thirty-four instrumental, plus two organs and continuo. The end of the period still found Bach opening and closing his *St. Matthew Passion* with large Venetian double choruses. The Venetian concept of terraced dynamics with its contrasting levels of intensity was also taken over into baroque organ music in the "echo" pieces of Sweelinck, Scheidt, and others.

The concertato idea with its dualism that paradoxically produces unity also became one of the ruling principles of the baroque style. This is manifest through the setting up of polar extremes—larger and smaller groups, solo and orchestral ensembles, soprano and bass registers, slow and fast tempos, regular and irregular rhythms, soft and loud dynamic levels, consonant and dissonant intervals, diatonic and chromatic harmonies, blocked chords and flowing counterpoint, homophonic and polyphonic textures, and the like—and through the maintenance of a continuous interplay between such opposing elements. The principle of supporting the upper melodic lines with the harmonies of basso-continuo accompaniments likewise became a universal practice. From Monteverdi to Bach and Handel the period employed the continuo as the foundation of ensemble writing, and baroque music consequently stood solidly on the powerful support of its basso-continuo feet.

The early beginnings of the idiomatic treatment of voices and instruments continued onward throughout the period. Such instruments as the lute, clavier, and lower strings were used mainly in supporting roles; while others, such as the violin, flute, and trumpet, were considered as principals in the melodic cast. In general the lines of keyboard practice followed those of the baroque style by moving outward from Venice and Rome, respectively. Frescobaldi, as the foremost organist of the Counter-Reformation, exerted a strong influence on the development of keyboard music, especially in Roman Catholic countries and more particularly through such outstanding pupils as Froberger who spread his ideas in Vienna and South Germany. Both Andrea Gabrieli and Zarlino were the teachers of Jan P. Sweelinck who carried the Venetian tradition northward to his native Holland where he established his reputation as the municipal organist of Amsterdam. He is identified with a type of toccata known as the *fantasy in the manner of an echo,* which represented a transfer of the Venetian polychoral practice to the keyboard. In such pieces a short motive is tossed back and forth from one manual and registration to another with neatly terraced, contrasting dynamic levels. Synthesizing both the Venetian and English keyboard traditions, Sweelinck's works show the baroque love of lively invention, complicated variation techniques, and opulent tonal effects. His fame attracted a host of students, including such important German composers as Samuel Scheidt of Halle, Heinrich Scheidemann of Hamburg, and others. These composers passed on the tradition to the generation of Pachelbel and Buxtehude who, in turn, became the principal influences on Bach and Handel.

Monteverdi, in his years at Venice, effected the transition of opera from its social position as a princely court entertainment to that of a public spectacle. Notable also was the toleration by both the Roman Catholic and Protestant Lutheran Churches of the opera idiom in sacred oratorios and cantatas. Secular operas and sacred oratorios were often so close in style as to be undistinguishable except for the texts and the intended place of performance. Opera thus moved outward from Venice to the cosmopolitan centers of Paris and London, while the oratorio was destined for glory in Italy with Carissimi; in France with Carissimi's pupil, Marc Antoine Charpentier; in Germany with Heinrich Schütz (a pupil of Giovanni Gabrieli and of Monteverdi, and without doubt the greatest of German composers before Bach) ; and in England with George Frederick Handel. This internationalization did not hinder the development of strong national styles. In Paris opera become indigenously French with Lully, even though Lully was by birth Italian. And in Germany the native-born Schütz furthered a national style in his Passion oratorios and *Symphoniae Sacrae* by combining Italian techniques with his unparalleled mastery of German prosody.

LULLY AND FRENCH OPERA[1]

Paris had experienced a taste of Italian opera when Cavalli —Monteverdi's younger colleague and successor at the Venetian opera— and Luigi Rossi of Rome were summoned to the French court in the 1640's to write and supervise several productions. Cavalli later received a royal command to stage a spectacular opera for the wedding festivities of Louis XIV in 1662. Since this was the great age of French baroque drama and the heyday of such literary luminaries as Corneille, Racine, and Molière, Cavalli's courtly French audience quite understandably refused to take his operatic extravaganzas very seriously either as drama or as music. Instead, to the composer's great indignation, they most admired the sumptuous ballet scenes that concluded each act. Cavalli, in his concern with his singers, had not even bothered with the ballet music, but had consigned it instead to the care of a young ballet master, Jean Baptiste Lully, who consequently emerged as the real hero of the occasion. Lully, though Italian-born himself, never lost sight of the fact that he was in the service of a French court; and to the ambitious young composer, the taste of his patrons always came first.

With indefatigable industry and a genius for organization, Lully, in his capacity as superintendent of the king's music, marshalled all the very considerable resources of the court of Louis XIV. With Molière he wrote a number of comedy ballets (*comédie ballets*) including the well-known *The Bourgeois Gentleman* (*Le Bourgeois Gentilhomme*) of 1670; and a series of lyrical tragedies (*tragédies lyrique*) in collaboration with the poet-dramatist Quinault. As conductor and disciplinarian Lully brought the court chamber orchestra known as the *Vingt-quatre Violons,* or Twenty-four Viols of the King, to a peak of technical precision. Its duties included playing for state dinners, balls, and chamber concerts, and it was also available for theater productions. If an operatic situation needed a trumpet fanfare for a triumphal entrance or some horns to embellish a hunting scene, Lully could always turn to the king's military band for wind instruments. Lully, in addition to his ballet company, was thus in command of the first permanent orchestral ensemble in Europe. He could also draw on the singers and chorus of the court chapel for vocal support; and with all of the ingredients of a flourishing operatic organization on hand, Lully proceeded to make the most of his opportunity.

Lully's opera *Alceste,* performed at the Versailles Palace during the summer of 1674, will serve as an example of his style. It opens with an instrumental number that Lully shaped into the form that has been known

---

[1] The earlier French *ballet de cour* and English court masque are discussed in Chapter 14, pages 170–171.

ever since his time as the *French overture*. Its first section is a slow, stately march with dignified dotted notes in duple meter resembling the manner of Example 20:4. A second section—lively in pace, fugal in texture, and triple in meter—follows. The Prologue then opens the stage proceedings, and a personification of the Nymph of the Seine River comes forward to make some pompous pronouncements in recitative style. A triumphal march now prepares for the entrance of Glory and the singing of a duet and solo air. A chorus of pastoral divinities and water sprites, symbolizing the fields and streams of France, then makes its entrance for some song and dance sequences that conclude the Prologue.

Ex. 20:4   Ritornel from *Alceste*, Act III, Scene 5. Lully.

Following the story line of the Greek myth, the plot unfolds throughout the course of the traditional five acts of classical tragedy. Each act is organized by means of a recurrent choral or orchestral ritornel such as Example 20:4, which is interspersed with recitative passages, solo songs (usually of the strophic type), vocal duets, and ballet sequences much in the manner of the above-described Prologue. French audiences always insisted that opera be good drama as well as good music, and they would no more tolerate singing just for the sake of singing than they would stand for a text being in a foreign language. Lully, therefore, had to make a thorough study of French prosody with its rising and falling inflections, word color, and rhythmic flow. His music, as Example 20:5 will show,

Ex. 20:5   Air from *Alceste*, Act III, Scene 5. Lully.

La mort, la mort bar - ba - re Dé - truit au-jourd'huy mille ap - pas.

is capable of rising to a point of considerable expressive power in spite of its baroque grandiloquence. Addressed as they were to the taste of an aristocratic circle, Lully's operas inevitably reflect the reserve and restraint of a formal way of life, based on a rigorous courtly etiquette. As a consequence they failed to develop a broad enough human appeal to assure their survival in the modern repertory. Lully's hand, however, is still felt in the French classical ballet and the standardized series of dances known as the French suite; his overture form, moreover, became the universally adopted French overture; and his organization of the opera was to be a determining force in France for well over two centuries.

PURCELL, HANDEL, AND ENGLISH OPERA

Henry Purcell,[1] born under Cromwell's Commonwealth and bred in the early Restoration years as a singer in Charles II's royal choir, came to maturity during the turbulent days of the downfall of James II, the Glorious Revolution of 1688, and the wars of William III. French influence had pervaded England under Charles II, who had acquired a taste for Continental grandeur during his long exile at the court of Louis XIV. A chamber orchestra, known as His Majesty's Violins, became the English equivalent of Louis XIV's *Vingt-quatre Violons*, and Purcell became its leader in 1677 as well as Composer in Ordinary to the King. Several years later he succeeded his teacher, John Blow, as organist at Westminster Abbey. Purcell thus had an outlet for chamber music, which he built principally on Italian models, and for church music such as the organ works, anthems, and choral motets that account for the preponderance of his output. In addition to his mastery of chamber and church styles, Purcell possessed a good sense of the theater, gained through years of experience with writing incidental music for London stage productions.

With the previously established precedent of the English court masque (a combination of pageantry, scenic spectacle, dancing, poetic recitation, and vocal and instrumental interludes), with Charles II trying to bring his country abreast of the latest baroque developments, and with the availability of all the necessary literary and dramatic resources, the stage would appear to have been all set for the cultivation of an indigenous form of English opera. However, the slenderness of the royal purse, the stubborn resistance of English audiences, and the opposition encountered among men of letters were to prove all but insurmountable obstacles. Several brave and historically important attempts had been made before Purcell's

---

1 See Chapter 7, page 87, *Dido and Aeneas*, "Ah, Belinda"; and Chapter 9, pages 111—112, *Fairy Queen*, "I attempt from love's sickness to fly."

time. *The Siege of Rhodes* (1656), with book by William Davenant and
music by Henry Lawes and Matthew Locke, for all its masquelike qualities, is generally considered the first English opera. Though John Blow
still called his *Venus and Adonis* of 1682 a "masque," it was really a small
but complete chamber opera. Charles II's death in 1685 was followed by
several unsettled years; and when Purcell came to write his only through-
composed opera, it was neither for a royal court nor a London theater,
but for an amateur performance by a girls' school of which he happened
to be the music master.

    Dido and Aeneas (1689), in spite of the curious circumstances of its
composition, the obvious weakness of Nahum Tate's libretto, and the
smallness of its scale, is nonetheless a masterpiece and still the ranking
serious opera by an English composer. With only the older masque tradition, the above-mentioned attempts at opera, and the current Continental ideas to guide him, Purcell's achievement is all the more impressive. At times with amusing naiveté and at others with profound sophistication,
Purcell put together his compact little lyrical drama by selecting what he
considered the more promising native and foreign developments of his
time. The Overture, for instance, with its contrasting sections of harmonic
and contrapuntal textures, is clearly of the French type established by
Lully. The recitatives, though sparingly used in deference to native taste,
nevertheless make vivid use of the Italian representative style to enhance
the dramatic projection of the text. A word such as "shake" (Ex. 20:6*a*),

Ex. 20:6   Recitative excerpts from *Dido and Aeneas*. Purcell.

for instance, is rendered by a nervous, fidgety line, while the word "storms"
(Ex. 20:6*b*) is represented by a sudden upward rushing gust of the C-minor
scale. The character of Anchises (Ex. 20:6*c*), the warrior father of Aeneas,
is delineated with a positive martial rhythm; Venus' voluptuous charms
(Ex. 20:6*d*) are rendered by heart-melting chromaticisms; and Aeneas' entrance (Ex. 20:6*e*) is heralded by a trumpetlike vocal fanfare.

    Dido, the tragic heroine, first sings an air over a ground bass which
seems to symbolize her unyielding fate.[1] On the words, "Fate and I are

---

[1] See Chapter 7, page 87, for further discussion of this aria and an example.

strangers grown," she seems to be relentlessly pursued by fate as the bass line follows in a series of canonic imitations, and the unbalanced lines of her phrases vis-a-vis their bass support clearly point to her eventual undoing. "Fear no danger" is a vocal version of the trio-sonata style with the two upper parts bound together and sounding over a continuo, which in turn becomes a concertino to the grosso of the full choir to make a concerted number. The first scene then ends in the French manner with a "Triumphing Dance," the music of which is a Lullian chaconne with free variations soaring over a repeated basso ostinato. With the sinister witches of the second scene, Purcell's audience was once more back on home territory; no Restoration play would have been complete without the presence of one or more of these "secret, black, and midnight hags." Though their choruses are mainly in the English madrigal style, two of the witches sing in trio-sonata fashion over a basso continuo; and "In our deep vaulted cell" they all prepare their charms to a typical Venetian double chorus (one onstage and the other off), complete with echo dynamics.

Act III begins with a typical English seaport scene with sailors dancing the hornpipe and giving voice to the customary salty comments of the common people. Purcell's partiality for basso-ostinato construction is admirably illustrated in Dido's moving "Farewell," an excerpt of which is found in Example 20:7. Such a chromatically descending bass was the universally accepted pattern to denote grief and mourning. Bach, for instance, uses one very similar to it for the "Crucifixus" of the B-minor Mass. Over this fixed figure, which bespeaks the foreboding force of her fate, Dido declaims her poignant lines in a free melodic obbligato of great expressive intensity.

Though *Dido and Aeneas* was Purcell's only through-composed lyric drama, one more opportunity to come to grips with the problem of English opera did present itself. John Dryden, the prime figure of Restoration drama, invited Purcell to collaborate on *King Arthur* in 1691. Dryden, as well as other contemporary authors, had grave misgivings about the place of music in drama in general and the recitative style in particular. His solution, a typical English compromise, was to let ordinary mortals discourse in spoken dialogue, and to allow such supernatural figures as gods and goddesses to declaim their lines in what he called a "songish part." Since the play literally abounded in superhuman characters, Purcell had as rich an opportunity as any composer could have desired. Some of Purcell's music for *King Arthur*—the Frost Scene, for instance, with its shivering chorus and realistic tremolando effects—rises to true communicative eloquence. Purcell, in spite of his Continental borrowings, composed with a strong personal style; and whether his surroundings are church, chamber, or theater, his writing always has a clear-cut musical profile. Not only

Ex. 20:7 "Farewell" from *Dido and Aeneas*. Purcell.

my fate, Re-mem-ber me, but ah!____ for-get my_fate!

is he a major composer in his own right, but his substantial influence on
both Bach and Handel qualify him as one of the most important of baroque composers.

An interval of but twenty years separated the Purcell-Dryden collaboration on *King Arthur* and the first performance in 1711 of one of George
Frederick Handel's [1] operas. Attempts to establish a native English opera
tradition had withered in the meantime, and Handel's presentations were
frankly Italian operas of the type that called forth Dr. Samuel Johnson's
famous definition of opera as "an exotic and irrational entertainment."
Others, such as Sir Richard Steele, rushed to Handel's defense and pointed
out that "an opera is the completest concert" to which one could go. Since
public orchestra concerts at this time were nonexistent and concerts of
any description were extreme rarities, this was a fairly accurate description
of the proceedings.

Handel's style was closely identified with the Neapolitan opera tradition which flourished during the late seventeenth and early eighteenth centuries under the leadership of Alessandro Scarlatti. As such, the chorus was

---

[1] See Chapter 9, pages 107–108, *Harmonious Blacksmith* variations.

relegated to the background and the texture of the writing was dominated principally by solo arias interspersed with liberal sequences of recitative. This was the golden age of the so-called *bel canto* voice culture, and the singing demanded vocal virtuosity of a high order. The baroque period was also one of great engineering, and the ingenuity expended on the complex machines and scenic architecture contributed to the spectacular aspect of opera.

According to the tenets of Neapolitan opera in general and Handel's procedure in particular, the dramatic continuity is carried on by the freely declaimed recitative in which the irregular metrical organization is adapted to prose speech rhythms. At certain points of the lyrical drama the action is temporarily arrested so that the characters can pour out in song their subjective reactions to the plot situation. The aria by this time had crystallized into the symmetrical da-capo design with its ABA arrangement of parts. Minute distinctions in type, however, were made, and the vocabulary abounds in such terms as *aria parlante* (recitative aria), *aria di bravura,* and *aria d'agilita* (virtuoso arias), *aria concertata* (concerted aria), and so on. A single "affection" governed a given aria, and each focused on one sharply defined emotion—joy, defiance, rage, sorrow, or the like. The da-capo aria with its ritornel introduction and conclusion, while static by nature, is nevertheless a complete emotional declaration that becomes dramatic by what precedes and what follows it; and in the hands of such a composer as Handel, it was capable of rising to great expressive power.

Handel's *Semele,* though technically described as a secular oratorio, is nonetheless an excellent example of his operatic writing. It has, moreover, the advantage of an English text of considerable literary quality by the distinguished playwright William Congreve. Act II opens with Juno venting her jealous fury in an impassioned passage of accompanied recitative (*recitativo stromentato*). Semele, by way of contrast, sings a serene solo aria, "Oh sleep, why dost thou leave me?" The eloquent melody rises over a lullabylike continuo accompaniment (harpsichord and cello) revealing the sleepless state of a woman overwhelmingly in love and longing for her lover—none other than the divine Jupiter himself. When he appears, their dialogue is carried on in dry recitative, or *recitativo secco* (voice and harpsichord), which leads up to one of Handel's most ardent arias, "Where'er you walk." After lavishing two such masterpieces on a single scene, Handel has still further lyrical revelations in store, such as Semele's aria, "Myself I shall adore." Her vanity, which is to be her downfall, has been cleverly prodded by Juno in disguise, and the aria is sung as she gazes fondly into her mirror. Handel chooses the concerted aria for this situation; and Semele's reflection is graphically described by the violins, which reflect her phrases in echolike imitations of the vocal line. With his constant flow of melodic invention, and by matching such technical devices as the concerted aria with significant insights into human character, Handel succeeds in drawing dramatic sparks from Congreve's text and in writing most convincingly for the lyric stage.

Handel, as others before him, found that his English audiences never took too kindly to the monumental Italian serious opera with its elevated tone, general grandiloquence, and what critics often described as "that perpetual singing." But though he failed in his operatic enterprises, Handel discovered that his adopted countrymen would tolerate in concert oratorios what they refused to accept in the theater. Unlike the passions and cantatas of Bach, Handel's oratorios were written for public concert halls; and even though they were usually settings of sacred texts, they were nevertheless billed on presentation as "Grand Musical Entertainments." The most familiar of these, the *Messiah*, is at the same time the least typical of the composer's oratorios. Completely devoid of dramatic plot and continuity of action, its three acts are in actuality three independent cantatas comprising an extended commentary and meditation on Christ's messianic mission. As such, it is the only one of Handel's great oratorios written on a *New Testament* text, since both Handel as well as his London audiences found more ready identification with the *Old Testament* events and characters in which they saw the reflection of the heroism of their own empire-building leaders.

The inward orientation and lyrical qualities of the *Messiah* contrast strongly with the Cyclopean sweep of such Biblical epics as *Israel in Egypt*. In this mighty oratorio the chorus represents the collective image of the children of Israel, and it is both the dramatic protagonist as well as the group narrator. Liberal use is made of the representative style, notably in such pictorial passages as those depicting the plagues. A leaping accompaniment figure to a solo aria, for instance, neatly describes the frogs mentioned in the text (No. 5).[1] Further graphic realism is found in the buzzing "Chorus of Flies" (No. 6), as well as in the "Hailstone Chorus" (No. 7). The lowering lugubrious harmonies of "He sent a thick darkness over the land" (No. 8) paint a vivid picture of nightfall; while the driving rhythms of "The Lord is a man of war" (No. 22) proceed in powerful sledge-hammerlike strokes.

It is, of course, the chorus, not the solo aria, that dominates a Handel oratorio, and it is in his complete mastery of the choral medium that Handel's baroque spirit is most transparently revealed. The scope of his choral writing in such a massively designed work as *Israel in Egypt* sums up as

[1] The numbers follow the order given in the Mendelssohn edition of the score published by G. Schirmer, Inc., New York.

well as consummates the practice of the two prior centuries; Handel always managed to achieve the mightiest of effects seemingly by the simplest possible means. In it there are survivals of the old motet style scaled, however, to larger proportions (No. 27, "And with the blast"); the monolithic harmonies of Protestant chorales (No. 15, "And Israel saw," and No. 30, "Who is like unto Thee"); the elemental power of the Venetian polychoral practice (No. 6, "Chorus of Flies," No. 7, "Hailstone Chorus," and No. 33, "The people shall hear"); the solid eight-part cantus-firmus chorus (No. 2, beginning on the words, "And their cry came up unto God"). Then there are such typical Handelian touches as the "Chorus of Darkness" (No. 8), in which the singers grope their way in harmonic space through a maze of remote keys; the solemn fugal choruses, "They loathed to drink" (No. 4), as well as "And believed the Lord" (No. 16); concerted choruses in which a solo voice is pitted against the combined forces of the double choir, "Sing ye to the Lord" (No. 39); and the ritornel choruses at the beginning of "Moses' Song" (Nos. 17 and 18) that function as gigantic da-capo structures.

It is, perhaps, the power and breadth of the jubilant sounds that Handel draws from his choruses that make the most unforgettable impression. And while his operas, for all their inherent beauty, failed to catch on, Handel's synthesis of his native German polyphony with the Italian operatic practice, French dance forms that he mastered in his journeyman years, and the English choir music of his adopted country did succeed in establishing an oratorio tradition that has continued with undiminished luster down to the present day.

BACH AND THE REFORMATION TRADITION

The warm, all-embracing human art of Johann Sebastian Bach [1] is deeply rooted in the soil of the German Reformation. Though he wrote chamber music, instrumental dance suites, and concertos for the pleasure of aristocratic patrons, though he wrote his monumental *B-minor Mass* for a Roman Catholic prince and subsequently held the title of Royal Polish and Electoral Saxon Court Composer, the vast quantity of his artistic output is to be found in the cantatas, oratorios, and organ pieces he wrote for the faithful congregations of St. Thomas' Protestant Lutheran Church in Leipzig. While the Reformation brought austerity in matters relating to the visual arts, and some pietistic sects even looked askance at professional musicians generally, the Lutheran tradition in the main was

---

[1] See Chapter 7, pages 90–95, sections on canon and fugue; Chapter 9, page 118, Partita No. 3 in E Major "Gavotte en Rondeau"; Chapter 11, pages 134–135, *Brandenburg* Concerto No. 3.

very liberal as far as music was concerned. Holding as it did to the tenets that every person through prayer may address God directly and that the Bible was the supreme authority in religious matters, Protestant churches were conceived as halls of instruction with a sermon-oriented liturgy, and as gathering places where all good Christians could raise their voices in song in praise of God. The Reformation first found its musical voice in the simple, unadorned congregational *chorales,* or hymns, which were sung in family circles and schools as well as in churches. The chorale thus became the nucleus of its musical tradition with such other expressions as organ chorale-preludes, cantatas, and oratorios growing around it. Martin Luther himself was the reputed author of many of these chorales, though the musical aspects of their composition can be more accurately ascribed to his musical collaborator, Johann Walther. These chorales had tremendous influence, and one of them, *A Mighty Fortress,* has aptly been called the "Marseillaise of the Reformation."

Bach's duties, as indeed those of all Lutheran choirmasters of his time, consisted of providing the music for the church services. Performancewise, this meant playing organ preludes, interludes, and postludes before, during, and after services; officiating as choir director at regular services; and rehearsing the band of instrumentalists who served as the orchestra. (All churches of the period, Catholic and Protestant alike, took the presence of orchestras in church for granted.) More important for posterity, however, was the creative aspect of Bach's position; he wrote cantatas for Sunday services, large-scale oratorios for Christmas, Passion Week, and Easter, as well as supplying music for marriages, funerals, the installation of a pastor, important civic occasions, and the like. Bach's fertile musical imagination and indefatigable industry led to his completing no less than five series of cantatas for each Sunday and feast day of the church calendar—some three hundred in all, of which about two hundred are now extant. The cantata was an integral part of the Sunday service, which proceeded with the reading of the Scriptural lesson, the first half of the cantata (written around a text related to the Epistle or Gospel for that Sunday), the sermon, then the latter half of the cantata ending with the chorale (the hymn of the day) in which the congregation joined. Just as the sermon was an interpretation of the meaning of the Scriptures, so also were the chorale and cantata musical commentaries.

Awake, the Voice is Calling (*Wachet auf, ruft uns die Stimme*), Bach's Cantata No. 140, written for the twenty-seventh Sunday after Trinity Sunday, will serve as a typical example. It is scored for solo soprano, tenor, and bass; four-part chorus; an orchestra of strings augmented by a solo violin, two oboes, English horn, French horn; and an unspecified continuo (probably for cellos and double basses plus the organ or harpsichord). The text has to do with the story of the Wise and Foolish Virgins, and the Bride (the conventional symbol for the church) preparing for the coming of the Bridegroom (Christ). Of its seven parts, the first five express longing and the last two fulfillment. The opening chorus is, appropriately enough, a festive choral march employing the full ensemble and with the sopranos, in high clear tones, announcing the hymn of the day as a cantus firmus.

The sturdy chorale provides the underlying material not only for the cantus firmus whenever it appears, but for the motives, themes, and obbligatos as well, and it is thus closely woven into all parts of the cantata's fabric. Italian opera now enters the picture with a short tenor passage in "dry recitative" (*recitativo secco*), that is, with bare continuo accompaniment. It leads up to a duet for soprano and bass, also with continuo accompaniment but now with an obbligato for solo violin that embroiders festoons of florid garlands around and over the voice parts. In the exact center of the design the chorale again appears; this time with the tenors carrying the cantus firmus, supported by the continuo below and the violins and viola above. This number is a typical chorale-prelude, a fact confirmed by Bach's own arrangement of it for organ solo. Now follows another recitative, this time of the instrumented, or *stromentato* type, written for bass voice, continuo, and strings. The penultimate number is a duet for soprano and bass with oboe obbligato and continuo accompaniment. Then finally comes the chorale once more, in this instance as a harmonized hymn in which the choir, orchestra, and congregation all join.

For the great church festivals Bach provided special music on a much larger scale. The tradition for such presentations goes all the way back to the mystery, miracle, and passion plays of the Middle Ages when, for instance, at Christmas time a manger scene, or *crèche,* was set up in the church for the re-enactment of the story of the Nativity. In such a liturgical drama the choir boys would represent angels; adult choristers, the shepherds; and members of the clergy, Joseph and the Three Wise Men. Bach's illustrious seventeenth-century predecessor, Heinrich Schütz, wrote a notable example called the Christmas Story; and Bach himself composed a *Christmas Oratorio,* consisting of a series of six cantatas designed originally for weekly presentations during Advent with the last one scheduled for the day after Christmas.

The Passion oratorios, similarly, grew out of the liturgical dramas performed during the week preceding Easter, particularly on Good Friday, and they are the epical counterparts of the more lyrical and intimate Sunday cantatas. Here Bach again had, among others, the precedent of Schütz's *St. Matthew Passion.* In keeping with established tradition, the Scriptural passages are intoned by the Evangelist, who is represented by a tenor singing in recitative style. In the course of the work, the recitatives,

solo and ensembles represent the dramatic action, which is balanced by
the more contemplative choral sections. The solo passages thus represent individual reactions, while the chorus symbolizes at various times the
crowd or mob, and ultimately the body of faithful Christians; the congregation joins in for the chorales, and thus they gain a sense of vicarious participation in the dramatization of the events in the life of the Lord. Bach's
St. Matthew Passion, with its unflagging intensity and never-failing musical invention, undoubtedly represents his supreme achievement in choral
music. A certain domestic intimacy associated with family festivals pervades the Protestant treatment of these Biblical stories, so that the Christmas story and Passion music become in turn the counterparts of the events
in family life—birth, marriage, suffering, and death—and in Bach's con-
tatas and oratorios the Reformation reaches its highest cultural realization.

BAROQUE SYNTHESIS: BACH AND HANDEL

Bach's mystical world view, embracing the restless search
for ultimate truths as found in his religious works, is offset by his rationalistic and comprehensive approach to composition, and together they combine to make him the universal figure he is. As a son of the Age of Reason,
the totality of his output is a musical reflection of the rationalistic spirit
of a period that witnessed the monumental systems by great philosophers
formulating all the religious, moral, mathematical, and scientific thought
of the time. Bach's searching mind was always on the alert for possible
syntheses, and he systematically explored all the stylistic and technical resources of his age. Each work he undertook, in fact, seems to have been
considered not as a single isolated instance, but rather as a part of a larger
whole that constituted an encyclopedia of all possibilities known to him.
The series of Protestant Lutheran cantatas and oratorios and the Roman
Catholic B-minor Mass, for instance, ran the gamut of religious expression. Within their internal organization one finds overtures of all types,
every variety of recitative and Italian solo and ensemble arias, as well as a
compendium of choral writing, all treated with the utmost completeness.

In the *Keyboard Practice (Clavierübung)* that Bach published serially
between 1726 and 1742, one encounters a cyclopedic survey of keyboard
writing. Part I presents six carefully diversified partitas, a series of dance
suites that Bach described on the title page as "consisting of Preludes,
Allemandes, Courantes, Sarabandes, Gigues, Minuets, and other Gallant-
ries, Composed for Music Lovers, to Refresh their Spirits, . . ." Each
partita, furthermore, opens with an introductory piece of a different type
variously entitled Praeludium, Sinfonia, Fantasia, Ouverture, Praeambu-
lum, and Toccata. Part II turns out to be a keyboard summary of the most

characteristic orchestral forms associated with the two major national styles—the *Italian* Concerto (in the style of Vivaldi) and the *French* Overture (a suite in the manner of Lully). Part III is devoted to organ music presented in a series of chorale-preludes, duets, and the monumental Prelude and Fugue in E Flat, popularly known as *St. Anne's*. Part IV returns to the harpsichord for the Aria with Thirty Variations, better known as the *Goldberg* Variations because they were written for Bach's pupil, J. G. Goldberg. The latter work is nothing less than a comprehensive synthesis of all contemporary variation procedures. In spite of the seeming spontaneity of its musical invention, Bach methodically arranged within the overall design an arithmetical series of canons in the third, sixth, and so on up to the twenty-seventh variation, which are canons at each interval from the unison, second, and third, on up to the final canon at the ninth, respectively. Even the modest *Two-part* Inventions, so familiar to beginning piano students, were originally arranged in a definite logical order of keys: C, d, e, F, G, a, b, B♭, A, g, f, E, E♭, D, and c (the capitals standing for major and the small letters for minor modes). Then, of course, there is that twice twenty-four series of preludes and fugues known as the *Well-Tempered Clavier* that is a veritable catalogue of key relationships (the keys are arranged on successive steps of the rising chromatic scale). The plan involves pairs of preludes and fugues in each major and minor tonality; and the intent was to write a manifesto for the efficacy of the tuning system known as well-tempering or equal temperament—a practical compromise permitting an unlimited choice of tonalities and freedom of modulation. When Bach was occupied with the problem of the keyboard concerto, he systematically set forth to provide examples for one, two, three, and four harpsichords. And the *Brandenburgs* show his survey of the concerto grosso scene from Corelli to Vivaldi,[1] as well as the many unique possibilities he himself was able to contribute.

The *Musical Offering* is a comparable compendium dealing in planned fashion with the major chamber-music forms of the baroque. The work had its inception during a visit paid by the composer to the Prussian court of Frederick the Great in 1747. The theme on which it is based was one proposed by the King as a subject for purposes of improvisation. The peculiar chromatic character of the theme was evidently a challenge to Bach, and he later compiled and caused to be printed the results of his improvisations and speculations on it. As Bach wrote in the dedication of this gift to his royal patron: "I resolved therefore and promptly pledged myself to work out this right royal theme more fully and then make it known to the world. This resolve has now been carried out as well as

---

[1] See Chapter 11, page 133, Corelli *Christmas Concerto;* Chapter 17, pages 221–224, Vivaldi concertos, *Four Seasons.*

possible . . ." The "modest" results of Bach's resolve turns out to be nothing less than a systematic survey of the chamber-music practices of his
time. The archetectonic design, like that of a triumphal arch, rests securely
on the pillars of an opening three-part *ricercare* (fugue) and closing six-
part *ricercare* (fugue). The keystone in the center is a four-movement trio
sonata flanked on either side by groups of five canons each. Briefly, the
plan is: ricercare—group of canons—trio sonata—group of canons—ricercare. The ten canons, the two ricercare-fugues, and the four movements
of the trio sonata are all either directly founded on Frederick's theme or
contain important references to it. Not only is the plan completely symmetrical, but its component parts are all related to one another in numerous and ingenious ways.

The *ricercare* (from the Italian, "to search") was the predecessor and
immediate progenitor of the fugue. Originally descended from the motet,
the instrumental ricercare may be regarded as a multisectional structure
devoted to the polyphonic elaboration of one or several themes. A monothematic ricercare could treat a single subject in one of two ways: the
theme itself could be either extensively modified and transformed, or else
retained in approximately its original state and combined with a succession
of new subjects. Now the entire *Musical Offering* is a multisectional structure devoted to the polyphonic elaboration of a single theme, and both
methods of monothematic ricercare elaborations are displayed in it. In the
first canon group, for instance, Bach retains the theme intact, combining it
with successive canonic treatments of new countersubjects; while in the
final movement of the trio sonata, he displays the theme in a daringly
transformed manner. The whole *Musical Offering* thus becomes an extensive and monumental monothematic ricercare. Bach undoubtedly had this
in mind when he added to the first page of the score a Latin superscription:
Regis Iussu Cantio Et Reliqua Canonica Arte Resoluta (By the King's
command, the theme and additions resolved in canonic style). The sentence is an acrostic, and combination of the first letter of each word spells
out the word *Ricercar*. (Such enigmatic strategems are not uncommon
with Bach.)

The ten canons—five before and five after the trio sonata—run the
gamut of this restricted and highly formalized art. A canon by definition
is a composition in which two or more parts are derived from one. The
first set of five contains in sequence a "canon at the double octave," a
so-called perpetual canon that admits of an indefinite number of repetitions; next a "canon in unison," one in which the second part enters on the
same note as the first, but a measure later; the third is a "canon in contrary
motion" in which the second part is upside down, or a melodic inversion
of the first; the fourth is a "canon in contrary motion and augmentation"

in which the second part proceeds in inversion as well as in notes of double value; and the fifth, a "circular canon" in which the canonic imitations follow a pattern of rising modulations that eventually return to the opening key. The second set of five begins with a "mirror canon" in which the royal theme is presented in canon twice, the second canonic imitation being an inversion or mirror image of the first. Next comes a "crab canon" in which the second or imitative voice plays the same notes as the first but backwards, or in retrograde order; the third is again a "canon in contrary motion," a so-called puzzle canon to which Bach appended a Latin inscription that translates "Seek and ye shall find"; the fourth is a canon in fourfold counterpoint, that is, in four parts; and the fifth is a "canonic fugue" in which the two upper parts are in strict imitation. This becomes a fugue when the bass part enters with the theme.

As the pre-eminent medium for the chamber music of the period, the trio sonata was aptly chosen by Bach for the centerpiece of the *Musical Offering*. Primarily the meaning of *trio sonata* in this case refers not to the number of instruments involved—actually four was customary, although it was quite possible to write them for a single instrument such as the organ—but to the number of clearly conceived parts in the music. Usually two high melodic instruments—sometimes matched (for example, two violins), sometimes unmatched (for example, flute and violin)—performed the upper parts; and a low stringed instrument performed the lower. To this ensemble, which carried the three obligatory, or *obbligato* parts, a harpsichord part was added in which the left hand doubled the bass line, and the right hand supplied improvised harmonies. This bass line, performed jointly by the harpsichord and the cello, was called the *continuo*. Bach specified in this case that the trio sonata was to be played by the flute (probably a subtle compliment to Frederick the Great who was an amateur flutist), violin, and continuo.

In style and structure this trio sonata of the *Musical Offering* is a church sonata (*sonata da chiesa*), comprising as it does a slow-fast-slow-fast succession of movements, none in dance rhythms and all polyphonically executed. All movements refer back in some fashion to the royal theme. In the first movement (Largo) it is outlined in the continuo part in the initial measures; and while the second movement (Allegro) opens with a new subject of considerable importance, a modified version of the royal theme appears subsequently in the continuo part. In the third movement (Andante) the presence of the royal theme is confined to references only to some of its salient features (for example, the characteristic downward leap of a seventh, and the stepwise descending chromaticism). For the basic subject of the final movement (Allegro) Bach chooses a radically altered variant of the King's subject.

While in the *Musical Offering* Bach sets himself the task of reviewing in characteristic comprehensive fashion the chamber-music idioms of his time, in the *Art of the Fugue* he codifies and classifies every possible fugal type from the early ricercare to the most complex contemporary fugues. As in a scientific demonstration, he carefully decides on his constants and variables. The constant in this case is a single subject for the entire series of fugues, one of stark simplicity and deliberate neutrality, designed to fit any fugal situation. Its sameness, therefore, points up all the differences of his contrapuntal manipulations. This scientific method applied to the craft of musical composition demonstrates conclusively that fugue is a principle and process rather than a form, much in the same way that equations and formulas are mathematical principles that can be applied to a number of specific situations, each calling for different sets of figures. Bach, then, attempts here a rational deductive logic of counterpoint, just as his French contemporary, Rameau (who was both a theoretical scientist and a practicing musician), had done for harmony. Bach's work in this light becomes the musical counterpart of the encyclopedic movement with the sum total of his works appearing as compendiums that account for all possible contingencies. The comprehensive character of his compositions thus reflect the entire range of baroque musical thought.

The two towering figures of the late baroque—Handel and Bach— invite comparison since, though they were compatriots and exact contemporaries, they were products of different external environments and different individual temperaments. Handel, for instance, was a cosmopolitan figure accustomed to being a celebrity, while Bach was a provincial personality content with a comparatively modest place in the social scheme of things. Handel was a free agent completely at home on the operatic and concert stages of the world capital of London, while Bach worked all of his life under direct patronage in relatively small positions principally within the church framework. Handel, as a robust man of the world, had a straightforward, vigorous mind, while Bach was more prone to brooding and introspective contemplation. Handel was more concerned with the joy and beauty of this life, while Bach beheld beatific visions of ultimate truth. Both were astute students of the Scriptures, but for Handel it was the *Old Testament* and the inevitable victory of the righteous cause, while for Bach it was the *New Testament* and the problems of death and redemption. Handel, in his choral music, approached a text much more directly and concretely, while Bach's thought ran in a more abstract vein, even at times to the complete disregard of the prosody of the text; and it has often been observed that Handel was essentially a vocal composer, while Bach was primarily instrumentally minded. Both, however, were masters of ex-

Fig. 20:3 *Performance of Lully's Alceste at Versailles.* (Engraving by Le Pautre, 1674.)

ternal forms as well as inner expression, and in the end they must be considered complementary rather than comparable figures. Both also, in any final evaluation, must be accorded equal eminence in their respective spheres, and together these twin musical suns of the baroque period sum up two centuries of accumulated creative experience and expression.

CLASSICAL CHRONOLOGY

Northern Germany

Georg P. Telemann	1681–1767	Hamburg
Johann Sebastian Bach	1685–1750	Leipzig
Johann J. Quantz	1697–1773	Berlin
Johann Hasse	1699–1783	Dresden
Karl H. Graun	1701–1759	Dresden
W. F. Bach	1710–1784	Berlin
C. P. E. Bach	1714–1788	Berlin
Johann A. Hiller	1728–1804	Leipzig
Johann F. Reichardt	1752–1814	Berlin

Paris

François Couperin (Le Grand)	1668–1773
Jean P. Rameau	1685–1764
Jean J. Rousseau	1712–1778
Johann Schobert	1720–1767
Pierre A. Monsigny	1729–1817
François J. Gossec	1734–1829
Giovanni Paisiello	1741–1816
André Grétry	1741–1813
Ignaz Pleyel	1757–1831
Maria Luigi Cherubini	1760–1842
Étienne Méhul	1767–1817
Gasparo Spontini	1774–1851

Vienna

Christoph Willibald Gluck	1714–1787
Georg Christoph Wagenseil	1715–1777
Georg Matthias Monn	1717–1750
Joseph Haydn	1732–1809
Michael Haydn	1737–1806
Karl Ditters von Dittersdorf	1739–1799
Antonio Salieri	1750–1825
Wolfgang Amadeus Mozart	1756–1791
Ludwig van Beethoven	1770–1827
J. N. Hummel	1778–1837
Franz Schubert	1797–1828

Italy

Alessandro Scarlatti	1658–1725	Naples
Domenico Scarlatti	1685–1757	Naples
Giovanni B. Sammartini	1698–1775	Milan
Padre Martini	1706–1784	Bologna
Baldassare Galuppi	1706–1785	Venice
Giovanni Battista Pergolesi	1710–1736	Naples
Niccolo Jommelli	1714–1774	Naples
Niccolò Piccinni	1728–1800	Naples
J. C. Bach	1733–1785	Milan
Luigi Boccherini	1743–1805	
Giovanni Paisiello	1741–1816	Naples
Domenico Cimarosa	1749–1801	Naples
Gioacchino A. Rossini	1792–1868	

Salzburg

Leopold Mozart	1719–1787
Michael Haydn	1737–1806
Wolfgang Amadeus Mozart	1756–1791

Mannheim

Franz X. Richter	1709–1789
Ignaz Holzbauer	1711–1783
Johann Stamitz	1717–1757
Christian Cannabich	1731–1798
Karl Stamitz	1746–1801

Bonn

Christian G. Neefe	1748–1798
Ludwig van Beethoven	1770–1827

The Classical Style

Chapter 21

___

THE STYLISTIC BACKGROUND

As the baroque style gradually began to break up in the early years of the eighteenth century, it was replaced by a multiplicity of artistic tendencies moving in a diversity of directions. The classical period, as music historians usually designate the latter half of the eighteenth and the first quarter of the nineteenth centuries, is a blanket term covering such intellectual and esthetic trends as the rococo, sensibility, Enlightenment, storm and stress, and so on. Whatever consistency it may be presumed to have must be diligently looked for in the balances and the syntheses of the various styles that its great representatives—Gluck, Haydn, Mozart, Beethoven, and Schubert—were able to achieve, rather than in any underlying unity of philosophical, social, and esthetic thought as such. The rococo style, for instance, was the final phase of the aristocratic baroque order as it left the grand avenues and marbled halls of the Versailles Palace on the death of Louis XIV in 1715 and took up its abode in the smaller salons of the urban aristocracy and upper bourgeoisie in Paris. Instead of serving a single sovereign and addressing their creative efforts to a single class at a unified court, writers, artists, and musicians had to take a new social order and the tastes of a variety of patrons into account.

When the baroque architect bowed to the rococo interior decorator, the long vistas and spacious chambers were replaced by intimate glimpses and small salons; the pomp and circumstance of baroque decoration yielded to the delicate ornamentation of the elegant rococo; royal purples and golds softened into a rainbow of pastel hues; the majestic mural became the precious miniature; monumental sculpture descended from its pedestal and shrank to the size of figurines for the mantlepiece; the center of life shifted from the grand ballroom to the boudoir; heroic passions and grand emotions melted into subtle shades of personalized expression and amorous intrigue; grandiloquent language modulated its voice and entered into witty, tête-a-tête conversations.

In music the transition from the baroque to the rococo, or the *style galant* as the latter is often called, shows many similar changes. From Paris, Rameau in his *Principles of Harmony* led the way from the tried-and-true avenues of polyphony into the newly paved streets of homophony. While the baroque strove for grandiose effects and pompous statements, the rococo tried for elegance and a minimum of material means. Instead of melody appearing at all levels, linear interest shifted to the thin treble register. The ponderous baroque basso continuo was streamlined into the slender Alberti bass. The lofty lyrical tragedy of Lully was engulfed by the rising tide of the theatrical divertissement, the purpose of which was to amuse rather than to edify. The mythological characters and historical heroes who struck their attitudes in baroque *opera seria* were felled by the frivolous coquettes of *opera buffa,* with their amorous swains, jealous vainglorious guardians, and meddlesome music masters. The old baroque concerto grosso was dieted down to the slim proportions of the sinfonia concertante; large cyclical instrumental forms yielded to short separate pieces; the inexorable progress of baroque tempos was interrupted by the capricious contrasts of rubato rhythms; baroque unity of emotion within single movements dissolved into mercurial fluctuations of mood from phrase to phrase. Instead of such forthright tempo indications as Allegro and Adagio, the qualifications of Allegro furioso and Adagio affetuoso began to appear; the broadly terraced levels of baroque dynamics were discarded in favor of capricious changes, abrupt alternations of forte and piano, as well as the gradual swelling and fading of crescendos and diminuendos; and the sweeping long lines of baroque melody were broken up into a series of undulating melodic curves whose contours were often barely discernible under an excess of embellishments.

While the rococo, or gallant style, was restricted for the most part to international aristocratic circles, it had a close relative in a middle-class counterpart known in France as *sensibilité,* in England as sensibility, and in Germany as *Empfindsamkeit.* This bourgeois edition of the rococo shunned high-flown histrionics for more down-to-earth statements; amoral eroticism for the soulful sentiments of sincere people; and the frivolous social attitudes of the aristocracy for the sterner virtues approved by solid citizens. In France Diderot declared that the purpose of art was to render "virtue adorable and vice repugnant." The painter Greuze portrayed homely scenes in pictures variously entitled *Innocence, Reading the Bible,* and *Return of the Prodigal Son.* And, of course, Rousseau called upon one and all to go "back to nature." Suddenly it became fashionable both in aristocratic and bourgeois society to love nature. Pastoral plays were mounted on the stage, and novels about idyllic country life found their way into the hands of eager readers. In them a nobleman usually disguises himself as a shepherd in order to commune more closely with nature. While tending his flock, he finds and falls in love with a charming shepherdess. The reader's heartstrings are gently pulled when he realizes that the nobleman cannot marry his shepherdess because she is so far beneath his social station. A visit to the fortune teller, however, reveals that the girl, when but an infant in arms, was spirited away from her castle by gypsies, and in reality she is a princess by birth. True love thus finds its way in the end. Rousseau's influential little pastoral opera of 1752, *Le Devin du Village,* is a variation of this stock plot, and it became the model for Mozart's first opera, *Bastien and Bastienne* (1768). Gluck, recognizing in Rousseau's style a more natural emotionalism, entertained hopes of collaborating with Rousseau, in order, as he put it, to arrive at "a melody noble, affecting and natural, with an exact declamation according to the prosody of each language and the character of each people . . ."

In England, meanwhile, a whole series of "sensibility" novels by Richardson beginning with *Pamela* (1740) portrayed poor but proud people struggling with the problems of life in the midst of modest middle-class surroundings. Their heroines were females of some education whom circumstances invariably forced to accept genteel employment as governesses in well-to-do households. The heroine's virtue is inevitably but vainly assailed by the master who is so impressed that he later decides to marry her and achieve his desires by more lawful means. Fielding, in such autobiographical novels as *Tom Jones* (1749), found that telling his tale in the first person intensified the subjective side of the story; the feeling of personal participation on the part of the reader was thereby enhanced. Oliver Goldsmith's *Vicar of Wakefield* (1766) was not far removed from a moral tract with the saving grace of some plausible characters and the semblance of a plot; and Laurence Sterne's *Sentimental Journey* (1768) was recounted in the form of an intimate diary.

As in France and England, the *Empfindsamkeit* movement in Germany was directed both in letters and music toward the new public made up of members of the increasingly articulate urban middle class as distinguished from the nobility on one side and the academic group on the other. Lessing established the new genre of the bourgeois drama with his *Miss Sara Samp-*

son in 1755, and two years later Diderot followed suit in France with his *Natural Son*. It is also no accident that the rising prosperity was accompanied by the acceptance and acquisition in middle-class households of the new pianoforte as the favored domestic instrument, replacing the more aloof and aristocratic harpsichord. Printed novels as well as engraved songs and keyboard works found a wide public, and compositions poured forth in a steady stream to fulfill the felt need.

A type of intimate emotional expression based on personalized experience, not previously heard in music, was explored. Honest sentiment, soulful sighs, and a touching melancholy bordering on tearfulness permeated the songs and instrumental works of the time. The new emotional orientation and the new social class to which the works were addressed are strikingly illustrated in some of the titles of the time. Whereas a rococo composer such as the Parisian Guillemain subtitled a set of six quartets *Gallant and Amusing Conversations between a Flute, a Violin, a Bass Viol, and Continuo* (1743), the German composer J. F. Reichardt called one of his song collections *Lullabies for Good German Mothers* (1798) and C. P. E. Bach named a touching tonal keyboard ode *Farewell to My Silbermann Clavier.* In the music of the sons of J. S. Bach, the new psychology of emotions was catalogued and codified into a new doctrine of affects. As C. P. E. Bach pointed out in his famous *Essay on the True Art of Playing Keyboard Instruments,* it was concerned with the fluctuation and flow of the affects or feelings. As his colleague J. J. Quantz put it in his *Essay on Playing the Transverse Flute,* "The player should change—so to speak—in every measure to a different affection, and should appear alternately sad, joyous, serious, etc., such moods being of great importance in music." These sentiments also found their way into the tract on violin playing that Leopold Mozart published in 1756, the same year his illustrious son was born. Each piece, he declared, must be played "in accordance with the passion prevailing in it." And he further cautioned that the performer "must spare no pains to discover and deliver correctly the passion that the composer has sought to apply and, since the mournful and the merry often alternate, he must be intent on delivering each of these in its own style. In a word, he must play everything in such a way that he will be himself moved by it."

After the turn of the nineteenth century the *Empfindsamkeit* became the full-fledged middle-class style that was known in Vienna as the *Biedermeier.* Taking its name from a popular comic cartoon character featured in the Viennese journal *Fliegende Blätter,* the Biedermeier typified a kind of honest Philistine figure, ingenuous and lovable. The art and music that falls into this category was addressed to other good-humored, comfortable burghers, who were self-indulgent but not frivolous, amiable but somewhat self-conscious about their taste for the "higher" things in life. In decoration it applied to billowing rosy garlands and clusters of true lovers' knots; in costume it meant full skirts with liberal ruffles and flounces; in music its voice was heard in tunes that belonged more in the beer garden than in the salon. In short, what had begun in France as a kind of drawing-room rococo was now the undisputed property of the comfortable middle class. The *Empfindsamkeit*'s doctrine of affects began to border danger-ously on the edge of affectation, and sensibility had come perilously close to sentimentality.

The Age of Reason or Enlightenment is still another designation given to the eighteenth century, and the philosophy of the so-called *Enlighten-ment* was a powerful stimulus in shaping the spirit of the time. *Sense and Sensibility,* the title of one of Jane Austen's novels, typifies the opposing ways of life—one based on reason, the other on intuition. The pure scien-tific speculation of such baroque intellects as Newton and Leibniz was now applied to problems that had a direct effect on daily living. Previously dis-covered principles and the new inventions based on them were turned into commercial channels and the production of new wealth. This broadening of the base of baroque rationalism spread the spirit of scientific inquiry to the educated classes generally, and it is perhaps best symbolized by the *Encyclopédie,* or *Classified Dictionary of Sciences, Arts, and Trades,* pub-lished serially by Diderot beginning in 1751. Even though Rousseau wrote the musical articles for Diderot, Rameau was the chief exponent of the Enlightenment as applied to musical theory. As a disciple of the philoso-pher Descartes, Rameau's expressed intention was to restore reason to musical thought, speculation, and composition. This rationalism is re-flected in the titles of such political tracts as Thomas Paine's *Common Sense* and the *Age of Reason,* and reached its apotheosis in the American and French Revolutions of 1776 and 1789, respectively, when the rule of the hereditary aristocracy was cast off and the age of republican democracy dawned. The spirit of sublime optimism it engendered is best expressed philosophically in Condorcet's book, *The Progress of the Human Spirit* (1794), which projected ten stages by which men had advanced from primi-tive savagery to the point where ultimate perfection was within his grasp. By the free exercise of his rational and moral powers, man could eventu-ally control his material and spiritual environment. This optimism found its most complete and articulate musical spokesman in Beethoven, who believed implicitly that the creative power of music could enlighten the spirit of man and guide him on his pathway toward eternal progress and ultimate perfection.

A strong stylistic counterforce to both sensibility and the Enlighten-ment is found in the so-called *storm-and-stress* movement in Germany beginning in the 1770's. Taking its apt name from Klinger's drama *Sturm und Drang,* this "Enlightenment-in-reverse" burst the bonds of propriety and politeness that had restricted the emotional range of the *Empfindsamkeit,* and embarked on an all-out emotional orgy. Instead of projecting an enlightened, predictable, and benign universe standing ready to unlock its secrets to the inquiring mind, the storm-and-stress world was obscure, incomprehensible, malignant, mysterious, and elusive in the extreme. Shrugging off the artificial etiquette of rococo as well as the tenets of middle-class morality, the movement recognized only the intellectual and emotional aristocracy of the genius and probed for his possible place in society. The most familiar literary representation is found in Goethe's *Sorrows of Young Werther* and his early *Faust,* first written during the peak of the storm-and-stress period and published later. Werther finds surcease from the tragedy of life in suicide; while Faust throws the objective detachment of the Age of Reason to the four winds and gives up searching for nature's secrets in books and tomes. Ultimate truth, Faust feels, is to be sought only in the world of experience and emotion. His operatic counterpart is Mozart's Don Giovanni, a kind of Latin Faust, who recognizes no rules of the game except those of his own making. Impetuous and defiant, he storms ruthlessly through life in search of an erotic freedom that turns out to be license. In their passions both Faust and Don Giovanni unchain the demonic forces that eventually devour them. The extreme subjectivity of the storm and stress perhaps found its most productive and enduring expression when sublimated into instrumental music. Haydn and Mozart in turn were both struck by its emotional lightning. This agitation is manifest in the urgent syncopations of the very opening measures of Haydn's stormy D-minor *Lamentation* Symphony (No. 26) and in the stark, angular, unison opening of his E-minor *Trauer* (Mourning) Symphony (No. 44). The emphasis on passion and personal individualism brought a more subjective type of expression to Haydn's music, and he was able to infuse the gallant-style symphony with greater emotional depth and thus to set its course toward the dramatic, all-embracing, and all-appealing musical form that it eventually became. The movement is also echoed in Mozart's music, the two G-minor Symphonies for example, where expressive pathos is punctuated with violent outbursts of passionate protest.

In addition to the above style tendencies, *classicism* in two of its many guises also puts in an appearance in the eighteenth century, and the impression it made was important enough to imprint its name on the period. The two sides of the classical coin in this case consisted of an academic head and an antiquarian tail—that is to say, a crystallization of formal principles on one side and a revival of antiquity on the other. Strict counterpoint as a basis for musical craftsmanship was still studied in spite of the increasing popularity of the lighter-textured, elegant rococo. The continuation of this academic tradition is often called the "learned" style, and as such it is to be considered as one of the several facets of this type of classicism. There was also the codification of new rules and a working out of more modern procedures that made the products of the period models of their kind. Classics in this sense are usually the end result of a long period of trial-and-error experimentation in which the rules of construction are formulated, and in which a balance of form and content is established. Whether the medium is verbal, visual, or tonal, such works tend to be humane in conception, clear in design, rational in execution, and objective in approach—all qualities that generally lead to their universal acceptance. Since the works of the Viennese composers qualify as high points in the craftsmanship of musical composition, and also in view of their central position historically, they have become classics in the sense of being classroom models for future generations to study and emulate. It is in this sense, then, that their sonatas, chamber music, concertos, and symphonies are to be considered classical. The so-called "neoclassical" style that crops up in the music of the twentieth century thus refers to new versions of the forms and images projected by the Viennese composers (Prokofieff's *Classical Symphony*, to cite an example), or the analogous French style (Ravel's suite, *Le Tombeau de Couperin*, or Debussy's *Hommage à Rameau* are cases in point here).

Antiquarian classicism, on the contrary, finds its expression in such manifestations as the new science of classical archeology, the revival of Greek and Roman art forms, and the reinterpretation of Aristotle's principles of drama as found in the plays and operas of the period. The excavations of Herculaneum and Pompeii that began in mid-century led to reverberations in all the arts. Two Englishmen, Stuart and Revett, visited Greece and published (in 1762) an influential book on the *Antiquities of Athens*. A German by the name of Winckelmann took a new look at Greek statuary and found it superior in workmanship to the later Roman models. His book, *History of Ancient Art* (1764), became the eighteenth-century equivalent of a best seller. The stalwart patriotism and civic virtues extolled by the ancients served the political purposes of the post-Revolutionary French governments, and the spirit of classical stoicism and individual self-sacrifice became the new social creed as well as the bourgeois answer to the wanton waste and reckless self-indulgence of the deposed aristocratic class. In the visual arts a veritable cult of ruins could be seen in the popular prints of Piranesi and the picturesque canvases of the French painter who has gone down in history by his nickname, Robert des Ruines. Architects built replicas of Greek temples and adapted classical motives for both

the exteriors and interiors of the town houses they erected for their aristocratic and wealthy middle-class patrons. A literary counterpart of this
archeological orientation is found in the work of the French lyric poet,
André Chénier, who adopted Greek metrical patterns rather than those
of Roman models for his paeans and odes. A desire to restore the principles
and spirit of Greek drama is found in the plays and operas of the period.
The new rules were derived from Aristotle's *Poetics* rather than the writings of his Roman successor, Seneca. The dramatist Lessing, the critic
Algarotti, the librettist Calzabigi, and the operatic composer Gluck all
entered with zest upon their dramatic and musical reforms. Phrases such as
the "imitation of nature" were bandied about and specifically applied to
the delineation of characters who were representative of true human nature rather than the stilted and stylized types found in Metastasio's dramas.
Gluck also echoed the phrases and sentiments of Winckelmann when he
stated that "simplicity, truth, and naturalness are the great principles of
beauty in all artistic manifestations." The key words of the time were always "nature" and what is "natural," and they were echoed over and over
again in the letters of Mozart and his contemporaries. Classicism in this
sense, then, means the attempt to recapture some of the glories of Greco-
Roman antiquity, and, by implication, the establishment of a new art that
achieves the ancient ideals of clarity, restraint, symmetry, balance, and
order.

VIENNA, THE CROSSROADS

The stage on which this great drama of music was enacted
embraced the entire European continent. The scenes in the several acts
shifted rapidly from one capital and provincial center to another, until
all the dramatic developments eventually converged on Vienna, the capital of the international Austro-Hungarian Empire. Here the final climactic
act took place from 1750 to 1828 with such players as Gluck, Haydn, Mozart, Beethoven, and Schubert in the leading roles. It is important always
to bear in mind that this configuration of great composers represents only
the highest peaks in a mountain range consisting of hundreds of talented
and well-trained musicians. Two of the principals in the cast achieved
their musical pre-eminence by taking diametrically opposite pathways.
Haydn, for instance, arrived at the peak of his creative powers late in life,
while Mozart flashed across the musical firmament in a brief but meteoric
career. Haydn, until late in life, never ventured further than a few miles
from Vienna and remained for the most part a provincial figure until he
set forth for London as he was approaching his sixtieth year. Mozart, however, was internationally prominent from his days as a child prodigy at the

early age of six, when he and his father toured the capitals and courts of Europe.

Haydn's ideas took shape only after a long period of gestation. He himself explained: "As a conductor of an orchestra I could make experiments, observe what produced an effect and what weakened it, and was thus in a position to improve, alter, make additions or omissions, and be as bold as I pleased; I was cut off from the world, there was no one to confuse or torment me, and I was forced to become original." It must, however, be added that, through publications and visits, Haydn was well aware of what was going on in Italy and such German capitals as Mannheim, Berlin, and Hamburg, from where the latest treatises, symphonies, and concertos reached him.

Mozart, however, as the most cosmopolitan of composers, was conversant at firsthand with all the contemporary developments of his time. In his native Salzburg he was the apt pupil of his wise and intelligent father, Leopold; and Michael Haydn, musical director to the Archbishop of Salzburg and younger brother of Joseph, regularly brought him copies of Joseph's latest works to study. Salzburg at this time was a bit of Italy transported to an Austrian province, and here Mozart grew up in an atmosphere of Latin lyricism, in which the singing voice, whether it was human or instrumental, was all important. Later in Naples Mozart absorbed the principles of *opera seria*, as well as its more fashionable competitor, *opera buffa*. In Bologna he learned counterpoint from the famous historian, Padre Martini. In Paris he came in contact with the operatic successors of Rameau; and he also became acquainted with the free improvisory keyboard style of Schobert, which was leading away from the tinkling harpsichord confections for the ear concocted by Couperin, Daquin, and Rameau. In London, J. C. Bach, the youngest son of the prolific Johann Sebastian, made an indelible impression on the eight-year-old Mozart, and instilled in him a lifelong love for the cantabile, or singing, style which he later used so freely in his own concertos as well as in his keyboard music. And finally in Mannheim at the court of the discerning patron, Duke Carl Theodor, he heard the finest orchestra in Europe, and through it the young composer saw opening up before him many new vistas of orchestral playing. The innovations there included the modern method of conducting, the shaping of the new symphonic form with its dramatic dualism of opposing themes, and important strides in amplifying the development section in sonata movements; the idiomatic treatment of various instrumental sonorities, especially in concertante situations; the brilliant use of wind instruments, which later assumed such prominence in Mozart's writing; the antiphonal alternation of strings and winds; and above all, the startling new dynamic shadings that ran the gamut of tonal gradations from pianissimo to fortissimo. As Schubart, a German poet, described the Mannheim orchestra, "Their forte is like thunder, their crescendo a cataract, their diminuendo the rippling of a crystal stream, their piano the soft breath of spring."

The paths of Mozart and Haydn crossed in Vienna in 1781 when Mozart left the unsympathetic court of the Archbishop of Salzburg to set up shop in the capital city as an independent, free-lance composer; and Haydn had begun to spend more time in his Vienna residence away from the employment of his patron. This was also the year in which Haydn brought out his series of six quartets, Opus 33, which bore the interesting inscription, "In an entirely new and special manner." Also known as the "Russian" quartets, because of their dedication to Grand Duke Paul, they contain some of Haydn's most profound discoveries in musical craftsmanship. This little revolution of Haydn's, which is discussed more fully in the section devoted to him (pp. 325–329), made a powerful impression on Mozart's musical thought, and he responded with six quartets of his own, which he dedicated to Haydn. Three of them were played on a memorable occasion in Mozart's house in Vienna in 1785, when his father was a visitor and Haydn the guest of honor. Leopold Mozart wrote home to his daughter in Salzburg: "On Saturday evening Herr Joseph Haydn and the two Barons Tinti came to see us and the new quartets were performed. . . . Haydn said to me, 'Before God as an honest man I can tell you that your son is the greatest composer known to me either in person or by name. He has taste, and, what is more, the most profound knowledge of composition.' " The tables were thus turned and the younger master now became a decisive influence on the older. This great musical dialogue continued for a full and fruitful decade, lasting until Haydn set out for London in 1790 and the death of Mozart the following year.

Many circumstances—historical, ethnographical, social, and economic —conspired to bring about the confluence of forces that led to the great cultural culmination in Vienna. A broader spread of the sources of patronage, for instance, prevented the imprint of a single standard or personality on the period, thus permitting a wider variety of styles and tastes to develop. While maintaining various court composers on modest stipends, the imperial court nevertheless dispensed only a fraction of the total patronage, preferring a less important role than that played by royal courts elsewhere. As a result composers were gradually emancipated from the restrictions of a single aristocratic employer. Through the eyes of a contemporary, it is possible to get a picture of the way Vienna appeared to a perceptive observer. Referring to the influx into Vienna of noble provincial families and the landed gentry of central Europe, J. F. Reichardt pointed out that "Some have established themselves with taste and not infrequently on a grand scale, and live here in great splendor and hospitality. This applies especially to Russians and Poles, who bring the good sociable spirit with them and amalgamate themselves with the Viennese the more easily. Aside from them, the great Bohemian, Moravian, and Hungarian families, like the Austrians, live regularly all winter long in Vienna, giving it the brilliance and magnificence that make it the great splendid imperial city, for the court itself prefers a retired family life to external pomp and show. Yet the court appears also with great dignity and no little brilliance at the few public festivities which it still maintains. The greatest brilliance consists, however, in the rich background provided by the higher nobility of the crown lands."

Thus it was that a Czech nobleman, Prince Lobkowitz, first brought Gluck to Vienna, and the Hungarian Prince Esterhazy became the patron of Haydn. Even the independent Beethoven, finding safety in numbers, accepted a lifelong pension subscribed to by a committee of aristocrats that included Prince Kinsky, Prince Lobkowitz, and one member of the imperial family, Archduke Rudolf. As noble families vied with one another for cultural prestige, men of ambition and genius were understandably attracted to Vienna by the larger number of available commissions and the variety of sources of employment. In addition to the nobility, Reichardt further noted that "The bankers and great landowners and manufacturers are included here; and so on through the bourgeoisie proper down to the well-to-do petite bourgeoisie; in the way that all the great public diversions and amusements are encouraged by all classes without any abrupt divisions or offending distinctions—in these respects Vienna is quite alone among the great cities of Europe." While much of the music-making in Vienna was in private households and open by invitation only, there was a thriving public concert life available to all who cared to participate.

Genius ranked high in prestige in the healthy international atmosphere that prevailed in this Central European crossroads; and men of talent, no matter what their point of origin, were accepted and encouraged for what they could contribute. The streams of folk and art music met and merged in this polyglot melting pot; in the process folk songs and dances lost their rusticity and roughness, and the musical forms in which they were incorporated likewise lost their artificiality thereby gaining new vigor and vitality. The country laendler, for instance, originally had a hop-and-turn step, but when it came to Vienna, the staccato stamping was replaced by a gliding glissando and it became the sliding, whirling waltz. As it rose on the social ladder it could be heard in the trios of the minuets, as for instance, in that of the E-flat major Symphony (No. 39) by Mozart. The bourgeois waltz was thus well on its way toward replacing the aristocratic minuet.

The unprecedented demand for the production of works by the contemporary composers of this period prevented the programs from becoming archives and made up principally of museum pieces from the past. The divining of the inherent dramatic possibilities of instrumental music, especially in the sonata form, was responsible for its subsequent rise to a position of equality with vocal works such as the opera. As Reichardt summed it up: "Vienna has everything that marks a great capital in a quite unusually high degree. It has a great, wealthy, cultivated, art-loving, hospitable, well-mannered, elegant nobility; it has a wealthy, sociable, hospitable middle class and bourgeoisie, little lacking in cultivated, and well-informed gentlemen and gracious families; it has a well-to-do, good-natured, jovial populace. All classes love amusement and good living, and things are so arranged that all classes may find well provided and may enjoy in all convenience and security every amusement that modern society knows and loves." Vienna thus experienced a florescence during this period that may well be compared to that of Periclean Athens, Medicean Florence, and Elizabethan England. But while these other eras brought the arts of architecture, sculpture, painting, and literature to unprecedented peaks of perfection, it remained for Vienna to do the same for music.

GLUCK AND THE OPERATIC IDEA

The year 1762 was a momentous one both in the history of Vienna as well as that of the lyric theater, as it marked the appearance of the first of Christoph Willibald Gluck's [1] so-called "reform" operas, *Orfeo ed Euridice*. As in all such esthetic movements innovation was liberally mixed with tradition, and the projected brave new operatic world was still populated principally by personifications of the contemporary eighteenth-century styles as well as by many survivals from the past. Preferring the muses of classical antiquity to some of the more seductive siren voices of his own time, the Bohemian-born Gluck and his Italian librettist Calzabigi were both highly articulate about what they were trying to accomplish. In order to build their lyric dramas on a solid authoritative basis, they harkened back to the precedents of Greek drama and the pronouncements of Aristotle. As to "unity of action," Gluck's operas do have a greater feeling of progress than previous examples because, for the first time in music history, he discards the harpsichord-accompanied dry recitative for a continuous, through-composed orchestral score from beginning to end. He also assigned both the chorus and orchestra a more prominent position by allowing them to comment on the action and reflect the emo-

[1] See Chapter 2, pages 24–25, for Gluck's orchestration techniques; Chapter 14, page 173, *Don Juan* ballet.

tional substance of the text in appropriate musical images. The action is also interrupted less often for long introductory ritornels and static da-capo arias. Gluck further attempted to return to classical clarity and simplicity by banishing coloratura roles as such and eliminating superfluous vocal virtuosity, though he did not disdain an occasional flourish or cadenza if it suited his purpose. He also reduced the number of characters in his casts —*Orfeo*, for instance, has only three principals, Orpheus, Eurydice, and Amor. Instead of striking heroic attitudes, strutting with grandiose gestures, and voicing conventionalized sentiments neatly packaged in standardized da-capo arias, his characterizations were more acutely drawn by the application of the Greek "imitation of nature" principle—meaning in this case, the representation of human nature. In spite of all his posturing in the classical toga, however, Gluck remained essentially a man of his own times, and a look now at his *Orfeo ed Euridice* will show how his theories worked out in actual practice.

The Overture, in spite of Gluck's announced intentions that it should prepare the audience for what follows, is still a mere curtain raiser. As such it is a type of functional music designed to establish a festive atmosphere and to sound a fanfare for the arrival of late comers. The only connection with what ensues on the rise of the curtain is its C-major key relationship to the somber C minor of the opening choral ritornel. This mourning scene around the tomb of Eurydice is, like the similar one in the later *Alceste*, a noble and convincing evocation of antiquity. The statuesque stances of the chorus and the restrained tone generally are representative of the spirit of antiquity as are many of the well-chiseled arias that follow. More important in a purely musical sense, however, is the immediate enunciation of a musical motive that appears again and again throughout the opera, changing each time to reflect the shifting moods and dramatic progress, yet recognizable enough to bind the work together in a tight motivic unity. After its initial appearance as a grief motive (No. 1, Ex. 21:1*a*[1]), the theme recurs in one of its many mutations in the recitative aria (No. 33, Ex. 21:1*b*) where, played by the plaintive oboe, it symbolizes Orpheus' longing for Eurydice. But since he is already in the Elysian fields, it sounds a more optimistic note, while in the following chorus (No. 34, Ex. 21:1*c*), it becomes quite buoyant in nature. After Orpheus has been united with Eurydice, he dares not look on her because of the injunction the gods have imposed upon him. Eurydice, convinced that he loves her no more, sings a Handelian rage aria (No. 41, Ex. 21:1*d*) in which the motive, now in an allegro tempo, takes a furious turn. When Orpheus relents and gazes upon her, she fades away in his arms, thus set-

[1] The numbering is in accordance with the score published by Novello and Co., London. Other versions and editions vary somewhat in their order.

Ex. 21:1 Excerpts from *Orfeo ed Euridice*. Gluck.

(a) No. 1, Bars 1-6.

Moderato

(b) No. 33, Bars 2-3.
Andante

(c) No. 34, Bars 1-5.
Andantino

(d) No. 41, Bars 1-6.
Allegro

(e) No. 43, Bars 1-4.
Andante con moto

ting the scene for the apotheosis of his grief, which is expressed in the well-known aria *Che farò senza Euridice* (No. 43, Ex. 21:1e). The motive now appears here for the final time in a transcendent lyric form.

Practically all of the current styles of the time make their appearance in appropriate places. The pantomime ballet (No. 3, Ex. 21:2a) that takes

Ex. 21:2 Excerpts from *Orfeo ed Euridice*. Gluck. (a) No. 3 (Bars 1–4).

Lento

place in front of Eurydice's tomb is an excellent example of the *Empfind-samkeit* with its sighing, tearful appoggiaturas. The appearances of the god of love, Amor or Cupid, are invariably accompanied by rococo music in the best Dresden china porcelain-figurine tradition. The Sicilian rhythm of No. 15 (Ex. 21:2b and c), for instance, bespeaks a pastoral character,

Ex. 21:2b No. 15 (Bars 1–4).   **Ex. 21:2c** No. 15 (Bars 25–28).

Lento e grazioso   Meno lento

and Amor gently tugs at our heartstrings with some sighing gallant-style appoggiaturas of his own (Ex. 21:2d). As Orpheus descends into the underworld, he is greeted by some menacing growls in the double-bass register, which portray Cerberus, while each of the three heads of this mytho-

Ex. 21:2d No. 13 (Bars 10–11).

logical watchdog of the nether regions barks in turn (Ex. 21:2e). This bit of "realism" on Gluck's part is an amusing continuation of the baroque

Ex. 21:2e No. 21 (Bars 15–17).

representative style, and he further intensifies the image by having his five-note rising figure span the diminished fifth, an interval known as the *diabolus in musica,* or devil in music.

The "Dance of the Furies" (No. 28) adds an appropriate touch of storm-and-stress demonology (Ex. 21:2f), while in contrast to it, the "Bal-

Ex. 21:2f No. 28 (Bars 1–5).

let of the Blessed Spirits" (No. 29, Ex. 21:2g) is once again in the elegant gallant style. Orpheus pleads eloquently with the Furies (No. 22) in the most melting Neapolitan-opera manner, and by the ardor of his music, the Furies (in Nos. 25 and 27) are moved to such unaccustomed emotions as pity and sympathy. The transition from the terrible abode of the Furies to the serene scenery of the Elysian Fields is full of dramatic contrast; while the recitative-aria *Che Puro Ciel* (No. 33), with its accompaniment describing the chirping of the birds, the running rivulets, and the radiant sunshine, is a worthy representation of Rousseau's "back to nature" in music.

Ex. 21:2g No. 29 (Bars 1–4).

While Gluck's musical characterizations are drawn with an ear for the thematic material that aptly reflects the mental and emotional outlook of his cast and is also capable of development as the dramatic action progresses, the survival of the artificial castrato contralto voice in the role of the male god Orpheus is a serious lapse in dramatic truth. Since the roles of Eurydice and Amor are both assigned to sopranos, there is a complete lack of deep male voices except in the chorus and a corresponding absence of contrast in timbre. This situation was later corrected when Gluck reworked the opera for a natural tenor in the Paris version, and the role can be sung by a baritone as well. Some other inner inconsistencies in Gluck's position can also be pointed out. While ostensibly he was criticizing Metastasian drama, he nevertheless continued to set librettos by Metastasio whenever he was commissioned to do so, because they were still admired in certain circles. For all his pious protestations against the "abuses in Italian opera," Gluck was and always remained an Italian-trained composer of opera in the Neapolitan style. For all his words about "reducing music to its proper function of seconding poetry," Gluck, as every other successful opera composer before and since his time, was primarily musically minded. For all his esthetic and musical authority, Gluck lacked the technical security and compositional craftsmanship of Haydn, Mozart, and Beethoven, though it must be admitted that as an opera specialist he had less need of it. As for his earnest reforms, his operatic successors—Mozart, Beethoven, and Rossini, for instance—paid them little heed; only by such romanticists as Berlioz, Liszt, and Wagner was he officially adopted as a forerunner. And for all the noble tragic utterances of his maturity, it is well to remember that in his unreformed days Gluck wrote some rollicking good comic operas in the French manner.

Gluck, finally, as an international figure often traveled to Paris where he had a friend at court in one of his former pupils—no less a personage than Queen Marie Antoinette, who always stood ready to put in a word for him with opera impresarios at the right moment. The opposing forces of innovation and tradition in his work were bound to clash, and Gluck's ideas led to one of the most heated esthetic debates of the century. Pitted against the Italian composer Piccinni, the operatic battle of the Gluckists versus the Piccinnists raged. The performances of *Orfeo* and *Iphigenie en Aulide* in 1774 and *Alceste* in 1776, however, carried the day for Gluck. Whether because of or in spite of his reforms, Gluck's operas have had sufficient vitality to insure their continuous survival on the stage, where they are today the oldest operas still regularly retained in the standard repertory. As the Preface to *Alceste* makes clear, Gluck sought a "beautiful simplicity" instead of a "useless superfluity of ornaments"; "heartfelt language, strong passions" in place of "florid descriptions . . . and sententius, cold morality." In this, Gluck represents that aspect of the Enlightenment that probed for the natural man under the veneer of artifice and convention.

HAYDN AND THE CHAMBER-MUSIC IDEA

Unlike the operatic specialist Gluck, Joseph Haydn [1] was a universal composer who contributed liberally to all the categories of musical productivity current in his time. Vocal church music in the forms of masses, cantatas, motets, offertories, and sacred arias occupied him from his early years onward and reached a final fruition in his two great concert oratorios, *The Creation* and *The Seasons*. But while he wrote a quantity of secular songs and no less than thirty-two operas, he is primarily noted as an instrumental composer and was happier working in the fertile fields of chamber music and the symphony. He also wrote prolifically in the genial genre of Viennese social music; and Haydn, more than any other composer, was responsible for the crystallization of the string quartet and symphony out of such casual ensemble combinations as the divertimento and serenade.

Social music of this kind was in demand for such occasions as wedding celebrations, birthday anniversaries, garden parties, and the visits of distinguished guests. Popular rather than serious in style, it was performed also as dinner or table music, dance music, conversation music, and background music in private households as well as in public taverns and coffee houses. Vast quantities of this social music came from the workshops of every minor as well as major composer of the time—Dittersdorf and Wagenseil, Leopold Mozart and Michael Haydn, as well as Joseph Haydn with over sixty examples and Wolfgang Mozart with more than forty.

Variously designated as divertimentos, serenades, and cassations, the titles carry little specific meaning. Leopold Mozart, for instance, called one of his works *Divertimento Militare sive Sinfonia* (Divertimento in the Military Manner, or Symphony). Divertimento, however, is generally used as a generic name for all works of this style; while serenade usually indicates a work intended to be played in the evening. Wolfgang Mozart, for instance, entitled several of his early examples by the Italian title *Serenata Notturna*, while the well-known later one bears the German equivalent, *Eine kleine Nachtmusik* (K.525)—literally "a little night music," figuratively a nocturnal serenade. Divertimentos could be written for any combination of three or more instruments of any kind, all the way up to a chamber or full orchestra. Sometimes specific instruments were called for, in other cases not. The instrumentation, of course, always depended upon what was available for the occasion since the music was written on order. Those scored for strings alone were most probably intended for the salon; those exclusively for winds would be located in the

---

1 See Chapter 4, page 50, *Creation* oratorio; Chapter 7, page 91, *Death is a Longer Sleep* canon; Chapter 9, page 112, Piano Sonata in D Major, Finale.

garden or park; and the vast quantity, combining a mixture of strings and winds with occasional percussion, could be played indoors or outdoors as the occasion arose. All sorts of odd combinations were possible. Because, for instance, Haydn's patron Prince Nicholas Esterhazy played the baryton (a large viol somewhere between the viola and cello in size), Haydn wrote a large number of trios and quartets for baryton and strings. They are all divertimentos, however, rather than trios and quartets in the later structural sense. Divertimentos could also include any number of movements from two to ten, the average falling around six or seven. Much freer in overall form than the baroque dance suite, the component parts followed no set order. Traditionally beginning with a march, the divertimento could be followed with an instrumental aria, several minuets or rondos, one or more sets of variations, and so on.

Theme and variation movements were apparently great favorites, for they offered the various members of the ensemble an opportunity for stepping forward as soloists, each variation featuring another instrumentalist in turn. The casual divertimento-serenade style was fundamental to early classical chamber music and symphony. Haydn's early string quartets (for example, Op. 1 and Op. 3) are really divertimentos, as is the so-called *Hornsignal* Symphony No. 31 in D Major. Echoes of divertimento-serenade idioms are still detectable in his late London symphonies and even in the *Qui tollis* passage from the Gloria of his Mass *In Time of War*. More than any other composer, however, Haydn was responsible for developing the independence of the string quartet and symphony as idioms of instrumental expression. In his maturer works, the string quartet and the symphony were no longer bound to the casual tone of a divertimento entertainment, although the divertimento idiom was occasionally retained to flavor a movement.

Divertimentos thus provided composers with frequent commissions; and while it was always a type of functional music, the more alert and ambitious among them seized the opportunity for experimentation in ensemble writing, trying out various instrumental combinations, and developing new technical ideas. The very fluidity and flexibility of the divertimento was thus ideal for this sort of trial-and-error composing. All of Haydn's early instrumental music falls in this flexible category, and it was the proving grounds of his mature style. It is of utmost importance to remember that this type of social music was never intended as a vehicle for a composer to make profound pronouncements, nor was it concerned in the slightest with his personal emotional outpourings or soul struggles. By its very nature it was social not individual, popular not serious, designed for easy listening not concentrated attention. Relying as it did on melodic invention rather than the development of ideas, it was occasional rather than permanent, everyday rather than eternal. Later, when the string quartet and symphony came to be works that were meant for repeated performances, composers took into account the need for weightier ideas in addressing a more attentive audience. Much of the total output of social music was the routine product of the time and as such it can be consigned to well-deserved oblivion. In other cases the fertility of the composer's inventive powers and the craftsmanship of execution in certain works lift them above their original purpose and make them welcome additions to the current concert repertory.

From this common source Haydn gradually evolved the ensemble combinations and the cyclical sonata forms that today are classified as duos, trios, quartets, quintets, and so on up to symphonies. His early string quartets, for example, were simply divertimentos for four stringed instruments with a wide variety of short movements. While literally dozens of other eighteenth-century composers shared in the development of the string quartet (two violins, viola, and cello) , it was Haydn, more than any other composer, who shaped the style and esthetics of string quartet writing on principles that provided the foundation for the work of other composers from his day to ours. Thus the urge to evolve a form that would encompass the cyclical character of the dance suite, the freedom of the fantasia, the lyrical quality of the aria, the opposition of one and several instruments of the concertante style, the contrasts of the concerto, the rationalism of contrapuntal techniques, and the emotionalism of the lyric drama led to the decades of experimentation that culminated in the sonata style. Out of the old baroque dance suite, the church and chamber sonatas, the toccata, the Italian overture, or opera sinfonia, the aria da capo, and the divertimento emerged the sonata, which, both technically and spiritually, is a composite affair synthesizing the forms, tendencies, styles, attitudes, and ideas of two centuries.

Chamber music in this sense is separated from social and dinner music in that the accent is now on the listening process, and its purpose is no longer to accompany polite conversation or to drown out the clatter of dinner dishes. Chamber music, as such, practices moderation in all things and argues with the logic of sweet reason. Each player is assigned his independent part within the whole and there is little doubling. The planes of sound have their separate identities and the parts rarely invade each other's territory by crossing registers. Chamber music is slim and sleek in its lines; its contours are well proportioned; its balances are symmetrical. Each voice, moreover, is intended to be heard in a give-and-take manner. Unlike large ensembles in which a leader imposes his will upon the orchestral masses, chamber music reflects the democratic image of equals among equals. Shorn of all bombast, it does not shout from the housetops nor speak in tones of violent emotionalism. Yet it can be as big in its conception as it is intimate in its manner of expression.

Haydn's particular contributions to the chamber-music field are legion, and it should be parenthetically pointed out that the bulk of his symphonies are to be considered in this category as well. Except for the twelve most mature examples (those usually numbered 93 through 104) that he wrote for the Salomon concerts in London from 1791–95, the vast majority were scored for the chamber orchestra of the Esterhazy household. Much the same is true of Mozart's essays in the form, and only the *Prague* and the final three written in 1788 are symphonies in the modern sense. In Haydn's hands, however, both chamber music and the symphony broadened out stylistically from the ultrarefinement and gracefulness of the gallant style to include the unexpected twists and witty turns of the sensibility, the gaiety and gusto of lusty peasant folk idioms, the impassioned emotional outbursts of the storm and stress, and the spiritual loftiness of church music.

Haydn brought a new and compelling logic to the overall cyclic form of the sonata design. From the loose concatenation of the multimovement divertimento, he retained just four movements—an opening in sonata form, a lyrical slow movement, a minuet, and a finale that was usually in either rondo or sonata form. In his hands the rococo minuet and rondo became full expressive members of the cycle, reflecting the prevailing mood of the whole composition. In this way the minuet served to bridge over the span between the slow movement and the finale; and beginning with the *Russian* Quartets, Op. 33, it lost its last rococo vestiges and was designated as a scherzo. The rondo also shed much of its playful character and all sorts of novel and ingenious ways to reintroduce the recurring opening section were devised. Above all, however, Haydn endowed the sonata form, as found in single movements, with new life and vitality. Taking the design as it first appeared in Neapolitan opera overtures, in the scintillating keyboard essays of Domenico Scarlatti, in the lighthearted but influential trio sonatas of Pergolesi, in the experiments of the Mannheim composers, and in the keyboard sonatas of C. P. E. Bach, Haydn proceeded to forge the new form. More than any other composer, it was Haydn who divined the latent possibilities of the development section, and he proceeded to make it the most important part of the design. At first it was only a central episode in which the previously presented thematic material was broken up and regrouped, thus creating a sense of suspense before it reappeared as a reassembled whole again in the recapitulation. But in the "new and special manner" of the *Russian* Quartets of 1781, as well as in the six *Paris* Symphonies of 1786, the thematic material was reduced to the smallest of musical particles, the *motive,* which now became the most vital unit of the form. It is indeed no accident that the word "motive" is derived from the verb "to move," since it is a tonal fragment that contains within itself an incipient directional tendency and the potentials for further melodic, rhythmic, and dynamic motion, and which lends itself to repetition and begs for adventure. Motivic development and expansion are now no longer confined to the central section but are a constant and continuous process throughout the composition. All instrumental voices, furthermore, share prominently in the developmental procedures and none any longer occupies a subordinate position. Even the bass part, which formerly filled only its appointed place in the harmony, is now released from its subservient role and shares equally in the presentation and development of melodic ideas. Thus it was that Haydn worked out the set of structural principles that did not confine, but instead brought a new freedom to music. The rare combination of lawfulness and liberty that he achieved in his creative approach and method is unmatched in the annals of music. No one knew as well as he the eternal paradox of art: namely, that freedom lies in the direction of discipline, and that only through the acceptance of limitations can the creative fires be released in such forms that make it possible for the artist to transmit his ideas to other minds. His music thus rests solidly on principles of form that progress and evolve rather than crystallize in the final or definitive sense. Haydn's forms are myriad, since no two works are ever alike, but there is unity in the underlying principles. The spirit of freedom and flexibility that he breathed into his music thus raised it above the elegant routine products of his time into the rarified atmosphere of eternal masterpieces with universal appeal.

MOZART AND THE CONCERTING IDEA

Wolfgang Amadeus Mozart,[1] as the greatest dramatist in the history of music, not only assimilated and refined all the contemporary styles of his period, but he also delved into the historical past to rediscover some of those that had been forgotten or overlooked by his colleagues. All the stylistic voices of his time are heard coming from his music—sophisticated rococo gallantry and back-to-nature rusticity, ingenuous naiveté and learned counterpoint, classical calm and tender sensibility sighs, lofty impersonal statements and intimate Rousseauian confessions, uproarious *opera-buffa* antics and aristocratic *opera-seria* aloofness, heavenly serenity and demonic storm-and-stress fury, passionate protest and tragic resigna-

---

[1] See Chapter 10, pages 125–131, Symphony No. 40 in G. Minor (K.550); Chapter 11, pages 137–142, Piano Concerto in D Minor (K.466); Chapter 15, pages 185–198, *Don Giovanni* opera; Chapter 16, page 209, serenades and divertimentos.

tion. Instead of becoming a mere international eclectic, however, he appropriated all this wealth of material, techniques, and ideas; adapted them to his own particular expressive purposes; and emerged within his short thirty-five-year life span as a composer of powerful individuality. No style or form of his time was left untouched or untransformed by the magic of his musical imagination, and his spirit transfigured and illuminated every page he wrote.

Of all instrumental media, the concerto proved the most congenial outlet for his unique dramatic gifts, and he proceeded to produce no less than half a hundred works in the form. With a truly Grecian genius for the reconciliation of opposites, Mozart saw the concerto as an ideal means of bringing about a harmonious unity in such dualities as the opposing demands of solo and tutti passages, the personal soliloquy of the soloist and the group orchestral commentary, the improvisation of cadenza passages and the through-composed sections, and the separate domains of the soloist proper and that of the other concertante instruments; he saw each of these as individuals in their own right, yet socially compatible within the concerting situation. More broadly, he extended this unity in duality even further by merging the oppositions of the gallant and learned styles; the emotionalism of the sensibility or of the storm-and-stress and the rationalism of the Enlightenment; comic and tragic elements; capricious and profound attitudes; the transitory and the eternal. All these opposites are integrated in specific instances in a masterly manner. This could come about, however, only in the hands of a composer who had immense technical resources at his beck and call, and whose workshop was so well stocked with tools of the trade that a freedom of choice from an almost infinite number of means could be brought to bear on a wide variety of desired ends.

Of Mozart's fifty concertos, about half are for piano. While others before him had written vast quantities of concertos for violin, flute, and harpsichord, Mozart is to be regarded as the creator of the piano concerto. Like all composers of his time, Mozart wrote works on order; but the piano concertos, while often commissioned also, were nevertheless intended expressly for the occasions when he himself played the solo part. Furthermore, the concertos he wrote for violin and various solo wind instruments occupied him only intermittently, while the piano concertos were a constant preoccupation from his prodigy years onward. Mozart's serious interest in concertos for single wind instruments probably dates from his visits to Mannheim. Here the most brilliant players of the time were employed, and composers such as Johann Stamitz began to exploit the timbres of the wind instruments as much in their symphonies as in their many solo concertos. (Stamitz, for instance, was the composer of one of the earliest concertos

for solo clarinet.) The prominent role and poetic usage that the woodwinds assumed in Mozart's later concerto, orchestral, and operatic writing
was the mature realization of a potential revealed to him at Mannheim.

In his concertos for wind instruments Mozart developed the various
timbres very much in the same manner in which he delineated dramatic
characters in his operas. Though he wrote two flute concertos (K.313 and
K.314), as well as several quartets for flute and strings, all on commission
for wealthy amateurs, Mozart seems to have heartily disliked the flute. For
all the lyrical beauty of these works, he apparently considered the flute's
pale pure tone incapable of serious dramatic treatment, and his flute writing always tended toward rococo gallantry, or at its emotional saturation
point, the gentle *Empfindsamkeit*. Even when the libretto of his *Magic
Flute* made its use mandatory, the instrument appears prominently in the
opera only twice, and even then it is more in a symbolic sense personifying
aristocratic *noblesse oblige* than as a coloristic entity in its own right. The
other wind instruments, however, assumed the status of real *dramatis
personae* in his concerted instrumental dramas, and Mozart was particularly sensitive to their color capacities as well as to their power to evoke
mood. By his divining of their innate possibilities and by his use of them
in idiomatic ways, they became full dramatic characters. The bassoon, for
instance, chants philosophically in K.191, and the French horn in four examples (K.412, K.417, K.447, K.495) exhibits an appropriately masculine
outdoor character in keeping with its uses as a hunting instrument, a
posthorn, and the like. The mellow lyrical qualities of the clarinet were
particularly favored by Mozart, who featured it in two of his finest works
—the Clarinet Quintet (K.581) and the Clarinet Concerto (K.622).

The eighteenth-century concerto, like the string quartet and symphony,
stemmed from the fertile soil of the social music tradition. Indeed, the
occasions on which they were usually played coincided with those on which
divertimentos were also performed. When Mozart inherited the concerto
from such of his older contemporaries as J. C. Bach and Wagenseil, it was
considered as a species of social music; and the usual festive, forthright
marchlike first movements, the contrasting lyrical slow movements and the
high-spirited rondo finales were very closely related to the divertimento.
Unlike the sprawling multimovement serenades and cassations, however,
the concerto earlier in the century had crystallized to the traditional three-
movement organization. In contrast to the older baroque concerto grosso,
the Viennese concerto had become dominantly a solo work, reflecting perhaps the higher degree of value given to individual personality. The soloist, however, did not depart from the orchestral crowd as, for instance,
in the case of such romanticists as Liszt. The individual always operated
within the sphere of polite social decorum in the chamber-music tradi-

tion. Haydn, in his preoccupation with other matters, did little, in spite of his thirty essays in the form, to change the basic character of the concerto; and it remained for Mozart to free the concerto from the limitations of rococo gallantry, to lift it out of the social-music tradition, to make it into a serious independent form, and to endow it with a significant new literature. Mozart's development of the latent possibilities inherent in the concerto thus parallels Haydn's contribution in the case of the string quartet and the symphony.

Subtracting Mozart's first four essays, which have proved to be youthful adaptations of solo sonatas by contemporaries, he wrote twenty-three concertos for piano and orchestra, including one for two and another for three pianos. It is also important to note that they were written for the piano, not the harpsichord. In the piano Mozart found the ideal instrument for the balanced antiphony between solo instrument and orchestra. The pitch range of the piano is roughly equal to that of the orchestra; and unlike the violin and wind instruments, it is capable of airy counterpoints and harmonic densities of its own, but like the violin and wind instruments, it can also sing lyrically when called upon to do so. Beginning in 1773 with his first original effort in the form (K.175), and continuing with a few intervening works, Mozart arrived at his mature conception in one bold stroke with the *Concerto* in E-flat Major (K.271), which Alfred Einstein aptly called Mozart's "Eroica." The soloist here occupies a prominent position in full possession of his virtuoso powers, instead of functioning as a chamber musician among equals. Later, after settling in Vienna in 1781, Mozart attained the peak of his instrumental writing with the twelve great piano concertos he wrote for the series of subscription concerts there. In the Viennese life of Mozart's time, it should be pointed out, the concerto was a more important vehicle for public performance than was the symphony. Only when these concerts ceased as a productive source of revenue did Mozart briefly, in the summer of 1788, turn his attention to the symphony.

Since the formal aspects of the Mozart concerto have been treated in detail in Chapter 11, it will suffice here to point out a few of the salient stylistic features of two of his most unique examples—the only two in minor modes, those in D minor (K.466) and in C minor (K.491). The D-minor Piano Concerto is the best known of all Mozart's works in the form and is notable for its dark moods as well as for its close resemblance, both in tonality and spirit, to the demonic sections of *Don Giovanni*. Storm-and-stress demonic fury mark its impassioned measures, and the duality of orchestral and soloistic elements is never fully reconciled. The soloist in this instance is cast in the role of a noble soul battling with the menacing orchestral furies.

Even more dramatic is the C-minor Piano Concerto (K.491), a work which goes completely beyond the confines of social music in the depth of its expressive content, and in which the tragic and lyrical elements are mixed in about equal measure. Significant also is the important role assigned to a full complement of wind instruments—a flute, two oboes, two clarinets, two bassoons, two trumpets, and two French horns—which are treated almost as the equals of the piano soloist. The transparency of the part writing, the discreet commentary the wind instruments make on the action, the way they participate in concertante lyrical sections in which they are accompanied by the piano, all mark a new departure and point to a growing kaleidoscope of orchestral color.

This C-minor Concerto is a heroic tragedy; and before its epic sweep, anguished outbursts, and granitic strength even Beethoven himself stood in awe. Its heroic outlook, however, is humane enough to make room for some quiet and touching serenade music in both the slow movement and in the final set of variations. This is the finale of a heroic concerto—Mozart was more interested in the emotional vicissitudes available through variation than in a display of wit with the mechanics of art. The variations are alternately majestic, decorative, dramatic, and serene. Some of them work close to the basic subject, others do not. The last variation is the most poignant and the most powerful. There is no happy ending here as in the D-minor Concerto, but a true climax to a heroic endeavor. Each man must have his own concept of the heroic. But there is surely something universally apt in Mozart's decision to conclude a concerto of this kind with a set of variations; for intrinsic to a humanistic heroism is an acquaintance with all the emotional climates in the world's weather, as well as a just regard for all of the seasons in a man's soul.

Thus it was that Mozart could divine dramatic possibilities in the concerto far beyond anything envisaged by his contemporaries. By writing concerted dialogues for piano and orchestra with both treated as equals in the cast and by ranging from witty repartee to violent conflict, the piano became the principal protagonist in a symphonic drama. Indeed, the dramatic spirit of Mozart the opera composer is most transparently revealed in these piano concertos. That he conceived them in an operatic manner is evident in the many passages that appear first in the concertos and then later in the operas themselves. The music for the entrance scene of Donna Elvira in *Don Giovanni*, for instance, first appears in the opening movement of the Piano Concerto in B Flat (K.238), a full decade before the opera was written. *Opera-buffa* elements abound in the frolicking finales and in many instances versions of them appear in the comic scenes of the later operas. Some of the substance of the C-minor episode of the Concerto for Two Pianos (K.365), for example, is "borrowed" by Mozart for Papageno's comic-tragic attempt at suicide in *The Magic Flute*. Some of the motives that accompany Papageno are also to be heard in the final bars of the C-major Piano Concerto (K.467), and in the presto finale of the G-major Concerto (K.453) Papageno is heard cavorting once more in a piano concerto. This is straight *opera buffa* with all the hilarity and slightly hysterical clamor of a comic opera final "curtain" ensemble.

In all the instrumental music of Mozart's Viennese period, he lavished most of his attention and affection on the piano concertos. Fully conscious of the contribution he was making, Mozart commented in a humorous letter to his father that they were "written for all kinds of ears, not just for the long ones." He further informed his father that the new concertos represented "a compromise between the too easy and the too difficult, pleasant to the ear and very brilliant without, of course, sounding empty. Some passages will appeal only to connoisseurs but others will also be satisfied and enjoy themselves without, perhaps, knowing why." There was thus something for listeners at all levels, and with full justification Einstein called the piano concerto Mozart's "most characteristic creation."

SCHUBERT AND THE LYRICAL IDEA

Franz Schubert,[1] the only native son among the Viennese composers, lived out his short span of thirty-one years completely immersed in a world of sound. So busy was he with composing, there was little time left in which to live a life, and romantic biographers ever since have had a field day inventing fictitious activities to fill the vacuum. Unlike Mozart and Beethoven he was not a distinguished performer and was almost never in the public eye. What little music-making he did in the external sense took place within an intimate circle of close friends. He shares with Mozart, however, the distinction of being one of the two most innately and naturally endowed musical geniuses of all time. When questioned, for instance, about his method of composition, he replied quite simply, "When I finish one piece, I begin the next." Everything, then, was inwardly oriented and took external shape only in the steady stream of scores that flowed from his pen. Schubert's life, therefore, can be found in only one place—his music.

Like his Viennese contemporaries, Schubert was a universal composer in the sense that he wrote in all genres—masses, operas, choral and solo songs, instrumental solos, chamber music of all combinations, and symphonies—but no matter what vocal or instrumental form he touched, it

[1] See Chapter 2, page 22, Symphony No. 7 in C Major, *Great;* Chapter 3, page 39, *Marche Militaire;* Chapter 3, page 42, *Erlking* and *To Be Sung on the Water;* Chapter 13, pages 158–160, *Death and the Maiden.*

always turned into the gold of song. It was his pure lyricism and absence of feeling for the theater that defeated his repeated attempts at opera, and he completely lacked the dramatic flair of Mozart. Yet the inner fire and passion he packed into his miniature music dramas, the lieder, and into his one-man operas, the song cycles, endowed them with a concentrated intensity unique in music literature. Though he lacked the epical qualities of Beethoven, his lyrical approach to the symphonic form resulted in at least two symphonies—the *Unfinished* in B Minor and the *Great* in C Major—that can stand unblushingly beside any of Beethoven's nine.

In his chamber music one is hardly conscious of the instruments, only of voices; and in his trios, quartets, and quintets not only the slow movements are lyrical but all the others as well. This lyrical approach was recognized by Schubert's contemporaries; and after the first performance of the String Quartet in A Minor, the painter Schwind commented in a letter, "It is very smooth and gentle, but has the kind of melody one associates with songs . . ." His treatment of the piano sonata is likewise almost purely melodic; and, of course, the shorter impromptus and *Moments Musicaux* (Musical Moments) are the prototypes of the songs without words. Nowhere is this lyrical approach to instrumental music more in evidence than in the numerous instances in which he took motives and melodies from his songs and used them as a basis for entire movements. This happened not only in such obvious instances as the *Death and the Maiden* Quartet, the *Trout* Quintet and the *Wanderer* Fantasia, but also in more subtle and disguised forms. His song to the words of Wilhelm Müller, *Die Götter Griechenlands* (The Gods of Greece), for instance, appears in the ballet music from *Rosamunde,* in the slow movement of the A-minor String Quartet, and once again in the piano Impromptu, Op. 142, No. 3. The Rondo finale of the posthumous Sonata for Piano in A Major is based on his song *Im Frühling* (In Springtime) ; and the melody of the opening movement of his last Piano Sonata in B-flat Major is closely associated with his setting of one of Goethe's lyrics from *Mignon*. Whatever programmatic implication, if any, this song material may have had for the composer is never explained. There can be little doubt, however, that a knowledge of the words, spirit, and mood of the songs can lead both performer and listener to a closer understanding of the instrumental music that is based on them.

The distilled essence of Schubert's art is almost always to be found in his songs, and perhaps nowhere is it more transparently revealed than in his two song cycles. The earlier, *Die Schöne Müllerin* (The Fair Maid of the Mill, 1823) is an example of the narrative type, which unfolds in a series of twenty lyrical episodes. Songs 1 to 13 represent various stages in the idyllic courtship of the miller's daughter by the young apprentice, ending in the rapture of his acceptance. In Song 14, however, his dashing rival, the huntsman, makes an unwelcome appearance; and Songs 15 to 20 then tell of the young miller's rejection, unhappiness, and death. All events are viewed through the hero's subjective eyes, and the other characters never appear in their own right. The principal contrast is to be found in the more objective part played by the piano as it personifies the voice of nature speaking through the symbol of the brook. At times the brook-let gurgles cheerfully (Song 1), chatters garrulously (2), slumbers soundly (4), splashes gaily (5), leaps with joy (11), roars angrily (15), and sings sorrowfully (19). In true romantic fashion the voice of nature thus reflects every nuance of the hero's innermost being. The brooklet is his guide and confidant, sharing his joys and comforting his griefs, and ultimately resolving his sorrows by drawing him to her maternal breast. The transcendental union of man and nature is touchingly symbolized in the piano postlude of Song 19, which in alternate measures weaves to-gether the last phrase of the young miller's song with the final appearance of the brook motive.

The poetic theme of the later *Winterreise* (Winter's Journey, 1827) is essentially the same—rejected love, the wandering man alone, the soli-tary soul seeking solace in nature—but the cycle is of the more contem-plative type. All events have taken place in the indefinite past, and the poetry recalls and describes everything in retrospect. Schubert's setting in this case is a masterly exposition of every conceivable aspect of a single somber mood. With sorrow in joy and joy in sorrow, and within an all-enveloping melancholy, each song represents a stage in life's dark journey into the night of death. With Schubert's penetrating power of portraying emotional states in music, the songs begin in sadness; progress through moods of nostalgia, conflict, frustration, self-pity, protest, defiance, illusory hopes, disappointment, courage, despair; and end in eventual resignation. Schubert, when inviting his friends to hear the work for the first time, cautioned them he was going to sing "a cycle of terrifying songs." He fur-ther added, "They have affected me more deeply than has been the case with any other songs." They are indeed so personal and subjective that they seem like an introspective autobiographical statement.

From a compositional standpoint, the unity of the *Winterreise* is con-tained in what can be called the "wandering" motive—an insistently re-peated ostinato rhythmic figure that is present at some point in every song and obviously symbolizes the weary tread of the tired wanderer. In the first song "Good Night," it is heard throughout in the accompaniment figure; it is featured prominently in "Rest," No. 10; but perhaps is no-where more poignantly stated than in the climax of "The Guide Post," No. 20, as seen in the example below.

Ex. 21:3 "The Guide Post" (Bars 69–74) from *Winterreise* (Winter's Journey). Schubert.

The dualism of the major and minor modes also plays an important role. The minor predominates, and the occasional excursions and modulations into the major occur at points where they symbolize the recollection of past joys (The Linden Tree, No. 5); the escape into the world of dreams (Dream of Springtime, No. 11); an occasional ray of hope (Illusion, No. 19); or the peace of the graveyard (The Wayside Inn, No. 21). Nature imagery in both the graphic and symbolic sense appears prominently in the piano part. The wind howls in "The Weather Vane," No. 2; leaves and branches rustle in "The Linden Tree," No. 5; the pounding of horse's hooves and the sounding of the posthorn are heard in "The Post," No. 13; dogs snarl and bark "In the Village," No. 17; and a storm rages in "The Stormy Morning," No. 18. All roads, however, lead to the twenty-fourth and final song, "The Organ Grinder." Paralleling the barren landscape implied in the text, the melody and accompaniment are reduced to the starkest simplicity. With the utmost economy of means, the recitative-like voice part alternates with the barrel organ's melancholy melody over a monotonous drone accompaniment. When Schubert was painting this bleak tonal picture, he may well have seen the reflection of his own last years in the image of the organ grinder whose plate was always empty and whose lyre was never still.

Wunderlicher Alter	Strange old organ grinder,
soll ich mit dir gehn?	if I go with you?
Willst du meinen Liedern	Will you play my music
deine Leier drehn?	on your organ too?

The organ grinder presents, of course, the grim visage of death, and with the premonition that his music would be heard only after he was gone, the song ends with a dissonant forte shriek and a shudder at death's icy grip.

Ex. 21:4 "The Organ Grinder" (Bars 58–61) from *Winterriese* (Winter's Journey). Schubert.

BEETHOVEN AND THE SYMPHONIC IDEA

Like a colossus the figure of Ludwig van Beethoven [1] be-
strides the turn of two centuries, both in respect to the temporal span of
his lifetime and in the scope of the ideas he represented. During his thirty
formative late eighteenth-century years, he was fired by the sun of the Enlightenment, the heat of the social and stylistic crosscurrents of the revolutionary years, and the reflected radiance of the music of his two predecessors, Haydn and Mozart. All of these helped nurture and bring his art
to its full fruition. During his twenty-seven mature early nineteenth-
century years, he produced the unique masterpieces that in turn cast their
lengthened shadow on the entire future course of music. Just as Kant's
"Copernican Revolution" changed the direction of modern philosophy,
so Beethoven's ideas became the turning point in modern musical thought.
Many intellectual, emotional, and esthetic influences of his time are reflected in his work, most especially perhaps the rationalism of the Age of
Reason, with its optimistic conviction that man could transcend all his
limitations if only he would exert his innate creative powers. The same
force that motivated the American and French Revolutions finds its musical counterpart in Beethoven's overriding concern with social, individual,
and artistic freedom of expression. This freedom, however, like that of
the founding fathers and revolutionary leaders, was the end result of an
overwhelming sense of self-discipline and stern moral responsibility.

Beethoven's individuality was so powerful that, like Napoleon, he
inevitably became the dominating personality who stamped his image not
only on his own time but also on the period that followed. Small wonder,
then, that he became the adopted godfather of the romanticists, who
claimed him as one of their own. In his titanic emotional power, heaven-
storming pronouncements, defiance of social convention, and mighty
struggle for individual freedom of expression, they saw the ideal of their
art. However, the sheer weight of the logical processes he brought to bear
on composition and the uncompromising rationalism of his approach to
formal problems preclude his containment within the dreamy world of
romanticism and point in the direction of the Age of Reason. Beethoven,
it is true, did bring a new subjective expressive power to music so that it
demands to be lived and experienced as well as understood. But even when
his personal emotional reactions were mirrored in his music, the very ob-

---

[1] See Chapter 1, page 6, Symphony No. 9; Chapter 3, pages 30–32, Chapter 4, page
49, Chapter 9, pages 112–113, *Sonata Pathetique;* Chapter 4, pages 49–50, *Ruins of Athens,*
"Turkish March"; Chapter 4, page 51, *Leonore* Overture No. 3; Chapter 7, pages 109–110,
String Quartet in A Major, Op. 18, No. 5; Chapter 9, pages 118–119, Piano Sonata in G
Major, Op. 31, No. 1; Chapter 9, pages 114–118, Violin Concerto; Chapter 13, page 161, *To
the Distant Beloved* song cycle.

jectivity of his approach raised his inner conflicts to the heights of universal significance. The roots of Beethoven's art, then, are firmly planted in the soil of the eighteenth-century Enlightenment, and as such he was the inheritor of the prophetic mantles of his Viennese predecessors.

Unlike Haydn and Mozart, however, Beethoven was not under the constant pressure of one or more imperious patrons to produce a steady stream of workaday scores. His finished products, therefore, are fewer in number, and as a result they bear the signs of a greater concentration of creative energy. Compared to Haydn and Mozart, for instance, his symphonies number only nine, to their one hundred and four, and forty-one, respectively. But in his time the symphonic idea had outgrown its divertimento beginnings and taken on heavier weight both in material resources and expressive power. Compared to Haydn's eighty-three string quartets, Beethoven's number but eighteen; against Mozart's twenty-three piano concertos, Beethoven produced but five; Mozart's twenty operas and six violin concertos are matched by only a single Beethoven contribution in each category. Yet Beethoven, no less than his predecessors, was a universal composer who made major additions to all the current forms of his period. All musicians since his time can claim him as their own. To conductors he is the author of the dramatic overtures and the nine symphonies with their stormy allegros, sublime slow movements, robust scherzos, and jubilant finales; to pianists he is the composer of the thirty-two solo sonatas, those great soliloquies in which he revealed his innermost thoughts; to violinists he is the creator of one of the cornerstones of the concerto repertory, as well as the ten splendid sonatas for violin and piano; to cellists he is the contributor of five fine sonatas; and to choral directors he is the issuer of the challenge of the immense *Missa Solemnis,* as well as the choral Finale of the Ninth Symphony.

Unfortunately no adequate biography of Beethoven exists, nor is one ever likely to be written because his external life is of little help in understanding his art. Only in his internal life as embodied in his music is true significance to be found. In order to understand Beethoven, then, he must be approached on his own terms, and these are musical terms that must be ferreted out in the creative workshop where the mighty monuments were wrought. The notebooks, for instance, tell of the fearful struggle it was for Beethoven to forge a chain of notes into the desired melodic and rhythmic shape. Thus it is that only in the great autobiography contained in the musical works themselves can the real creative life and thought of the master be discovered.

As with all artists of stature, the materials, mediums, and forms in which he wrote are not so important in themselves as how he adapted, shaped, and transformed them. The piano sonata and violin-and-piano duo, for instance, were both humble species of house music when they came into his hands. By breathing elements drawn from the symphony and concerto into such works as the Sonata *Pathétique,* Op. 13, the *Wald-stein* Sonata, Op. 53, and the *Kreutzer* Sonata, Op. 47, as well as readdressing them to a public assembled in the concert hall, he raised the stature of these two comparatively modest genres to heroic size and transformed them into larger mediums with expressive potentialities never before realized. The piano concerto, in spite of Mozart's dramatic treatment, was still a dialogue in which the piano and orchestra discoursed on equal terms. In a work such as Beethoven's Fifth Piano Concerto, Op. 73, however, the virtuoso pianist now possessed a triumphant vehicle for the conquest of vast audiences. From his commanding position, the soloist's proclamations completely dominated the masses of orchestral humanity in an epic panorama that extended from the ringing opening chords to the closing whirlwind of scales.

A similar evolution took place within the framework of the symphony. Here as elsewhere the foundation of Beethoven's art was entirely traditional, since both Haydn and Mozart had blazed the trails leading into new fields. But it remained for Beethoven to extend the frontiers still further and to break through into vast new musical terrain. The first two symphonies were, in many respects, individual in conception, although they remained within the boundaries of eighteenth-century practice. But beginning with his third essay in 1804, the immense *Eroica* Symphony, he crossed the Rubicon dividing the eighteenth and nineteenth centuries. Continuing with his Fifth, Seventh, and Ninth, he cast the symphony in the heroic mold of great human documents in which the symbolic image of the emergence of a free and triumphant humanity was envisaged. Between the scaling of these mountain peaks, he paused for breath in the Fourth and Eighth and managed to recapture once again the clarity and universality of the eighteenth-century spirit; in the pastoral idyll of the Sixth he explored the antiphony of self and nature in the search for unity between the individual and divine being.

While space does not permit a complete study of even a single example, some of Beethoven's conceptions of the symphonic idea can at least be pointed out for further exploration. In the *Eroica,* for instance, Beethoven in one stroke arrived at the view of the sonata form as an all-encompassing, ever-progressing structure compounded out of expanding melodic constellations, rhythmical groupings, dynamic climaxes, harmonic patterns, and contrapuntal complexities—all shaped into a closely integrated whole. The initial subject (Ex. 21:5a), which becomes the prime mover in the process, is hardly a melody at all. It is just a fragment that announces the tonality, defines the lower and upper dominant limits, and establishes the

Ex. 21:5   Symphony No. 3 (*Eroica*). First Movement. Beethoven.

(*a*) Bars 2–7.

(*b*) Bars 15–25.

(*c*) Bars 186–193.

(*d*) Bars 300–308.

(*e*) Bars 338–359.

(*f*) Bars 408–421.

(*g*) Bars 640–647.

rhythmic pattern. Beethoven often preferred to open with workable construction formulas rather than with lyrical inspirations. For him melody
existed at its inception largely in terms of its future promise and as a cause
for the effects that follow. His choice of melodic material here, as elsewhere, was always dictated by its structural relation to the work as a
whole; consequently the focus of interest is not on melody as an end in
itself but on what it is to become. The theme here, then, is one of common
currency that anyone could compose. A premonition of future developments, however, is heard in the chromatic downward direction of the three
tones in Bars 4 and 5 of the example. From this point onward this thematic
fragment is swept up in a flood of opposing directional forces, and as it
interacts with the surrounding materials its various transformations take
place. Never complete but always seeking to go beyond itself, it starts to
rise in Examples 21:5*b* and *d*, only to fall back again; in Example 21:7*c* it
oscillates indeterminately; while in Example 21:5*e* it starts the upward

climb toward the climaxes of Example 21:5*f* and *g;* here it soars to a series of plateaus, each higher than the last.

The gigantic dimensions of the 691 measures of this movement go be-yond anything heretofore attempted. All is developmental, including the transitions between subjects; and the development section proper now swells to such size that it dominates the form. In this movement it accounts for 245 measures; and in true Beethovenian fashion the composer, after stating his initial premises and propositions, throws the forum open, so to speak, for a free discussion and analysis of all the implications of the previ-ously presented ideas. The argumentation here, as in other development sections, proceeds by *modulation,* in which changes of mode and a shifting of key centers to near and distant points take place (see Ex. 6:19) ; by *fragmentation,* in which the various subjects are broken down into their constituent parts for purposes of analysis; by *combination,* in which the subjects are compounded and woven together by various contrapuntal techniques; by *reiteration,* in which the material is repeated for the sake of emphasis; by *digression,* in which one or more episodes are introduced, or some tangential observations are made; and by *contrast,* in which conso-nance is opposed by dissonance, harmonic textures interchanged with con-trapuntal, loud levels of intensity alternated with soft, and in which anti-phonal responses are made by shifting from higher to lower registers and from one orchestral choir to another.

The full force of the process is then felt in the recapitulation, which in Beethoven's vocabulary is never a verbatim repetition of the beginning. Instead of returning to its point of origin, the movement continues inces-santly onward in the restless process of seemingly endless evolving. After the revelations of the development, the listener can now see how far he has come and by what roads he has arrived, before he takes off in the new di-rections set by Beethoven's extension of the coda into a terminal devel-opment.

The *Eroica* has, in fact, become so much a part of the symphonic vo-cabulary of the nineteenth and twentieth centuries that it is important to point out that it was, for its own day, intensely and even violently con-temporary. For the *Eroica* is, in its full splendor, perhaps the most im-posing example of what is now called—in referring to the painting and architecture contemporary with it—the "grand style." This was the domi-nant manner of Beethoven's generation, serving academicians and radicals, republicans, court flatterers, and nonpoliticals alike. It was a vehicle for the torrential heroism of this symphony, for the impassioned humanism of Shelley's *Prometheus Unbound,* and also for the austere didactic republi-canism and later the Napoleonic flattery of the painter Jacques Louis David. Composers no less than poets and painters were well acquainted with the style, for it was an inheritance from the eighteenth century re-shaped to suit the needs of a new generation. It came of age at a moment when the grand style tended to be strongly identified as a Napoleonic style, and, indeed, the *Eroica* was originally conceived as a work dedicated to the ideal of the heroic which Napoleon then represented. Set in alignment with such possible orchestral models as the Mozart *Jupiter* Symphony or C-minor Piano Concerto, the most immediate and startling difference is the enormous enlargement of the time scale. The *Eroica* is double the size of the Mozart works. Time, of course, is the composer's canvas, and he works with the articulation of duration as a painter does with the organi-zation of space. If, in 1804, the time scale of the *Eroica* was unprecedented for symphonic music, its very size was one of the conventions of Napoleonic painting and sculpture. The analogues to the *Eroica* are to be found not in the contemporary orchestral practice, but in David's coronation painting, *Le Sacre,* and in Canova's colossus of Napoleon posed nude like a Greek god. And the moment this comparison is made, the exceptional character of the *Eroica* becomes manifest. For there is no empty posturing in the *Eroica,* but a genuinely vast and all-engulfing heroism esthetically com-parable in its equation between scale and scope not to the frozen rhetoric of David and Canova, but to the humanistic heroism of Michelangelo. Future generations have become accustomed to the scale of the *Eroica,* but what is forever new is the musical substance that requires every mo-ment of the time expanse which Beethoven organized to contain it. In its vast size it is wholly efficient, and in its way as fine an example of econ-omy of structure as any four-minute Bach fugue.

The *Eroica* is one musician's declaration of faith, born at a particular moment in history, and consonant with the uncorrupted idealism which many in his generation sustained for their own sake and for ours. With Beethoven, this declaration was a triumphant one. Characteristically, the funeral march, as agonizing as it is in its last broken moments, is the second movement. The Finale to this heroic drama is a typical victory finale, and one with a resounding popular marching-band tune to mark one of the stages of its triumphal progress. No doubt this document was for Beetho-ven a deeply personal one. There are men such as Beethoven who reach for and seize upon universals by an intense participation in the drama of their own lives. If the world within is vast enough, they find there such generalities as are urgent for their generation, and sometimes timeless truths for all men. Whatever Beethoven's needs, there is no doubt that his generation also needed an *Eroica*. And its timelessness has been simply this: that if no subsequent generation has been spared its tragedy, neither has any subsequent generation sustained itself without its expectation of ultimate triumph.

In the Fifth Symphony a still tighter sense of unity is achieved by the use of a single germinal motive which brings together not only the component parts of the first movement itself, but all four movements of the entire cyclic design. The sonata form as found in single movements had been predicated on a dualism of two opposing subjects in a kind of bithematic organization based on contrast and conflict. These subjects, during the course of the composition, became harmoniously reconciled in a dramatic union of opposites. With the mature Beethoven, in such instances as the Piano Sonata Op. 10, No. 3, as well as in the Fifth and to a certain extent the Ninth Symphonies, the contrast of parts is just as complete; but for the dualism of thematic material, he substitutes a dualistic treatment of various versions of the same subject. Turning now to the Fifth Symphony, a glance at the first, second, and closing subjects of the opening exposition will quickly reveal their basic identity. After the initial motive is established by repetition, its manifold possibilities and directional tendencies begin to unfold through the development section, and continue onward into the recapitulation and coda. But instead of reaching fulfillment at this point, rhythmic references to the motive are heard during the slow movement, and the thread is caught up again in the trio and coda of the Scherzo; and from this point it goes onward to the triumphant affirmation of the Finale. The entire symphony is thus an outgrowth of this central motivic force. The initial idea has determined the shape of the whole work, and the formal contours have emerged out of the inherent character of the basic materials. Starting with the germinal elements of subject and phrase, all ramifications of the initial idea are realized through progress and expansion in accordance with the laws of organic growth. The Fifth Symphony is proof once again of Beethoven's position as a supreme rationalist, daring in his choice of ideas and patient in his pursuit of their ramifications. The symphony is an admirable illustration of the rational control of a heroic passion, the imagination to conceive such magnificent ideas, and the untiring search for the most remote and esoteric coherences in musical structure to contain and clarify them. Intensity of emotion and intensity of formal discipline meet here, and merge, and the one is known only in terms of the other. The severity of structural discipline in the first movement is the logical urgency, the unencumbered coherence of pure heroism. Its passion is not blind but illuminated, not willful in aberration, but willful in control.

Thus in the work of the Viennese composers an ideal of composition is achieved in that a maximum of variety emerges from a minimum of material, and in that there is complete coincidence of matter and form, technique and inspiration. The medium of abstract sound in instrumental

Fig. 21:1 Watteau. *The Music Party.* (French eighteenth-century rococo.)

music became a means of expressing ideas powerfully conceived and force-fully realized. Beginning with Gluck, continuing with Haydn, Mozart, and Schubert, and culminating in Beethoven, the Viennese composers, through the language of tone, projected a convincing and universal image of man that is as valid today as it was in the eighteenth century.

ROMANTIC CHRONOLOGY

Italy

Muzio Clementi	1752–1832
Maria Luigi	
Cherubini	1760–1842
Gasparo Spontini	1774–1851
Nicoló Paganini	1782–1840
Gioacchino Rossini	1792–1868
Gaetano Donizetti	1797–1848
Vincenzo Bellini	1801–1835
Giuseppe Verdi	1813–1901

Paris

Daniel Auber	1782–1871
Giacomo Meyerbeer	1791–1864
Hector Berlioz	1803–1869
Frédéric Chopin	1810–1849
Franz Liszt	1811–1886
Charles Gounod	1818–1893
Jacques Offenbach	1819–1880
César Franck	1822–1890
Édouard Lalo	1823–1892
Camille Saint-Saens	1835–1921
Léo Delibes	1836–1891
Georges Bizet	1838–1875
Emmanuel Chabrier	1841–1894
Jules Massenet	1842–1912
Gabriel Fauré	1845–1924
Vincent d'Indy	1851–1931
Ernest Chausson	1855–1899

Germany and Vienna

E. T. A. Hoffmann	1776–1822
J. N. Hummel	1778–1837
Louis Spohr	1784–1859
Carl Maria von	
Weber	1786–1826
Karl Czerny	1791–1857
Heinrich Marschner	1795–1861
Carl Loewe	1796–1869
Franz Schubert	1797–1828
Albert Lortzing	1801–1851
Johann Strauss Sr	1804–1849
Felix Mendelssohn	1809–1847
Robert Schumann	1810–1856
Richard Wagner	1813–1883
Anton Bruckner	1824–1896
Johann Strauss Jr	1825–1899
Johannes Brahms	1833–1897
Engelbert	
Humperdinck	1854–1921

Czechoslovakia

Bedrich Smetana	1824–1884
Karl Goldmark	1830–1915
Anton Dvořák	1841–1904

England

John Field	1792–1837
Arthur Sullivan	1842–1900

Norway

Edvard Grieg	1843–1907
Christian Sinding	1856–1941

United States

Stephen Foster	1826–1864
Louis Morreau	
Gottschalk	1829–1869
John K. Paine	1839–1906
Victor Herbert	1859–1924
Horatio Parker	1863–1919

Russia

Michael I. Glinka	1803–1857
Anton Rubinstein	1829–1894
Alexander P. Borodin	1834–1887
César A. Cui	1835–1918
Mili A. Balakirev	1837–1910
Modeste Moussorgsky	1839–1881
Peter Ilich	
Tchaikovsky	1840–1893
Nicholas Rimsky-	
Korsakoff	1844–1908

The Romantic Period

Chapter 22

STYLISTIC BACKGROUND

T<small>HE</small> battlefield for the new artistic, social, and political struggles that were stirring men's minds in the 1820's was to be found in the theaters, opera houses, salons, cafes, and eventually in the streets of Paris. While the beginnings of romanticism are encountered in earlier developments elsewhere—notably in England and Germany—the style first moved into the international arena in France. Paris at this time was literally teeming with poets and playwrights, painters and composers. Franz Liszt came from Hungary in 1823, Frédéric Chopin arrived from Poland in 1830, and the poet Heinrich Heine from North Germany in 1831. Here they brushed shoulders with such native French intellectuals and artists as the painter Eugène Delacroix, the poet Victor Hugo, and the composer Hector Berlioz.

Romanticism projected a new emotional spectrum that reflected the ways composers interpreted their world and how they reacted to the revolutionary, literary, dramatic, and pictorial events of their time. The French Revolution of 1789, for instance, had emphasized the ideals of liberty, equality, and fraternity; instilled a humanitarian interest in the rights of man; and given promise of a more liberal social framework in which the individual could realize his personal ambitions. Paris in the year 1827 saw many events that presaged a new order of things. An English Shakespearean troupe, for instance, created a sensation with their performances of

Romeo and Juliet, Macbeth, and *Hamlet;* hitherto the bard had been considered too uncouth and unclassical for the polished French stage. New voices were heard coming from Germany with the first French translation of Goethe's drama, *Faust,* and the first performance of Weber's opera, *Der Freischütz* (The Free Ranger), both of which bespoke a new attitude toward man and nature. Victor Hugo published his play, *Cromwell,* with a lengthy Preface that was to become the manifesto of the romantic movement, and but a few years later, Hugo's *Ernani* was to be the play that delivered the deathblow to the already moribund French classical drama.

In the following year, 1828, Berlioz' Opus 1 first saw the light of day with his *Eight Scenes from Faust,* a work he later expanded into the *Damnation of Faust.* And this was the year when Daniel Auber once again captured the operatic spotlight for Paris with his *Deaf-Mute of Portici,* the first so-called "grand" opera. It impelled Gioacchino Rossini to revise his style completely in the work he was composing for the Paris Opera, *William Tell* (1829). The cause for grand opera was then settled once and for all by Giacomo Meyerbeer who, though German by birth, became the leading exponent of romantic-historic grand opera with his *Robert the Devil (Robert le Diable,* 1831), *The Huguenots* (1836), and *The Prophet* (1848). The Meyerbeer formula for grand opera included five-act plots liberally bestrewed with powerful melodramatic episodes, dark and devious conspiracies, dashing deeds of derring-do, and pompous cavalry marches with the hero on his prancing steed in their midst. Technically they wove together recitative sequences, passionate arias and duets, several large ensemble numbers, frequent ballet entries, milling mass choruses, spectacular stage mountings, and a large orchestra. Such grandiose and bombastic goings-on prompted the young Richard Wagner to characterize them as "effect without cause." In spite of his sarcasm, however, Meyerbeer's operas influenced Wagner's own thinking more than he cared to admit, and the cause of grand opera can be seen marching along through the century in Wagner's *Tannhäuser,* and also in Verdi's *Aïda* as well as in a host of other sumptuous stage spectacles.

Such fanciful flights of the imagination were among the many manifestations of a new psychology of escapism that is summed up neatly in the slogan, "any time but now and any place but here." Romanticism in this sense amounted to a reaction to rationalism and a withdrawal from reality in order to envision a roseate dream world through the intuitive eye of the artist. In so doing he sought to go beyond sense experience and view the world in the light of an ideal. The Middle Ages, for instance, was seen as a colorful golden age of the past far removed from the sordid materialistic struggle of the present. In England a reading public had been long conditioned to reading the so-called "Gothic" novels such as Horace Walpole's *Castle of Otranto* (1765), to hearing comic operas with medieval trappings at Covent Garden such as *Banditti; or Love in a Labyrinth* (1781), as well as to attending melodramas such as *Raymond and Agnes; or The Bleeding Nun of Lindenberg* (1797).

   This prepared the way for the sensational popular success of Sir Walter Scott's novels whose influence was felt in France through Victor Hugo's novel, *The Hunchback of Notre Dame* (1831), as well as in the works of Alexandre Dumas. Dante became to the romantic movement what Homer had been to the classicists; Shakespeare's popularity eclipsed the French tragic dramatists Corneille and Racine; and the poetic stars of Byron and Goethe were in the ascendancy. The composers of the time had strong literary interests, and music drew much closer to poetry. Berlioz was busy writing a symphony on *Romeo and Juliet*, a viola concerto (*Harold in Italy*) on Byron's *Childe Harold*, as well as overtures to *King Lear* and Scott's novels, *Waverly* and *Rob Roy;* Liszt, in turn, was composing piano pieces on Petrarch's sonnets, symphonies on Dante's *Divine Comedy* and Goethe's *Faust*, as well as the bloodcurdling fire-and-brimstone inferno of his *Dance of Death* (*Totentanz*) for piano and orchestra; Donizetti found the story for his most successful opera *Lucia di Lammermoor* in Scott's novel *The Bride of Lammermoor;* and Wagner was tapping the rich sources of old Celtic sagas and the Arthurian legends of the Holy Grail for the subjects of his *Tristan and Isolde, Lohengrin,* and *Parsifal,* as well as the medieval epics for his *Ring of the Nibelung.*

   All this led, of course, right to the doorstep of *programme music,* and the desire for the closer union of literature and music was also accompanied by a felt need for freedom from such traditional forms as theme and variations, rondo, and sonata. If, for instance, a composer set out to base a work on *Romeo and Juliet* or *Mazeppa* (a subject treated by both Byron and Hugo), no ready-made forms were available and no preconceived patterns were expected, hence the need to invent them. Or, to put it the other way around, if a composer abandoned the established forms, he needed the compensation of some literary unity to keep his episodes in line and make them dramatically convincing. Hence literary sources became handy suggestive material; and since no two literary works unfolded in identical sequence, a symphonic poem became a convenient way for a composer to avoid crystallizing his forms, as well as giving him the desired excuse for having each work different from the last. In general it can be said that while other centuries took occasional programmatic pieces in their stride, it was in the nineteenth century that programme music actually began to dominate the scene, particularly after the romanticists attempted to establish a theory of composition on it and to make it the basis of a musical style.

Another of these escape mechanisms is found in the rejection of beauty in the eighteenth-century sense and the acceptance of the ideals of the sublime, grotesque, and fantastic into the canons of romanticism. Edmund Burke, as early as 1756, had admitted the awesome and ugly into the realm of art by distinguishing the two concepts in his *Essay on the Sublime and the Beautiful*. The sublime, he wrote, is vast in dimension, rugged and negligent, dark and gloomy. The sublime embraces vast power including the terrible, and the emotional reaction to it is that of astonishment and even horror, rather than admiration and respect. Hugo went a step beyond Burke into the grotesque. "The ugly," he declared in the Preface to *Cromwell*, "exists beside the beautiful, the unshapely beside the graceful, the grotesque on the reverse side of the sublime, evil with good, darkness with light." "The grotesque," he continued, "fastens upon religion a thousand original superstitions, upon poetry a thousand picturesque fancies. It is the grotesque which scatters lavishly in air, water, earth, fire, those myriads of intermediary creatures which we find all alive in the popular traditions of the Middle Ages; it is the grotesque which impels the ghastly antics of the witches' revels, which gives satan his horns, his cloven feet, and his bat's wings." It is this spirit of the grotesque that finds such vivid musical expression in the "Wolf's Glen" scene from Weber's *Freischütz* and the last two movements of Berlioz' *Symphonie Fantastique*.

This implied a new concept of nature, which to the romanticist was nothing in itself, but rather a complement to human nature. In this sense nature provided a picturesque and resonant sounding board reflecting back, and at the same time revealing, to the self all the complicated states of the tortured human soul as, for example, in the "Scene in the Country," the third movement of Berlioz' *Symphonie Fantastique*. The predictable, benign universe of the Enlightenment, in short, yielded to the capricious, often malignant world of romanticism. Such forces were beyond man's control, and as such they were personified by the romanticists in a demonology conjured up from the witchcraft and superstitions of the Middle Ages as well as out of their own fevered imaginations. Examples are readily found in the "Invocations to Nature" from Berlioz' *Damnation of Faust*, as well as in the storm scenes, witches' sabbaths, and macabre dances of romantic operas and symphonies.

The regressive aspects of romanticism, as seen in these various escape mechanisms, were counterbalanced by the progressive effects of the times which the artists were quick to turn to their advantage. In the wake of the Industrial Revolution, for instance, had come a rapid change from an agrarian to an industrial economy, as well as a shift from a rural to an urban society. The large new city populations became potential patrons of the arts, and, after the French Revolution had drastically curtailed the powers of aristocratic patrons, artists perforce had to become free lancers. Music-making, consequently, moved out of the aristocratic salons into the public concert halls, where a new, largely middle-class audience gathered. This was the culmination of a process already well advanced during the eighteenth century; and, as will presently be seen, this shift to a more democratic base had its effect on both the form and content of romantic composition.

With the advent of the Industrial Revolution also came greater technical precision and standardization in the manufacture of musical instruments. The new valve mechanisms in brass instruments, for instance, made it possible for players to command a wider range of instrumental color and to produce effects never before heard. Composers consequently had a vastly expanded orchestral color palette at their finger tips, and it is only to be expected that they would make effective use of it. Pianos, too, gained with the replacement of wooden frames by those made of cast iron: the cost of their manufacture was reduced, they stayed in tune longer, and it was possible to ship them about for touring virtuosos. This was also the time of the industrialization of printing, and the mass distribution from the press vastly enlarged the circulation of journals, novels, and sheet music. The influence of the press was also reflected in the rise of the modern concept of journalistic music criticism, and composers such as Weber, Berlioz, Schumann, and Liszt took to the pen as critics and propagandists.

In the face of this growing collectivism came a vigorous reassertion of individualism. Novelists wrote their books in the first person; and since there was no universally recognized style, each artist had to create his own. A new aristocracy of genius replaced that of the hereditary dynasties in the public mind, and the era of the great individual was the result. It was also a time in which a composer's creative work no longer spoke for itself alone, and it became incumbent on composers to be great personalities and to lead fascinating, or as in the case of Paganini, even lurid lives. At the psychological moment, of course, the artist's autobiography, memoirs, or confessions, as the case might be, appeared in print (for instance, Berlioz and Wagner). Liszt wryly commented on this development by observing that he never had time to write about his own life because he was too busy living it.

This romantic individualism, moreover, also extended into the sphere of nationalism. A poet or composer, for instance, was expected to become the voice of his people, shaping their unconscious aspirations toward the more conscious goals of self-discovery and self-determination. Byron the poet and Chopin the composer were thus found espousing the heroic causes of Greek and Polish independence, respectively; and national self-determination became almost a religion. The spirit of a people, moreover, was thought to be reflected in their native languages and literatures. The new reading and listening audience, for instance, did not have the command of the international languages of Italian and French as had been the case with aristocratic eighteenth-century audiences. This gave a new impetus to the development of a national and indigenous drama and opera for each country. The effect of nationalism was also felt in the admiration for local color in painting, for the use of regional dialects in literature, and for the use of native songs and dances in music as well as in the exploration of folklore and folk ballads.

Much has been made in the history books about the romantic revolt against classicism, when it would be far more accurate, in the case of music at least, to say that romanticism was primarily opposed to academicism. Romantic music was "modern" music to the ears of nineteenth-century audiences, and as such its appearance in opera houses and concert halls was an exception rather than the rule. The repertory of the time was dominated by such conservative figures as Cherubini, Spontini, Hummel, and Reinecke, as well as a host of now-forgotten composers. Pianists, for their part, played pieces by Clementi, J. B. Cramer, Kalkbrenner, Czerny, and Moscheles—all now remembered principally as purveyors of finger exercises—and the programming of a work by Beethoven, Schubert, or Weber was a comparatively rare event. The music of Ludwig Spohr is a case in point. Since it was always agreeable, well mannered, and at times quite elegant, he enjoyed wide success during his long lifetime. Occasionally he introduced innovations, but his mild-mannered radicalism was always so carefully couched in conservative terms his audiences were rarely startled. The real romantics—Weber, Berlioz, Schumann, and others—were at this time the wild men of music. Their revolt, however, was never against genuine inspiration, whether of the past or present, but rather against the slavish adherence to formal stereotypes that the conservatories held up as models. Any romantic artist worth his salt was capable of recognizing inspiration and genius, whether it appeared in his own or any other century. Berlioz' lifelong championship of Gluck's cause, Mendelssohn's and Schumann's ardent admiration of J. S. Bach, as well as Weber's and Chopin's enthusiasm for Mozart are all cases in point. However, when the academic mind went into action and reduced the works of C. P. E. Bach, Haydn, and Mozart to a series of pedantic textbook prototypes, the ire of the romantics was understandably aroused, and they led the revolt for formal freedom, not against Bach and Mozart, but against academic conventions and clichés.

The obverse side of this romantic coin, however, shows some curious inconsistencies, and an academic approach seems to have been present in the most ardent romanticist. Berlioz, for instance, wrote a textbook treatise on orchestration; Mendelssohn directed the Leipzig Conservatory; Chopin projected, but never finished, a "piano method"; Robert Schumann, Ph.D. (University of Jena), was one of the founding editors of the Bach Society, the group of careful scholars that prepared the monumental publication of the master's complete works; and Wagner was a voluble and verbose writer of didactic and critical essays. In similar fashion the effusive romantic historical novels were accompanied by the solid discipline of modern historiography; the interest in folklore and ballads of the people, by the science of philology; the admiration for the artistic monuments of the past, by classical and medieval archeology; and the "back to Bach" movement and revival of past musical periods, by the foundation of musicology.

In sum, the romantic revolt against rational and methodical thinking ushered in a new wave of emotional outpouring. The romantics, in other words, would have altered Descartes' dictum, "I think therefore I am," to "I feel therefore I am." Instead of emphasizing the general, universal, and superpersonal, the romantics stressed the particular, transitory, and personal. Intuition superceded reason, the subjective was in the ascendancy over the objective, and individual soliloquy replaced social dialogue. Out of this panorama of revivals of the past, the regressive and progressive tendencies of the time, and the evolutionary and revolutionary factors came the constellation of ideas that led to the new emotional spectrum and the new technical vocabulary for its expression.

NEW VOICES AND VOCABULARY: BERLIOZ; WEBER; SCHUMANN

Romanticism, after its beginnings in other centers, first moved onto the international stage in Paris. With the July Revolution of 1830 it became the official French style, and it was destined to remain such until the February Revolution of 1848. The flamboyant figure of Hector Berlioz, with his shock of red hair and the burning intensity of his eyes, illuminated the cafes and concert halls of Paris in 1830, just as the red glare of Revolutionary rockets lit up the Parisian streets that same year. How far things had come since the days of the polite eighteenth-century social music can be measured by the spectacle of this ardent twenty-six-year-old composer proclaiming his personal passion for an Irish actress to one and all at the top of his symphonic lungs. The *Symphonie Fantastique,* as this orchestral autobiography was called, served as the musical manifesto of the new movement, just as the plays of Victor Hugo and the paintings of Delacroix were its literary and pictorial equivalents. "Bizarre and monstrous," wrote one of the reviewers, but the *Symphonie*

Fantastique commanded such attention that no one to this day can disregard its challenge.

Berlioz' lively imagination was fired as much by the dominant literary enthusiasms of the romantic movement—the Gothic novel, the Shakespearean and Dante revivals, and Goethe's *Faust*—as it was by the current musical developments—romantic opera as exemplified in Weber's *Freischütz,* the "grand" style as found in Beethoven's *Eroica,* as well as the programmatic elements in Beethoven's *Pastorale* Symphony. Others of Berlioz' works, such as the *Romeo and Juliet* Symphony (1839) and the *Damnation of Faust* (1846), are made even more explicit in their literary connection by the incorporation of texts. Though he called the former a "dramatic symphony" and the latter a "dramatic legend," both are actually hybrid forms obtained by crossing the opera and oratorio with the symphony.

The *Symphonie Fantastique* projected a large-scale design in five movements, and the composer's problem was how to keep such a big and varied work together without letting it dissolve into a loose collection of episodes. Like his fellow romanticists, Berlioz was at his best in quick flashes of inspiration and deft strokes of the dramatic. His dilemma was how to build something monumental out of such inspired but fragmentary materials. The solution was typical of his compositional procedures, being half literary and half musical—a poetic programme prefacing a fanciful story line to each of the movements, and a melodic motive he called an *idée fixe* (or fixed idea) running through each of the several movements. By a technique not unlike that used by Gluck in his *Orfeo* (compare Exs. 21:1*a through e* on p. 322), Berlioz devised a theme to be identified with his heroine and varied it with each of the symphonic vicissitudes. Later, Liszt and Wagner appropriated this fixed-idea scheme, modifying and expanding it to suit their own systems.

Ex. 22:1   *Symphonie Fantastique.* Berlioz.

(*a*) First Movement (Bars 72–79).

(*b*) Second Movement (Bars 107–113).

(*c*) Fifth Movement (Bars 22–25).

The first movement—"Reveries, Passions"—is the only one that follows the outlines of the classical sonata form. The slow, dreamy Largo introductory section, redolent with romantic longing, leads directly into an *Allegro agitato e appassionato assai* in which the fixed idea (Ex. 22:1*a*) is first sounded by the flute and violins. In the subsequent development section the motive is exposed to a series of musical experiences much in the manner of Beethoven. According to Berlioz' rather lurid programme, "A young musician of morbid sensibility and ardent imagination poisons himself with opium in a fit of amorous despair. The narcotic dose, too weak to result in death, plunges him into a heavy sleep accompanied by the strangest visions, during which his sensations, sentiments, and recollections are translated in his sick brain into musical thoughts and images. The beloved woman herself has become for him a melody, like a *fixed idea* which he finds and hears everywhere." The literary source in this case was De Quincey's psychological study called *Confessions of an English Opium Eater,* which had appeared earlier that year in a French translation by Alfred de Musset. A scene invented by the translator serves as the programme for the second movement where "he sees his beloved at a ball, in the midst of the tumult of a brilliant fete." This becomes a brilliant concert waltz in which the heroine, bedecked with diamonds, is seen in the arms of another. Here the theme (Ex. 22:1*b*) is likewise caught up in the swirl of the waltz time.

The hero's wild despair can be assuaged only in the bucolic arms of Mother Nature, and the third movement thus becomes a "Scene in the Country." In spite of the pastoral dialogue of the two shepherds (symbolized by the English horn and oboe, "*She* appears once more, his heart stops beating, he is agitated by painful presentiments . . ." With the fourth movement the real phantasmagoria begins. According to the programme, "He dreams that he has killed his beloved, that he is condemned to death and led to execution. The procession advances to the tones of a march which is now somber and wild, now brilliant and solemn . . . At the end, the fixed idea reappears for an instant, like a last love thought interrupted by the fatal stroke." This mock march of triumph, with its raffish rhythms and nightmarish atmosphere, tells much about the relation of the romantic artist to his society. Here the hero is misunderstood by the jeering mobs and marched off to the guillotine just as the Revolutionary lyric poet André Chénier had been during the reign of terror in 1792. Also in Berlioz' *Harold in Italy* (1834) the noble and sensitive artist is found in the midst of uncomprehending savages in the final "Orgy of the Brigands."

The hell-fire and brimstone of Dante's *Inferno* as well as the wild imagery of Goethe's grotesque "Walpurgisnight's Dream" from *Faust* are heard in the "Witches' Sabbath" of the fifth movement as the howling demons come to claim the hero's soul. Like Victor Hugo's poem, *Rondo of the Sabbath,* this piece seems to be set in a Gothic church at the mysterious hour of midnight. The smell of sulfur is in the air, the holy water boils in the fonts, and the fantastic congregation—specters, ghouls, monsters, and, from the graveyard, the souls of the damned—gathers from all directions. Satan himself sings the Black Mass, and the fearsome assembly joins in the mad capers. The fixed idea enters here in a grotesque version (Ex. 22:1c). The one who has been bewitching him was apparently a witch all along; with a shriek he recognizes the beloved on her broomstick just before the doomsday theme is intoned. As Berlioz' programme promises, this is a "burlesque parody" on the *Dies irae,* that fine old Gothic chant that was and is an integral part of every solemn Requiem Mass. This parody on the sacred service is one of the many touches of romantic irony in a period that was enamored of the supernatural, fascinated by the grotesqueness of gargoyles, and beguiled by the demons depicted in medieval Last Judgment scenes. The movement concludes with a fugue based on the witches' dance and the *Dies irae* melody. The *Symphonie Fantastique* incorporates many of Berlioz' original discoveries in instrumentation and orchestral tone color. Though written but three years after the death of Beethoven, the orchestra is greatly increased in size and scope, and it was destined to be still further expanded to colossal proportions in such later works as Berlioz' *Requiem* (1837).

Der Freischütz by Carl Maria von Weber, when first performed at Berlin in 1821, was a real victory for the new style as well as for a national German opera. Subtitled "A Romantic Opera in Three Acts," it departs in significant ways from the mainstream of Italian and French models and strikes out on its own. Like Mozart's *Magic Flute,* it is a union of the folklike and fantastic, and an opera of genuinely popular appeal. The theme is idyllic love and the people's freedom in God's realm of nature. The form is that of the *singspiel,* or song-play of the indigenous German tradition with its spoken dialogue. Parts, to be sure, employ recitative, but it is always of the orchestrally accompanied type and so closely connected with the arias or choruses that follow that it begins to break down the rigid divisions of the old number opera. The setting is that of the Bohemian forest; the tale is that of the simple life without goddesses or heroic personages; the heroine is a gamekeeper's daughter, the hero a forest ranger; the choruses are those of peasants, villagers, and hunters. The play, an adaptation from a book of popular ghost stories, was originally entitled "The Huntsman's Bride," and the somewhat obscure term *Freischütz* can, perhaps, best be rendered as the "Free Ranger." The term in this case designates one who has sold his soul to the Devil in return for seven magic bullets, six of which will hit the target he determines but the seventh (the free shot) that which the Devil directs. Nature is here seen as a force which can either destroy or heal, and both its demonic and divine aspects are explored, both the sorcery of black magic and the innocent joy of nature worship. Zamiel, the Black Huntsman, is the personification of the Evil One who commands the malignant elements, while his counterfoil is the old Hermit who knows the secrets of nature's healing power. Against this play of forces the young lovers grapple with their fate.

The Overture, still a staple in the symphonic repertory, sings the song of the German forest with the voice of the hunting horns and woodwinds. The principal melodies of the opera are heard, including the sinister Zamiel motive with its shuddering orchestral tremolando, pizzicato basses, and fatalistic drumbeats. This is the type of music that the German writer, critic, and composer E. T. A. Hoffmann described as being "The mysterious essence of nature expressed in sounds; through it [music] alone can be understood the divine singing of the trees, of flowers, of animals, of stones, and of waters."

In the course of *Freischütz* a mixture of styles is encountered. Agatha's Scene and Aria No. 8, for instance, suggests the form of Italian opera, but the aria contains the *Leise, leise, fromme Weise,* a folklike ballad with strophic repetitions in the tradition of the German domestic lied. The influence of French opera is heard in Ännchen's Romance and Aria No. 13 as well as in the haunted "Wolf's Glen Scene" (No. 10). However, the Chorus of Bridesmaids (No. 14) and the Huntsman's Chorus (No. 15) with the sounds of hunting horns are as German as the *Gesangverein.* The operatic core is contained in the weird scene in Wolf's Glen to which Caspar lures the hero so that they can pronounce the incantation that conjures up the spectral figure of Zamiel, an orchestral evocation that runs the gamut of romantic demonology. The foreboding trombones, the dark low clarinet register, and the agitated tremolo string effects vividly describe the fantastic visions involved. This is a romantic horror piece that has aptly been described as the arsenal of romanticism, a scene from which both Berlioz and Wagner freely borrowed some of their most potent orchestral weapons. The stage directions indicate the macabre atmosphere this aspect of romanticism sought to evoke, "A weird, craggy glen, surrounded by high mountains, down the side of one of which falls a cascade. To the left a blasted tree, on the knotty branch of which an owl is sitting. To the right a steep path by which Max comes; below it a great cave. The mood throws a lurid light over all. A few battered pine trees are scattered here and there. Caspar, in shirt sleeves, is making a circle of black stones; a skull is in the center; near by a ladle, a bullet mould, and an eagle's wing. A thunderstorm is coming on."

Weber's sensitivity to orchestral and vocal coloration, as well as the compelling force of his melodic invention, placed him in the vanguard of romanticism; and it was in *Freischütz* that he first realized his ideal of opera as "An art work complete in itself, in which the partial contributions of the related and collaborating arts blend together, disappear, and, in disappearing, somehow form a new world." Though his lifetime fell entirely within that of Beethoven, and he died two years before Schubert, Weber was one of the principal prophets of romanticism. With *Freischütz*, as well as with the later *Euryanthe* (1823) and *Oberon* (1826), Weber laid the foundations for the future Wagnerian music drama, just as his bravura piano pieces made him a significant precursor of Mendelssohn, Chopin, Schumann, and Liszt.

Robert Schumann's youthful enthusiasms, like those of Berlioz, were about equally divided between literature and music. And like Weber and Berlioz, he also turned to musical criticism as a means of furthering his views. The influence of the fanciful dreamworld of E. T. A. Hoffmann is felt in Schumann's *Phantasiestücke* (Fantasy Pieces, 1837), *Nachtstücke* (Night Pieces, 1839), and the *Kreisleriana* (1838), the titles and substance of which are taken directly from Hoffmann's imaginative short stories. The latter work, for instance, has to do with anecdotes about an eccentric conductor named Kreisler, a wild genius who was the literary prototype of the mad musician. Without exception Schumann's early published works up to his Opus 23 are written for piano. Like his fellow romanticists he placed inspiration first and foremost; and with the courage of his convictions, he stuck principally to smaller forms. These were, in the main, short lyrical fragments or character pieces that have a spontaneous freshness of approach associated with improvisations. For publication he grouped them into various series, but beneath their fancy-dress titles they bear some resemblance to the traditional keyboard dance suites. Only after 1840 did Schumann turn to larger forms that include the great song cycles, the Piano Quintet and Piano Concerto, as well as the four fine symphonies. (For an analysis of Schumann's song cycle, *Dichterliebe,* see Chap. 13, pp. 161–164.)

The *Carnaval* (1835) is a colorful combination of the old dance suite and a free adaptation of the variation principle. This "rogue's gallery" of romanticism contains the distilled essence of Schumann's early life—a life in which all experiences, friendships, literary ideas, feeling for his fellow artists, infatuations, and dreams are turned into a music full of Puckish humor and animated by romantic warmth. The organization of the whole structure is definitely subordinated to the parts, and the general impression is that of a collection of miniature scenes, fleeting glimpses, and kaleidoscopic shifts of color. Schumann added the somewhat enigmatic subtitle, "Little Scenes on Four Notes," and often referred to it in his letters as the "masked ball." It is indeed a masquerade, and as such it reveals the whimsical side of Schumann's nature as well as his love of indulging in little mysteries. It becomes, then, a kind of cult of romanticism in this case, full of secret allusions known to the initiated. Only after the eighth piece, and then as a kind of parenthesis in the score, does Schumann disclose the four-note figure on which his variations are built; and even here it is propounded in the form of a riddle entitled "Sphinxes." This touch is not unlike the eccentric practices of Schumann's literary idol, Jean Paul Richter, who once put a preface in the middle of one of his books.

The three "Sphinxes" read S–C–H–A, As–C–H, and A–S–C–H. Since S, in German nomenclature, is a pun on Es (E flat), As is A flat and H is B natural, the reference is to the notes of the scale that form the motive. The solution of the anagram is found in the fact that Schumann's lady love at this time lived in the small town of Asch, and the letters also happen to be the only musical ones in his surname, SCHumAnn. In the tenth number, "A.S.C.H.—S.C.H.A.," the letters join hands in a lively dance. As seen in the following examples, each piece is based on some constellation of this four-note motive, which is varied rhythmically and melodically to suit each instance.

Ex. 22:2 Excerpts from *Carnaval*. Schumann.

After the "Préambule"—a preamble or prelude that establishes the festive atmosphere—comes a series of scenes and portraits that are done with brief bold strokes and often with incisive psychological insight. Many are stock masquerade characters out of the Italian *commedia dell' arte* who conform to their prototypes. "Pierrot" (No. 2) is ever the ardent but awkward lover; "Harlequin" (No. 3), the gaudily dressed acrobatic clown; "Coquette" (No. 7), the frivolous, flirtatious, eternal feminine; and Pantalon, the jealous old husband, and the coquettish Columbine are en-

gaged in one of their incessant quarrels in No. 15. Schumann explains in
one of his letters that " 'Reconnaissance' (No. 14) is a scene of recognition,
'Aveu' (No. 17) an avowal of love; (and) 'Promenade,' a walk such as
one takes at a German ball with one's partner."

Concurrent with these general characterizations is a series of particular
portraits that reveal much about Schumann's world. "Valse Noble," a
title from Schubert who guided Schumann's music along the lines of instrumental lyricism, is apparently a portrait of the master whom Schumann admired so ardently. Schubert's short piano pieces—the *Moments
Musicaux,* Impromptus, and dances—were models not only for Schumann
himself, but for Mendelssohn, Chopin, and Liszt as well. One is also reminded that it was Schumann who was the discoverer of the "Great" C-
major Symphony of Schubert amid a pile of neglected manuscripts. "Eusebius" and "Florestan" (Nos. 5 and 6) are two of the pseudonyms under
which Schumann published his early works. In these obvious self-portraits
he reveals the two sides of his temperament, with the dreamy, reflective
Eusebius representing him as a quiet man of contemplation, and the bold,
aggressive Florestan as the vehement man of action. In the latter piece
there is a quotation from Schumann's highly original youthful work, the
Papillons, Op. 2. "Chiarina" is a piece with bravura and dash portraying
the young pianist, Clara Wieck, who was later to become his wife. The fluency and grace of Chopin's nocturne style are heard in No. 12, and one is
again reminded that Schumann was one of the first to hail that young composer in his famous critical review that began, "Hats off, gentlemen, a
genius!" "Estrella" (No. 13) was his affectionate name for his flame at the
time, Ernestine von Fricken, the lady who lived in Asch. In the midst of the
"Valse Allemande" (No. 16) there is an apparition of Paganini with all
the diabolical virtuosity of his fiddling. Schumann, it is recalled, became
the first composer to transcribe some of Paganini's caprices for the piano.

Just before the finale comes the "Pause" (No. 19), a hurried picture
with everyone frantically scurrying about and mounting the barricades
to do or die for the cause of romanticism. Then ensues the "March of the
'Davidsbündler' against the Philistines," the battle royal of Schumann's
self-declared war on the enemies of art. The ranks of the latter include the
purveyors of dry academic stereotypes, the upholders of outmoded traditions, as well as the smug middle-class conservatives who were the bulwark
of the mediocre and commonplace. The Davidsbündler, or David's League,
was a mythical society of romantic reformers banded together to fight
the Goliaths of Philistinism like David of old. Schumann quite freely acknowledged that it was "a purely abstract and romantic society" and a
figment of his own imagination. The officers of this ideal and progressive
"organization" included Berlioz, who was never informed of the honor ac-

corded him, and Beethoven, who had been dead nearly a decade. "In every time," remarked Schumann, "there reigns a secret league of kindred spirits. Tighten the circle, you who belong to it, in order that the truth in art may shine forth more and more brightly, everywhere spreading joy and peace." Schumann's critical articles sometimes assumed the form of minutes of this "society," and his review of a performance of Beethoven's Ninth Symphony began with Florestan climbing onto the piano and haranguing the group, "Assembled Davidsbündler, that is, youths and men who are to slay the Philistines, musical and otherwise, especially the big ones—." This "March of the 'Davidsbündler' " in the *Carnaval* has all the optimistic ring of a crusader's song, while the composer's contempt for the academic conservatives is contained in the "Grandfather's Dance," the traditional tune that closed wedding festivities and German balls.

THE RISE OF VIRTUOSITY: PAGANINI, LISZT, CHOPIN

The legendary violinistic career of Nicolò Paganini, as well as those of his pianistic counterparts Franz Liszt and Frédéric Chopin, is synonymous with the growth of a new audience for solo instrumental music, the emphasis on specialization in composition, as well as the romantic interest in individuality as expressed by a great virtuoso. Instead of composing and performing for an intelligent and discriminating minority, the romantic virtuoso had to take the wide variety of tastes of his new, enlarged audience into account. No longer was it possible to command admiration for subtle and intricate manipulations of a formal design; instead the composer and performer, in order to awaken an enthusiastic response, had to astonish and astound. The age of the universal composer at home in all media was over, and the era of the specialist had begun. Practically the entire creative output of Berlioz, for instance, was cast in the orchestral mold; that of Paganini, in the violinistic; Chopin, in the pianistic; and Wagner and Verdi wrote almost exclusively for the operatic medium.

Paganini's meteoric career became a symbol of musical virtuosity, just as he himself became a legend in his own lifetime. This traveling celebrity, matchless showman that he was, performed at concerts that drew vast crowds who were willing to pay fantastic admission fees to hear him. With his gaunt figure and feverishly burning eyes, he was thought, like Faust, to have sold his soul to the devil in return for his uncanny technical prowess. His prodigious violinistic feats included mysterious high harmonics (often with the addition of double and triple stopping), and a dancing bow that bounced nimbly off the strings. The sparks he ignited with his left-hand pizzicatos, as well as the playing of entire pieces on a single string, were all highly inventive effects that the majority of his listeners were experiencing for the first time. His astonishing virtuosity, however, captivated not only the crowds of curiosity seekers, but inspired the careers of his younger contemporaries as well. He received the unreserved admiration of Schubert, Rossini, and Berlioz; and Chopin once remarked, "Paganini is perfection." His Twenty-four Caprices, one of the few works he actually published, had wide influence. These short, polished technical and character studies had much to do with increasing the vogue for short aphoristic forms, and they undoubtedly influenced Chopin's corresponding sets of Twenty-four Etudes and Twenty-four Preludes, as well as the many Paganini transcriptions for piano by Schumann, Liszt, and others. The vitality of his melodic invention is likewise confirmed by the choice of one of his tunes for such great sets of variations as Brahms' *Twenty-eight Variations on a Theme of Paganini,* and Rachmaninoff's *Rhapsodie for Piano and Orchestra on a Theme of Paganini.*

Liszt's fabulous pianistic career followed in the path blazed by Paganini. With a trace of good-humored envy, Berlioz describes in his *Memoirs* a Liszt recital. After the grand entrance, he comments, "The silence speaks; the admiration is intense and profound . . . Then come the fiery shells, a veritable bouquet of grand fireworks, the acclamation of the public, flowers and wreaths showered upon the priest of harmony as he sits quivering on his tripod, beautiful young women kissing the hem of his garment with tears of sacred frenzy; the sincere homage of the serious, the feverish applause wrung from the envious, the intent faces, the narrow hearts amazed at their own expansiveness! And the next day the inspired young genius departs, leaving behind him a twilight of dazzling glory and enthusiasm. It is a dream; it is one of those golden dreams that come to one when one is named Liszt or Paganini."

Contrary to precedent, Liszt became the first pianist to present solo recitals. At that time, a concert always called for a wide variety of appearances and personages, including several singers, assorted instrumental soloists, as well as the presence of an orchestra. Liszt's programs, however, made up the deficiency by supplying Beethoven symphonies, songs by Schubert and others, whole opera scenes and operatic fantasies, musical travelogues such as his *Years of Pilgrimage (Années de Pélerinage)* and the *Album of a Voyager,* an art gallery with musical commentary on Raphael's *Marriage of the Madonna (Sposalizio)* and Michelangelo's statue of Lorenzo de' Medici (*Il Penseroso*) , as well as his latest literary musings (*Après une Lecture de Dante*) —all for piano alone. As one contemporary put it, "Liszt does not merely play piano; he tells, at the piano, the story of his own destiny, which is closely linked to, and reflects, the progress of our time . . . To him the piano becomes an approximate expression of his high mental cultivation, of his views, of his faith and being . . . how far inquiry has reached into the domain of science; how far speculation has fathomed musical thought; how it goes in the world of the intellect . . . Such a brain must be rated higher than a piano, and it is an accidental circumstance of no importance that Liszt plays the piano at all."

As with Paganini, there was indeed a seriousness of purpose behind the external glitter, and Liszt envisioned himself as a modern incarnation of Orpheus and as a high priest of harmony (he later took the Holy Orders of Roman Catholic priesthood). His own literary programme for the symphonic poem, *Orpheus,* has an authentic autobiographical ring: "Men's brutal instincts are silenced; the very stones are softened; hearts, harder perhaps than the stones, are melted to burning, but grudging, tears; the singing birds, the murmuring waterfalls, suspend their melodies; laughter and pleasure are hushed at these sweet sounds, which reveal to humanity the beneficent power of Art; its glory and civilizing influence . . ."

Chopin, in contrast to Paganini and Liszt, played in public rather rarely, and then only to the select few in the elegant salons of Parisian society. He consequently had more time for composition, and his creative work proves the truth of Goethe's observation that a master reveals himself through his limitations. Except for a few early songs and several chamber compositions, everything he wrote was for the piano. His complete works, moreover, occupy no five-foot shelf; on the contrary, they are small in number, compact in size, fine-grained in texture, lustrous in their polish, and masterly in their workmanship. Unlike so many of his more vocal colleagues, he makes no fetish about formal freedom; instead, he quietly achieved a fluidity of form without sacrificing the clarity of his designs.

In his scherzos, for instance, Chopin adopts the form that Haydn and Beethoven had evolved out of the old minuet and trio, but while his predecessors had surrounded it with the cyclical sequence of sonata movements, Chopin lets it stand alone. The essential dance character and minuet-and-trio form are still present, but they appear in the costume of a romantic masquerade. The "choreography" is now that of the *danse macabre,* the form a flexible A-B-A-Coda affair, and the humor colored by more than a trace of romantic irony. The Scherzo in C-sharp Minor, Op. 39, for example, was written during the composer's winter journey of 1838 to the Mediterranean island of Majorca. The moods that he incorporated in it are, perhaps, revealed by his letters of the time. "Tomorrow," he wrote, "I go to that wonderful [abandoned] monastery of Valdemosa, to write in the cell of some old monk, who perhaps had more fire in his soul than I, and stifled and extinguished it, because he had it in vain." His cell, he commented, was in "the shape of a tall coffin," and his view overlooked "the most poetic of cemeteries" and a ruined crusaders' church. The stage, in other words, was all set for a scherzo of the ironic type. First a challenging chromatic introduction ushers in a wild, whirling-dervish macabre dance in the traditional triple meter. As it subsides, a trio section in the style of a chorale ensues, in which a procession of melancholy dark chords is illuminated by mysterious moonbeams of pianistic figurations. The macabre dance resumes to round out the design and leads up to the free fantasia of an extended coda. The idea of a diabolical dance in sacred surroundings, of course, was a favorite romantic device dating from the shock tactics of Berlioz' parody on the Gregorian funeral sequence, the *Dies irae* (Day of Wrath) , and the scandal of Meyerbeer's ballet of nuns in his opera, *Robert the Devil*. After the solemnity of the chorale, Chopin indicates in the score that his finale is to be played "with fire" (*con fuoco*) ; and the sulfurous smoke of the fire-and-brimstone passages leaves none in doubt as to its location in the hereafter.

It can hardly be considered accidental that most of the major as well as the minor romantic composers were pianists. Weber, Mendelssohn, Chopin, Liszt, and Schumann (through his wife, Clara Wieck) all reached their audiences more readily through piano recitals and the circulation of their printed pieces than did composers such as Berlioz and Wagner who tried for weary years to storm the bastions of the more conservative opera houses. Besides providing a more immediate prospect for getting their works heard, the piano was a new instrument with a still-unexplored spectrum of tone color. It was, furthermore, completely under the control of one individual and therefore ideal for subjective self-expression, intimate soliloquies, and autobiographical confessions.

LISZT AND THE SYMPHONIC POEM

Programme music—the attempt to intensify music with some of the power of the other arts such as drama, poetry, painting, and the like—found its most articulate spokesman in Franz Liszt. Though its basic principles had been worked out long before and many shining examples had been written before his time, it was in Liszt's comments and orchestral compositions that programme music first became an unabashed, self-conscious, stylistic reality. It was he who first coined the term "symphonic poem" to signify the mystical marriage of orchestral music to a poetic idea. Later the name was modified by others to "tone poem" to imply that any instrumental combination could harvest the fruits of this process of hybridization. "The programme," as Liszt pointed out, "has no other object than to indicate preparatively the spiritual moments which impelled the composer to create his work, the thoughts which he endeavored to incorporate in it."

Liszt's stated objective was thus to infuse music more and more with poetry so as to preserve its circulatory system from a hardening of its formal arteries—a mortal danger he professed to see in composition as it was taught by the academicians in conservatories. He well knew that in music's state of classical health, the design of a sonata was extremely flexible. So he took violent issue to the formulation of a set of "Express rules, which are considered inviolable, although the composers who originated them had no other precept for them than their own imagination, and themselves made the formal dispositions which people wish now to set up as a law. In programme music, on the other hand, the return, change, modification, and modulation of the motives are conditioned by their relation to a poetic idea." His principal quarrel with the purists of his time is contained in his statement that, "All exclusively musical considerations, though they should not be neglected, have to be subordinated to the action of the given subject. Consequently, action and subject of this kind of a symphony demand a higher interest than the technical treatment of the musical material . . ." As such, Liszt's innovations represent a tempering of the cold logic of technique with some warmth of human feeling, as well as a revolt against formal stereotypes.

Far from disregarding formal procedures, Liszt's method was based on a specialized application of developmental principles as worked out in the sonatas of the Viennese composers from Haydn and Mozart to Beethoven and Schubert. In a very free way, the exposition-development-recapitulation plan of a sonata design is still discernible in his symphonic poems. All verbatim repetition, however, is studiously avoided in favor of free variation and continuous development from beginning to end. Since the external outline and the internal arrangement of parts may be adjusted in each case to suit the dramatic necessity of the subject in hand, the symphonic poem can be considered a type rather than a form. The only thing that all symphonic poems have in common is that they are continuous rather than divided into separate movements as with the sonata or symphony, and that they are based on a central motive.

This motivic writing was essentially the same process that the classical composers had considered to be one of the more important devices in the craft of composition. In the nineteenth century, however, it began to acquire a host of different names. To Berlioz it was the "fixed idea," to Wager the *leitmotif* or "leading motive"; and Liszt, with one of his characteristic rhetorical flourishes, calls it the *metamorphosis of themes,* or *theme transformation.* All, however, are essentially the same process, if allowances are made for the personal idioms of the respective composers and the various usages they made of it. This metamorphosis, or growth principle, permeated much of the scientific as well as esthetic thought of the period. To paraphrase a poem of Goethe called the *Metamorphosis of Plants* (1789) : observe how the plant, little by little progressing, step by step guided on, changes to blossom and fruit; first the seed unfolds itself as soon as the fruitful womb of the earth releases it; simply slumbers the force of the seed, a germ of the future; upward then it strives, trusting in gentle moisture; and, from the night wherein it dwelt, straightway ascends to the light. The motive, then, in this natural history of composition, is the thematic germ cell containing within itself all the embryonic potentialities of future growth. Each musical seed unfolds differently according to the individual laws of its genus and species, yet each follows in its own way the laws of external harmony.

Liszt's method is perhaps best exemplified in his well-known symphonic poem *Les Preludes,* for which he provided a programmatic point of departure adapted from the poetry of Lamartine. "What is life," the poem asks, "but a series of preludes to that unknown song whose first solemn note is sounded by Death?" The basic motive, contained in the first three notes (Ex. 22.3*a*) , thus poses the question of the meaning of life with the ascending interval of the fourth; and the remainder of the first section, Andante maestoso (Ex. 22:3*b*) , continues with some of the implications and consequences of the motive. "The blissful dawn of every life is heralded by love," continues the programme, and appropriately enough the second section dissolves into the amorous duet of Example 22:3*c* (observe that the asterisked notes add up to a transformed version of the motive) . Next, a storm, Allegro tempestuoso, interrupts "with a deadly blast that dispels youth's illusions" (Exs. 22:3*d* and *e*) . This is followed by an Allegretto pastorale interlude (Ex. 22:3*f*) , in which the rustic oboe sounds the motive and recalls "the memories of the pleasant calm of rural life." Yet man should not linger too long "in the idyllic lap of Nature, but must hasten to his post when the trumpet sounds the warning," and an Allegro marziale then begins on a warlike note (Ex. 22:3*g*) . The final section now functions like a symphonic recapitulation, and the various mutations of the motive yield to its triumphant restatement by the full orchestra, signifying that man has achieved victory over all the adversities of fate.

In a symphonic poem, then, the motive is the vital unit which lends itself to repetition and variation and which begs for adventure. After its initial presentation all the subsequent themes and melodic entities must be derived directly from this motive or be closely related to it. Each reappearance is marked by thematic alterations—variants, melodic elaboration,

Ex. 22:3 Excerpts from *Les Preludes*. Liszt.

harmonic and contrapuntal contrasts, and the like—according to the exigencies of the dramatic circumstances. The motive is thus the unifying force while the surrounding series of episodes provides the variety.

Curiously enough, after this first flush of formal freedom had time to wear off, composers returned with fanfares and flourishes to the pre-established forms. In the early part of the nineteenth century no self-respecting romantic composer would have dreamed of writing an obvious rondo or theme and variations. Yet Richard Strauss gave just such subtitles to his tone poems of 1895 and 1897—*Till Eulenspiegel's Merry Pranks, after the old roguish manner, in rondo form;* and *Don Quixote, fantastic variations on a theme of knightly character.* Gustav Mahler, for his part, wrote weighty philosophical discourses for orchestra, bundled several of these metaphysical tone poems together into a single cyclical package, and called them symphonies once again.

NATIONALISM

Another of the characteristic expressions of the romantic era was the rise of *nationalism*. Like programme music, nationalism as such was by no means new to the nineteenth century. Regional differences and ethnic attitudes can be detected in all historical periods; the important thing, however, is the particular form it assumes at this time. The liberating force generated by the French Revolution continued in the wake of the Napoleonic wars and led to the desire on the part of ethnic groups for national self-determination. Its political expression can be seen in the series of popular struggles within various countries to throw off the tyrant's yoke, and its artistic counterpart is found in the efforts of the people to free themselves from foreign influences and importations that hitherto had dominated their cultural life. Men of letters, artists, and composers were often in the intellectual vanguard of such movements, and the increased interest in folklore, ballads of the people, national epics, and local color provided a powerful stimulus. In music it meant an awakening to the beauty of folk songs and dances and their possible use in art music, as well as the encouragement of native composers.

Nationalism likewise applied to the seeking out of indigenous sources for a flourishing national art and listening for "the voice of the people." As Dvořák once wrote, "When a musician takes a walk, he should listen to every whistling boy, every street singer, or blind organ grinder. I myself am often so fascinated by these people that I can scarcely tear myself away, for every now and then I catch a strain or hear the fragments of a recurring melodic theme that sound like the voice of the people. These things are worth preserving, and no one should be above making a lavish use of all such suggestions. It is a sign of barrenness, indeed, when such characteristic bits of music exist and are not heeded by the learned musicians of the age."

The nationalistic movement in the nineteenth century, as generally understood, applied principally to the Continental countries previously outside the main centers—Hungary, Bohemia (Czechoslovakia), the Scandinavian countries, and Russia. In Italy, France, Germany, and Austria, on the other hand, there had been a continuous musical tradition for centuries; and while the operas of Weber, Berlioz, Verdi, and Wagner admittedly had nationalistic overtones, the fact was a minor manifestation within a major movement. Hitherto, however, there had been no self-conscious body of music and musicians specifically bearing a Hungarian, Bohemian, Scandinavian, or Russian label. Liszt thus began writing Hungarian rhapsodies, and his twentieth-century successors—Bartók and Kodály—still continued in his footsteps. Poland was handsomely represented by Chopin's polonaises and mazurkas; Bohemia by such works as Smetana's opera *The Bartered Bride* (1866), his collection of six symphonic poems *My Country* including *The Moldau* (1874), and Dvořák's *Slavonic Dances;* Norway by Grieg's incidental music to Ibsen's drama, *Peer Gynt,* and other works; England by the music of Sterndale Bennett, Edward Elgar, and more recently by Vaughan Williams; America by Edward MacDowell and Charles Ives; and Finland by Sibelius' tone poems and symphonies, which will be discussed in the following chapter.

The most noisy of all the nationalistic movements was probably that of the Russian "Five," who broke with the international Italian, French, and German opera tradition and set out to establish a specifically Russian school of thought. Michail Glinka had shown them the way with his operas, *A Life for the Tsar* (1836) and *Russlan and Ludmilla* (1842), the latter based on a play by Alexander Pushkin. "The Five"—Mili Balakirev, César Cui, Alexander Borodin, Modeste Moussorgsky, and Nicholas Rimsky-Korsakoff—were, with the exception of the latter, self-taught amateurs who made up for their lack of technical equipment by the freshness and vitality of their ideas. Borodin's *Prince Igor* (1869) and Moussorgsky's *Boris Godounov* (1874) certainly rank as operatic achievements of the first magnitude; and as such, they transcend their narrower nationalistic implications and are now accepted as masterpieces in the international repertory. (See Chap. 17, pp. 224–226, Pictures at an Exhibition; "Promenade" Chap. 3, p. 39; "Bydlo" Chap. 3, p. 42).

In contrast to "The Five," Tchaikovsky, as well as his successors Glazunov, Scriabin, and Rachmaninoff, stood apart by adhering to the international tradition, though they did not hesitate to utilize folk material when it fitted into their operatic or symphonic designs. The music of the nationalists is far too diversified for a detailed or even generalized discussion at this point. It invites exploration, however, by the listener with an ear for exotic melody, an eye for local color, and an interest in ethnic influences.

ITALIAN OPERA: VERDI

From his first-produced opera of 1839 to his *Falstaff* of 1892, the incredibly creative career of Giuseppe Verdi spanned a full and active fifty-three years.[1] As the logical successor to Rossini and Bellini, he quickly established himself as the principal exponent of Italian opera in the nineteenth century, and no serious challenges appeared on the horizon to contest the pre-eminence of his position. His operas, however, inevitably invoked comparison with those of his exact contemporary on the other side of the Alps, Richard Wagner. When questioned, for instance, about the contrast between his sunny music with that of his darkly brooding northern colleague, he replied, "Do you think that under these skies I could have composed *Tristan* or the *Ring?*" Unlike Wagner, it would never have occurred to him to write abstruse philosophical essays or indulge in abstract esthetic speculation. "Not theory but music" was always his self-declared motto.

Verdi was also little concerned with nature as such, and musical landscapes like Wagner's "Forest Murmurs" and "Siegfried's Rhine Journey" held little interest for him. As a Latin humanist, he always put human

[1] The principal works in between were: *Ernani*, 1844 (after V. Hugo); *Luisa Miller*, 1849 (after Schiller); *Rigoletto*, 1851 (after V. Hugo); *Il Trovatore*, 1853 (after Lope de Vega); *La Traviata*, 1853 (after A. Dumas, Jr.); *Masked Ball*, 1859 (after E. Scribe); *Aïda*, 1871 (Ghislanzoni); *Requiem*, 1874 (oratorio on Mass for the Dead); *Don Carlo* (revised version), 1884 (after Schiller); and *Otello*, 1887 (after Shakespeare).

nature first and foremost, and in his operas it carries all before it. Since he always deals in basic human types rather than metaphysical personifications, his characters react to their dramatic conflicts with such basic emotions as love and hatred, rage and repentance, rather than with philosophical discourses and high-flown histrionics. His heroines, moreover, die of accidental or natural causes rather than mysterious love deaths or heroic self-immolations on funeral pyres. Verdi, good Italian that he was, instinctively felt that the material of opera should be human voices, not musical instruments; and in answer to Wagner's operatic symphonic poems, he disarmingly observed, "Opera is opera, symphony is symphony." The Wagnerians, of course, likened Verdi's orchestra to a gigantic guitar, but it is much more articulate and it contains more musical substance than his critics cared to admit. With Verdi the orchestra, to be sure, plays a supporting role, and the vocal lines invariably carry the dramatic weight.

La Traviata (1853) will serve as an illustration of Verdi's operatic procedures. It was one of the first operas on a contemporary subject (thus anticipating Bizet's Carmen of 1875 with its realistic subject matter by almost a quarter century), and its setting and passions were neither historical nor heroic in the usual sense. Violetta, the heroine who, as the title delicately suggests, has "lost her way," was a well-known figure of the Paris demimonde who had died but five years before the younger Alexandre Dumas wrote his novel and play Camille (La Dame aux Camélias) on which it was based. It was, in effect, a domestic tragedy involving the conflict between middle-class morality and free love; and, as such, it was not far removed from a moral tract on the sanctity of the home and family life. Alfredo's father, Germont, for instance, describes his son's romance with Violetta by saying, "This is passion in its most terrestrial and human form," in contrast with the sterner truth that marriages, presumably, are made in heaven. Inevitably, the woman with a past must yield to the woman with a future in holy wedlock. Verdi, however, sees only the poignant human situations, and the moralistic platitudes are taken in stride.

The Prelude to Act I of La Traviata, which serves Verdi in lieu of an overture, is a lyrical evocation that introduces the various themes that are to be associated with Violetta and her love for Alfredo. Some high pianissimo chords, sounded by the divided strings, cast a long tragic shadow and lead to the full, shapely, descending line that reveals the tender side of Violetta's nature—that of a lonely spirit longing for true love (Ex. 22:4a). Her more worldly and frivolous attitude is reflected in the succeeding passage in which the melody of her inner self is now complemented by a rising staccato counterpoint (Ex. 22:4b) —a bubbling, champagnelike obbligato that hints at the gay drinking song soon to follow. After Alfredo's declaration in Act I, she wonders, in two arias that reflect her mercurial changes of mood, whether it is possible to surrender to true love (*Ah, fors'è lui*) or whether she should whirl her life away in gay waltzes (*Sempre libera*). When she overhears Alfredo singing under her balcony window, the insistent throbbing melody now acquires a counterpoint of rising and descending scales, revealing her mounting emotional conflict (Ex. 22:4*c*). The Prelude to Act III is complementary to that of Act I, but completely contrasting in spirit. A variant of the warm, ardent opening phrase (Ex. 22:4*a*) is now broken up into short, panting fragments that hint of her mortal illness and foreshadow the inevitable tragic conclusion (Ex. 22:4*d*). Verdi with his true Latin temperament is seen here lavishing the utmost care on one of his heroines, who are usually much more complicated characters than his heroes. The way in which he portrays human character through such manipulations of his melodic lines is truly one of the major miracles of music.

Ex. 22:4 Themes from *La Traviata*. Verdi.

THE ROMANTIC SYNTHESIS: WAGNER; BRAHMS

Richard Wagner's art matured later than that of his more precocious contemporaries, and from this perspective he could survey the entire romantic scene.[1] His restless searching eye and acute critical faculties

[1] See Chap. 1, p. 7, Prelude to *Das Rheingold*; Chap. 4, pp. 50–51, Prelude to *Lohengrin*.

told him that in spite of the many inspired ideas and magnificent moments the romanticists had provided to date, none as yet had led to permanent public acceptance. Music-making such as Schubert's was, for Wagner, on much too small a scale, even though his union of romantic poetry, vocal melody, and instrumental collaboration in the lied contained a germ of artistic truth. Beethoven's only opera, *Fidelio,* for all its great music and clear-cut social message, had enjoyed only a success of esteem. Its dramatic overtures, as well as those to the plays *Egmont* and *Coriolanus,* however, were orchestral poetry of the highest dramatic intensity, and Beethoven seemed to be on the right track when he brought vocal soloists and a chorus into his heroic Ninth Symphony. Weber had made a brave beginning toward establishing a national German opera, but his librettos lacked focus and he was still too close to the idioms of Italian opera for comfort. Nevertheless Weber's *Euryanthe* would be usable material for *Lohengrin.* Berlioz had been a noble failure, but his original experiments in hybridizing the drama, symphony, and opera could prove very useful; and the themes and erotic atmosphere of Berlioz' *Romeo and Juliet* could be expanded for *Tristan and Isolde.* Schumann's secret-society romanticism, with its hidden meanings revealed only to the initiated, was, perhaps, too refined and obscure, but the cult idea had for Wagner a certain attraction. The success of Paganini and Liszt as performers had certainly been sensational enough, but personal virtuosity was a highly perishable commodity. Liszt's programmatic principles and symphonic poems, however, seemed sound enough. Chopin's urbane salon style was, in Wagner's opinion, too restricted, but his chromatic harmony might be good grist for the Wagnerian mill. Peering backward into history, the dramatic sweep of Shakespeare and the colossal-baroque qualities of Handel also did not escape his notice. No one approach in Wagner's view, however, was sufficiently successful in itself, yet all contained enough vital elements to assure success if carefully selected, blended, and combined by him in the proper proportions. The production of those complete works of art, to be known as music dramas, was thus Wagner's calling as he saw it; and he set forth on his esthetic mission with religious fervor and messianic dedication.

This self-declared musico-dramatic successor to Shakespeare and Beethoven brought forth in turn *Rienzi, Last of the Tribunes* (1840) —an operatic adaptation of Bulwer-Lytton's historical novel—and *The Flying Dutchman* (1842) , based on a poetic ballad by Heinrich Heine. From this point onward, however, Wagner was to be his own poet and playwright, as well as composer and producer. *Tannhäuser* (1845) began the procession of national pageants founded on the lives of historical figures, and its hero was a medieval minnesinger, just as the hero of *Die Meistersinger von Nürnberg* (The Mastersingers of Nuremberg, 1867) was to be the Renaissance cobbler poet, Hans Sachs. Both the early *Lohengrin* (1848) and the late *Parsifal* (1882) have the quasi-religious tone of medieval miracle plays. The *Ring of the Nibelung* (1853–74) is derived from the early Germanic pagan epic, the *Nibelungenlied;* and *Tristan and Isolde* (1859) stems from an old Arthurian romance.

Wagner's mature music dramas are closer to the symphonic idea than they are to Italian operatic conventions. The principal lyrical element is transferred to the orchestra, and the general effect is that of a vast symphonic poem, with visualized stage spectacle and a verbalized as well as vocalized running commentary on the orchestral action by the singers. Since the music runs on in an unbroken continuity, arias and recitatives effectively disappear as such, and only rarely is a self-contained aria introduced. The orchestra alone can maintain such unbroken continuity, and much of the superstition about the "unvocal" character of Wagner's voice writing derives from a rather elementary misconception of the relationship of the voice parts to this continuous orchestral flow. The vocal line must necessarily grow out of this symphonic core or else be superimposed upon it, but it decidedly does not entail a voice part that is either subservient or unvocal. It does mean, however, that the singer must project within the context of a continuous musical development which began, perhaps, before he arrived on stage, and which may well continue after he has, in operatic parlance, "sung his say" and gone. He may not have a "number" to sing, but he has his fairly allotted time share of the drama.

In lieu of aria, recitative, or ensemble numbers, then, the essential convention in Wagnerian music drama is the *leading motive,* or *leitmotif.* These short aphoristic fragments may vary in length from a motive to a melody, and are designed to characterize individuals, aspects of personality, abstract ideas, the singular properties of inanimate objects, and the like. The entities that can be so characterized are limited only by the composer's ability to conceive convincingly appropriate motives. Wagner is astoundingly skillful in his ability to create such musical-dramatic characterizations. The forthright ringing sound of the leading motive for the invincible sword in the *Ring* cycle, for example, has a martial snap, buglelike melodic intervals, as well as the sharp, gleaming tone quality of the trumpet, all of which help to convey the image (Ex. 22:5*a*). Contrast it now

Ex. 22:5   Motives from the *Ring* Cycle. Wagner. (*a*) The Sword Motive.

with the strange, mysterious harmonies that signify the helmet of invisibility (Ex. 22:5*b*). Or compare Siegfried as the healthy young hero (Ex.

Ex. 22:5b   Helmet of Invisibility Motive.

22:5c) with Isolde's memory of Tristan, ill from a wound sustained in

Ex. 22:5c   Siegfried Motive.

combat as well as sick within his soul (Ex. 22:6).

Ex. 22:6   Excerpt from *Tristan and Isolde*. Wagner.

These motives, moreover, are by no means static entities, and they undergo a constant symphonic development. The gay 9/8 time of Siegfried's jaunty horn call (Ex. 22:7a) portrays the buoyant mood of the youthful hunter. But when this child of nature reaches mature manhood, the rhythm is transformed into that of a march with incisive off-beat accents (Ex. 22:7b). Finally, when Siegfried attains his true heroic stature, the same theme is amplified by full harmonies and reinforced by the whole brass choir and rolling drums (Ex. 22:7c).

Ex. 22:7   Siegfried's Horn Call Motive from the *Ring* Cycle. Wagner.

With a fairly large number of such motives to work with, the role of the orchestra as a participant in the drama is vastly enlarged. Furthermore, a motive sounded in the orchestra can recall an earlier event and clarify the root motivation behind a given action on the stage. In a tetralogy such as the *Ring*, which takes four evenings to complete, events of the first night (*Das Rheingold*) can be so recalled in the subsequent installments. Similarly, the orchestra can anticipate the future for the listener. At the end of the second evening (*Die Walküre*), for instance, when Wotan puts Brünnhilde to sleep on a mountain ringed with magic fire and the promise that only an intrepid and fearless mortal will awaken and claim her, the orchestra first announces (and then Wotan takes it up) the motive subsequently to be associated with Siegfried as hero. Actually, at this point in the drama he is not yet born, but in the fatalistic predestination of mythology the prediction can safely be made. The orchestra, moreover, can interpret for us states of mind not yet explicit in overt action on stage. Thus when Siegmund and Sieglinde meet (Act I of *Die Walküre*) the orchestra makes clear that they are falling in love, though from their conversation they themselves are not yet entirely aware of it. And finally the leading-motive system proves its efficacy at the end of the cycle in *Götterdämmerung* (Twilight of the Gods). In Act III, when the mortally wounded Siegfried recalls his past and in the subsequent orchestral funeral oration, all the motives previously associated with him pass by in biographical review: fate; his mother, Sieglinde; the heroism of his paternal ancestors, the Wälsungs; the sword; Siegfried's own theme; Siegfried as hero; and finally the women in his life, Brünnhilde and Gutrune. Such a procedure thus lends itself to biography in music and at the same time summarizes the entire dramatic cycle.

In Wagner all the intellectual trends, all the technical devices, and all the emotional directions of romanticism meet and merge. In addition to summing up the past and synthesizing the nineteenth-century motivic system of writing, Wagner, in the score of *Tristan and Isolde,* pushed the frontiers of Western harmony to its outermost limits. This sensuous seductive chromaticism, with its tangled web of motives, never-ending chains of chordal progressions, and complex continuous counterpoints carried right through to the ecstasy of its rapturous conclusion, was destined to have profound effects on the future course of music. Recognizing the essential symphonic core of Wagner's writing, many of the post-Wagnerian composers subsequently dispensed with the stage business altogether and wrote their dramatic music in other mediums. Bruckner, Mahler, and the early Richard Strauss, for instance, translated the Wagnerian idioms into the symphonic poem and programme symphony; César Franck and Max Reger into organ and orchestral works; Hugo Wolf into his "songs for voice and piano"; and Arnold Schoenberg into programme chamber music such as his *Verklärte Nacht* (Transfigured Night) and orchestral song cycles such as his *Gurrelieder* (Songs of Gurre) .

Johannes Brahms,[1] Wagner's junior by some twenty years, had a still higher vantage point from which to view the strengths and weaknesses of his century. Starting his artistic life as an ardent romanticist, and hailed as such by Robert Schumann, he later steered a more conservative middle course between the academic formalism of Spohr and Mendelssohn [2] on one side, and the romantic emotionalism of Schubert and Schumann on the other. From this position he could admire the inspired lyricism of his romantic elders, and at the same time see that there were serious lapses in their technical craftsmanship. He also recognized that spontaneous lyricism was not solid enough ground on which to base large symphonic edifices. Even Wagner, he felt, had failed because he tried to build his monumental music dramas out of those miniature scraps of material known as leading motives. After a thoroughgoing study of his classical Viennese forebears—Haydn, Mozart, Beethoven, and Schubert—he built his safe-and-sane style on a return to formal construction. He also tried to escape the limitations of the pianistic, orchestral, and operatic specialists by returning to the spirit of universalism he saw in music's state of classical health. In his collected works, therefore, one encounters piano music and songs; chamber music for all combinations, from duos to sextets; concertos, orchestral overtures, serenades, and symphonies; as well as a wealth of choral music. Even the modest genre of house music for amateur performers, as evidenced in his sets of waltzes and *Hungarian Dances* for piano duet, was not neglected. Only the opera, in spite of his many projected and rejected plans, was left untouched.

One aspect of his century, however, Brahms could never escape—the conviction that somehow the composers of the past had soared to greater heights than could be attained by those of the present. Many of his most significant works show that he delved deep into the historic past. One hears the influence of Schütz, for instance, at some places in his *German Requiem,* and that of Handel (the large pedal-point choral fugue at the end of the third number) in others. His Double Concerto for Violin, Cello, and Orchestra harks back to the old concerto grosso, while the Fourth Symphony concludes with a solid set of structural variations in the manner of baroque chaconnes and passacaglias. The great shadow of Beethoven fell on Brahms as it did on the whole century, and set all its composers to wondering who among them would write the "Tenth Symphony." Brahms thus remained a lonely and somewhat anachronistic figure, darkened by the shadow of the past, and his overenthusiastic critical champions prob-

---

[1] See Chap. 3, pages 43–44, *German Requiem.*
[2] See Chap. 15, pages 199–203 for a discussion of Mendelssohn's oratorio, *Elijah.*

Fig. 22:1   Delacroix. *Dante and Vergil in Hell*. This painting, done in 1822 in Paris, anticipates the Berlioz *Symphonie Fantastique* and Liszt's *Dante* Symphony.

ably hampered more than they enhanced his career by mistakenly coupling his name with those of Bach and Beethoven. Brahms, however, did succeed in breathing new life into the older forms; and just as Wagner leads to the harmonic and tonality crisis of the twentieth century, Brahms laid the foundation for the neoclassical return to formal constructive methods.

Gabriel Fauré	1845–1924	Enrique Granados	1867–1916
Charles Widor	1845–1937	Umberto Giordano	1867–1948
Henri Duparc	1848–1933	Max von Schillings	1868–1933
Vincent d'Indy	1851–1931	Granville Bantock	1868–1946
André Messager	1853–1929	Albert Roussel	1869–1937
Arthur Foote	1853–1937	Hans Pfitzner	1869–1949
Leoš Janáček	1854–1928	Franz Lehár	1870–1948
George Chadwick	1854–1931	Florent Schmitt	1870–
Anatol Liadov	1855–1914	Henry Hadley	1871–1937
Sergei Taneyev	1856–1915	Frederick Converse	1871–1940
Edward Elgar	1857–1934	Alexander Scriabin	1872–1915
Ruggiero Leoncavallo	1858–1919	Ralph Vaughan Williams	1872–
Giacomo Puccini	1858–1924	Max Reger	1873–1916
Mikhail Ippolitov-Ivanov	1859–1935	Sergei Rachmaninoff	1873–1943
Hugo Wolf	1860–1903	Daniel Gregory Mason	1873–1953
Isaac Albéniz	1860–1909	Jean Roger-Ducasse	1873–1954
Gustav Mahler	1860–1911	Gustav Holst	1874–1934
Ignace J. Paderewski	1860–1941	Josef Suk	1874–1935
Gustave Charpentier	1860–1956	Arnold Schoenberg	1874–1951
Edward MacDowell	1861–1908	Charles Ives	1874–1954
Charles M. Loeffler	1861–1935	Samuel Coleridge-Taylor	1875–1912
Claude Debussy	1862–1918	Maurice Ravel	1875–1937
Frederick Delius	1862–1934	Reynaldo Hahn	1875–1947
Gabriel Pierné	1863–1937	Italo Montemezzi	1875–1952
Pietro Mascagni	1863–1945	Reinhold Glière	1875–1956
Eugen D'Albert	1864–1932	Manuel de Falla	1876–1946
Richard Strauss	1864–1949	Ermanno Wolf-Ferrari	1876–1948
Alexander Grechaninov	1864–1956	John Alden Carpenter	1876–1951
Carl Nielsen	1865–1931	Carl Ruggles	1876–
Paul Dukas	1865–1935	Ernst Dohnányi	1877–
Alexander Glazunov	1865–1936	Franz Schreker	1878–1934
Jean Sibelius	1865–1957	Ottorino Respighi	1879–1936
Ferruccio Busoni	1866–1924	John Ireland	1879–
Erik Satie	1866–1925	Cyril Scott	1879–
Francesco Cilea	1866–1950	Nicolai Medtner	1880–1951

Contemporary Styles I

Chapter 23

T IME is an artist whose theme is history, an illusionist whose deep perspective shrinks all but a few to a common dimension, a painter whose broad brush strokes blur a thousand disagreements into a calm tonality of things past. As the music of any era—present or past—recedes in time, a vast leveling process begins to resolve the dissonant clashing of its ultra-individualistic personalities. Decade by decade, the passing of time tends to place in perspective, and seemingly to unify in a common cultural context, the sharp divergence of ideas that characterize the music of a period. It is customary to express this apparent unity in the music around 1900 by referring to its mutual and immediate inheritance. In this view, Puccini, Mahler, Debussy, Strauss, and Sibelius are all "late romantics." It is equally usual to read history backwards, and by referring to these composers as "premoderns," to unify their accomplishment as a preparation and a background for the self-consciously "modern" phase of twentieth-century music that followed.

Although the interval between the death of Mahler (1911) and the death of Sibelius (1957) is very nearly a half century, the eldest in this group (Puccini, b. 1858) was the senior of the youngest (Sibelius, b. 1865) by only seven years. By the turn of the century each had already achieved a distinctive style, and each had already earned the right to be regarded as a major figure. What unites them is not only an approximate simultaneity of their coming to maturity, but curiously, the diversity of their origins. For each composer was deeply rooted in his own national tradition, and each achieved definition of himself as an artist in settling accounts with his own inheritance. A curious compatibility underscores the disunion of this generation. It derives, among other things, from the fact that Puccini fell heir to Italian opera through Verdi, just as Richard Strauss inherited the German tradition through Wagner; that Mahler, though born in Bohemia, was as inveterately Viennese as Debussy was Parisian; and that, in music at least, Finland and Sibelius are synonymous.

THE NATIONAL IDEA: SIBELIUS

With Jean Sibelius the national music of Finland came of age. It is no small tribute to his personal genius that both at home and abroad the national style should be so exclusively identified with his name. And this despite the self-evident fact that no man unaided can invent or discover the musical consciousness of his country. Yet apart from perhaps Kajanus, his forerunners (like Von Schantz, Collan, and Ingelius) are unknown abroad and scarcely remembered in the concert halls of their own country. Upon the specifics of Sibelius' musical style their influence was indeed negligible, but as a result of their labors, young Sibelius fell heir to an audience conditioned to the "national idea" in music, and eager to applaud signs of exceptional talent in this direction. His apprentice work was watched with interest, and his emergence as a national composer greeted with enthusiasm.

One may date this emergence with the *Kullervo* Symphony completed in the spring of 1892. This was a vast work for orchestra, chorus, and soloists, based upon several cantos in the repository of national folk legend known as the *Kalevala*. Its first performance was received with a storm of enthusiasm which Nils-Eric Ringbom (a recent biographer) feels may in part "be laid to the national awakening and the patriotism generated by other causes." The "other causes" were a series of distasteful measures taken by Russian Imperial authority during the 1890's—from the Russification of the Finnish postal and monetary system early in the decade (1890), to military conscription, and attacks upon the press toward the decade's close. In short, Sibelius emerged as a "national" composer during the very decade when national feeling was growing more stubborn and more fervent.

Two familiar works from the close of this decade are *Finlandia* and his Symphony No. 1 in E Minor. The Symphony engaged him during the autumn and the winter of 1898–99 and *Finlandia* was composed in 1899. They are companion pieces not because they resemble each other (for really they do not), but because, taken together, they delineate a man who was a Finnish nationalist and simultaneously an individualist. And this lack of contradiction between the two goes to the heart of all his music. *Finlandia* was a piece written to emphasize a patriotic occasion. During 1899, a freedom of the press campaign developed in Finland in response to a series of restrictive measures which Russian Imperial authority sought to impose upon Finnish and Swedish newspapers. A number of patriotic theater benefits were arranged to raise both financial assistance and moral support. To one such theater benefit Sibelius contributed a rather hastily contrived musical accompaniment for a series of tableaux illustrating the glories of Finland's past. The following year (1900) he extracted and revised a section of it, which he titled *Finlandia*. Intended as a piece of exhilarating, popular patriotism, it is as raucous, strident, and belligerent as a work of this sort ought properly to be. The First Symphony, because of its heroic and often tragic tone, had initially been understood as a reflection of the patriotic fervor of the time. It may well carry connotations of this sort, but Ekman who talked to Sibelius about this and other matters, assures us that Sibelius had an entirely personal document in mind. The two are perhaps not entirely distinguishable. As subjective a work as this Symphony undoubtedly is, "his dreams, his melancholy, his longing, his undaunted acceptance of life, his indomitable will to assert himself" (Ekman) found personal expression at a moment when such qualities characterized not just one man, but a nation. Without consciously seeking Sibelius found the mood of a historic moment within himself, and therein lies the singular strength of his early music. No doubt, this was "his own ego he confessed in sound," but a Finnish critic, noting the impact of the First Symphony on native audiences, stated quite simply, "It is our symphony."

It is significant that Sibelius neither announced nor maintained his standing as a national composer via such contrived primitivisms as folk-song imitation or orchestrated national dances. Few symphonists have succeeded in treating folk material with integrity. Sibelius consistently preferred to rely on his own invention, to create imaginatively an orchestral color and a curve of melody which his countrymen could immediately sense as their own. Expert scholarship, as well as Sibelius' own word, denies the existence, to any significant degree, of actual folk melodies in his scores. One may presume, perhaps, a folk basis, unwittingly acquired and not consciously remembered, imbedded in his composer's sense of the logic of sound. In any case, in his emergence as a national composer he chose not to don folk tunes in symphonic format as one would a suit of clothes likely to prove fashionable among right-thinking citizens. Necessarily, the road to a national idiom had to be more personal and, indeed, intuitive. In the fusion of a personal and a national style, Sibelius was wholly successful. A knowledgeable musician can identify Sibelius as a dis-

tinct personality simply from the sound of his music. This very same sound
is recognized as distinctly Finnish (and without benefit of folk tune) by
his countrymen and by his major critics either in Finland or abroad. Perhaps it is, in general, true that the more profoundly national a work of
art is, the more profoundly personal it will be for the man who creates it.
Just as the more deeply a work of art sinks its shafts into the national consciousness, the more nearly it touches those fundamental human meanings which legend and landscape have for all men in all nations.

Like many another romantic nationalist, Sibelius found continual inspiration for his tone poems in the legends and the landscape of his own
country. Some of these tone poems are specifically programmatic while
others are only generally so. In *En Saga* (Op. 9), composed in 1892 and
extensively revised in 1901, Sibelius was concerned essentially with the
ruminating, rhapsodic tone which one associates with the narration of a
northern saga. The famous *Swan of Tuonela,* composed in 1893 and originally designed as a prelude to an opera, was subsequently incorporated
into a cycle of four orchestral legends dealing with the Lemminkäinen
myth. It is an evocative tone picture, suggesting a scene rather than narrat-
ing an event. A note on the score identifies the subject and the scene:
"Tuonela, the Kingdom of Death, the Hades of Finnish mythology, is
surrounded by a broad river of black water and rapid current, in which the
Swan of Tuonela glides in majestic fashion and sings." *Lemminkäinen's
Homeward Journey,* a companion piece to the *Swan of Tuonela,* is likewise general in its programmatic annotation. A note prefixed to the score
identifies Lemminkäinen as a "warrior hero, the Achilles of Finnish mythology," whose "fearlessness and beauty cause him to be greatly admired
by women." Fatigued by his military exploits, the hero decides to return
home. He transforms his "sorrows and solicitudes" into war steeds and
after an adventurous journey arrives at the scene of his childhood. Here,
as in so much of his other music, Sibelius found his source of inspiration
in the reading of the *Kalevala.*

Throughout the decades of his creativity Sibelius' progress as a composer was steady and assured. Utterly indifferent to the modernisms developing apace in Paris and Vienna, and unmindful of the echoes of controversy that greeted the new music of Stravinsky and Schoenberg, Sibelius
enclosed himself in his music as if within a magic circle of his own ac-
complishments. Despite the rhapsodic freedom that characterizes the style
of his communication, the man was a patient and painstaking craftsman,
and, in his own way, an original one. This is perhaps most evident in the
two works that are very likely the culmination of his achievement as a
composer: the Symphony No. 7 in C Major, Op. 105, and the tone poem
Tapiola (Op. 112), both of which date from 1925. The Symphony is a one-

movement work, at once compact and spacious in the way that large-scale structures are in the hands of a mature master. The essence of musical form is the organization of movement in music. In this work, Sibelius is at his most personal in his conception of the time scale within which the pace of a symphonic drama unfolds. The four-movement time scale and the sonata-form pacing of musical events do not fit the Sibelius scheme. He chose rather the more esoteric discipline of building up the structure through an accretion of musical events, each strongly and deeply felt; and an event in this symphony may be anything from a short phrase to an extended paragraph spreading over several pages of the score. It is an emerging structure, and it is well to be forewarned against expectations adduced from experience with other late romantic symphonies. Like a no-man's land that takes shape as each slowly explored mile follows another, the ultimate structure of this symphony emerges measure by deliberate measure. Despite the 1925 date on the score, this work is one of the possible end points in the nineteenth-century romanticist's yearning for that type of continuous symphonic expression designed to record the uncharted and ever-unfolding geography of a man's soul.

Tapiola is deeply kin to Sibelius' Seventh Symphony. A nature study and national legend in one, its name derives from Tapio, the ancient god of the Finnish forests. A quatrain prefixed to the score locates Sibelius' inspiration in the wide-spread Northern forests, with their ancient, mysterious, brooding dreams. A casually masterful work, as austere intellectually as it is gracious to the ear, it is monothematic in structure (or so nearly so as to make little difference), with the identifiable motivic fragments ultimately deriving from the opening measures. This transformation process is so continual that the work seems often to unfold almost objectively out of itself. There is a "self-contained" quality about the music, almost as if, like the forest it represents, it were not a man-made artifice, but a fact of nature.

IMPRESSIONISM AND SYMBOLISM: DEBUSSY, RAVEL, DE FALLA, AND RESPIGHI

The term *impressionism,* used so commonly to characterize the music of Claude Debussy, is borrowed from painting, and suggests an analogy between Debussy's music and the art of a number of diverse and strongly individualistic painters whose work is grouped, more or less loosely, under the common designation of "impressionism." As applied to Debussy, the term can scarcely be construed simultaneously in all of the several senses in which it is separately applied to artists as divergent as Monet, Renoir, and Seurat. Moreover, since sound and pigment are very

different media, differences between composer and painter are bound to
be considerable. Analogy is not a form of exact reasoning, and if pursued
as such, the result is liable to prove poor logic or nothing more than a
clever pun. But it is a limited, though useful, way of pointing to similar
elements in seemingly unrelated situations. And sometimes such a way of
pointing, intuitive though it may be, acts like a flash illumination, bringing suddenly into focus a strongly felt relationship in the creative attitudes
of an era. Since in the making of comparisons, words must necessarily be
used with a degree, at least, of controlled inexactitude, it is well to observe
this caution: some of Debussy's techniques, and a few of his esthetic beliefs
may be *like* techniques and beliefs manifest in this or that aspect of impressionism. But to be *like* is not to be *the same as;* and comparison should
not be confused with identity.

It is just as pertinent to characterize Debussy's work as "symbolist";
and, again by analogy, to point to a deep kinship between certain aspects
of his art and certain underlying tenets in the work of the French symbolist poets. It is usually helpful to consider a composer's work in the
context of related ideas developed in the other arts. In Debussy's case, it
is well-nigh disastrous to do otherwise. There are moments when the arts
of an era seem especially close to one another; and in France, in the latter
decades of the nineteenth century, an ambiguity of boundaries, the spill-
ing over from one art to another, was a conscious element in the esthetics
of the day. If music was a point of reference for a Gauguin or a Van Gogh,
in his turn, Debussy spoke of his music as if he were a painter. And if
music was the ideal of symbolist poetry, Debussy returned the compliment
by finding in such poetry the ideal inspiration for his music.

Debussy's account of his Nocturnes for orchestra shows how instinctively he tended to express himself as a painter. Originally, the work was
planned for violin and orchestra. In a letter to the famous violinist Ysaÿe,
for whom the work was intended, Debussy described it as, "An experiment
with the different combinations that can be obtained from one color—
like a study in gray in painting." Later, when the work took its present
shape as three orchestral pieces, the last with female choir, the composer's
descriptive vocabulary became even more explicitly that of an impressionist painter. The title, Nocturnes, he explained, was *"not* meant to designate the usual form of the nocturne," but was intended in the sense of "the
variety of impressions and the special effects of light that the word suggests." By careful exclusion, neither its literal meaning as a night piece,
nor its common musical meaning in romantic piano music (for instance,
the Chopin Nocturnes) as an indrawn mood piece is intended. The notion that the word *nocturne* suggests "special effects of light" obviously is
derived not from music, but from painting. From Debussy's day to our

own, writers have been quick to point to the obvious analogy between Debussy's Nocturnes as "special effects of light," and the Nocturnes of James McNeill Whistler—paintings conceived as studies in the *harmonies* of blue and silver. That Debussy admired Whistler's work goes without saying, and that the composer should refer to light and the painter to harmony must be assumed as natural if one is to find oneself in any relationship of sympathy to the work of either. It is fairly futile to insist that such a use of language is ambiguous and would fail to stand up under exacting analytical dissection. If there is any one attitude most typical of Debussy, it is a sorrowful head shaking, touched with perceptible irritation that grown-up people should have forgotten, as he once remarked, "that as children they were forbidden to open the insides of dolls."

In the first Nocturne, titled *Nuages* (Clouds), Debussy explained that he sought to "render the immutable aspect of the sky and the slow solemn motion of the clouds, fading away in gray tones lightly tinged with white." The second is called *Fêtes* (Festivals), and here Debussy's interest was, as he wrote, "the atmosphere vibrating with sudden flashes of light." During the *Fêtes* there is the episode of a procession (described by the composer as "a dazzling fantastic vision") first heard dimly in the distance, and eventually merging with the festive scene. Debussy visualized it as a "blending of music and luminous dust." [1] The last piece, called *Sirènes* (Sirens) "depicts the sea and its countless rhythms." "Amid the waves silvered by the moonlight," wrote Debussy, "the mysterious song of the sirens is heard as they laugh and pass on." Such impressionist descriptions, since they are the composer's own, have been construed, quite naturally, as an invitation to later writers to extend the comparisons with impressionist painting. The juxtaposition of Debussy and Whistler has already been noted. Further, Lockspeiser finds *Nuages* like a Monet, *Fêtes* the counterpart of a southern landscape by Renoir, and *Sirènes* the equivalent of a water color by Turner.[2] Each will find the equivalents that suit him; and while normally strong objections should be entered against such pictorial equivalents for music, in this instance it may be held that Debussy himself suggested precedent for the procedure.

Among its early practitioners, impressionism was a kind of primitive, bed-rock realism; for the painter, viewing the object in open air, rather than in artificial studio arrangement, made a total equation between the object and his immediate and unanalyzed sense impression of it. Stress was

---

[1] See Chap. 4, p. 50, for a further discussion of *Fêtes*.

[2] Such interpretations are not confined to fanciful biographers. In his excellent manual on *The Art of Orchestration*, a technical handbook on the subject, Bernard Rogers, himself a distinguished composer, provides the following note on Debussy's *Nuages:* "Evocative painting with slender means. Reed colors in parallel planes. Influence of Japanese wood prints—as in the pictures of Degas and Whistler."

Ex. 23:1   *Tragic* Overture. Brahms.

Ex.
23:2

on the fresh, informal immediacy of the impression, and the translation of
it onto the canvas almost inevitably took shape as a spontaneous, ultrasub-
jective record, realized in rapid strokes and streaks of color. Often the
colors were not mixed on the palette, but applied pure, sometimes in un-

Ex. 23:3 *Iberia* (Bars 6–10) . Debussy.

modulated and even in vibrantly unharmonized juxtaposition. This involved a breakdown in preconceived, academically instilled precepts based
on the studied analysis and the deliberate composition of a scene and of
the function of shadow and color in the clarification of shapes. Necessarily,
the impression was but a transitory moment in the ever-changing aspect of
the scene. Since the impression varied at different times of the day, and
since the variation could be accounted for by differences in the conditions
of light, two solutions quickly suggested themselves, both in turn suggesting points of analogy with Debussy. First, several paintings were done of
the same scene at different times of the day, in an effort to record the
altered impressions of the object under differing conditions of light. Second, the relationship between light and color began to be studied for its
own sake, as an independent discipline, and hence in relation to shapes
much more abstract than those normally given to the senses when an object
is empirically under observation.

The emergence of this second point of view marks a clear antithesis between the earlier spontaneous, sense-data impressionism of Monet, and the
later, formalistically controlled "scientific impressionism" of Seurat. In the
process, intuitive techniques became fixed principles, and of one such
principle Debussy made superb application in his orchestral scoring. The
earlier impressionists had already had recourse to the lively juxtaposition
of pure colors. With the scientific impressionist it became a fixed principle
that colors mixed together on the palette were dulled in the process. When
dots of pure color were placed in predetermined juxtaposition on the
canvas (a technique known as *pointillism* or *divisionism*), they were
mixed in the eye, or mind, of the viewer. One of the cardinal tenets of the
new impressionism was the belief that such optical mixtures were more
luminous than palette mixtures.

The likeliest analogy to this divisionist juxtaposition of pure color is
in orchestration, a discipline that deals with what is commonly called the
tone color of musical sounds. A simple inspection of two pages chosen
nearly at random, one from Brahms and the other from Debussy, shows
the distinction between Brahms' classical use of choir color as blocs of
blended color (Ex. 23:1), and Debussy's divisionist scattering of points
of pure instrumental color (Ex. 23:3). Note that in the Brahms example
the instruments are grouped into clear blocs, and the blocs dramatically
juxtaposed one against the other. Within the bloc, the separate instrumental colors tend to be fused or mixed together. Thus the flutes and the
oboes are fused by the fact that the top oboe line duplicates the bottom
flute line. Similarly, the clarinet color is fused onto this mixture by writing
the top clarinet part (read a whole step down) as a duplicate of the lower
oboe part. A diagram of the first woodwind chord may perhaps clarify this

(Ex. 23:2). In place of a solid choir color bloc achieved by mixing and fusing the colors of the separate instruments within the choir, notice in the Debussy example how each instrument is stippled in as a fleck of pure color, and even the homogeneous strings are desynchronized to achieve an uncommon degree of color separation. In an analogy of this kind, it becomes possible to talk of a musical impressionism, and to make articulate (though not necessarily exact) certain intuitively felt similarities between music and painting.

Like the earlier impressionist painters, Debussy was concerned with the crystallization of sensations deriving from objects to be found in the open air (*Clouds, Reflections on the Water, The Wind on the Plain, Footprints in the Snow,* etc.). An effort to capture these vague and spontaneous impressions in music led Debussy to short forms like the improvisational prelude. He revived the whole-tone scale, with its vague, peaceful ladder of equal steps.

Ex. 23:4 *Veils* (Bars 1–2). Debussy.

He insisted on a device common in medieval diaphony, but forbidden in classical music—that is, movement in parallel intervals of the fourth and fifth (Ex. 23:5). Most important, he moved chords up and down the scale (Ex. 23:5) as if they were points in a single melodic line, destroying the ability of their component parts to become related horizontally and to set up the tensions and the relaxations which make music dramatic.

Ex. 23:5 *Engulfed Cathedral.* Debussy. (*a*) Bars 14–15. (*b*) Bar 84.

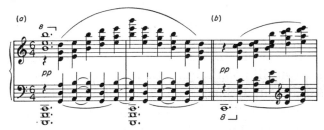

This last point was of enormous consequence in that it opened up new vistas in harmonic usage. The organization of these vistas into well-defined roads came after his death and perhaps in ways which he may neither have anticipated nor approved. But his position as a pioneer in this aspect of twentieth-century musical development is assured beyond question.

In his own harmonic usage, the destruction of the sense of clear, chord function resulted in progressions best characterized as ambiguous harmonic drift. But what his harmony lost in solidity and well-defined contour, it made up for in power of suggestion. An analogy (and again, an admittedly inexact one) here suggests itself between Debussy's chord juxtapositions, where chords are immune from the necessity of defining the harmonic mass or motivating its movement, and the free color juxtapositions in earlier impressionist painting, where color is exempt from its obligation to clarify the shape of an object, and where the object itself is not obliged to assume proper shape as in a well-defined drawing. Very like Debussy, Monet made up in atmosphere, spontaneity, and suggestion what he lost in clarity of contour and solidity of forms.

In Debussy's piano music, the immediate sense impressions conveyed by his harmonic usage are immeasurably enhanced by his enchanting use of piano tone. The pianist's ears, fingers, and feet are working constantly at a mitigation of the hammer action of the piano. A brushlike, caressing touch, a sensitive use of the tints and half tints to be found in a combination of damper and soft pedals, and infinite care in the production of the softest possible tone are absolute necessities in the performance of his piano music. He took great pains to make his requirements clear in a wealth of dynamic markings and textural instructions. A few of these instructions must be quoted; but first an outlining of the contexts in which they occur is necessary.

Previously in this discussion, there was passing notice of the early impressionist painter's interest in doing several renditions of the same scene at different times of the day. The effort was to record the diversity of impressions given by the same object under differing conditions of light. Actually, music is an ideal art for capturing the continuity in mood variation produced as the object is transformed in the passing of time. The painter, perforce, must seek to record each moment on a separate canvas; whereas the composer's canvas is itself in flux, and can always coordinate with the altering aspect of the subject. This, at least, was Debussy's tacit assumption in the opening movement of *La Mer* (The Sea) which he entitled "From dawn till noon on the sea"; and implicitly one finds this assumption manifest in Debussy's affection for such pictorial subjects as lend themselves to a continual evolution of transitory tonal impressions. Thus the title of a piano piece like *Reflets dans L'Eau* (Reflections in the Water), instantly explains the composer's concern for the ever-changing interplay of keyboard and pedal light and color, and his interest in the ever-changing ambiguities of reflected tonal shapes.

Debussy's *La Cathédrale engloutie* (The Engulfed Cathedral) is another such example. It is based on an old Breton legend, treated also by

Debussy's contemporary Edouard Lalo in an opera called *Le Roi d'Ys.*
According to the legend, the cathedral of an ancient city long submerged
in the sea may, on clear days, rise momentarily out of the past. Debussy's
piano prelude is a sonorous presentation of the changing cathedral as it
rises out of the mist into the sunshine. It is a continuity of merging and
emerging impressions for which Claude Monet required several canvases
when he sought to capture the Cathedral at Rouen under differing conditions of light. As instructive as this analogy may be, it is nevertheless
worth remembering that this piano prelude is a piece of music. It does
no violence either to a sensitive use of language or to Debussy's own conception of his music to describe him as a painter, provided it be further
specified that his medium was musical tone. His point therefore was not
to describe a picture, but to evoke the changing mood of a scene, and this
through an imagery of tone. Thus the visual story of the sunken cathedral
is transformed into a study in the gradually changing sonority of bells
as they emerge from profound undersea enchantment to full glory in the
sun.

It may seem, at this late date, a poetic license firmly crystallized into
cliché to speak of the sound of bells in the sun. But this fusion or confusion
of sense impressions is precisely the point. In his own words, he requires
the pianist to begin with "a sweetly sonorous mist." The instruction is a
blend of taste, touch, sight, and hearing; the simultaneity of all senses is
suggested to the performer—a subtle unity of experience to be projected in
tone. Such correspondences between the senses offered Debussy a new dimension in programme music, and required of the performer an added
sensibility in understanding and realizing the composer's instructions.
Thus in the slow movement of *Iberia,* the orchestra is asked to translate
into sound "The Perfumes of the Night"; and in *Footprints in the Snow,*
the pianist is instructed concerning the dominating *rhythm,* that it "should
have the sonorous value of a sad and frozen landscape."

This transference of suggestion from one sense medium to another is
a concept which Debussy acquired from the French symbolist poets. His
affection for Baudelaire, Mallarmé, and Verlaine is evident enough in the
settings, both instrumental and vocal, which he did of their work. One
source for the symbolist esthetic is the following poem by Baudelaire:

Correspondences

Nature is a temple where living pillars
Let sometimes emerge confused words;
Man comes there over forests of symbols
Which watch him with intimate eyes.

Like those deep echoes that meet from afar
In a dark and profound harmony,
As vast as night and clarity,
So perfumes, colors, tones answer each other.

There are perfumes fresh as children's flesh,
Soft as oboes, green as meadows,
And other, tainted, rich triumphant,
Possessing the diffusion of infinite things,
Like amber, musk, incense and aromatic resin,
Chanting the ecstasies of spirit and senses.

                              (Translated by Geoffrey Wagner)

Whether the consequences of this in Debussy and in later symbolist poetry are entirely consonant with Baudelaire's point of view is not entirely relevant to this discussion. What was suggestive here was a notion of correspondences in the imagery crystallized through different senses. The relationship between Debussy's musical evocation of the perfumes of the night and Baudelaire's perfumes "soft as oboes" is scarcely coincidence. Further what was involved here was a concept of the multi-sense image as "symbol." The images that impinge upon consciousness were construed as intuitions of a reality beyond reality. The image became then a symbol, a mechanism of correspondence, via which one journeyed from the peripheral reality of immediate things to an ultimate reality of pure beauty. This ultimate reality was not a describable thing. It could only be evoked or suggested by a juxtaposition of sense impressions. To name a thing was then necessarily to destroy it. And further, experience as commonly understood in everyday life, was an irrelevant if perhaps unavoidable distraction.

The hero of a symbolist novel (Des Esseintes in Huysmans' *A Rebours*) undertakes a trip to England. But before the first stage of the journey is over, he returns home. In anticipation he experiences imaginatively the flavor of English life through countless indirect associations. When it comes to an actual inspection of the reality of England, the imaginative experience is preferred and he turns back. "What is the use of moving, when one can travel in a chair so magnificently? . . . I have been filled with English life since my departure. I would be mad indeed to go and, by an awkward trip, lose these imperishable sensations."

The analogy with Debussy's *Iberia* is plain enough. For Debussy, Spain was a collection of associations, and a trip to that country less important than the picture post card that suddenly evoked a complex of purely imaginative experiences. As Vallas, his biographer, remarked, "It was not Debussy's aim to write Spanish music, but rather to express truthfully his own impressions of Spain, a Spain of which he knew little or nothing, but which his imagination depicted with marvelous accuracy."

André Gide's objection to symbolist poetry was its "lack of curiosity about life." Maeterlinck's *Pelleas and Melisande,* which Debussy chose as the text for his opera, offered the composer an opening scene remarkable for the manner in which the heroine reiterates, in the barely audible intensity so characteristic of her and of Debussy, that any curiosity about her life is irrelevant and intolerable. The scene is set in an unknown part of a forest located in an unidentified kingdom. Throughout the opera, the music transmits the feeling of a kingdom, ancient and remote, a place of trembling silences where a quiet tragedy is enacted almost unnoticed by the very people involved in it. Golaud, the ancient king's elder grandson, is lost in the forest. He comes upon Melisande weeping at the edge of a pool. The conversation between them is a sequence of direct questions from Golaud about things an audience ordinarily would want to know, and a series of frightened evasions in reply. Thus to Golaud's question, "Why do you weep," Melisande only trembles. Upon its repetition, she answers, "Do not touch me." When he asks, "Has anyone wronged you?" this normally would be sufficient provocation for an aria. But Melisande simply says, "Yes." He continues, "Who has wronged you?" She says helpfully, "Everybody." And when Golaud, doing his best, asks, "And what wrong has been done you?" she tells him that she will not answer, and that she cannot answer. This topic exhausted, Golaud tries another tack. "Where do you come from?" The answer is, "I ran away." Patiently, he rephrases the question, "Where did you run away from?"; and the answer is, "I am lost." Eventually Golaud provides the customary information about himself, and Melisande returns the confidence by finally pronouncing her name.

In the entire course of the opera we know nothing of her beyond what the music evokes and suggests. Debussy is in his element here, for his music offers to our intuition, via the symbols of its tonal imagery, a correspondence to an ultimate and unnamable reality in Melisande's love and death. In the pianissimo sounds wherein the reality of Melisande is enclosed, there are moments of terrifying tenderness, unknown to the rather tiresome young lady in Maeterlinck's play. Music, the symbolist poets themselves freely granted, was for their purposes the ideal art; and in its later stages symbolist poetry, with Paul Valéry, turned to abstract formalism in the effort (so Valéry phrased it) to take back from music what the poets had lost to it. Debussy's opera compared to Maeterlinck's play is a prime example of the essence of a poetry that had been surrendered to music.

Although the premiere of this opera was given as far back as 1902, Melisande is still a difficult role to project from the conventional operatic stage. "I had done my best," wrote Debussy, "to express in music her fragility and her elusive charm; but there was also her attitude to be considered, her long silences, which a single wrong gesture might frustrate or render meaningless." In a symbolist creation it is always questionable whether any specific realization can accord entirely with the artist's inner vision. "The scenic realization of a work of art," wrote Debussy of the opera, "no matter how beautiful, is always contrary to the inner vision which drew it in turns from its alternatives of doubt and enthusiasm." Experience had taught him to be a pessimist about performances, for his music is truly the ideal symbolist intimation of correspondences: a continual meditation between what is actually heard and what is audible only to the inner ear. To one degree or another this is a quality to be experienced in almost all music, and Debussy's preciousness outlives the limitations of its symbolist environment by refining a quality which, in music, is universal.

There are works by Debussy which fall outside the range of either a symbolist or an impressionist approach to experience, and he was rather harsh with such critics as were prone to use a pat word like "impressionism" indiscriminately for whatever he did. Actually what runs through all of his music is a traditional French flavor, difficult enough to define and easy enough to point to while his music is being played. In some of his keyboard miniatures there is a kinship to harpsichord pieces of an eighteenth-century French composer like Couperin. In the sensuous sweetness of much of his music there is the touch of Massenet which Debussy felt every French composer had within him. And if precision and craftsmanship and a sense of humor are traditional French traits which Malraux can observe in a painter like Jacques Louis David, they are also characteristics readily observable in Debussy. In *Golliwog's Cake Walk,* there is a delicious dig in the middle part at Wagner's *Tristan and Isolde,* and in *Minstrels* a delight in the humor of minstrel show tunes. Both works reflect an early interest in ragtime and preview a later Parisian interest in jazz. In the *Dance of Puck,* when the voluptuous music of the ill-matched lovers, Bottom and Titania, is at its height, Bottom turns back into a donkey and brays. The charm broken, Puck blows his horn, giggles, and is gone. In *The Interrupted Serenade* the frustrated performer keeps tuning his instrument while trying to sing a lovely if slightly sentimental song. And in *Les Collines d'Anacapri,* a Neapolitan scene, the liveliness of the tarantella and the genuine loveliness of popular song are interrupted by a gem of premeditated and carefully planned banality—an epitome of sentimental Italian melody with strummed accompaniment. This unsentimental affection for popular melody and this delight in the arabesque of absurdity unite Couperin, Debussy, Satie, and that impertinent sextet known during the 1920's as *Les Six* (Poulenc, Milhaud, Auric, etc.) .

When cliché is the method of criticism, Maurice Ravel is described as an impressionist composer of the school of Debussy. There are more misconceptions here than are worth bothering about. That Ravel wrote a few impressionist pieces, as did nearly every young composer who came of age during Debussy's maturity, is a token of how deep an impression Debussy made on music generally. As for a school, this was as much anathema to Debussy as it was plainly ridiculous to the long list of important composers who read his scores with undeniable profit. The list includes not only Ravel, but Respighi, Manuel de Falla, Stravinsky, Bloch, Bartók, Aaron Copland, Walter Piston, and (though this be heresy in some high places) even Schoenberg. What Debussy offered to this international assemblage of successors was an example in conceiving a new imagery of tone, fundamentally unorthodox in respect to inherited tradition, and yet controlled by a painstaking and impeccable craftsmanship.

Ravel eventually achieved a musical personality quite different from Debussy's, harsher in its expressionistic distortions, as in *La Valse;* more blatant in the reduction of craftsmanship to a *tour de force,* as in *Bolero;* and tinged at times with a surrealist fantasy, as in *L'Enfant et les Sortilèges* (The Child and the Sorceries) ; all of these were written after Debussy's death. If they seem close to Debussy's style, despite strong differences, it is —as with Schoenberg and Mahler, or Kodály and Bartók—a closeness in affection for a common tradition. Both Debussy and Ravel, despite their occasional use of Spanish idioms, are deeply French in their musical style. In this, they are closer to each other than to Manuel de Falla, even when the latter, a Spanish composer, writes as an impressionist.

The national aspect of impressionism is clearly evident in the *Nights in the Gardens of Spain* by Manuel de Falla, and in the *Fountains of Rome* by Respighi. The first is a Spanish work, the second Italian, and in each instance, the impressionist idiom is strongly modified by the national one. The work by Falla, scored for piano and orchestra, was described by the composer as "symphonic impressions" written "to evoke places, sensations, and sentiments." The first movement is devoted to the famous gardens of the Generalife overlooking the Alhambra in Granada, and the last to the gardens of the Sierra of Cordova. Between the two is a movement entitled "A Distant Dance." "The music," writes Falla, "has no pretensions to being descriptive; it is merely expressive. But something more than the sounds of festivals and dances has inspired these 'evocations in sound,' for melancholy and mystery have their part also." The denial of descriptive intent and the phrase "evocations in sound" indicate that Debussy's esthetic is shared by Falla. Yet the *Nights in the Gardens of Spain* is deeply

Spanish in its idiom. The short, repetitive phrases and the crisp rhythms characteristic of Spanish folk music are ever present, and in the last movement the passionate and precise coloraturas of the *cante hondo,* a popular type of Andalusian melody, make their appearance.

In Respighi's *Fountains of Rome,* the lushness of texture and the opulence of sound seem at variance with the fragility and the refinement of Debussy's music. But these are characteristics which unite Respighi to Puccini and to late Italian romanticism. Despite the non-Debussyist (more accurately, non-French) traits in his music, Respighi's *Fountains* is impressionist in conception. To summarize the composer's program for the work, each of the four fountains is presented as a musical evocation of "sentiment and vision" associated with the hour of day when each fountain seems "most in harmony with its surrounding landscape," or when its "beauty appears most impressive to the observer." Thus the opening evokes a "pastoral landscape," with droves of cattle passing and disappearing before the Fountain of Valle Giulia. The scene is transmitted through tonal images suggested by "the fresh, damp mists of a Roman dawn." The second is a vision of naiads and tritons pursuing one another in a frenzied dance through the jet and spray of the Triton Fountain. It is joyous music, an evocation of the fountain in the bright exuberance of the morning light. The third section is more "solemn," for it is the Fountain of Trevi at mid-day and upon "the radiant surface of the water there passes Neptune's chariot, drawn by sea horses." This triumphal mid-day scene is succeeded by the subdued appearance of the Villa Medici Fountain at "the nostalgic hour of sunset." Dawn, morning, mid-day, and now the "tolling bells," when "all dies peacefully into the silence of the night." For Debussy, it was the sea from dawn till noon, for Respighi the fountains of his beloved city from dawn till dusk. Both had been schooled in the impressionist's sensitivity to mood as it changes in the flux of time. But in the sense of mood, and in the choice of tone image to transmit it, each was faithful to his inheritance.

REALISM (VERISMO): PUCCINI

There are scarcely two conceptions of realism more utterly divergent than the symbolism of Debussy's *Pelleas and Melisande* and the *verismo* of Puccini's *Tosca.* In effect, Puccini's truth comprised, in the main, such details as Debussy was concerned to suppress. The two were contemporary. Puccini's dates are 1858–1924, and Debussy's 1862–1918. *Tosca* was given its premiere in 1900, and *Pelleas* in 1902. Not only do they seem worlds apart, but Debussy appears the more "modern" of the two. *Pelleas* owes little to an immediately inherited opera tradition, and its unorthodoxy as theater is underscored by a harmonic and orchestrational practice which opened the road to the future. *Tosca* is rooted in the tradition of the Italian stage as Verdi had shaped it. Moreover the veristic traits which are so violent a feature in *Tosca* are derived from a well-established tradition in nineteenth-century Italian literature, and had already won sensational success on the Italian opera stage in Mascagni's *Cavalleria Rusticana* (premiere 1890) and in Leoncavallo's *Pagliacci* (premiere 1892). Puccini's originality consists not in a break with tradition, but in a personal treatment of it.

Literally, *verismo* refers to an art dedicated to truth, to a projection of reality. This tells us very little, since there are scarcely two concepts more subject to divergent interpretation than "truth" and "reality." Puccini's *verismo* is a complex of abstracts from reality, viewed in a special way. The stress is on the ordinary, and on the violence, the tenderness, the suffering, and the humor contained in everyday life. This is not entirely inconsistent with the choice of an exotic locale—China for *Turandot,* Japan for *Madama Butterfly,* the Latin Quarter in Paris for *La Bohème,* the American west for the *Girl of the Golden West;* but the veristic naturalism of *Tosca* is perhaps the more direct for its Roman setting, and the more convincing in *Il Tabarro* (The Cloak) for the unfolding of its tragedy amid the life of the water front.

Tearing the passions to shreds—another component of *verismo*—is all the more poignant in that the passions are not those of gods or emperors, but of ordinary people who, unlike gods or emperors, cannot control their own destinies. In *Pagliacci* the victims are the indigent theater folk who ply the provinces with their tawdry glamour; and in *Cavalleria Rusticana* the participants in the tragedy are the Sicilian poor. Puccini's favorite was the woman victimized, a singularly poignant and sympathetic creature caught in the conflict of forces larger than her small, intimate world, and too powerful for her to cope with. Behind Rodolfo's falling out with Mimi (*La Bohème*), Pinkerton's betrayal of Butterfly (*Madama Butterfly*), and Scarpia's brutality to Tosca (*Tosca*), there are the larger forces of social, economic, and political injustice which bring Mimi to an early death by consumption, and Butterfly and Tosca to suicide. Always, however, the tragedy is a personal one. The larger forces are aloof from the drama and are present only by implication. They are beyond the reach of the victimized heroines, for they lie outside the enclosed stage upon which the helpless personal tragedy is enacted. The ultimate political reasons for the entanglements in *Tosca* are remote from the immediate drama. Cavaradossi, the hero, is a liberal, and Scarpia, the villain, is head of the secret police. Each does as he must, and Tosca, in love with Cavaradossi and desired by Scarpia, is caught between them in a horror she cannot understand. In the torture scene, with the cries of Cavaradossi ringing in her ears, and the image of him mutilated and defiant still before her, Tosca can only plead in bewilderment that she has always brought flowers to the church altar, and jewels for the mantle of the Madonna. "I have lived only for love and music" (*Vissi d'arte, vissi d'amore*), she cries helplessly, "I never harmed a living being." In the last scene of *La Bohème*, Mimi is dying of consumption. Nothing can be done to help her; and when she dies, there is nothing to do but weep. No doubt this was a good box-office finale, but the people who made money out of it also believed in its truth and were moved by it. As Puccini's publisher wrote to him, "The last act and the death of Mimi, especially, ought to call forth torrents of tears. I myself was much, much moved."

The harrowing torture of Cavaradossi in Act II of *Tosca* is, however, just one aspect of Puccini's *verismo*. He was shrewd enough and human enough to realize that naturalism of this sort was meaningful only as a heightened focus for deeper psychological truths. Thus Tosca's *Vissi d'arte,* already mentioned, acquires poignancy in the context of the crude naturalistic horror of the scene. Likewise, when Cavaradossi is brought in after torture, mangled and (however sympathetic one may be) repulsive, Tosca's first instinct is to turn away. The moment is governed by the interplay of confused reactions in Tosca's mind: disgust, shame at her revulsion (for it is her lover who has been thus mutilated), love for Cavaradossi, and the urgent need that she feels to kiss and to comfort him. The essence of the entire act is the interplay of the two levels of torture. Scarpia desires to know the secret hiding place of Angelotti, an escaped political prisoner. He has reason to suspect that either Cavaradossi or Tosca can provide him with the answer. His aim is twofold, to secure Angelotti for the state and Tosca for himself. Tosca has been invited to his private apartment, adjacent to which he maintains the torture chamber where Cavaradossi is held. The physical torture to which Cavaradossi is subjected offstage reaches our ears and Tosca's, and is the immediate context for the psychological torture to which Tosca is forced to submit. She breaks under the strain and provides both the required information and a promise to give herself to Scarpia in payment for a safe conduct for Cavaradossi and herself. When Scarpia approaches to embrace her, she stabs him and literally howls with ecstacy to see him choking in his own blood. Yet a moment later, just as the act closes, she reverts to her essential character; and as a properly brought up Italian girl, reverent in the presence of the dead, she places lighted candles on either side of Scarpia's head, a crucifix on his breast, and departs closing the door quietly.

This interplay of naturalistic setting and psychological truth is the key to Puccini's interest in such details as authentic Japanese melody in

Madama Butterfly. For the first act of *Tosca,* a church ritual is designed as the setting for Scarpia's erotic visions. This mixture of sex and religion is a standard romantic formula which Hollywood inherited and converted into one of its most profitable clichés. (Salome's erotic dance of the seven veils occurs in a film whose final scene is the Sermon on the Mount.) Mephistopheles seeks to seduce Marguerite in church; Tannhäuser invokes the Virgin Mary when he tires of the eroticism of Venus; and Parsifal, only by virtue of his being both pure and a fool, escapes the seductions that have decimated the guardians of the Holy Grail. For Scarpia's eroticism, Puccini wanted a church setting, and he applied to a priest (Pietro Panichelli) for help in selecting suitably naturalistic material. During the procession to the altar, and amid the murmuring in Latin that envelops the church, Scarpia sings *con passione erotica* (with erotic passion) of his vision of possessing Tosca. During a pause in the *Te Deum,* he cries out, "Tosca, for thee I would renounce my hopes of Heaven," and the next instant falls on his knees *con entusiasmo religioso* (with religious fervor) joining his voice with the others in intoning the Latin prayer.

EXPRESSIONISM: STRAUSS, MAHLER

With Richard Strauss, the aberrational aspects of psychological drama are even more strongly accentuated. In a sense, exaggeration is the clue to the Strauss personality. His work, around the turn of the century, aroused storms of controversy, not because what he attempted was unheard of, but because the Strauss version of it was so nakedly extreme. Thus when he chose to indulge in veristic naturalism, as in his *Don Quixote* (a set of orchestral variations with the Don as a solo cello), a wind machine was introduced to depict the Don's transportation through space, while the episode with the sheep was illustrated by the most naturalistic baaing ever to emerge out of a symphony orchestra. And when a tongue-in-cheek (perhaps) naturalism was combined with the romantic, or more specifically Wagnerian, religion of ego worship, the result was a full-length concert-hall symphony, the *Symphonia Domestica,* devoted to the private routine of an ordinary day in the Strauss household. The glockenspiel sounds seven times at the close of the adagio, for it is assumed that audiences will be edified to learn that the Strauss household is awake at seven o'clock in the morning. The fugue that follows takes the baby's theme as its subject, the contrapuntal dispute representing the Strauss family at loggerheads over the child's future. The baby, incidentally, is an oboe d'amore, and the relatives who come to admire him are represented in conversation among the wind parts. Over a figure for muted trumpets and clarinets, Strauss writes, "Aunts: just like his papa"; while over the answering figure given to trombones, horns, and oboes, he notes, "Uncles: just like his mama." (Trombones may be standard for uncles, but a muted trumpet for a certain kind of aunt is verism with a vengeance.) It was customary, incidentally, for Strauss to insist that he really wanted his music to be listened to for its own sake as pure music.

Such details in the *Symphonia Domestica* may be nothing more serious than the composer's innocent enjoyment of his own rather pompous sense of humor. But Strauss was in earnest, as were so many in the post-Wagnerian generation, concerning the religion of art and the religion of ego worship. *Ein Heldenleben* (A Hero's Life) is the epitome of this late romantic point of view. Strauss, of course, is himself the hero, the noble artist beset by the philistine world, the conqueror of the petty people who interfere with his sacred mission to write great music. The titles (later withdrawn by Strauss) for the several sections of this symphonic poem are as follows: The Hero, the Hero's Adversaries, the Hero's Helpmate, the Hero's Battlefield, the Hero's Works of Peace, the Hero's Retreat from the World and his Fulfillment. In the first section, Strauss portrays himself in a trinity of themes, as courageous, high-minded and noble in bearing, as a high-spirited fellow with a fine sense of humor, and as a sensitive, meditative soul. The adversaries or critics who intrude upon his dedicated life are represented in shrill, scrawny dissonances. The hero's noble theme rises from the depths of the orchestra more in sorrow than in anger, assailed on all sides by a nasty little cacophony of critics. Eventually he sweeps them aside, and sits brooding among the lower strings while the hero's helpmate, a solo violin, executes kittenish virtuoso arabesques to amuse him. The adversaries, however, will not be silent. Their slaughter on the battlefield involved some of the boldest expressionistic dissonances to which audiences around the turn of the century were subjected. The victorious hero now exhibits his works of peace, which are, naturally enough, a collection of themes taken from Strauss' previously composed works (*Don Juan, Death and Transfiguration, Don Quixote,* etc.). At last, having conquered, the hero bids the world farewell, and retires to fulfill himself in peace.

Strauss is a most efficient master of the mechanisms of music. If his frankness in the presentation of his material seems strongly overstated, it is because his subject matter is often intrinsically already an exaggeration. Thus *Ein Heldenleben* is really a daydream view of reality. The exaggeration intrinsic to it as a daydream may enliven its poignancy and deepen its profundity for the composer who experienced it; but it may well seem obvious melodrama to an unsympathetic outsider for whose edification it is so frankly described. Reactions to some of the strongest pages in operas such as *Salome* and *Elektra,* like reactions to *Ein Heldenleben,* are often polarized at the extremes of deep sympathy or deep disgust. For Strauss was, above all, an artist who saw no use for half measures in realizing the exaggerations intrinsic to his chosen material.

In *Salome* and in *Elektra,* Strauss devoted himself with total mastery and with characteristic lack of inhibition to the musical realization of psychotic personality. There is at least one scene in each opera impressively horrifying in this respect. In *Salome,* it is the final scene following the dance of the seven veils, when Salome, given the head of John the Baptist in reward, makes love to it. This perversion, known in abnormal psychology as necrophilia, is transformed by Strauss into a voluptuous love scene. The sensual ecstasy of the music is too revolting even for Herod to tolerate. The curtain comes down as heavy, grinding chords describe how the body of Salome is crushed, by Herod's order, beneath the shields of his palace guard. In *Elektra,* it is the scene where Elektra has sent her brother Orestes within to murder Klytemnestra, their mother. Strauss' point in removing the act of murder off stage is not to spare the audience its horror, but to concentrate more intensely upon where the horror truly lies, within Elektra. She speaks but once, to remember the axe she had forgotten to give to her brother. For the rest, the orchestra speaks for her. This is the drama within Elektra herself—a psychosis too deep for human voice or word to express or explain. As she rages in silence, like a crazed beast, through the shadows of the empty stage, the orchestra communicates how the whole of her contaminated soul hungers for the death cry of her mother. When it comes, she shrieks, "Strike her again." After the second prolonged scream from within, the stage fills with excited servants. Only after Aegisthus appears and the servants scatter, does Elektra find sustained voice to rejoice, and to prepare for her eventual, heavily exhausted, dance of death.

Subject matter of this sort demands exceptional artistic treatment, and the customary term for it is *expressionism.* A brief discussion of the esthetic principle underlying an expressionistic approach is in order, for it will prove useful in a study not only of Strauss, but of Mahler, Schoenberg, Berg, and certain aspects of Stravinsky as well. It is one of the more commonly encountered approaches in contemporary culture, evident among painters and sculptors as well as among composers.

Like many another approach, *expressionism* rests on the premise that the work of art is an externalization of an emotional state—the objective correlative of a state of mind. The expressionist's prime focus is upon a state of overexcitement; he is interested in discovering the objective equivalents of states of extreme passion; and often he seeks for such technical components in a work of art that will stand for states of neurosis or psychosis—for unendurable agony or an equally unendurable joy. A simple tree, an ordinary sky, or an anatomically correct head can scarcely represent such extremes of disordered and distraught emotionality. A technique of distortion seems inevitable. The tree trunk must twist and its branches writhe; the sky becomes a swirling tumult of wild stars; and in the head of a human being, the eyes are dislocated and the mouth torn with broken teeth. These are the expressionistic exteriorizations of volcanic passions, and in music they take shape as wide, dissonant, interval leaps in the melody; harsh or strained coagulations of instrumental color; violent desynchronizations in the normal rhythmic pulsation; and acutely disturbing dissonances in the harmony. Such distortions are effective only with respect to an accepted norm. In an art like music, where the norms of melody and harmony are in continual flux from generation to generation, the expressionism of one age may become the standard practice of another. At the moment it is standardized, it loses much of the strength of its expressionistic disorder. The progress from the musical techniques displayed in the battlefield scene in Strauss' *Ein Heldenleben*, or in scenes from his *Salome* and *Elektra*, to the techniques in Mahler's Ninth Symphony, and eventually to those in Schoenberg's *Pierrot Lunaire* and in Stravinsky's *Rite of Spring* illustrates how frantically the search for more violent expressionistic resource was conducted in the decade and a half prior to World War I.

The expressionism of Gustav Mahler emerges out of tendencies that were in process in German romantic music for nearly a century. Mahler's art is based as fundamentally as Schubert's upon the *lied* (the German art song). Traditionally, the lied is a vehicle for the externalization of indrawn states of mind. In essence, it is the most intimate type of private music; for the one individual who sings it can also play the piano part, and by himself, be a sufficient audience. Much in the transformation of the character of the German romantic symphony after Beethoven can be traced to the growing importance of the intimate lied miniature as the basis for large-scale public composition. A basic feature in Mahler's maturest work is the extension of the lied to an overly large symphonic dimension—for example, in the enormous opening movement of his Ninth Symphony. In *Das Lied von der Erde* (The Song of the Earth), material which an earlier romantic composer would probably have treated as a short cycle of six songs, Mahler amplified into a vast song cycle for two voices and orchestra which he subtitled a symphony. This in itself entails an expressionistic distortion, for under magnification details often assume a startling and even aberrational urgency. When the intimacies of an utterly private world are projected through the enlargement apparatus of a symphony, shifts in mood emphasis are sometimes suddenly distended to the extremes of ecstasy and despair.

Mahler's point was to intensify the poignancy, and indeed, the agony of his inner world by means of such enlargement. And there are moments when he is overpoweringly successful, as in the first movement of the Ninth Symphony where a manic-depressive break occurs from a peak of luminous, ultra-Wagnerian ecstasy down to the very depths with some of the grimmest, blackest, and most despairing sounds to be heard in twentieth-century music. The tempo of the opening movement is andante, appropriate to its character as an orchestral song, and it opens in a state of almost dragging spiritual exhaustion. (In structure, the movement is planned, interestingly enough, not in the traditional dramatic sonata form, but as an elaborate song form with several interludes.) The final movement is even slower, an adagio, its sonorous lyricism acting as a solace to the dissonant and embittered second and third movements which precede it. The overall scheme of the symphony is more psychological than organic, for Mahler's concern is with the accentuation of intensely emotional states of mind.

The two middle movements are given over to types of musical material for which Mahler felt the deepest personal love—peasant dances in the second movement, and the heritage of Bach and Beethoven in the third. Yet, in each instance, the beloved music is broken, torn, and distorted. Mahler suffered from a sardonic pessimism which, most often, he turned in on himself. The deliberately ungraceful banality of the folk dances, and the distortion (Mahler titled it "Burleske") of Bach fugue and the Beethoven heroic scherzo style are grim examples of expressionistic self-laceration. The final adagio resolves these embittered moods into a simple, wholehearted flow of warm, ultraromantic melody. The symphony concludes on a barely audible level of sound (*pppp*). Over the final measure, Mahler placed a *fermata* (a hold) and the word *ersterbend* (dying away). In a sense, the music does not end; it is just that beyond a certain point it is no longer audible. After the expressionistic agonies of the first three movements, it is as if ultimate solace lies only in pure consonant sounds, in the quiet beauty of music itself prolonged into an inaudible eternity.

The *Song of the Earth* ends in like fashion, and it resolves a sequence of similarly embittered pessimisms. The texts are translations from old Chinese poetry and the solo voices used with orchestra are tenor and contralto. There are six songs. The first, the "Drinking Song of the Earth's Sorrow," is marked by the recurrence of a beautiful, descending melodic phrase set to a line of text which reflects the ultimate quality of Mahler's pessimism, *Dunkel ist das Leben, ist der Tod* (Dark is life and dark is death). For the second song, "The Lonesome One in Autumn," Mahler's tempo instruction reads, "Slightly dragging, as if tired." The tone color is cued to the "drifting autumn mists," and the mood to the line, "My heart is weary." A buoyant tribute to youth and a resplendent one to beauty—

"Of Youth," "Of Beauty"—are the concerns of the third and four songs, respectively. Expressionistic agitation returns with the fifth song, "The Drunkard in Spring," while the last movement "The Farewell" is the deeply moving departure of the world-weary wanderer. It is not at all far-fetched to suppose that for Mahler this farewell was symbolic autobiography, for he had premonitions of his own departure, and he saw himself as the earth's wanderer approaching his rest in eternity. Like the last movement of the Ninth Symphony, this last song is a music of solace which dies away ($pppp$) into inaudibility. The text for the closing pages evidently touched the composer deeply. The wanderer "no longer seeks the far horizon," for "his heart is still," and awaits its deliverance in the eternal renewal of the earth. The last word to be heard amid the hushed orchestral sounds made luminous by the light tones of harp and celesta is the word *ewig* (forever).

Fig. 23:1   Seurat. *Sunday Afternoon on the Island of La Grand Jatte* (1884–1886). An example of "scientific" impressionism, or *pointillism*.

Fig. 23:2 (above). Picasso. *Guernica* (1937). Collection the Artist. Courtesy Museum of Modern Art, New York. An example of formalized expressionism.

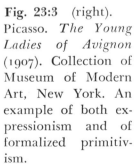

Fig. 23:3 (right). Picasso. *The Young Ladies of Avignon* (1907). Collection of Museum of Modern Art, New York. An example of both expressionism and of formalized primitivism.

CONTEMPORARY CHRONOLOGY II

Ernest Bloch	1880–	Virgil Thomson	1896–
Ildebrando Pizzetti	1880–	Jaromir Weinberger	1896–
Béla Bartók	1881–1945	Henry Cowell	1897–
Charles Wakefield Cadman	1881–1946	Alexander Tansman	1897–
Nicolai Miaskovsky	1881–1950	Eric W. Korngold	1897–
Georges Enesco	1881–1955	Quincy Porter	1897–
Heitor Villa-Lobos	1881–	George Gershwin	1898–1937
Joaquín Turina	1882–1949	Ernst Bacon	1898–
Artur Schnabel	1882–1951	Roy Harris	1898–
Zoltán Kodály	1882–	Vittorio Rieti	1898–
Francesco Malipiero	1882–	Silvestre Revueltas	1899–1940
Igor Stravinsky	1882–	Carlos Chavez	1899–
Karol Szymanowski	1883–1937	Francis Poulenc	1899–
Anton von Webern	1883–1945	Alexander Tcherepnin	1899–
Alfredo Casella	1883–1947	Randall Thompson	1899–
Arnold Bax	1883–1953	Kurt Weill	1900–1950
Charles T. Griffes	1883–1920	George Antheil	1900–
Louis Gruenberg	1884–	Aaron Copland	1900–
Alban Berg	1885–1935	Ernest Krenek	1900–
Rudolf Reti	1885–	Otto Luening	1900–
Wallingford Riegger	1885–	Werner Egk	1901–
Deems Taylor	1885–	William Walton	1902–
Edgar Varèse	1885–	Boris Blacher	1903–
Egon Wellesz	1885–	Aram Khachaturian	1903–
Heinrich Kaminski	1886–1946	Luigi Dallapiccola	1904–
Marcel Dupré	1886–	Dmitri Kabalevsky	1904–
Ernst Toch	1887–	Goffredo Petrassi	1904–
Jacques Ibert	1890–	Marc Blitzstein	1905–
Frank Martin	1890–	Paul Creston	1906–
Bohuslav Martinu	1890–	Ross Lee Finney	1906–
Sergei Prokofieff	1891–1953	Normand Lockwood	1906–
Arthur Bliss	1891–	Dmitri Shostakovich	1906–
Arthur Honegger	1892–1955	Olivier Messiaen	1908–
Giorgio Ghedini	1892–	Paul Nordoff	1909–
Darius Milhaud	1892–	Samuel Barber	1910–
Eugene Goossens	1893–	William Schuman	1910–
Alois Hába	1893–	Gian-Carlo Menotti	1911–
Federico Mompou	1893–	Alan Hovhaness	1911–
Douglas Moore	1893–	Igor Markevich	1912–
Bernard Rogers	1893–	Benjamin Britten	1913–
Willem Pijper	1894–1947	Morton Gould	1913–
Walter Piston	1894–	Norman Dello Joio	1913–
Mario Castelnuovo-Tedesco	1895–	René Leibowitz	1913–
Paul Hindemith	1895–	David Diamond	1915–
Carl Orff	1895–	Leonard Bernstein	1918–
Leo Sowerby	1895–	Gottfried von Einem	1918–
William Grant Still	1895–	Lukas Foss	1922–
Howard Hanson	1896–	Peter Mennin	1923–
Roger Sessions	1896–	Karlheinz Stockhausen	1928–

Contemporary Styles II

Chapter 24

EXPRESSIONISM AND THE TWELVE-TONE METHOD: SCHOENBERG, BERG, WEBERN

THE most celebrated of modern Viennese expressionists is Arnold Schoenberg. Wagner's music and Mahler's personality were both strong influences during his formative years. Early works like the *Verklärte Nacht* and the mammoth *Gurrelieder* are still in the orbit of late romantic chromaticism, although the Wagnerian overtones are treated with sensitive individuality. Another early work, a *Kammersymphonie* (chamber symphony) for fifteen instruments, reflects an early interest in conciseness of expression and in the formal problems attendant thereon.

The tone-row method of composition eventually evolved by Schoenberg is now sufficiently in perspective so that it can be understood as the single most systematic effort to solve a sequence of historical problems in composition. However, as the music of Debussy, Strauss, and Mahler indicates, the development of post-Wagnerian harmony was not confined to any one composer or any one musical center. While this development was initially motivated by the search for new expressive resources, the further reaches of dissonance could no longer be contained within the chromatic extensions of the traditional tonal system. Beyond a certain point new concepts were required to help explain and discipline their use. Composers as well as theorists found themselves involved in problems of the extension of tonality, the suspension of tonality, or in the possibility of its conscious abrogation. Debussy turned to a whole-tone scale in place of a diatonic major or minor scale, and contributed notably to the weakening of the structural harmonic functions of chords through his habit of moving a chord group up and down the points of the scale.

Before World War I, Charles Ives in the United States and Bela Bartók in Hungary had already begun to experiment with a polytonal music—that is, a music in two or more keys, played simultaneously. In Russia, Alexander Scriabin produced a notable "synthetic" harmonic system to subserve a rather obscure mysticism. Scriabin's system was too personal for general use. In his music, he is a man absorbed in remote ecstasies (*The Poem of Ecstasy*); in mystical postsymbolist experiments with color and sound (*Prometheus: The Poem of Fire* contains an especially constructed "keyboard of light" as part of the score); and in visions of the eternal struggle between Good and Evil (*The Divine Poem* and *The Satanic Poem*). His last work was to be an ultimate music whose sounding would collapse the walls of the world, whereupon the cycle of creation might start afresh. His harmonic system reduces to a "mystic chord," wherein the six notes C, D, E, F♯, A, B♭ are disposed usually in fourths—that is, C, F♯, B♭, E, A, D. It is a curious by-product of the search for new harmonic systems, and an interesting forerunner of subsequent approaches to chord construction by fourths instead of by thirds.

There are a number of works by Schoenberg leading up to *Pierrot Lunaire* in which the harmonic practice is perhaps best described as a suspension of tonality. In the welter of new ideas which emerged in a chromaticism liberated from the constraints of traditional tonal thinking, one can in retrospect detect the appearance of new concepts in compositional discipline which were later to be formulated into a method. It is worth emphasizing that Schoenberg's tone-row method was not an arbitrary invention, but a series of concepts evolved work by work. The method took shape in the course of the solution of specific creative problems in composition. The full method is not yet in evidence in *Pierrot Lunaire*, but this is a work that is extreme in the use of chromaticism and expressionistic dissonance. It was completed in 1912, and for the next few years Schoenberg busied himself with the evolution of a set of principles representing a codification of accumulated experience, and suggesting possibilities for the development of his music beyond the point reached in *Pierrot*.

Pierrot Lunaire is a cycle of twenty-one songs, divided into three sections with seven songs per section. The "vocal" part is taken by a *Sprechstimme*, literally a "speaking voice." The voice technique is that of speaking on indicated pitches—an expressionistic distortion of both speech and

song called *Sprechgesang,* an effective device for yielding a strange variety
of speech-song colors. A small group of instruments, varied for each song,
cooperates with the *Sprechstimme,* and the instrumental treatment is such
that dissonance of color and texture is as much an expressionistic resource
as a harmonic friction. Because of the brevity of each song, Schoenberg
practices an extreme economy of composition, each note calculated for
maximum tension, and each interval for maximum distortion of line. The
texts for the songs are German translations from the work of the French
symbolist poet Albert Giraud. The imagery is strained—it is an affected
fin de siècle decadence, reveling in gruesome gaieties and a moon-struck
state of hysteria. Pierrot, disregarding Cassander's shrieks, bores a hole in
his skull, stuffs it with tobacco, affixes a reed to the base, and smokes con-
tentedly (No. 16). The moon is sick (No. 7) and its stain upon Pierrot's
jacket (No. 18) is a contamination that no amount of scrubbing can remove. The poet's verses are crosses upon which he lies bleeding (No. 14),
and Pierrot, regarding the crescent moon with anguished horror, imagines
it a turkish scimitar and himself decapitated by it (No. 13).

Schoenberg's music is more than a match for such texts. Curiously, the
naked hysteria in this combination of music and poetry is often the product of the most precisely logical arrangement of tone patterns. In one
piece (No. 17) the viola imitates the *Sprechstimme* which the clarinet part
is an imitation by contrary motion. This is followed by a canon between
Sprechstimme and piccolo and in contrary motion between viola and
clarinet. In another piece (No. 18) the formalisms are even more extract-
ing. A double canon (one canon between piccolo and clarinet, and a
second between violin and cello) runs its course and is then played retrograde, all parts reading backwards from last note to first. All this goes on
simultaneously with a free part for the *Sprechstimme,* and a three-part
fugato for the piano. This union between an expressionism pushed to the
point of hysteria and an abstract musical formalism refined to the last precise point of musical logic is characteristic of Schoenberg both before and
after his formulation and conscious application of the disciplines of a
tone-row method. It was a habit of mind which he transmitted to his disciples, although when one encounters it in the work of Alban Berg, the
quality of the emotion and the type of formalism are necessarily altered
in ways that are individual to Berg.

Traditional harmony discriminates between the seven diatonic tones
that belong to a stipulated tonal system (a key) and the five chromatic
tones that are peripheral to it. (For clarification of this point, a rereading
of pp. 67 to 82 is recommended.) In a music as densely overgrown with
chromaticism as Wagner's, the range of harmonic reference within a tonality (a given key) is enormously enlarged. In a few works prior to

Pierrot, and in *Pierrot* itself, the chromaticism has grown beyond the boundaries of tonality; the discrimination between what is diatonic and what is chromatic disappears, and with it all sense of clear tonal orientation. This phase may be described as a suspension of tonality, and it presents the composer with the obvious need for alternatives to tonal organization. The intensive recourse to formalistic device already noted in *Pierrot,* is, in part at least, motivated by the need for some governing concept to discipline the free association of the twelve tones. Such devices are, however, temporary expedients, and following *Pierrot,* Schoenberg set himself seriously to the task of evolving a firm set of principles with which to order a music composed on the basis of twelve equal tones.

The point to be especially noticed is that the twelve tones are equal. They are no longer divided into seven diatonic and five chromatic tones, nor is there necessarily any stipulation intrinsic to the system (as there is in tonal harmony) that one tone is to be accorded pre-eminence and regarded as the tonic. The system is not limited, then, to chromatic harmony or to tonal harmony, but is founded on such general principles as can be said to underlie the total range of relationships possible among twelve tones.

Theoretically the system is not committed to tonality. Neither is it committed to the denial of tonality. Tonality relationships are among the many possible relationships which the new system can suggest and govern. In any given work, the composer will exercise a personal option as to the extent to which it pleases him to accept tonality relationships as part of the plan for the piece. In his first applications of his new method, Schoenberg was somewhat overly concerned with the avoidance of any suggestion of tonality relationships, and thus emphasized the aspects of his system which were most aggressively different from traditional practice. However, since the system is general enough to include tonality relationships as a sector of its harmonic possibilities, Schoenberg's practice eventually began to take cognizance of tonality as a wholly legitimate resource with much still to recommend it. (The use of the term "atonality" to describe the twelve-tone system does not appear to contribute anything to an understanding of the system, either of its practice or its potential; it seems best simply to avoid it.)

As for the principles of the system, they may be summarized as follows. A row of tones is posited as the basic substance of a given piece. A row is simply a particular arrangement of the twelve tones, and all twelve tones are to be first stated in sequence before any tone is repeated. The following, for example, is the row Schoenberg uses for the first movement of his Fourth String Quartet, Op. 37.

D, C♯, A, B♭, F, E♭, E, C, A♭, G, F♯, B

The time values and the rhythmic organization give contour to the row—
that is, convert it into a melody (see first violin part, Ex. 24:2*a*). The
third and seventh notes (A and E) are given as three eighth notes, and
the eleventh note (F♯) as two eighth notes. But these are repetitions
within the sequence. The tone row as an entity is not disordered initially
by the reappearance, for example, of the third note after the seventh. If a
note is repeated (as it may well be, for the row is not only an abstraction
but also a melodic line), the repetition will be at the point in the sequence
where the tone occurs. In short, the shaping of the row in accordance with
the composer's sense for line cannot be at the expense of the integrity of
the row as such.

   The integrity of the row is not considered to be in any way jeopardized
by the octave position of a tone. Thus a given note can be transposed an
octave or two up or down. It is still the same note, and the row, as a row, is
intact, although the melodic configuration is severely altered. Thus the
basic row for the first movement of Anton von Webern's Concerto for
Nine Instruments, Op. 24, may be stated as follows:

Ex. 24:1a   Concerto for Nine Instruments. Webern.

However, it is first heard in the following dispersion of octave registers:

Ex. 24:1b

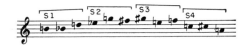

Like Schoenberg and Berg, Webern was strongly expressionistic in his
orientation, and this dispersion of octave registers converts mild half steps
into aggressively dissonant minor ninths.

Ex. 24:1c
(Bars 1–3).

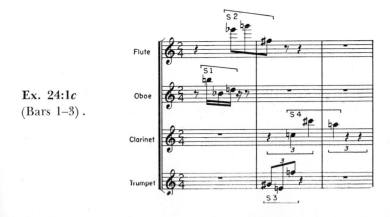

The row is most often treated as a unity of segments. A commonly encountered segmentation is to consider the row as comprising four segments of three notes each. This suggests to Webern a color pattern for his row, each segment of three notes given to a different instrument. (The row or series is represented by the letter "S." The numbers 1, 2, 3, and 4 stand for the succession of the segments.) See Example 24:1c, page 411.

The row can be transformed by a number of simple operations. For example, the entire row can be played backwards, beginning with the last note and ending with the first.

S series			1	2	3	4	5	6	7	8	9	10	11	12
SR series in retrograde	12	11	10	9	8	7	6	5	4	3		2		1

Or else, if the series is segmented, each segment can be given in retrograde:

S	1	2	3	4	5	6	7	8	9	10	11	12
SR	3	2	1	6	5	4	9	8	7	12	11	10

In the Webern row, the latter procedure, the retrograde of each segment in turn, yields the following row:

Ex. 24:1d

This new row is then distributed over the piano keyboard as follows:

Ex. 24:1e

In similar fashion, the row can be inverted; for instance, a half step upward (B to C) becomes a half step downward (B to B♭) ; or the retrograde of the row can be inverted. Regardless of the forms of the row that can be produced by the manipulation of the segments, there are then four versions of the row: its fundamental position, its inversion, its retrograde form, or the inversion of its retrograde. Each of these versions of the row can be duplicated starting on any one of the twelve degrees of the scale, yielding then no less than forty-eight simple versions of the row.

In the first movement of the Webern Concerto, the following procedures are encountered in the first thirteen measures.

No. 1: The row in fundamental position (Bars 1–3):

B Bb D	Eb G F♯	G♯ E F	C C♯ A
1	2	3	4

No. 2: Retrograde of each segment in turn (Bars 4–5):

D Bb B   F♯ G Eb   F E G♯   A C♯ C

No. 3: Duplication of No. 2 (retrograde of each segment) transposed down a half step and starting on C♯ (Bars 6–7):

C♯ A Bb   F F♯ D   E Eb G   Ab C B

No. 4: The row in fundamental position (as in No. 1), transposed up a half step and starting on C (Bars 7–8):

C B Eb   E G♯ G   A F F♯   C♯ D Bb

No. 5: An inversion of No. 4 (inversion of the foregoing transposition), (Bars 9–10):

C C♯ A   G♯ E F   Eb G F♯   B Bb D

No. 6: The foregoing inversion (No. 5) transposed to F as the starting tone (Bars 11–13):

F F♯ D   C♯ A Bb   Ab C B   E Eb G

Both harmonic and contrapuntal procedures are readily suggested by the method. The opening movement of Schoenberg's Fourth String Quartet, Op. 37, provides convenient examples. The opening measures present the row in the first violin part. It is a segmented row, four groups of three notes each (represented in the example as S_1, S_2, S_3, S_4). While the first violin plays the first segment (S_1), the three other strings accompany with S_2, S_3, and S_4 in that order. When the first violin moves to the second segment (S_2), the accompaniment continues the progression in order (S_3, S_4, and S_1). And so on in sequence: Violin I on S_3, accompaniment on S_4, S_1, S_2; Violin I on S_4, accompaniment on S_1, S_2, S_3. The row is always in order although it is simultaneously disposed in two opposite ways: as a line of melody, and the notes within each segment arranged vertically to form chords (Ex. 24:2a). Later on the row is transposed to G as the start-

Ex. 24:2a   String Quartet, Op. 37 No. 4 (Bars 1–6). Schoenberg.

ing tone (Ex. 24:2b) and this row on G is inverted (Ex. 24:2c). The in-

Ex. 24:2b

Ex. 24:2c

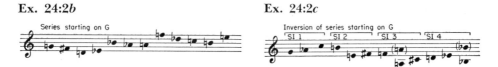

version of the G row is then dispersed contrapuntally as a series of canonic
entrances (Ex. 24:2d). By staggering the entrances one segment apart, the
row becomes vertically complete when the cello enters.

Ex. 24:2d

The row can be constructed to avoid all tonal suggestion; or it can be constructed to intimate tonal relationships as a possibility; or it can be designed explicitly to incorporate a wide range of traditional tonal resource. The row from Alban Berg's Violin Concerto shown in Example 24:3 indicates how a row can be constructed to contain within it traditional tonic and dominant chord relationships, all traditional basic chord formations (major, minor, augmented, and diminished) , and the resources of the whole tone scale as well.

Ex. 24:3 From Violin Concerto. Berg.

Toward the close of the Violin Concerto Berg introduces a Bach chorale, *Es ist genug* (It is enough) , which fits quite naturally within the fabric of the twelve-tone music, for the first four notes of the chorale are identical with the last four notes of the row.

The procedures in tone-row composition are no more mathematical than those to be found in Bach's counterpoint or in Beethoven's harmony. As a method it offers, as any method does, a range of suggestion. If this method has the singular virtue of suggesting to the composer an extraordinarily large number of relevant tone patterns from which to choose, in the last analysis the value of the music, as music, depends upon the choice. And in choosing among possibilities—which is what Josquin des Prez did when he wrote modally, Beethoven when he wrote diatonically, Wagner when he composed chromatically, or Schoenberg when he manipulated tone rows—the composer, in every case, is exercising an esthetic judgment. For this there is fundamentally no substitute for taste, experience, and the mysterious quality called inspiration. For the mediocrity in any age, method is an excuse for lack of creativity; the method, in a sense, writes the music. For the creative composer in any age, method is simply a framework of relevant relationships. It does not constrict the composer's musical imagination, although it does condition it by the nature of its suggestions. The point to be emphasized about the music of Schoenberg, Berg, and Webern is that it was written as music, not as illustrations of a method.

The musical style of Schoenberg and Webern derives only in part from the tone-row method of composition. Styles other than expressionism are quite feasible in the tone-row technique, and Schoenberg's musical personality was already substantially formed before he evolved his method. Actually, this penchant for expressionistic techniques strongly conditioned the manner in which both composers made use of the method. Theirs was an expressionism that had been formalized; and Schoenberg's course from intuition to formalism was, for expressionism, a parallel to the similar history of impressionism and symbolism (from Monet to Seurat in painting, and from Mallarmé to Valéry in poetry). In this post-Mahlerian circle of Viennese expressionists, Webern is the most indrawn, Berg the most accessibly fervent and indeed flamboyant in his emotionality, and Schoenberg, upon occasion, almost necessarily the most doctrinaire.

Apart from his Violin Concerto, two of the best-known works by Alban Berg are his *Lyric Suite* and his opera *Wozzeck*. The expressionistic emotionality of the *Lyric Suite,* a string quartet, is a violent intensification of a Mahlerlike sequence of emotional states. The overall psychological design and the character of this enormously compelling music are indicated in the titles for the six movements:

I. *Allegretto gioviole,* which translates as lively and jovial.
II. *Andante amoroso,* which may be construed as moderate in tempo and amorous in tone.
III. *Allegro misterioso,* fast and mysterious.
IV. *Adagio appassionata,* slow and with passion.
V. *Presto delirando,* very fast and delirious.
VI. *Largo desolato,* very slow and in utter desolation.

Every two movements represent a stepping up of the level of alternating emotions. Fast and slow movements alternate in sequence, the fast movements becoming progressively faster (Allegretto, Allegro, Presto), and the slow movements slower (Andante, Adagio, Largo). As the tempos culminate in expressionistic extremes, so likewise do the emotional levels to which the tempos correspond: from joviality, through mystery, to delirium for the sequence of increasingly fast tempos; and from amorousness, through passion, to desolation for the sequence of slow movements. Characteristic of the course of an expressionistic music, delirium and desolation are the ultimate goals.

Berg's opera *Wozzeck,* a setting of Georg Büchner's drama by that name, displays to the fullest the highly formalized expressionism so characteristic of the Viennese circle clustered around Schoenberg. It is a tragedy that ends in madness, murder, and death; and the moon plays the role a Viennese expressionist expects it to in abetting Wozzeck's madness and his murder of Marie. Yet nothing could be further from the moonstruck hysteria of Schoenberg's *Pierrot Lunaire,* or from the abstract psychotic states projected in Strauss' *Salome* and *Elektra*.

Berg remained faithful to the profoundly compassionate view which

Büchner took of those who live and suffer and die in his drama. Wozzeck is a poor soldier, and he and Marie have a child out of wedlock. As Wozzeck explains to his captain, people without money cannot afford morals, and the lives of Wozzeck and Marie are displayed against the backdrop of the brutalizing circumstances in which they are condemned to live. As Wozzeck ruefully observes, "People like us can't be holy, either in this world or the next. If they ever let us into heaven, it would only be to help with the thunder." Marie plays fondly with her child, and indulges in a tawdry affair with a flashy, blustering Drum Major who adds injury to insult by trouncing the humiliated Wozzeck. Marie reads the story of Mary Magdalene and weeps. Later, while walking near a pond in the woods with Wozzeck, she watches the moon and they reminisce about how long they have been together. She is oblivious of Wozzeck's growing insanity, for her feet hurt; and she approaches the moment of her murder absorbed, as she has always been, in the small nuisances of being alive. Following her death, Wozzeck seeks to forget his crime in a cheap dance hall. But the blood on his arm excites suspicion and he rushes off to recover the knife which he had left behind. Attempting to wash the knife, he wades deeper and deeper into the pond. A few passers-by, hearing some disquieting sounds from the pond (Wozzeck drowning), go away. It is none of their business. At the close of the opera, Marie's child, playing unconcernedly on his hobbyhorse and utterly without comprehension, receives from another child the news that his mother is dead.

All through Act III, from the scene where Marie reads the Bible to the close, the music underscores this poignant blend of the aberrational and the ordinary. Berg never attempts to convert Büchner's characters into conveniences for the embodiment of expressionistic soul states. For Wozzeck and for Marie, the details of their poor humanity are their only possession, and Berg does not rob his characters of them.

Büchner's drama presents difficulties, for it is a sequence of twenty-six short scenes, some just a few lines each. The expressionistic intensification of both the social and psychological realism of the drama owes much to its short, fragmentary nature. To a considerable degree Berg preserved this quality, although he reorganized Büchner's work into three acts of five scenes each. As Berg saw the problem, "The necessity for pulling the scenes together and juxtaposing them so that they could be grouped into several acts confronted me, whether I liked it or not, with a problem of a musical rather than literary nature; that is, by a problem to be solved not by the laws of dramaturgy, but by musical construction." Music, of course, is always the central dramatic mechanism in any opera. In this opera, each act, as well as each scene within the act, achieves coherence and continuity (despite its fragmentary literary quality) through the abstract formalism of the music.

Act I, presenting five characters in their relationship to Wozzeck, is designed as a set of five musical character or genre pieces. The five scenes present, in order, the Captain, Andres, Marie, the Physician, and the Drum Major. The parallel musical construction for each scene is, respectively: (1) a Suite, (2) a Rhapsody (3) a Military March and a Lullaby, (4) a Passacaglia, and (5) an Andante affetuoso (quasi Rondo). The Suite, which serves as setting for the scene between the Captain and Wozzeck, begins and ends with a Prelude. The second Prelude is, however, the first in retrograde; and between these two Preludes, Berg interpolates a Pavane, a Gigue, a Gavotte, and a three-part Aria. As transition to Scene Two, various canonic elaborations of material from the Suite occur. However emotional the music, this type of formal discipline is never relaxed.

Act II is a five-movement symphony: a sonata form serves for the opening scene in which Wozzeck's suspicions of Marie are first exposed and developed; a Fantasia and Fugue are used for the second scene in which Wozzeck is mocked; a slow movement (largo) is used for Wozzeck and Marie; a Scherzo serves for the fourth scene between Marie and the Drum Major; and a Rondo marziale for the Finale (the scene where the Drum Major trounces Wozzeck). Act III is a sequence of six inventions, the added invention serving as an extended interlude after Wozzeck's suicide and before the final scene with the children. Marie's remorse (Scene One) is constructed as an invention on a theme; her death (Scene Two), as an invention on a tone; the scene in a dance hall, when Wozzeck tries to forget his crime, as an invention on a rhythm; Wozzeck's suicide and the extended interlude that follows, as inventions, respectively, on a chord and on a key; and the final scene with Marie's child and the hobbyhorse, as an invention on a persistent rhythm.

Wherever possible the formal construction serves not only as the abstract architecture that governs the integrity of the act, but also as a projection of character and situation. The invention on a persistent rhythm for the child playing, oblivious to the meaning of his mother's death, is conceived as a musical symbolism for a child's unheedingly egocentric world; while an orientation to the traditional Viennese storm-and-stress key of D minor (for instance, the death of Don Giovanni in Mozart's opera, and Schubert's song and quartet on *Death and the Maiden*) is evident and, indeed, almost inevitable in the episode of Wozzeck's drowning and in the interlude that follows. It should, however, be emphasized that Berg is a dramatist and, as fascinating as the musical formalisms may be, it is Berg's compassion for the human condition that is primarily in focus.

ANTIROMANTICISM: THE PRIMITIVIST REVOLT—STRAVINSKY

One of the challenging curiosities encountered seemingly at every moment in music history is the fact that a Rachmaninoff—to choose a well-known name at random—is always the contemporary of a Schoenberg, and both are always, apparently, the contemporaries of a Stravinsky. The present seems to be continually in the process of settling accounts with the past. There is no reason to expect unanimity in this matter, nor any compelling need to suppose it is even desirable. Divergent approaches to technical problems are the symptoms of deeper disagreements in attitude; loyalties and antipathies are often pushed to extremes. Interestingly enough, one can probe more extensively into the twentieth-century relationship to romanticism through an ill-assorted trio like Rachmaninoff, Schoenberg, and Stravinsky than one can through the work of more compatible groupings such as Schoenberg, Berg, and Webern; or Sibelius, Rachmaninoff, and Respighi.

At the stage where Schoenberg was still finding himself amid the post-Wagnerian ecstasies of a *Transfigured Night,* Rachmaninoff was defining himself in his popular Concerto No. 2 for Piano and Orchestra within the context of a sensuous post-Tchaikovskian melancholia, and Stravinsky was just emerging via his *Fire Bird* from the effulgent, late-romantic exoticism of his master, Rimsky-Korsakoff. Each first found himself with respect to his inheritance, and within a few years each came to terms with the romanticism from which he emerged. Rachmaninoff was a conservative, which is to say that in essence he found his romantic inheritance good. The slow changes in the technicalities of his style, which are evident over several decades of distinguished creativity, were refinements that were bound to occur within the work of a sensitive composer. But Rachmaninoff never felt the need to move beyond the orbit of a late romantic idiom which, early in his career, he defined as his world. By contrast, Schoenberg's romanticism was of the radical variety, rather than conservative. All through his career, he remained faithfully wedded to a flamboyantly romantic expressivity. However, the sheer power of his expressionistic compulsions drove him to extend the limits of traditional romantic emotionality, and eventually to transform it. With Stravinsky, however, attitudes that are basically negations of romanticism can be seen emerging as early as *Petrouchka,* and this despite the persistence of certain traditional elements in the score, such as a national folk style of melody. Thus the two most arresting and influential of the radicalisms of twentieth-century music reveal themselves as a contrary settling of accounts with the nine-

teenth-century inheritance—an extension of romanticism with Schoenberg; and, for an important period at least, its negation with Stravinsky.

The setting for *Petrouchka* is a Russian fair. From the very outset
Stravinsky confronts his audience with a wholly new attitude toward traditional romantic material. The pulsation of the crowd, the drunkards
that stagger across the stage, the side-show barker's raucous fanfare, the
organ-grinder's innocent banality, and the music box with its tinkling in-
sipidity are all reported with journalistic matter-of-factness. Divested of
its romantic glamour, the scene is noisy, vulgar, banal, but endowed with
a new and wonderfully unsentimental vigor. During the enactment of the
puppet show, a whole collection of clichés, so precious to romantic ballet,
are unceremoniously stripped of their magic, their sugary charm, and their
fairyland elegance. The curtain rises on the puppet booth to a blatant percussion accompaniment appropriate not to the romantic ballet but to a
cheap carnival side show. The animation of the puppets begins with a few
phrases that are still within the conventions of romantic magic-transfor-
mation music. But the magician is a charlatan, and on his magic flute he
plays a little virtuoso solo which is a masterpiece of pure banality. The
puppets come to life for their Russian Dance, for which the orchestra cuts,
shapes, and polishes the dance patterns with all the accuracy and the unsentimental efficiency of a precision-tool instrument.

The characterizations that then emerge are the very antithesis of romanticism. Petrouchka is unceremoniously kicked onstage for the Second
Tableau. He is awkward, unattractive, and his ludicrous self-pity (heard
in the wailing dissonances that open the scene) is worked up into a fury of
foul-mouthed cursing (the *furioso* passage for muted brass marked "male-
dictions of Petrouchka" in the score). So much for the handsome, noble
ballet hero. The Moor is a mere voluptuary, and the Ballerina a dancing
girl who would be more at home in the gaudy vulgarity of a Toulouse-
Lautrec dance hall than in a ballet theater. She makes her appearance in
the Moor's apartment (in the Third Tableau following the Moor's
Dance), announced by a rat-tat-tat of dry percussion and a cornet tune that
is a ballet cliché reduced to an extreme of blatancy and banality. The
Valse of the Ballerina and the Moor, which then follows, is a merciless
exposé of a collection of stale romantic clichés, the vulgarity of its charm
and the tawdriness of its elegance being underlined by a brash cornet commentary interpolated at intervals during the duet. (Other aspects of
Petrouchka are discussed in Chap. 14, pp. 174–176.)

In *Petrouchka,* which dates from just before World War I, Stravinsky
created that unglamorous, hard-boiled, monosyllabic world so familiar to
the American reading public through the unromantic, expatriate novels
of the 1920's. This enormously vital music, released from its burden of

fragile, fairyland charm, cavorts with unbounded exuberance amid banalities. There is also a primitivism in *Petrouchka* that reappears in various and sundry transformations in *The Rite of Spring* (1913), *The Story of the Soldier* (1918), *The Wedding* (1917–23), and in *Renard* (1922). The primitivism of *The Rite of Spring* (*Le Sacre du Printemps*) is an expressionistic extreme. By the turn of the century, Gauguin's exotic pictorial primitivism took shape as a conscious attack upon Europe—its civilization and its polite Christianity. More than the hot color of Tahitian skies lured Gauguin to the South Seas. Gauguin's complaint against the romantic revivals of the past was that none of them went back far enough. His was a true primitivism that gloried in being called savage, in being not only non-European but even pre-Christian. Before the first decade of the twentieth century was over, Picasso had not only redirected the sources of Parisian primitivism to African masks and primitive Iberian sculpture, but in his painting. *The Young Ladies of Avignon,* had already turned expressionistic primitivism toward the formalities of cubism.

Stravinsky's *Rite of Spring* emerged in the year 1913 out of the context of this Parisian primitivism. It is a ballet designed as a series of rituals from pagan Russia, more barbaric than the pictures of Gauguin, and more extreme in its expressionistic violence than the pre-World War I paintings of Picasso. None of the musical imitations of it (Prokofieff's *Scythian Suite,* for instance, was composed for another pagan ballet designed to capitalize on the sensation caused by the *Rite of Spring*) have quite the raw cacophonous power of Stravinsky's final scene, *Danse Sacrale* (Sacrificial Dance). It is significant that two composers so deeply sensitive to the world around them—Schoenberg and Stravinsky—should have produced, just prior to World War I, the two most violently expressionistic works of this century. These two disparate companion pieces—*Pierrot Lunaire* (1912) and *The Rite of Spring* (1913)—appeared, moreover, within a year of each other and in different musical centers (Vienna and Paris). They were thus the opposite vectors of the same emotional explosion. Also the composers of these two works were intuitively more truthful than the presumably well-informed statesmen of those years, who soothingly declared that Europe was too civilized to have another war.

The primitivism of *The Wedding* (*Les Noces*) takes the inevitable step beyond that of the *Rite,* for it is a primitivism made efficient and economical—in short, a formalized primitivism. A choreographic cantata in four tableaux, *The Wedding* was the major work to occupy Stravinsky during the war years 1914–15. Completed in 1917, the instrumentation was delayed until very near its performance deadline in June of 1923. If the *Rite* is based on pagan Russia, the *Wedding* is an equivalent primitivism based on peasant Russia. In his autobiography, *Chronicles of my Life*

(1936), it is precisely during his account of *Les Noces* and the war years that Stravinsky digresses into a discussion of his musical esthetic, in which "construction" and "achieved order" are postulated as the fundamentals of his musical art, and the flat assertion is made that "music is, by its very nature, essentially powerless to *express* anything at all . . ." In literally every minute detail of this score, construction with sound is pursued and order therein achieved. The ground plan of the sonority is a stark division between the vocal forces on the one hand (solo and ensemble), and on the other a percussion aggregate comprising four pianos, four kettledrums, xylophone, bass drum, tambourine, triangle, cymbals, and drums both with and without snare. This mechanized ensemble is a logical evolution out of the orchestra of the *Rite,* which may be taken as very nearly the ultimate in precision-tool percussiveness for an orchestral mechanism of that vast dimension. It is possible to conceive of expansion beyond the *Rite,* and, for a while, Stravinsky did consider scoring *The Wedding* for a force of some one hundred and fifty performers. But the ultimate choice of a condensed percussion ensemble emphasizes the essential severity and primitivistic starkness of the music, which, in turn, reflects (despite Stravinsky's suspicion of cultural correlations) the general antiromantic esthetic of the early 1920's.

In the visual arts as well as in music, the new esthetic, reacting against the opulence and the megalomania of late-romantic music and art, stressed a puritanical economy of means and a flat precision in the treatment of detail. In *The Wedding,* for example, the interval of a fourth, broken into a minor third and a major second, accounts for an astounding amount of motivic detail throughout the score. And upon occasion, a single one-measure unit, with a kind of pure momentum gained by driving repetition and variation, generates an entire melodic line.

Ex. 24:4   *The Wedding* (Bars 140–153). Stravinsky.

This intricately constructed simplicity—this severe "dynamism" (the word is Erik Satie's) —serves to illustrate the rather special flavor of this score. There is here an intricately stylized folk primitiveness, which so often marks the sophisticate's approach to the manners and music of the folk, rather than the "naturalism" of a peasant ceremonial. A "hard" primitivism, so-called, characterizes *Les Noces,* for Stravinsky strips from peasant ceremonial its picturesque camouflage of quaintness and bucolic charm.

ANTIROMANTICISM: THE NEOCLASSIC REVOLT—STRAVINSKY, THE SIX

The emphasis on formal construction in sound that began to appear during the war years reached perhaps its purest and most engaging expression in Stravinsky's Octet for Wind Instruments composed during 1922–23. The work is literally a musical architecture—an edifice of sonority and pattern. In Stravinsky's own words, his point was "to establish order and discipline in the purely sonorous scheme to which I always give precedence over elements of an emotional character . . ." The Octet is light in sonority, transparent in texture, casual in manner, and popular in melodic tone. These are qualities that also began to emerge during the war years, and that relate the Octet to *The Soldier's Tale* (*L'Histoire du Soldat*), and to an assortment of minor works from 1914 on.

The Soldier's Tale is a modern retelling of the Faust story—the Devil seeking possession of the Soldier's soul, which is symbolized by a fiddle. The Devil, in this case, appears in a variety of disguises (a cattle merchant, an old woman peddler, a virtuoso violinist, and a card sharp). He offers the Soldier the conventional inducements and eventually carries him off when the Soldier, not content with wealth, glory, and the hand of a princess in marriage, leaves his kingdom to seek his native village. The work is a pantomime, and the instrumentalists are present on stage along with the narrator and the dancers. The vast orchestra of the *Rite* is here reduced to just seven performers. Woodwinds are reduced to one clarinet and one bassoon; the brass, to a trombone and a *cornet à pistons* (a short-tubed trumpet); the strings, to a violin and double bass; while the one percussionist manages cymbals, tambourine, triangle, and drums of various sizes with and without snare. The music is light and informal, except for the ponderously discordant "Great Choral" during which the Narrator moralizes: a man must not desire more than he has; he must choose between what he is and what he was, for to be both is impossible.

The Soldier's Tale marks one of the main musical events in the intense antiromanticism that developed during and after World War I. The plush and brocade textures of the romantic orchestra, the tantrums and the transfigurations, the yearnings for innocence, infinity, solitude, and the world's adulation give way here to an economical street-gamin ensemble, tooting tangos, and ragtime, intoning the sacred chorale, "A Mighty Fortress" (*Ein feste Burg*), with deliciously discordant solemnity, marching gaily to fresh rhythms, and to well-scrubbed and cleanly dressed dissonances. In place of a religion of art, and expressionistic post-Freudian accounts of the soul of twentieth-century man, the listener is invited to have fun.

Seldom since the eighteenth century had a major master of the orchestra offered the musical public popular entertainment of this sort. Stravinsky seemed to have been thoroughly aware of this, for if there are models for this work, they are the eighteenth-century dance suite, and, less so perhaps, the divertissement. The internationalism of the eighteenth century is transformed into the internationalism of 1918. In place of a courante, an allemande, or a minuet, Stravinsky provides (in the "Little Concert") a tango, a waltz, and a ragtime piece, and (in the "Marche Royale") a Spanish *paso doble*. Apart from the source of the text, which is from a collection of Russian folk tales, and a brief reference to a Russian tune in the motto for the Soldier's violin, Stravinsky has left his Russian background behind him. In *The Soldier's Tale* he emerged as an exponent of the light, clever, aerated entertainment known sometimes as the "International Style," and very popular among the avant-garde in postwar Paris.

The Paris scene during this period was a complex of heterogeneous trends. In the following account, which is necessarily schematic, misconceptions will be avoided if it is understood that each trend in itself was a complex of diverse motivations and origins. In certain of their aspects, these trends intersected freely with one another, forming temporary unities out of diverse musical impulses. And since they did intersect freely, they were also dissociated quite readily, following a course of development at times intrinsically logical, at others influenced by nothing more profound than the momentary caprice of this or that composer. This free and tolerant association of styles and ideas was centered in Paris which was, during the 1920's and early 1930's, an international expatriate center. Significantly, Stravinsky, a Russian, was the dominating figure. While French composers were active and important to be sure, the assemblage of talent was international in character. Under such circumstances the musical developments in Paris could scarcely be confined to French music alone. The echoes of developments in Paris were heard in musical centers all over Europe and in the Americas.

The antiromantic tone that pervaded a sector of this complex is well illustrated in the work of *The Six,* a group that included such notable composers as Francis Poulenc, Darius Milhaud, and Arthur Honegger. Their spiritual grandparent was Erik Satie, a gremlinish character who was a precursor of, and a participant in, the short-lived dadaist style in the visual arts and letters of World War I and the postwar years. Satie had an infallible eye for humbug, and a quietly beautiful instinct for the absurd. He knew how to load his delicate music with stage directions as well as any Viennese expressionist or Parisian symbolist. It was typical for him to instruct the performer that a given passage in his music was to be played "like a nightingale with a toothache." To Debussy he remarked concerning the "From dawn till noon on the sea" section of *La Mer* that he liked the part around a quarter to eleven. Satie's piano music is an informal extemporaneous cafe style. It rambles along on a kind of free-association principle from one consonant chord structure to another. When criticized for the lack of formal design in his music, his reply was *Three Pieces in the Shape of a Pear.*

The romantic doctrine that one must be serious at all costs was negated by *The Six* into a new antiromantic catch phrase, "Against seriousness at all costs." The informal spontaneity, and the uncomplicated pleasantries of Satie's music was a convenient point of orientation. Much of the music produced by *The Six* is charming, delightful to listen to, and refreshing as a musical entertainment for its own sake. Their melodic material is jaunty and popular, and their instrumentation light and clear. French cabaret music and American jazz were both welcome, as were the styles and forms of preromantic eighteenth-century music. The clear counterpoint of Bach, and the fresh, experimental sonorities of small-ensemble jazz were discovered to be delightfully compatible. The symphony was contracted to the light-weight serenade or divertimento style that had characterized it in some of the early works of Haydn, and diminutives became fashionable.

Arthur Honegger's engaging three-movement work for piano and orchestra, with a jazz idiom featured in the Finale, is called a Concertino; while Darius Milhaud composed a three-movement Symphony (No. 3, subtitled a "Serenade") lasting in its entirety but three minutes. Absurdity was the order of the day, and Poulenc's "grand" Concerto for Two Pianos and Orchestra is a yoking together of a Lisztian virtuoso style with music borrowed from Mozart's "storm-and-stress" D-minor Piano Concerto. The favorite instruction to the performers in this grandiose work is *très sec* (very dry). Curiously, for all his comedy, Poulenc is a delicate miniaturist, and there are exquisitely sensitive moments in this score, just as there are in many of his beautiful songs. Echoes of this Paris manner can be heard in Prokofieff's *Sarcasms* for piano, and in Hindemith's *Kleine Kammermusik,* Op. 24. The idiom is, however, transformed, for in both Prokofieff and Hindemith the high-spirited irreverence is often etched with acid.

ECLECTICISM: MUSIC HISTORY REVISITED

Paris at this time was bound to be friendly to the small-ensemble jazz style that found its way there after World War I. The new jazz was unconventional, non-European, and primitive in the sense of its being academically uneducated; and Parisian sophisticates had already been trained to appreciate the untutored primitivism of African wood sculptures as well as that of painters like Henri Rousseau. Furthermore, jazz ensembles were refreshingly original in their choice of instruments, and remarkably imaginative in exploiting instrumental sonorities in unorthodox ways. Every instrument served in a maximum capacity, for each was, in turn, a soloist as well as an efficient member of the ensemble. There was no romantic padding, and yet the music was warmly emotional (and to Parisian ears, unsentimental). Above all, jazz, at this time, was frowned upon in the conservatories and regarded as a lower-class vulgarity by the smug members of a bourgeois audience who sat through fairy-tale ballets and congratulated themselves on their refined taste. In short, the appeal of jazz lay in the fact that it was spontaneous, unsophisticated, and unconventional. Actually, a composer like Stravinsky had no real interest in writing jazz as such, or in contriving a music that sounded like the authentic product. But he did have a great deal of interest in appropriating from it such qualities as he found personally serviceable. Stravinsky's "Ragtime" pieces, his *Ebony Concerto* (written for Woody Herman's jazz band), Milhaud's ballet, *Creation of the World,* Honegger's Concertino for Piano and Orchestra, and Aaron Copland's Piano Concerto (the so-called "Jazz Concerto") are not works which the true jazz devotee is likely to listen to with either comfort or comprehension. The idiom became an abstract musical substance; the composer worked with it as he pleased, with no obligation either to understand it or to reproduce it faithfully. It was conventional, for instance, to make concerto finales out of Hungarian idioms. But Mozart, Beethoven, Liszt, and Brahms were no more interested in the authenticity of Hungarian idioms than Stravinsky, Milhaud, Honegger, or Copland were in fidelity to true jazz style.

A similar development characterized the widespread borrowings from the preromantic past. The so-called "back to Bach" movement attracted perhaps the greatest critical attention, but the reusing of various period styles spread eventually from the classical and baroque styles, to fifteenth-century Burgundian polyphony, the *ars nova* of Machaut, all the way back to medieval organum. At no point was there any desire to imitate or recreate; only to reuse earlier styles and techniques as fresh musical substances. This ransacking of past music history, generally called *eclecticism,* is perhaps symptomatic of a broader eclecticism in all the arts, in which every conceivable idiom is welcome for whatever fresh ideas it can suggest. More than ever, style is the man. Style is, in short, the collection of personal habits shown by the composer, regardless of the idiom—Bach or jazz, Pergolesi or a Lutheran chorale—he chooses to use in any given work. This point of view is as characteristic of Stravinsky as of Aaron Copland. It is also characteristic of Picasso and other modern artists.

Baroque polyphony was one of the substances used by Stravinsky in his *Symphony of Psalms;* and Burgundian polyphony, with intimations of the style of Machaut, in his Mass. A generalized Bach style became the substance of the slow movement of Stravinsky's Capriccio for Piano and Orchestra, while traces of Bach's Third *Brandenburg* Concerto are evident in Stravinsky's *Dumbarton Oaks* Concerto for Sixteen Wind Instruments. Pergolesi's music served as the material for Stravinsky's ballet *Pulcinella,* and, as Stravinsky himself has said, the "conventions of old Russo-Italian opera" were the materials for his own opera, *Mavra.* A combination of both Bach and South American dance music is included in Milhaud's ballet *Creation of the World,* while the union of Bach and national Brazilian idioms provided Heitor Villa-Lobos with the musical materials for his *Bachianas Brasilieras.* Respighi in Italy, Vaughan Williams in England, and Roy Harris in the United States were all interested in the revival of early modes: Respighi in his *Gregorian Concerto,* Vaughan Williams in his *Fantasia on a Theme by Thomas Tallis,* and Roy Harris in his String Quartet, No. 3 (the four movements of which are preludes and fugues in such modes as the Dorian, Aeolian, Lydian, Ionian, and Phrygian). In like fashion, instruments long obsolete were found to be singularly compatible with new musical idioms. Hindemith wrote a Sonata for Viola d'Amore and Piano (Op. 25, No. 2), and Manuel de Falla a Concerto for Harpsichord and small chamber ensemble.

This eclecticism served many purposes and was the consequence of a multiplicity of motivations. It opened the door to some of the freest experiments in music history. Microtonal music (based on more minute divisions than the half tone, such as quarter tones) was investigated by Hába, Barth, and Carillo; and a pure percussion music was established on a secure footing by Edgar Varèse and Carlos Chavez; electronic instruments such as the Theremin were constructed; and the production of tone by modifications of magnetic-tape recording and other electronic processes is still being investigated by Otto Luening and Vladimir Ussachevsky in New York, and Karlheinz Stockhausen in Germany. Theoretically, all musical directions were valid, and one or another new development produced strong partisanships. Thus, for some, the orientation toward the "internationalism" of the eighteenth century was a conscious denial of nineteenth-century nationalism (Stravinsky and Walter Piston). For others, the reversion to the preromantic past was, on the contrary, a reassertion of nationalism and the means, for example, of uniting a historical European tradition to indigenous national melody (Villa-Lobos); or the means of calling attention to the forgotten musical treasures of a national heritage (Respighi and Vaughan Williams). For some, the forward direction was neoclassicism, the revival of a clean, clear, and freely treated diatonicism, unsentimental and unencumbered by romantic chromaticism (Prokofieff's *Classical Symphony* and Ravel's Sonatine). For others, the strength of baroque formal constructions and the discipline of its polyphony seemed especially attractive. Many found this neobaroque idiom an avenue for the reintroduction of a warmly emotional music, free of the coagulations of thick romantic harmony and tone color. In this latter development, a settlement of a long-standing quarrel with romanticism is evident, and eventually composers such as Stravinsky, William Walton, Paul Hindemith, Roy Harris, Aaron Copland, and Serge Prokofieff made their peace with the traditional large-scale symphony and even with the old-fashioned grand opera. The list is international and the motivations in each case are different. But works like Stravinsky's opera *The Rake's Progress,* Walton's Viola Concerto and Violin Concerto, Hindemith's opera *Mathis der Maler,* Harris' Third Symphony, Copland's Third Symphony, Roger Sessions' Second Symphony, Prokofieff's opera *War and Peace* and his Fifth Symphony effectively mark the end to the self-conscious witticisms and the carefully contrived miniatures of the so-called "modern" phase of the twentieth-century music that characterized the post-World War I period.

With this reorientation, twentieth-century music, in a sense, comes of age. A new and more balanced perspective emerges with respect to fundamental attitudes. While there are today only small survivals of a self-conscious "cult of modernism," the antiromantic revolt of the 1920's served its purpose. Art is no longer a precious psychic mystery, a word to be uttered in a reverent hush or written always in italics. The composer is under no obligation to offer his audience a piece of his immortal soul in return for the price of admission to the concert hall. In the last few decades, the composer has become increasingly concerned with the hope of restoring composition to the status of an honorable and decently paid profession. The conditions of the market are distressing to be sure, but garrets are now too expensive to starve in; and towers, ivory or otherwise, are apt to be in use as radar stations.

There has been a production boom in music for use; for since the antiromantic clarification of the 1920's, the present-day composer no longer shares Schumann's scorn toward the "untalented daughter" market in piano music, nor Tchaikovsky's chronic suspicion of a commissioned work. Béla Bartók has written a fine six-volume graded method for the beginning piano student, the *Mikrokosmos;* Hindemith and Benjamin Britten have composed operas to be performed by children in elementary grades; Britten has prepared a *Young People's Guide to the Orchestra;* while Hindemith has composed works for chamber orchestra which take into account the simpler finger positions for string players in schools or ama-

teur community orchestras. Trumpeters, trombonists, organists, and vio-
lists need, and no doubt deserve, a respectable modern repertory for their
respective instruments, and Hindemith has undertaken to provide them
with one. This is a new kind of realism and a welcome one; for Hindemith's music is not only marketable, it is good. Not every composer is permitted to write a decent musical score for a Hollywood film, but a few
have managed to do so, and the level of Broadway musical comedy is
high. Alternate orchestrations are no longer uncommon. Ibert's *Concertino da Camera* for saxophone and eleven instruments, for instance, can
be readily converted from chamber music to concert hall use through
the simple expedient of enlarging the string quintet to a full section for
each string part. Similarly, Honegger's oratorio, *King David*, was originally
scored for seventeen instruments and later reorchestrated for large orchestra and organ. The original limitation was one of the stipulations of the
commission. Honegger, at first, was dismayed by the restriction, but following Stravinsky's advice, he solved the esthetic problems by the simple
expedient of imagining that this arrangement was what he wanted all
along.

This revised perspective is all to the good, for it is a hopeful token
of a better reciprocal relationship between composer and audience. The
road ahead for composers and audiences is still a long and problematical
one; but there is at least the hope that concert programs and opera seasons
may eventually become like current publishers' lists, or as with a normal
theater season, an avenue for the continuous display of recent creative
expression.

THE NEW NATIONALISM: IVES; BARTÓK

While the realism of the 1920's is still a part of the current
scene, international neoclassicism is largely defunct. Nationalism cannot
be cajoled or argued out of existence. Its survival in music depends not so
much upon music itself as upon the social and political climate within
which music is created. As long as there is urgent reason for strong national
feeling to exist among millions of human beings, then such feeling will
inevitably loom large in an art such as music. For music is a sensitive
barometer to states of emotion, and it can hardly remain impervious to an
emotion so dominant in the twentieth-century world. Béla Bartók in Hungary and Charles Ives in the United States are perhaps without any serious
challenge in their astonishingly creative use of national idioms.

Ives is far less disciplined, although no less exciting, than Bartók in
his imaginative exploitation of indigenous materials. Ives' sources are
those of an omnivorous New Englander, generous in his appreciation of

the world's culture but loyal to the loveliness of the local countryside. Nonconformist and plain-spoken, Ives has been at times succinct and at others long-winded to the point of incomprehensibility. No triad was too simple or consonant for him to use, and no dissonance too extreme to find a place in his music. When a traditional diatonicism was in order, he used it; yet he wrote pieces for a quarter-tone piano, and as early as 1891 or 1892 he experimented with a polytonal fugue in four keys simultaneously. As for the sources of his inspiration—hymns, cowboy tunes, ragtime, Civil War songs, and barn-dance melodies—all served in turn. His *Central Park in the Dark* shows him treating New York City as tenderly as his local river, the *Housatonic at Stockbridge*. Boyhood recollections of national holiday celebrations served for a Symphony (the movements of which are called "Washington's Birthday," "Decoration Day," "Fourth of July," and "Thanksgiving Day," respectively); and an interpretation of Concord, Massachusetts, in the 1840's for a Piano Sonata (the movements entitled "Emerson," "Hawthorne," "The Alcotts," and "Thoreau," respectively). His work is astonishing in its range of subject matter, and in the radicalism of his techniques. However far afield he may have gone in the search for sources of inspiration, any dozen of his works put together prove him a product of New England.

Béla Bartók's work is better known than that of Ives, for he was more disciplined as a composer and more professional in his address to compositional problems. As a result, his work was more profoundly thought out, and, difficult as it is, more playable. Folk sources of Central Europe provided Bartók with the basic substance of his music. These sources he collected and studied assiduously, and his scholarship in this regard was in itself a tremendous achievement. In general, the matured stage of his method no longer consisted in "settings" of folk tunes, but in the address to larger media, such as the string quartet and the concerto, in terms of a new sense of sonority, novel rhythmic patterns and instrumental colors, as well as melodic lines deeply conditioned by years of exposure to Hungarian, Romanian, and Bulgarian folk idioms. Folk music served to re-educate his ear, and this new sense for the line and color of sound led to radical departures on his part in the treatment of a string quartet or the percussion section of an orchestra. As personal as such a music must necessarily be, the vigor and the strong emotional drive of folk song and folk dance are intrinsic to his music. Further, in the writing of a concerto or a string quartet, everything had to be thought out afresh, for the formal structure, as well as the harmonic idiom, had to grow naturally out of these new, folk-conditioned sonorities. The fundamental radicalism of Bartók's music lies, then, in the reorientation of his ear away from traditional sources and toward new concepts of form, line, color, and harmonic texture. Bartók brought to his task the ardor and the heroic patience of a truly great composer. His later quartets (Nos. 4, 5, and 6), and concertos (including the Concerto for Orchestra), are, in their austerity and passion, monuments not only to a national art but also to the nobility of the man himself.

As rich as the work of Bartók and Ives undoubtedly is, no one composer can contain the creativity of a nation. Bartók's Hungarian compatriot, Kodály, and such Czech colleagues as Janáček lend a broader dimension to his creative uses of Balkan materials. Ives, despite his enormous range, is still a New Englander, and a composer such as Roy Harris provides a necessary Western dimension. Yet despite differences, both Ives and Harris are rooted in the tradition of Walt Whitman and Abraham Lincoln. Furthermore, there are inevitably strong temperamental differences, larger than the personalities of individual composers, that illuminate aspects of national character. Aaron Copland, for instance, can never quite shed his New York City background, even if his subject for a ballet happens to be *Billy the Kid, Rodeo,* or an *Appalachian Spring;* while Boston, as distinguished from New England, makes its special tone felt in the urbane, cosmopolitan, and literate style of composers as different as Charles Martin Loeffler and Walter Piston.

"MODERN MUSIC"—PAST AND PRESENT

About one hundred years ago, a distinguished English music critic, Henry Chorley, visited the Continent and returned convinced that modern German romanticism was a "fever which, should it last, will superinduce an epilepsy fatal to music." One of the prime sources of Chorley's despair was Robert Schumann who, distressed by the philistinism of the present, sought "to recall the old times", and to regenerate modern music out of the "pure sources" of the past. Toward the middle of the sixteenth century an enormously erudite musician named Glareanus could find little in the music of living composers worthy of mention, much less of praise. Looking back to the music of Josquin des Prez who was already dead, Glareanus found there "the perfect art . . . after which nothing but decline is to be expected." Some decades later, Vincenzo Galilei (the father of the famous astronomer) delivered himself of an impassioned diatribe against modern music, and demanded most urgently a return to the high moral purpose manifest in the ancient Greek conception of the art. However, among the ancient Greeks, as Romain Rolland once reminded his readers, "Aristoxenus of Tarentus . . . made the decadence of music begin with Sophocles, and Plato . . . found that no progress had been made since the seventh century [B.C.] and the melodies of Olympus. From one age to another, people have said that music has reached its apogee, and that nothing but its decline can follow." In short, as a poet in this century discovered, we are "the too late born," and as a poet some two thousand years ago observed, "The times are bad, and this is an ignorant generation."

Curiously, it would be trivial to construe the history of such opinion on contemporary music as a record of the inveterate denseness of people who refuse to face up to what is new in the world. For if Plato, Glareanus, and Chorley were conservative in temperament, they were also intelligent men; and, moreover, Aristoxenus, Galilei, and Schumann were among the avant-garde of the enlightened and progressive thinkers of their age. The outcry against contemporary music heard so often and so urgently in this century is neither the first, nor will it be the last instance of man's dissatisfaction with the shortcomings of the present moment.

In the arts, such dissatisfaction tends strongly to be aggravated, for there is always the irritant of a past perfection to point to. Unlike the scientist whose victory is always a partial one, still to be extended and consolidated, the work of a Michelangelo, a Monteverdi, or a Beethoven stands as an achieved perfection in the coordination of the quintessential aspirations of an era. For the art of an era does not express a truth about the formation of the earth's center; but it can in itself be a truth, a once-and-forever rendition of the deepest feelings and the noblest ideals of a moment in the history of humanity. No matter how soon after its creation the perfection of a work of art is recognized, all too soon the world changes. And all too soon this perfection is a relic of longings fast losing ground, an eloquence of men no longer living. Because it is of the past, it is always for the present a lost perfection—irretrievable, inimitable, and unreplaceable. And herein is the human agony when an opera by Monteverdi or a wall painting by Leonardo is lost, or soiled, or destroyed. When an *Eroica* or an *Art of the Fugue* lives on as a perfection in any present occasion, it is at once the nostalgia of its admirers, as well as the inspiration and betimes the despair of those with lives to live and music to make in a new world. The newness of it is always with the composer, and the contemporaneity that he seeks to transfix is always a process or a becoming. However much he may entrance his contemporaries, and however richly they reward him with applause, such perfection as he abstracts from the moment of becoming will stand as a monument only in posterity.

No important piece of music is complete the first or second time it is performed, and more than unfamiliarity explains the need for its rehearing. It is what it is only in its entirety, and its contribution of itself is complete only when the potential of all things in it have been realized. Part of its entirety is the heritage that helped shape it, and another part is the heritage it will help to create. Thus it becomes ever more complete as its consequences become recognizable decade after decade, and thus does it realize itself slowly in the music of other composers and in the lives of later men. It is a truism that a new image of the past emerges with every generation, and that every age finds in the music of a Beethoven a somewhat different composer. Each generation is convinced that it has discovered a new dimension to Beethoven's work which renders his musical personality more complete. Whether there is a new Beethoven still to be made manifest, our children and our grandchildren will tell us. And whether this process of Beethoven becoming more completely himself shall endure until eternity, only those who live in the last hour of the world will know.

In each generation masterpieces of music become new monuments unto themselves, and become new mirrors wherein the present finds, idealized or distorted, an image of itself. When such a masterpiece first appears, what is sensed in it is its strength for the future, and this is agreeable or alarming to the degree that for some it shakes the small equilibrium they have managed to make of their lives, while for others it offers hope of an eventual clearing in the blind wilderness of the present. Such recognition is an intuition of understanding, and in the first moment it is marked by extravagances of enthusiasm or of dismay. Debate breaks out rarely about the music itself, but rather upon the good or evil it may yet do in the world. The works of Monteverdi, Beethoven, Berlioz, Schumann, Schoenberg, and Stravinsky are all cases in point of a music whose importance was quickly sensed and slowly understood. None were neglected composers among their contemporaries. Yet with each, the music promised much to some, while to others it was an augury of evil.

We live in a century given, with sufficient reason, to the sounding of alarms. Thus the intimation of a new direction produces, in the beginning, much in the way of accusations of anarchy and anger over seemingly uncalled-for unpleasantness. Initially, critics are often more concerned with anxious annotations of the symptoms of incurable psychic disease than with an open-hearted hopefulness for the adventure with new sounds, or an open-minded confidence that the future of music is in the hands of capable and responsible composers. The experience of H. G. Wells at the London premiere of Stravinsky's *Les Noces* was typical of the musical situation during the 1920's and 1930's. "It was an amazing experience," he reported, "to come out from this delightful display with the warp and woof of music and vision still running and interweaving in one's mind, and find a little group of critics flushed with resentment and ransacking the stores of their minds for cheap trite depreciation of the freshest and strongest thing that they had had a chance to praise for a long time." There is small comfort in assuming that this was ever so; and, in any case, it is a comfort available to the millenniums of experience possessed only by the very young who were living when the art of music was born. It is a pity that such comforting people are rarely mature composers with reputations and livelihoods at issue. The detachment and the long patience with which they view the tribulations of music in our time may be a prophetic wisdom bespoken unto futurity, but it may well seem a wickedness to composers whose need it is to be reasonably understood and fairly evaluated while they are yet among the living.

Similarly, it may be entirely true that an imaginative projection back to any point in the past would find us amid the warring *isms* of that moment. Yet it is the necessary and inevitable bias of any age to find its own musical conflicts the most urgent, and the most critical for the future of the art. A new musical work unites—whatever the compatibility of the union—composer, performer, and audience under the auspices of a mutual occasion; and all three are constrained to participate in it amid, and often in terms of, the clamorous contradictions of that moment. The exceptional nature of the music is received amid the irritants and the excitations of everyday living. "The young man seated behind me in the box," reported Carl van Vechten of the Paris premiere of Stravinsky's *Rite of Spring,* "stood up during the course of the ballet to enable himself to see more clearly. The immense excitement under which he was laboring betrayed itself presently when he began to beat rhythmically on the top of my head with his fists. My emotion was so great that I did not feel the blows for some time." Through the pacifying tolerance of time, we look back with indulgence at the Comtesse de Pourtalès, "her face aflame and her tiara awry" rising during the performance of Stravinsky's *Rite* to assure all and sundry that this was the first time in sixty years that anyone had dared make fun of her. Since the issues are no longer urgent, audiences no longer hiss a Schoenberg composition, and an outraged conductor no longer rams it down their blasphemous throats by a prompt repetition of the offending piece.

It is a truism that time is a great healer, for moral immediacy will tomorrow find a new object for its irritation. A worthy work can outlive nearly everything but indifference, and when it survives the first enthusiasm and the first indignation that may mark its appearance upon the contemporary scene, it displays itself thereafter in a friendlier sort of way, less angelic and less satanic than it first appeared to be. Thus has the friendship of time quietly dissolved the contractions between Wagner and Brahms, between Beethoven and Weber, between Bach and Pergolesi, between any past pairing of divergent contemporaneities. And thus at mid-century, the heritage we have but recently acquired is slowly coming into focus. William Walton, it turns out, never had any serious point to dispute with Ralph Vaughan Williams; Sibelius and Bartók are becoming tolerable together on the same program; Berg's *Wozzeck* and Puccini's *Il Tabarro* are no longer poles apart; and even the music of Stravinsky, earlier critical mythology to the contrary, turns out to have been written —all of it—by the same composer.

Such outbursts as those described above are more than the amusing freakishness which lends spice to history; for in the record of such conflicts, and in the progress of their resolution, each will find his favorite fable wherein he reads clearly the confusions of other generations. Music history is also moral and social history, and each will make his own parable for the fifty-odd years since Strauss' *Salome* was removed from the blessèd boards of the Metropolitan Opera following its New York premiere. For it was then an indecency, but now it has become afternoon television broadcast material fit for mature neo-Freudians as well as for the unwary young who were undismayed to find it a replacement for a wrestling match. Lest it be imagined that debate on moral issues is an irrelevance confined to an ignorant lay public, it is worth noting that Debussy's hostility to Wagner's *Parsifal* was partially owing to his opinion that it promulgated the "falsest of moral and religious theories."

It is common enough to find in music the illness of an age, and parents still locate in a new jazz fad the source of the disturbing postures their teenage children assume while talking on the telephone. Hisses, moral indignation, and even fisticuffs are the weapons of music criticism when more than the music is at stake. It is just liable to be the case, that in settling accounts with contemporary music, one settles accounts with one's self, and with the world in which one lives, or in which one aspires to live.

Index

Certain features of a Glossary are combined with the Index. When technical terms are defined in the text, the reference is given in **bold face** type. The definition to which it refers will in almost all cases appear in *italics* on the page of the text. Examples and figures have been indexed, but the Chronologies at the beginning of each historical chapter have not. Birth and death dates of composers, as well as their first names, will be found in the Chronologies.

Cymbals

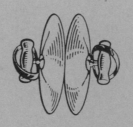

Triangle and beater

Snare drum

Tympani

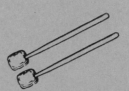

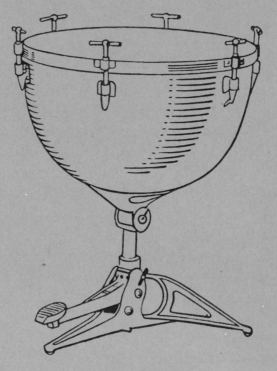

PERCUSSION